COST ACCOUNTING DESK REFERENCE BOOK

Common Weaknesses in
Cost Systems
and How to Correct Them

COST ACCOUNTING DESK REFERENCE BOOK

Common Weaknesses in
Cost Systems
and How to Correct Them

THOMAS S. DUDICK

with

Lawrence C. Best
Partner, National Office of Ernst & Whinney

and

George Kraus
President, DJR Associates

VNR VAN NOSTRAND REINHOLD COMPANY
_____ New York

Library of Congress Catalog Card Number: 86–7836
ISBN 0–442–21790–0

Manufactured in the United States of America

Published by Van Nostrand Reinhold Company Inc.
115 Fifth Avenue
New York, New York 10003

Van Nostrand Reinhold Company Limited
Molly Millars Lane
Wokingham, Berkshire RG11 2PY, England

Van Nostrand Reinhold
480 Latrobe Street
Melbourne, Victoria 3000, Australia

Macmillan of Canada
Division of Gage Publishing Limited
164 Commander Boulevard
Agincourt, Ontario MIS 3C7, Canada

15 14 13 12 11 10 9 8 7 6 5 4 3 2 1

Library of Congress Cataloging-in-Publication Data

Dudick, Thomas S.
  Cost accounting desk reference book.

  Includes index.
  1. Cost accounting. I. Title.
HF5686.C8D88 1986   657′.42   86–7836
ISBN 0–442–21790–0

Preface

In many companies, once the cost accounting system is put in place, many accountants are reluctant to introduce changes. As the years go by, traditional methods of costing become so ingrained in the costing routines that they become inviolate.

Automatic equipment is introduced to minimize and, in some instances, completely eliminate the need for direct labor in some departments. But there is a tendency to continue using direct labor as a base for allocating overhead to products—often on the basis of a single plantwide rate. The same arbitrariness applies to methods used in allocating SG&A costs to product lines. Such peremptory practices result in product costs that are inaccurate and product line profitability figures that are deceptive. It is to these kinds of weaknesses that the first section of this book, "Product Costing Deficiencies," is addressed.

Inventory represents one-third to one-half of factory investment. Companies that have adopted computerized material requirements planning techniques are still vulnerable to large physical-to-book adjustments, as well as overstocking, obsolescence, and negative balances on stock status reports. Section 2, "Managing and Mismanaging Inventories," discusses these weaknesses and presents solutions.

In this age of advanced technology, investment in highly automated equipment exceeds the inventory investment in many companies. This points up the importance of optimizing utilization of expensive facilities and the related high-cost overhead support services; hence the title "Productivity and Profits" for Section 3. This section also demonstrates, in two easy steps, how the portion of the profit due to productivity can be isolated from the portion due to changes in the cost/selling price relationships.

Section 4, "Key Management Reports and How to Produce Them," goes beyond the factory management level by asking corporate management the question, "Is your manufacturing services staff earning its keep?" This section also demonstrates how the performance of Manufacturing and Marketing can be more effectively monitored by creating separate profit centers, each with its own income statement.

This book is addressed to all levels of management that share responsibility for improving profitability. The techniques for correcting weaknesses in costing and improving the company's position in our highly competitive marketplace have proved to be successful and can be tailored to meet the requirements of the reader's business.

Thomas S. Dudick

101 Topics Addressed by This Book

1. If your company has a machine-paced as well as a labor-paced operation, a direct labor base for applying overhead can greatly distort product costs. Read the case example relating to two types of incandescent lamps. Chapter 1.
2. The fact that all products pass through every production department does not preclude the need for individual departmental overhead rates. See a case example for the manufacture of fluorescent lighting fixtures in which the overhead of product A can be as much as 40% more than that of product B, even though the same type of processing is required for both. Exhibit 1, Chapter 1.
3. Too many overhead rates, like too few, can distort product costs. See Exhibits 2 and 3, Chapter 1.
4. Don't rule out the use of material-based overhead rates for material-related costs. Material-based rates can be advantageous in documenting requests for reimbursement for canceled contracts when material has been purchased, processed through the Receiving Department, inspected, stored, and issued to the factory floor with only a small amount of labor expended in fabrication and assembly. Chapter 1.
5. Material-based overhead rates are also useful when the manufacturing process requires all material to be cleaned prior to use. See a case example of removal of scale and corrosion from coils of rod used for wire drawing. Chapter 1.
6. When using a material-based overhead rate, determine whether material cost or material weight is the more appropriate base. See a case example of a company manufacturing heat exchangers. Chapter 1.
7. Small items of material, such as nuts, screws, rivets, washers, and grommets, can be issued in bulk and charged to the product as a percentage of the larger items of material. But make tests before using an across-the-board material rate. See a case example of a company making communications equipment. Chapter 1.
8. When products are hung on conveyors and automatically spray-painted (or otherwise coated), direct labor as a basis for applying costs could have a distorting effect on product costing. A better measure is square inches or square feet of surface to be coated. Chapter 1.
9. In firing operations, the mass (weight) of material being fired is a better method for applying overhead than the use of direct labor.
10. When packing operations are an integral part of the production line, overhead can be applied on the same basis as it is applied to the conveyorized line on

which the product is assembled. If the packing is done in the warehouse as orders are shipped, see Exhibit 9, which illustrates how standards can be used. Chapter 1.

11. Remember that one company's overhead can be another company's G&A. Such corporate (and divisional) services as payroll, billing, purchasing, and accounts receivable should be charged to the factory operations and included as part of the overhead cost of the products being produced. Chapter 1.

12. Before undertaking the development of overhead costing rates, prepare a schedule showing a breakdown of the annualized manufacturing costs by category. This will provide an excellent overview to assure that maximum attention will be focused on the major items. Exhibit 1, Chapter 2.

13. How to calculate the available machine hours for machine-paced operations and reduce them to the net machine hours for use in calculating the machine hour rates. See Exhibit 2, Chapter 2.

   How to calculate the available labor hours for labor-paced operations and reduce them to net labor hours for use in calculating labor hour rates. See Exhibit 2, Chapter 2.

   Calculating the direct labor cost for machine-paced and labor-paced operations. See Exhibit 2, Chapter 2.

14. Since indirect labor is a major cost, it warrants major attention. See how this is done in Exhibits 3 and 4, Chapter 2.

15. How the president of a large textile company used Exhibits 3 and 4 in his company as a tool for cost reduction. See Chapter 2.

16. For guidelines in allocating various overhead costs to production departments, see Chapter 2.

17. How overhead and direct labor costing rates are calculated for machine-paced and labor-paced departments. See Exhibit 5, Chapter 2.

18. A simplified method for increasing the number of costing rates in a production department. See steps A through D, Chapter 2.

19. Does your company make overhead studies on a piecemeal basis and then fail to integrate the pieces? If so, read the Printing-Binding, Inc., case example. This illustrates how the same overhead costs used for calculating the costing rates are also used for developing the budget formula used for flexible budgeting and profit-volume studies. Chapter 3.

20. Why a company making components for commercial applications and using standard costing had to use a job costing system when similar components were made to tight specifications required for highly engineered products. Read "Impact of Tighter Specifications" in Chapter 4.

21. How one company's gross profit was distorted by using a standard cost system for both commercial and highly engineered products. See Exhibit 3, Chapter 4.

22. How a nuclear component manufacturer controlled costs through the use of "Estimates to Complete." Chapter 4.

23. Two formats for a cost history record for more effective cost estimating of new jobs. See Exhibits 4 and 5, Chapter 4.

24. Deficiencies in product line profitability when SG&A costs are allocated on the basis of sales. Chapter 5.

25. Allocating SG&A costs on the basis of conversion costs: advantages and disadvantages. Chapter 5.

26. Impact of small allocation inaccuracies on low-volume products. Chapter 5.
27. The same expense can vary by market for an equivalent sales volume. Exhibits 1 and 2, Chapter 5.
28. See how the OEM market with the lowest return on sales yielded the highest return on investment. Exhibits 1 and 3, Chapter 5.
29. If your company incurs large differences between physical and book inventories, Chapter 6 is "must" reading.
30. Differences between physical and book inventories are due more to improper accountability for production than to theft. Chapter 6.
31. How the Rago Company incurred a $190,000 inventory difference because of improper reporting of rework. Chapter 6.
32. How improper handling of customer returns caused the Hydraulic Valve Corporation to incur a $43,000 inventory discrepancy. Chapter 6.
33. How the KGO Company double-charged freight on incoming steel by improper coding. Chapter 6.
34. Why JTC Company's 11-month profit of $1,650,000 was reduced to $375,000 after the year-end inventory was taken. Chapter 6.
35. How one company's die casting production was being overreported. This reporting problem could occur in other types of molding as well. Chapter 6.
36. Incomplete accountability of production losses is a major cause of inventory differences. A good solution is to book only good production accepted into the work-in-process and finished goods stockrooms. Chapter 6.
37. An illustrative example of how the buildup of phantom inventory can be monitored during the year. Exhibit 3, Chapter 6.
38. Read a material manager's complaint that his newly computerized inventory control system merely automated the existing manual procedures. Chapter 7.
39. The computerized MRP system of another company requires forecasting of finished products only. The finished products represent 24% of the 18,500 items in inventory. The MRP system automatically forecasts the remaining 76% of the inventory items. Exhibit 1, Chapter 7.
40. The MRP system can be extended to forecast direct labor requirements and to provide shop floor control. Exhibits 2 and 3, Chapter 7.
41. Many computerized inventory management systems are highly transaction oriented and lack the analytical capabilities to highlight errors. Chapter 7.
42. Read "Setting the Record Straight," which discusses cycle counting as a systematic approach to ferret out errors in status reports. This reduces complete reliance on the once-a-year physical inventory. Chapter 7.
43. Illustrative examples of errors commonly found in sophisticated computerized inventory systems. Exhibits 6 through 13, Chapter 7.
44. Exhibit 13 in Chapter 7 illustrates how the analytical feature can highlight errors through exception audits.
45. How manufacturing process sheets are structured to provide accounting cost data as well as data required for computerizing the MRP inventory management procedures. Exhibit 4, Chapter 8.
46. A cost routing sheet demonstrates how the cost roll-up is used to accumulate costs upward from level 05 to level 01. Exhibit 5, Chapter 8.
47. How the computer calculates material and direct labor costs. Exhibits 6 and 7, Chapter 8.
48. See the section titled "By-Product Control Reports," which discusses by-prod-

uct reports that can be produced from data needed for cost accounting and inventory management. Chapter 8.

49. See a summary of journal entries, ledger accounts, and breakdown of variances. Exhibit 17, Chapter 8.

50. An illustration of cumulative costing wherein material, labor, and overhead in each department are transferred in total as material entering the succeeding department. Cumulative costing simplifies costing of the components of the product at various stages of completion. Exhibit 1, Chapter 9.

51. The cost system also requires noncumulative costs to fulfill other accounting applications. Exhibit 2, Chapter 9.

52. Note in Chapter 8, "Computerizing the cost accounting system," that all transactions have been costed on the basis of pure costs. Exhibit 5 in Chapter 9 is illustrative of a company that costs its products both ways.

53. Advantages and disadvantages of LIFO. Chapter 10.

54. Points to consider before adopting LIFO. Chapter 10.

55. Applying the specific goods method. Exhibit 1, Chapter 10.

56. Advantages and disadvantages of the specific goods method. Chapter 10.

57. Pricing the increments by three methods. Exhibit 2, Chapter 10.

58. Application of double-extension techniques of dollar value LIFO. Exhibit 3, Chapter 10.

59. Link chain technique compared with double-extension. Exhibit 5, Chapter 10.

60. LIFO reporting in industry—actual examples

Specific goods	Exhibit 6, Chapter 10
LIFO using chain link method	Exhibit 7, Chapter 10
LIFO for a distributor	Exhibit 8, Chapter 10

61. Making LIFO adjustments to standard costs. Exhibit 9, Chapter 10.

62. Selecting the dollar value pools. Chapter 10.

63. Optimum utilization of facilities—a key factor in profitability. Chapter 11.

64. Impact of expanded capacity on profits if anticipated volume fails to materialize. Exhibit 2, Chapter 11.

65. Programming expansion in stages to "test the waters" before making a full commitment: (a) overtime in lieu of physical expansion and (b) increasing the productivity of existing facilities. Chapter 11.

66. Fallacy of excess equipment. Chapter 11.

67. Importance of monitoring utilization of equipment. Exhibit 3, Chapter 11.

68. Interplay of utilization and machine efficiency. Exhibit 4, Chapter 11.

69. How the Erco Company erred in projecting the cost savings in its purchase of an automated assembly machine. Chapter 12.

70. The common errors made in projecting cost savings in the purchase of new equipment. Chapter 12.

71. Rebuilding old equipment versus purchasing new equipment. Chapter 12.

72. Past history contains a wealth of information on errors in judgment which should not be overlooked in future planning. Chapter 12.

73. Pictorial illustration of the problems encountered by the Durard Company in its rush to grow faster. Exhibit 1, Chapter 12.

74. Read the Guidelines for Profitable Expansion in Chapter 12.

75. Advantages and disadvantages of different measures of productivity. Chapter 13.

76. How labor efficiency was overstated in one company by charging nonproductive direct labor to an indirect category. Exhibit 1, Chapter 13.

77. Avoiding distortions in productivity measurements caused by changing dollar values. Exhibit 2, Chapter 13.

78. A simple two-step method for calculating the portion of the profit due to productivity and the portion due to changes in the cost/selling price relationships. Chapter 13.

79. What corporate executives with profit responsibility expect from the manufacturing services staff. Chapter 14.

80. The ESKO Division illustrates the type of problem the manufacturing services staff should be able to ferret out. Chapter 14.

81. What are the staffing and qualification requirements of the corporate manufacturing services staff? Chapter 14.

82. What one manufacturing superintendant had to say about "that guy from Corporate." Chapter 14.

83. The corporate services staff cannot fulfill its mission by long-distance telephone and questionnaires. Chapter 14.

84. Read "Steps in an Operations Audit," which outlines a systematic program that should be followed by the corporate manufacturing services staff. Chapter 14.

85. Importance of the plant tour. Chapter 14.

86. Conducting interviews with key factory personnel. Chapter 14.

87. Preparing the report of findings and recommendations for management. Chapter 14.

88. Ten commandments for more effective manufacturing services staff work. Chapter 14.

89. Need for individual internal income statements for Manufacturing and Marketing. Chapter 15.

90. See Exhibit 1 for the format of these statements. Chapter 15.

91. Charging interest on investment to the two functions—using budgeted corporate expenses as the base for the rate. Chapter 15.

92. Comparing the corporate expenses incurred with the aggregate of the interest charges made to Manufacturing and Marketing. Chapter 15.

93. Advantages of the functional income statement. Chapter 15.

94. Modern computerized business graphics are perpetuating existing deficiencies in manually prepared graphs. Chapter 16.

95. Business graphics software must provide for the use of semilogarithmic (percentage) scales. Exhibits 1 and 2, Chapter 16.

96. Software should also provide for relating one variable as a percentage of the other. Exhibit 3, Chapter 16.

   How one set of figures can tell two different stories. Exhibits 4 and 5, Chapter 16.

97. How the message can be distorted by omitting part of the scale. Exhibits 6 and 7, Chapter 16.

98. Note the deceptiveness of Exhibit 8 in Chapter 16 when the "profits" scale is expanded and the "assets" scale is contracted.

99. Note the difficulty in comparing the sales for five metals when more than two pie charts are displayed. See how bar charts provide a more meaningful comparison. Exhibit 14, Chapter 16.

100. Makers of business graphics software should follow the General Guidelines for Presenting Graphics. Exhibit 15, Chapter 16.

101. Many accountants need to develop a greater familiarity with their manufacturing operations. Read the 10 guidelines for improving this familiarity. Chapter 17.

Contents

Preface/v

100 Topics Addressed by This Book/vii

SECTION 1/PRODUCT COSTING DEFICIENCIES/1

1. Need for Better Product Costing/3
2. Developing Overhead Costing Rates/22
3. Importance of Integrating Costing and Cost Controls/42
4. How a Standard Cost System Can Distort the Cost of Highly Engineered Products/55
5. Present Methods of Accounting for SG&A Costs: A Distortion of Product Line Profitability/71

SECTION 2/INVENTORY MANAGEMENT AND MISMANAGEMENT/83

6. Common Pitfalls in Accounting for Inventory/85
7. Computerized Inventory Management: Strengths and Weaknesses/99
8. Interface of Inventory Management and the Computerized Cost Accounting System/117
9. Integrating Inventory Management with Cost Accounting and Fulfilling Dual Costing Needs/150
10. Inventory Valuation in an Inflationary Economy/161

SECTION 3/PRODUCTIVITY AND PROFITS/195

11. Production Capacity and Utilization of Investment/197
12. Common Errors in Projecting Productivity of Capacity Increases/204
13. Productivity Management by Level of Responsibility/216

SECTION 4/KEY MANAGEMENT REPORTS AND HOW TO PRODUCE THEM/225

14. Is Your Manufacturing Services Staff Earning its Keep?/227
15. Management's Need for Separate Income Statements for Manufacturing and Marketing/234
16. Computerized Graphics: Will They Correct the Deficiencies in Manually Prepared Graphs?/241
17. Summing Up/256

Index/261

COST ACCOUNTING DESK REFERENCE BOOK

Common Weaknesses in Cost Systems and How to Correct Them

SECTION 1
PRODUCT COSTING DEFICIENCIES

The three major cost deficiencies in product costing discussed in this section are:

- Using direct labor as a basis for allocating overhead to machine-paced operations.
- Using the incorrect cost accounting system.
- Improperly allocating selling, general, and administrative (SG&A) expenses.

Machine hour rates were known and used in the first decade of this century. Yet, in this day and age of highly automated operations, many companies with machine-paced (capital-intensive) operations still cling to direct labor and the use of a single plantwide rate based on direct labor.

Chapter 1 illustrates the cost distortions that can occur if a plantwide, labor-based overhead rate is used, rather than a machine hour rate for automated operations and labor-based overhead rates for manually assembled products. The illustrative product used in this example is the incandescent light bulb. Also discussed in this chapter is the use of material-based overhead rates.

Chapter 2 shows how overhead costing rates can be developed in five steps. The rates are based on both machine hours and labor hours. This case example provides a good guide for anyone attempting to establish costing rates for the first time.

Many companies that establish overhead costing rates fail to integrate them with other overhead-related procedures such as flexible budgets and profit/volume relationships. Chapter 3, in addition to illustrating the development of costing rates for a book printing company, shows how the overhead was recast to provide flexible budgets for use in controlling the various items of overhead. It also shows how to calculate the breakeven point in order to test the acceptability of the costing rates.

Some cost accountants look upon job costing as a throwback to a bygone era. Chapter 4 explains why highly engineered products that appear to be a mirror image of their commercial counterparts require a job cost system, while a standard cost system satisfies the costing needs of the commercial version.

The distortions in product line profitability, caused by haphazard methods of allocating SG&A expenses, complete the triumvirate of cost deficiencies. Chapter 5, the final chapter in this section, discusses these deficiencies in allocating this burgeoning item of cost. It also describes alternative methods that will provide a more accurate determination of product line profitability.

1
Need for Better Product Costing

Prior to the introduction of labor-saving equipment, overhead represented only a minor portion of the manufacturing cost, while material and direct labor made up the bulk of it. With the onset of the Industrial Revolution, as more and more labor-saving equipment was introduced, direct labor became the smallest of the three cost elements. Overhead, in some companies, has beceome the largest of the three—it can be as much as three to four times the amount of direct labor. Overhead costs cannot be precisely identified for individual products through the use of standards, as is done with material and direct labor. It is therefore essential that good business judgment be exercised in the development of overhead costing rates. This chapter identifies the common pitfalls and shows what corrective steps must be taken to ensure better product costing.

Operating executives with profit responsibility are often frustrated because of inaccurate product cost information. They complain that too many accountants consider their management costing needs as a by-product of the normal routine accounting procedures. The general manager of one company made the following comments regarding this problem:

> I could never rely on the product costs prepared by my accounting department. The material and direct labor were not a problem because we had engineered standards for material and direct labor. The problem, then, had to be with overhead. I called in my accountant one day and had him explain how he worked up the overhead costs. Would you believe he was spreading the total pool of overhead on the basis of the labor content of the products? The more direct labor a product or process required, the more overhead it was made to bear.
>
> We have 12 high-cost automatic machines. The production output of these is tremendous, but we need only three operators—one for each group of four machines. The direct labor cost of the products made on these machines dropped very sharply, but the total plant overhead costs more than doubled.
>
> It should have been obvious to my accountant that he could not continue to use the traditional method of allocating overhead. After our discussion, he realized that he had to split the pool of overhead into two parts and distribute the two overhead pools on the basis of the two separate pools of labor.

This chapter will discuss five types of deficiencies in allocating overhead to products. These are:

1. Failure to distinguish overhead cost differences between capital-intensive (machine-paced) and labor-intensive (labor-paced operations).
2. Failure to recognize overhead cost differences within capital-intensive or labor-intensive operations.
3. Using too many overhead rates.
4. Incorrect use of material-based costing rates.
5. Incorrect association of nonmanufacturing costs with products and/or product lines.

In addition to this chapter, Chapter 2 will discuss in greater detail deficiencies 1 and 2 listed above. It will break out the machine-paced and labor-paced operations and will illustrate how overhead costing rates are developed for each type of operation. It will also include a robotic type of operation (special automatics) that involves no direct labor. Deficiencies 3 and 4 will be covered only in this chapter, while no. 5 will be discussed in greater detail in Chapter 5.

FAILURE TO DISTINGUISH OVERHEAD COST DIFFERENCES BETWEEN MACHINE-PACED AND LABOR-PACED OPERATIONS

The ratio of overhead to direct labor for machine-paced and labor-paced operations is quite different. Machine-paced work requires substantially more depreciation, maintenance labor, repair parts, energy, and indirect support labor. Labor-intensive work, on the other hand, requires substantially more direct labor but relatively little overhead because operations are performed on work benches with simple tools and equipment when machines are used.

The following case example of the manufacturing process in assembling the mount for incandescent lamps illustrates the cost distortions that can occur when a direct labor base is used for automated operations.

Manufacturing the mount assembly on automatic equipment

The automatic mount assembly machine, requiring only a single direct labor operator, consists of a narrow moving conveyor that runs around the perimeter of the machine. The conveyor, into which mount parts are fed automatically, carries these parts through a series of operations. The sequence of these operations is described in steps 1 through 4.

Step 1: A piece of glass tubing, flared at one end, is positioned automatically and vertically in the machine, with the flared end up. Two lead-in wires, fed through cylinders, are placed inside the flared glass and come to rest in positioning guides. Then a piece of exhaust tubing (hollow glass about $3/16$ inch in diameter) is also placed inside the flared glass to about one-half its length and forced down against a stop. Fires are played on this assembly just below the flared part until it reaches the softening stage (1800°F) (see Fig. 1).

Step 2: Clamps move in and form a flat solid section called a "press" (see Fig. 2). Just before the press solidifies, a puff of air through the exhaust tube provides an opening in the press through which air will be removed later from the assembled bulb and mount.

Step 3: At the next position on the conveyor, the exhaust tube, under fire, is shaped into a button ¼ in. in diameter and ⅛ in. thick. Three molybdenum support wires are inserted in this button (see Fig. 3).

Step 4: The top ends of the two lead wires are shaped and separated to a distance of a millimeter or two less than the length of the tungsten coil. Finally, the coil is lifted into position as the glass-lead wire assembly arrives opposite it and the coil is mechanically clamped to the two lead wires. Two of the molybdenum support wires are folded around the main lead wires, and the third is folded into a loop around the center of the filament but does not touch it. The mount assembly, which is entirely automatic, is then transferred to the machine that seals it into

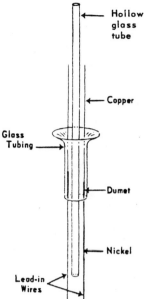

Hollow
glass
tube

Copper

Glass
Tubing

Dumet

Nickel

Lead-in
Wires

Fig. 1. Mount parts assembled.

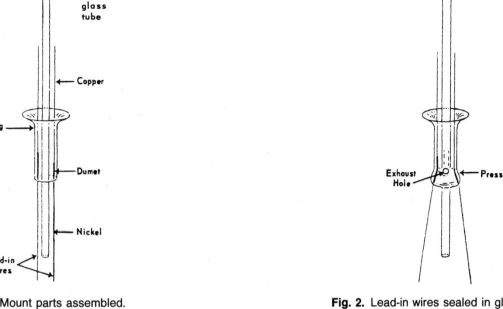

Exhaust
Hole

Press

Fig. 2. Lead-in wires sealed in glass press.

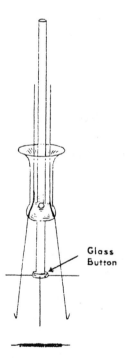

Glass
Button

Fig. 3. Support wires buried in a glass button.

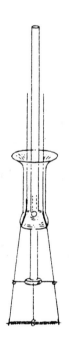

Fig. 4. Completed mount.

the bulb (see Fig. 4). Figure 5 shows how the mount is inserted into the bulb before sealing, exhausting, and basing.

This completes the description of the automatic mount assembly operation, which requires one operator for each of two shifts.

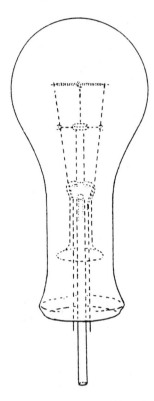

Fig. 5. Mount inserted into bulb.

Manufacturing more complex low-volume mount assemblies

The more complex low-volume mount configurations, shown in Fig. 6, are assembled at work benches using simple equipment and fixtures. Although the number of employees can vary, depending upon the complexity, let us assume an average of five direct labor employees working a single shift.

Calculating a Single Plantwide Overhead Rate Based on Direct Labor

A surprisingly large number of accountants still favor the use of a single plantwide overhead rate in which the overhead is allocated to all products on the basis of the labor content.

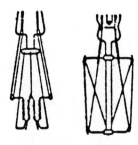

Fig. 6.

In the interest of simplicity, four of the major items of overhead will be used for illustrative purposes. These are:

Depreciation	$ 8,600
Maintenance (labor and parts)	7,400
Electricity and gas	5,500
Rent equivalent costs	5,600
Total overhead/year	$27,100

Calculating the direct labor base:

Automated mount assembly for two shifts:

Two operators $\times$ 1,936 hours/year	3,872	hours

Manual mount assembly for one shift:

Five operators $\times$ 1,936 hours/year	9,680	hours
Total annual direct labor hours	13,552	hours

Calculating the plantwide overhead rate:

$$\frac{\text{Total annual overhead}}{\text{Total annual direct labor hours}} = \frac{\$27,100}{13,552 \text{ hours}} = \$2.00 \text{ per hour}$$

Allocating the total overhead to both operations:

Automated mount assembly	(3,872 labor hours $\times$ $2.00)	$ 7,740	29%
Manual mount assembly	(9,680 labor hours $\times$ $2.00)	19,360	71
		$27,100	100%

The single plantwide rate of overhead based on direct labor allocates 2.5 times as much overhead ($19,360/$7,740) to the manually assembled mounts as it does to those assembled on the automatic equipment. This would result in large distortions in the cost/selling price relationship of the two types of mounts. Distortions such as this preclude the possibility of determining true product profitability—not to mention inventory valuations.

Calculating Individual Overhead Rates for Automated and Manual Assembly Operations

The more correct method would be to determine how much overhead is actually chargeable to each of the two production centers discussed in this case example. The accounting records should provide a breakdown of the depreciation. Maintenance and repair part costs should be determinable by an analysis of maintenance job tickets showing where time was spent by the maintenance men and the material that was used. Often this information must be supplemented by judgmental estimates. The electricity would be estimated by the electrician by calculating the connected load and weighting it for both centers by the number of hours of usage. Gas would similarly be estimated by the use of flow meters to measure the rate of usage and weighting the usage by both production centers according to the hours involved. Rent equivalent costs would be allocated on the basis of the floor space occupied. Using this breakdown, the applicable figures for the two types of operations are as follows:

	TOTAL PROD. HOURS	OVERHEAD COSTS						OVHD. RATE PER HOUR
		DEPRE- CIATION	MAINT. AND REPAIR PARTS	ELECTRICITY AND GAS	RENT EQUIV- ALENT	TOTAL	%	
Automated assembly	3,872	$8,170	$6,030	$5,225	$3,360	$22,785	84	$5.88
Manual assembly	9,680	430	1,370	275	2,240	4,315	16	0.45
Total	13,552	$8,600	$7,400	$5,500	$5,600	$27,100	100	$2.00

Note that the single plantwide overhead rate apportions only 29% of total overhead to the automated assembly operation and 71% to manual assembly. The apportionment based on separate rates alters the percentage breakdown to 84% for the automated operation and 16% for the manual operation—a more realistic breakdown.

The preceding case example illustrates how product costs can be distorted by the use of a single plantwide rate. Some accountants insist on using a single rate because the product line made in their plant requires operations to be performed in all departments. The controller of one company commented on this subject as follows: "We have four production centers, all of which are dedicated to making only fluorescent lighting fixtures. So why do we need four overhead costing rates when the present single rate absorbs the total overhead within 1 or 2%? This 1 or 2% of under- or overabsorption corresponds to fluctuations in volume of production."

The fallacy in this type of reasoning is a failure to recognize:

1. That the overhead costing rates are higher in some production centers than in others—ranging, for example, from $8.16 per labor hour to $11.08.
2. The number of labor hours required in the various production centers can vary greatly from product to product. The case example that follows demonstrates this.

FAILURE TO RECOGNIZE OVERHEAD COST DIFFERENCES WITHIN CAPITAL-INTENSIVE AND LABOR INTENSIVE OPERATIONS

Overhead rate differences must be recognized in different manufacturing operations whether they are all capital intensive, all labor intensive, or a combination of both. The case example shown below is entirely labor intensive because it has no machine-paced operations. The product line is fluorescent light fixtures. The four departments (production centers) are:

Large presses: The sheet metal work for the larger lighting fixtures is done on these because heavier gauge steel is used.

Light and medium presses: The fixtures used for lighting smaller areas are formed on these presses because a thinner gauge steel is used.

Anodizing and coating (also referred to as the "paint shop): All fixtures are anodized and coated here.

Assembly: All fixtures are assembled here. Assembly includes wiring together of the various components, as well as cutting and threading suspension tubing when fixtures are hung from the ceiling.

If the time spent in the four production centers were proportionately the same for all products, a single plantwide overhead rate would suffice. However, this is not the case, as illustrated by products A and B.

Product A is a large fixture used for factory and corridor lighting, while product B is a smaller fixture used for office lighting. The percentage breakdown of time spent in the four production centers by these two products is as follows:

	PRODUCT A (%)	PRODUCT B (%)
Large presses	47	15
Light and medium presses	6	40
Anodizing and coating	32	13
Assembly	15	32
Total	100%	100%

Although two fixtures might require exactly the same amount of labor in one of the press shops and in the paint shop, the amount of labor required in assembly would be substantially greater for the fixture that contains four light bulbs than for the fixture that has only two. The reason is that four lamps call for substantially more wiring than two. Bathroom fixtures are another example. The fixture with an outlet for plugging in an electric shaver will require more wiring than a similar fixture having no such outlet. The application of a single plantwide overhead rate would overstate the cost of the fixtures that require a greater amount of wiring because the additional labor in the wiring operation would absorb more than its due share of the higher overhead costs in the press and paint shop operations.

Exhibit 1 illustrates the principle for developing overhead costing rates per direct labor hour for the four production centers in this company. Here, as in the preceding case example, several major overhead costs were used to demonstrate the overhead rate differences. In actual practice, all overhead items must be considered.

Column 1 breaks down the labor hours expended in each of the four production centers. Columns 2 through 6 represent the major overhead items selected for this illustrative example. The total of these is shown in column 7.

The total in column 7 is divided by the total labor hours shown in column 1 to arrive at the overhead cost per labor hour shown in column 8. Note that the overhead rates range from a high of $11.08 per labor hour for the large presses to a low of $8.16 per labor hour in the assembly area. The rate for the lighter presses is so close to the rate for anodizing and coating that they could be averaged and the same rate used for both.

The lower half of Exhibit 1 illustrates the application of the production center rates to two products. Product A is a large fixture with a minimum amount of wiring. Product B is a small fixture with a large amount of wiring. Note, in comparing the average overhead rate for Products A and B, that there is a difference of $0.74 per labor hour ($10.16 for product A minus $9.42 for product B). The dollar effect of an erroneous accounting treatment of overhead is shown below for a month's production of products A and B:

	FOUR INDIVIDUAL RATES	SINGLE PLANTWIDE RATE	DIFFERENCE
Product A	$51,544	49,988	(1,556)
Product B	33,906	35,462	1,556
Total	$85,450	85,450	–0–

EXHIBIT 1
OVERHEAD COST DIFFERENCE BETWEEN TWO PRODUCTS

Production Departments	Total Labor Hours	Deprecia- tion	Indirect Labor	Rent Equivalent Costs	Electricity	Maintenance Labor and Repair Parts*	Total (2) Through (6)	Overhead Cost Per Labor Hour (7) ÷ (1)
	(1)	(2)	(3)	(4)	(5)	(6)	(7)	(8)
Large presses	2,936	$ 7,294	$11,360	$ 7,718	$2,210	$ 3,960	$32,542	$11.08
Light and medium presses	1,768	3,351	5,223	3,640	1,492	3,400	17,106	9.67
Anodizing and coating	2,077	2,832	10,942	1,742	1,860	2,980	20,356	9.80
Assembly	1,893	285	2,675	9,233	378	2,875	15,446	8.16
Total	8,674	$13,762	$30,200	$22,333	$5,940	$13,215	$85,450	$ 9.85

* Includes dies as well as equipment

APPLICATION OF OVERHEAD TO PRODUCTS A AND B

	Total Labor Hours	Overhead Cost Per Labor Hour	Total Overhead
Product A			
Large presses	2,396	$11.08	$26,549
Light and medium presses	328	9.67	3,172
Anodizing and coating	1,609	9.80	15,768
Assembly	740	8.16	6,055
Total	5,073	$10.16	$51,544
Product B			
Large presses	540	$11.08	$ 5,983
Light and medium presses	1,440	9.67	13,925
Anodizing and coating	468	9.80	4,586
Assembly	1,153	8.16	9,412
Total	3,601	9.42	$33,906
Total Products A and B	8,674	$ 9.85	$85,450

USING TOO MANY OVERHEAD RATES

The attempt to correct errors in existing methods of costing sometimes results in corrective measures which produce equally erroneous results. An example would be the abandonment of a costing procedure that uses 6 overhead rates in favor of one using 12 rates. This should not be construed to mean that 12 rates should never be used or that more than 12 would always produce incorrect results. The intention of this statement is to point out that judgment and common sense still play a large part in the determination of meaningful product costs.

Exhibit 2 illustrates a case in which one company, using 6 overhead rates, decided to increase the number to 12, feeling that this would provide more accurate costing.

In apportioning overhead to departments (cost centers) for the purpose of developing overhead costing rates, one will usually find that the substantial portion of this cost which makes up the overhead originates from areas outside the jurisdiction of the production departments. This "immigrant" overhead consists of such service as production scheduling, stores, receiving, factory engineering, industrial relations, quality

EXHIBIT 2
OVERHEAD RATES FOR SIX DEPARTMENTS

Department	Direct Labor	Overhead	Overhead Rate (%)
A	$ 232,892	$ 290,034	124
B	300,771	414,709	138
C	244,857	462,630	189
D	332,108	326,547	98
E	201,953	195,620	98
F	217,297	242,546	112
	$1,529,878	$1,932,086	126

EXHIBIT 3
WHEN THE NUMBER OF OVERHEAD RATES IS DOUBLED

Department	Direct Labor	Overhead	Overhead Rate (%)
1 (A)	$ 198,702	$ 220,223	110
2 (A)	34,190	69,811	204
3 (B)	4,769	25,633	537
4 (B)	106,100	200,611	189
5 (B)	189,902	188,465	99
6 (C)	132,450	242,409	183
7 (C)	112,407	220,221	196
8 (D)	12,200	38,488	315
9 (D)	319,908	288,059	90
10 (E)	101,950	100,800	99
11 (E)	100,003	94,820	95
12 (F)	217,297	242,546	112
	$1,529,878	$1,932,086	126

Note: Letters identify the previous six departments.

assurance, purchasing, cost accounting, and manufacturing administration. In many companies, these service activities make up as much as half of the overhead rate.

Since overhead consists of expenses that cannot be specifically identified with individual products, it must be allocated to production departments and then distributed to products as was demonstrated earlier in Exhibit 1. Allocations like any estimate, always contain a certain amount of inaccuracy. In some instances, when the vehicle used for charging overhead to the product is small, a very small percentage error in allocating the overhead can have a great impact on the rate in a department with a small direct labor or machine hour base.

Note that in departments 3 and 4, which were originally department B, department 3, with $4,769, has the lowest direct labor base of all 12 departments. In breaking down department D into departments 8 and 9, the latter, with $319,908 in direct labor, has the highest direct labor base of the 12. (The company from which this illustrative example was taken used direct labor dollars, rather than hours, as its vehicle for applying overhead to the product.) The total overhead to be allocated over the 12 new departments amounts to $1,932,086. A 1% error in either direction would amount to $19,321. The overhead rate of department 3, as calculated, is compared with the rate that would result if the estimated overhead had been $19,321 higher or $19,321 lower. This comparison is as follows:

	DIRECT LABOR	OVERHEAD	OVERHEAD RATE (%)
Overhead as calculated	$4,769	$25,633	537
Overhead $19,321 higher	4,769	44,954	942
Overhead $19,321 lower	4,769	6,312	132

Note in the above comparison that a 1% error in allocating the total overhead could make the overhead rate range from a high of 942% to a low of 132%. If we make the same comparison for department 9, which has a relatively large direct labor base, the amount of distortion in the overhead rate is insignificant.

	DIRECT LABOR	OVERHEAD	OVERHEAD RATE (%)
Overhead as calculated	$319,908	$288,059	90
Overhead $19,321 higher	319,908	307,380	96
Overhead $19,321 lower	319,908	268,738	84

As illustrated, the overhead ranges from a high of 96% to a low of 84%. This range falls within an acceptable margin of error that can be expected in any overhead rate calculation.

The important question raised by expanding the number of overhead rates is: "How does one cope with the problem presented in department 3, in which a small percentage error in allocating overhead can have such a great impact on the overhead rate?" There are two alternatives.

Evaluating the Alternatives

Department 3 is a degreasing operation in which the metal stampings produced in department 4 are degreased prior to transfer to department 7 for plating.

Alternative 1: Merge departments 3 and 4 for overhead calculation purposes inasmuch as the degreasing operation is performed on all metal stampings produced in department 4. The volume of parts stamped is directly related to the amount of activity in the degreasing operation.

Alternative 2: Merge department 3 with department 7, which is the plating department. Degreasing operations are performed in the plating department in most companies that do plating.

MERGING DEGREASING AND METAL STAMPING (DEPARTMENTS 3 AND 4)

	DIRECT LABOR	OVERHEAD	OVERHEAD RATE
Department 3	$ 4,769	$ 25,633	537%
Department 4	106,100	200,611	189
Departments 3 and 4 combined	$110,869	$226,244	204%

MERGING DEGREASING AND PLATING
(DEPARTMENTS 3 AND 7)

	DIRECT LABOR	OVERHEAD	OVERHEAD RATE
Department 3	$ 4,769	$ 25,633	537%
Department 7	112,407	220,221	196
Departments 3 and 7 combined	$117,176	$245,854	210%

From a cost accounting point of view, the above test indicates that it makes little difference in the overhead rates whether degreasing is combined with metal stamping or with plating. This illustration also points out that overhead rates cannot be developed mechanically without taking into account the nature of the production processes and their relationship to the steps in manufacturing the product.

INCORRECT USE OF MATERIAL-BASED COSTING RATES

Some companies utilize a material overhead rate to recover their material handling costs. The items ordinarily included in the material overhead classification are purchasing, stores, inventory control, receiving, and incoming inspection. The material overhead rate is developed by dividing the total of such material-associated costs by the total material normally handled. The rate is applied to the material content of the various products in arriving at the production cost.

This type of overhead rate became popular after World War II when contracts which were canceled by the government created problems in reimbursement for materials which were either unprocessed or only partially processed. Because little or no labor had been expended, application of a labor overhead rate would not yield a sufficient amount of recovery of the material handling costs which had been incurred.

How a Wire Drawing Company Makes Effective Use of a Material-Based Overhead Rate

Wire drawing is a method of reducing ductile metals from a larger to a smaller diameter. This is accomplished by pulling the wire through a series of reducing dies. These are carboloy or diamond dies which contain a carbide compound or diamond stone with a contoured hole through the center. The die is housed in a circular steel disc about the size and appearance of the wheel of a child's roller skate. Dies are placed in the wire drawing machines in progressively smaller sizes so that the wire can be threaded and pulled through at the optimum speed required.

The rod used for drawing wire in this company is received in coils weighing about 10,000 pounds. These coils, when received, are not protected from the elements. They are stored in the open until they are ready for processing into wire. When the coils are brought into the plant, they must first be cleaned to remove the scale and corrosion. The coils are run through a series of baths which remove the scale and leave the coil with a clean, smooth surface.

In developing the material overhead rate to cover this operation, the annual cost of the cleaning operation is divided by the number of linear feet to be cleaned. This provides the material cleaning cost per linear foot, which is added to the inventory value of the coil ready for processing into wire.

Calculating the Material-Based Overhead Rate Requires the Same Kind of Business Judgment Required in Any Overhead Costing Rate

The preceding example showing how the wire drawing company calculated its material overhead rate for the cleaning process is illustrative of effective costing because good business judgment was exercised in developing the rate. Many companies using a material rate do not take the time to determine whether the mechanics of applying the rate will result in good costing. A case example follows.

A company manufacturing heat exchangers

This company, which manufactured heat exchangers used in heating and cooling equipment, used a large quantity of both stainless steel tubing and copper tubing of the same diameter. In developing a material handling rate to cover such overhead costs as receiving, incoming inspection, and purchasing, it arrived at a material overhead rate of 3.5% of the materials purchase cost. This meant that when either product was received, 3.5% of its cost was added to the inventory value to account for the handling costs.

The problem with using a percentage of the cost was that the copper tubing cost about five times as much as the stainless steel tubing, even though the weight and bulk of the two materials were reasonably close. Because of the use of a percentage of the cost, the copper tubing carried five times as much of the handling costs as the stainless steel tubing. The proper method would have been to determine the material handling cost per linear foot or per pound, thus eliminating the distortions caused by the difference in the purchase price.

Material-based rates are not always used for allocating overhead. They may also be used to allocate small items of direct material that do not warrant precise calculations. This is illustrated by the following case example.

A company making communications equipment

This company, in an effort to reduce record keeping, decided to account for its small low-unit-value items on a bin reserve (min/max) basis. This included such items as screws, nuts, contacts, washers, grommets, and rivets. Instead of counting the exact number of these items needed for the specific run, the company issued them in standard packages that were replenished when used up. The cost of these small items was charged to the product by adding 5% to the larger items of material that were issued in the conventional manner.

One should always be wary of across-the-board percentages, whether they are plantwide overhead rates, material handling rates, spoilage allowances, or selling, general and administrative (G&A) allocations. Some type of test should be made, as it was in this case example. The company made two products with two basic assemblies in each. The parts lists are shown in Exhibits 4 through 7:

Exhibit 4—Relay Mounting Frame $\left.\right\}$ Control terminal
Exhibit 5—Fuse Panel Assembly

Exhibit 6—Base Assembly
Exhibit 7—Contact Assembly $\left.\right\}$ Telephone module

Each exhibit lists all the parts used in the assembly, both small and large. The total cost is shown for all the parts. At the bottom of the exhibits, the grand total is broken down into the total cost of the small and large parts. Then a percentage is calculated by dividing the cost of the small parts by the large ones. A summary of the calculations is shown in Exhibit 8.

EXHIBIT 4
RELAY MOUNTING FRAME

Quantity	Description	Material Cost
9,000	Screw KTU*	$ 64.08
6,000	Rh Wood Screw-Conn*	24.54
6,000	Screw KTU*	25.82
2,000	Screw KTU*	70.05
9,000	Teenut*	171.44
2,000	Mounting Plate KTU	157.08
1,000	Bracket KTU	306.77
3,000	Bracket KTU	541.28
4,000	Receptacle KTU	509.44
2,000	Stud KTU	322.65
1,000	Bracket KTU	169.81
1,000	Back Board KTU	3,587.33
1,000	Frame KTU	7,715.93
1,000	Mounting Support	2,610.90
		$16,277.12

* Total Small Items	$ 355.93	
Total Basic Material Cost	15,921.19	
% Small Items	2%	

EXHIBIT 5
FUSE PANEL ASSEMBLY

Quantity	Description	Material Cost
14,000	Washer KTU*	$ 14.00
14,000	Screw KTU*	42.00
14,000	Lock Washer KTU*	75.65
14,000	Hex Nut KTU*	172.08
14,000	Terminal KTU*	270.50
14,000	Stud KTU	2,095.12
14,000	Bushing KTU	1,064.60
7,000	Fuse Mounting Block KTU	1,645.61
1,000	Fuse Mounting Assembly	504.65
		$5,884.21

* Total Small Items	$ 574.23	
Total Basic Material Cost	5,309.98	
% Small Items	11%	

EXHIBIT 6
BASE ASSEMBLY

Quantity	Description	Material Cost
7,000	Rivet*	$ 9.40
2,000	Cabinet Lock Screw*	5.47
4,000	Foot*	25.90
4,000	Rivet*	10.26
1,000	Base	174.96
1,000	Dial Bracket	7.82
1,000	Dial Bracket	8.39
1,000	Cradle Switch Assembly	334.94
		$577.14

* Total Small Items	$ 51.03	
Total Basic Material Cost	526.11	
% Small Items	10%	

EXHIBIT 7
CONTACT ASSEMBLY

Quantity	Description	Material Cost
1,000	Grommet*	$ 3.08
1,000	Positioning Bar	7.43
1,000	Operating Bar	7.43
6,000	Insulator*	6.67
3,000	Insulator*	6.06
2,000	Bushing*	20.38
2,000	Screw*	5.07
1,000	Cover	1.32
1,000	Nut*	1.08
1,000	Wire Assembly	10.22
1,000	Wire Assembly	10.07
1,000	Wire Assembly	10.15
1,000	Wire Assembly	10.15
1,000	Wire Assembly	10.22
1,000	Wire Assembly	9.70
1,000	Wire Assembly	10.08
1,000	Mounting Frame	80.92
1,000	Contact Spring Assembly	16.10
1,000	Contact Spring Assembly	14.62
1,000	Contact Spring Assembly	14.62
1,000	Contact Spring Assembly	14.62
1,000	Contact Spring Assembly	15.13
1,000	Contact Spring Assembly	14.62
1,000	Contact Spring Assembly	25.49
		$325.23

* Total Small Items	$ 42.34	
Total Basic Material Cost	282.89	
% Small Items	15%	

EXHIBIT 8
SUMMARY OF MATERIAL COSTING RATES

| | Control Terminal | | Telephone Module | | |
	Relay Mounting Frame	Fuse Panel Assembly	Base Assembly	Contact Assembly	Total
Total Small Items	$ 355.93	574.23	51.03	42.34	$ 1,023.53
Total Basic Material Cost	15,921.19	5,309.98	526.11	282.89	22,040.17
% Small Items	2%	11%	10%	15%	4.6%

Note that the overall material percentage rate for the small items is 4.6%—reasonably close to the 5% being used by the company. However, the individual percentages for the four assembly parts lists range from as low as 2% to as high as 15%. It is obvious from this that the relay mounting frame is overcosted, while the remaining three are undercosted. The solution is to use separate percentages for each assembly.

Coating Operations

Companies having coating operations in which the products are placed on conveyorized hangers to be automatically spray painted, for example, find direct labor to be an inaccurate vehicle for costing this type of operation. The reason is that direct labor is utilized for loading and unloading the conveyor, and therefore bears no direct relationship to the amount of coating material used. A better method would be to determine the cost per square inch or per square foot of surface to be coated. This method could also be used to allocate overhead and direct labor to the product.

Firing Operations

Firing operations, in which porcelain insulators are automatically conveyed through a high-temperature kiln, are similar to coating operations. In the kiln operation, however, the measure is the mass of material being fired rather than the surface dimensions. Here, too, the direct labor and overhead of the kiln could be allocated by the weight of the parts being fired.

The foregoing examples show how some companies charge smaller material costs to the product by using the larger material cost items as the vehicle for making the apportionment. Next, we will discuss nonmanufacturing costs and the problems associated with their proper allocation.

INCORRECTLY ASSOCIATING NONMANUFACTURING COSTS WITH PRODUCTS

It is important that nonmanufacturing costs be correctly associated with the products that incur such costs, even though these nonmanufacturing items may not be included in the inventory value of the product. Packaging is an example of an incurred cost that is usually inventoried as part of the product cost when it must be packaged before it can be stored in the stockroom. Some products are sent to the stockroom in bulk and packaged at a later date as customer orders are scheduled for shipment. In this circumstance, the packaging and shipping operation would normally not be considered an inventoriable cost, although there are companies that consider packing and shipping as one of the overhead service centers that should be allocated to the various production centers and included in their overhead costing rates.

Packing and Shipping Expenses

One company's general manager, recognizing the deficiencies of spreading packing and shipping expenses over production cost centers through what he termed "guesswork percentages," made the following comment:

> My accountant insists on allocating packing and shipping expenses to the various production centers so that each center will share in a portion of the cost of this expense. I realize that each part we manufacture is part and parcel of the finished product that must be packaged and shipped to the customer. But who knows how much to allocate to each center? We do a good deal of plating of metal parts. How much of the packing and shipping expense should be allocated to the plating department? How about the purchased castings that become part of the finished product? Do we add an overhead surcharge to cover the packaging and shipping costs? We have a final testing operation for our electronics products. Do we allocate such costs to this center? If we make all these allocations, does this give us reliable product costs? I doubt it. In fact, I would have less faith in the accuracy of my product costs.

A recommended solution that the general manager agreed to was the development of standards for the eight major product lines. These standards would, understandably, not be as precise as those established for the production operations but would be more meaningful than allocations made to the various production departments. Exhibit 9 illustrates how the standards were developed.

Step 1: Determine the year's total budgeted costs for the packing and shipping department for the number of units of the eight product types to be shipped. The total budget, $83,538, is shown at the bottom of column 5. The total units by product type are shown in column 1.

Step 2: Determine the estimated standard hours per 100 units of each of the product types to be shipped (column 2).

Step 3: Multiply the number of units of each of the eight product types in column

EXHIBIT 9
PACKING AND SHIPPING STANDARDS

Product Types	Number of Units	Std. Hrs. Per 100 Units	Total Std. Hours	Std. Hrs. as a % of Total	Total Packing & Ship. Cost	Std. Cost Per 1,000 Units
A	40,000	2.2908	916	19.5	$16,290	$407.25
B	214,000	1.2500	2,675	56.9	47,532	222.12
C	38,000	1.5724	598	12.7	10,608	279.15
D	13,000	.8670	113	2.4	2,004	155.07
E	5,300	.8670	46	1.0	834	155.07
F	6,300	1.5724	99	2.1	1,755	278.58
G	7,800	1.8921	148	3.1	2,592	332.31
H	7,500	1.4164	106	2.3	1,923	256.41
Total	331,900	1.4164	4,701	100.0	$83,538	251.70
	(1)	(2)	(3)	(4)	(5)	(6)

1 by the standard hours per 100 units shown in column 2 to determine the total standard hours required for each product type. Example: 40,000 units of product A × 2.2908 hours per 100 = 916 standard hours, as shown in column 3.

Step 4: Divide the total standard hours for each product type in column 3 by the total standard hours for the eight product types to arrive at the percentage breakdown of the standard hours by individual product type. Example: 916 total standard hours for product A divided by 4,701, the total standard hours for all eight product types, gives 19.5%, as shown in column 4.

Step 5: Use the percentages shown in column 4 to break down the total packing and shipping budget of $83,538 by product types to be shipped. Example: $83,538 × 19.5% = $16,290 for product A, as shown in column 5.

Step 6: Divide the dollar breakdown in column 5 for each product type by the number of units of each type to be packed and shipped to determine the standard cost per 1,000 items. Example: Divide $16,290 in column 5 by 40,000 units to arrive at the standard cost of $407.25 per 1,000 units, as shown in column 6.

The standard costs shown in column 6 would be used to determine the total standard allowance for the various product types shipped each month. This figure could then be compared with the total actual costs incurred by the packing and shipping department as a measure of efficiency.

Problems in Setting Standards for a Wide Range of Low-Unit-Cost Products

The parts manufacturing division of a large electronics company produces thousands of varieties of low-unit-cost metal stampings and plastic molded parts. Standards were developed for those items in which there were differences in the size of the parts and the fragility of certain configurations. These items required specialized packaging with dividers strategically spaced to prevent crushing. Silver-plated parts had to be packed with camphorized material to retard tarnishing. These all required individual estimates to ensure that the packaging costs were correctly determined.

For the many remaining parts that required no special packaging, a standardized per unit cost of $0.05 per 1,000 parts was established. Even though this small charge seemed ridiculously low, it was discovered that its use put certain parts in a noncompetitive position. The product involved was wire cuts. The operation was a highly automated process in which wire was fed through cutting dies and cut in lengths of about ⅛ to ½ inch. A typical order of this type would call for quantities of 500,000. Using a $0.05 per 1,000 cost for recovery of packing costs, this amounted to $25 for a lot of 500,000. In analyzing the actual operation, it was found that these parts could be measured on a counting scale, poured into a $0.15-cent carton, sealed, and labeled in less than two minutes at a total cost of less than $0.50 including overhead. This seemingly small charge of $0.05 per 1,000 parts amounted to about one-fourth of the selling price of 500,000 small wire cuts. This case illustrates an example in which the costing basis was not tested. To correct the distortions, the parts requiring no special treatment were categorized into families based on the type of part and its packaging requirements. A representative item in each family was selected to determine the correct packing cost. Upon completion of this study, a packing cost schedule was prepared for each family of parts.

Packing and shipping, usually the least complex step in the manufacturing operation, is illustrative of the costing problems that can arise in our highly competitive business community.

Selling, General and Administrative (SG&A) Expenses

When a company is small, such functions as payroll, billing, purchasing, personnel, and administration are usually housed in the same facilities as the manufacturing operation. Employees are typically expected to wear more than one hat. The book-keeper, in addition to preparing the payroll, may also operate the switchboard. The general manager may not only be the chief executive but the sales manager as well.

As the company grows and adds more manufacturing plants, with a greater diversity of products, a large segment of these functions becomes centralized in a corporate headquarters. Such functions as payroll, billing, accounts receivable, and sales analysis become a corporate data processing service rendered to the plants. An industrial relations group is formed to deal with wage and salary policies as well as union matters. A purchasing manager may be located at the headquarters to consolidate purchases of materials used by more than one plant. The sales function is expanded and housed at the headquarters as well as in regional locations. Competition and a desire for further growth often dictate the establishment of a market research and product development group.

One Company's Manufacturing Overhead May Be Another Company's SG&A

Categorization of what is included in overhead and what is considered a corporate expense can vary from company to company even within like industries. In the interest of proper determination of all inventoriable manufacturing costs, it is necessary to identify those corporate expense items that should be charged back to the plants based on the amount of services rendered. If, for example, a purchasing group at headquarters is making purchases of a major commodity, steel for example, this cost should be charged back to the plants on the basis of the amount of steel consumed. The question might arise as to whether the "amount" of steel means dollar value, weight, or some other denominator. Which denominator is correct depends on which one reflects the degree of purchasing effort required. The cost accountant should not make this determination arbitrarily without consulting with the purchasing manager responsible for making the purchases. In fact, in allocating any manufacturing overhead or SG&A expense, the cost accountant must consult with those most qualified to know how the allocation should be made to reflect the expenditure properly.

Sales costs can frequently be identified by product family. Although such costs should be allocated to the appropriate product line, they would not be considered inventoriable costs because of their nonmanufacturing status. However, they would be considered in the development of product line profit and loss statements. The same principle applies to new product development. If the new product or a variation of an existing product is being developed, the costs should be identified with the specific product and reflected in the product line income statement for both the current month and the year to date. Conceivably, the income statement for a new product in the process of development would show only the development cost and would result in a loss during the period of development. It would be more meaningful to management to see that the development costs for product 2163 were $325,000 for the first six months rather than arbitrarily spreading this amount over other products and misstating their true profitability.

Any remaining residual costs, such as for company officials, public relations, and the legal department, would be considered as an override to the various plants to ensure that product line profitability reports reflect all costs and do not overstate the profit.

SG&A expenses are important enough to warrant a separate chapter. This is Chapter 5, titled "Present Methods of Accounting for SG&A Costs are Distorting Product Line Profitability."

LAYING THE GROUNDWORK TO MINIMIZE DEFICIENCIES IN PRODUCT COSTING

The increasing demand for more and more products and the pressure among competitors for a larger share of the market have led to intensified automation to cut labor costs. With the reduction of direct labor as a percentage of the total manufacturing cost, there has been a concurrent increase in the percentage of overhead—which includes large increases in indirect support labor. Direct labor required to make a product is relatively easy to measure. Overhead is more difficult because it requires judgmental decisions in determining the proper allocation bases for each item. These decisions, in turn, require a reasonably good knowledge of the product and how it is made. If followed, the guidelines shown below will make the learning process easier.

1. Don't try to develop overhead costing rates from behind a desk. Get out on the factory floor and learn what's going on.
2. Don't go it alone. Have a knowlegeable operations-oriented individual explain the various processes.
3. Inquire about problem areas in the manufacturing process that must be taken into account.
4. Don't be embarrassed to ask questions, however simplistic they may seem.
5. Don't worry about the calculations. Once you are familiar with the manufacturing process, the figures will fall in place.

These guidelines are shown in expanded form at the end of Chapter 17.

2
Developing Overhead Costing Rates

This chapter describes a five-step method for calculating overhead and labor costing rates for machine-paced and labor-paced operations.

A major area of weakness in the cost accounting procedures of many companies is the haphazard manner in which overhead is assigned to the product. Chapter 1 provided several examples in which inventoriable manufacturing overhead was not properly allocated, with the result that cost/selling price comparisons were meaningless. Some will ask, "Since the marketplace determines the selling price of the product, why be concerned with the cost/selling price relationships of individual products?" The answer is that such information will identify those products whose costs are too high in relation to the selling price. Many companies, knowing where their costs were out of line, have introduced lower-cost substitute materials such as plastics for steel. Others have standardized the components used in assembling the finished products. Standardization has two advantages: (1) it reduces the size of the inventory, thus eliminating the high carrying costs of excess stock, and (2) it facilitates automation. Subassemblies previously assembled by hand can now be assembled on automatic equipment with substantial savings in labor. Often products can be redesigned to achieve cost savings.

An illustration of product redesign is the manufacture of the shovel carried in the backpacks of infantrymen in the armed forces. At one time, the gauge of steel used in these shovels was heavier than it is at present. The army desired to lighten the weight of the shovel to speed up mobility, and the contractor was told to come up with a lighter shovel without sacrificing strength. The answer was to form several "ripples" in a lighter-gauge steel. This not only lightened the shovel but brought about cost reductions in the material.

Automobile manufacturers have found it possible to use lighter-gauge steel by introducing contours that add to its strength. Metal brackets used as supports have likewise been reduced in cost through use of lighter gauges contoured to provide greater strength. Plastics have often been substituted for steel to reduce material costs, particularly in appliances where plastic parts in various colors have eliminated the need for painting or plating. Reductions in labor costs through the use of automated equipment for metal forming, plastics molding, die casting, assembly and testing are well known.

This chapter deals with the development of manufacturing overhead costing rates for the same product used in Chapter 8. There are two differences, however: (1) the figures used in this chapter are based on a later time period and (2) the calculation of costing rates is based on more advanced manufacturing equipment to reflect improvements in manufacturing technology.

The procedure for developing overhead costing rates should be broken down into the following steps:

1. Prepare an overview of all manufacturing costs by category to provide a better perspective.

2. Determine the level of activity to be used in the various production cost centers using machine hours for capital-intensive operations and direct labor hours for labor-intensive operations.
3. Identify the personnel requirements by number and job title in the production cost centers and service departments needed to achieve the projected level of activity determined in step 2.
4. Determine the appropriate allocation bases to be used in allocating each of the overhead items to the various production cost centers.
5. Calculate the overhead costing rates.

PREPARING AN OVERVIEW OF ALL MANUFACTURING COSTS BY CATEGORY (STEP 1)

This step, illustrated in Exhibit 1, might also have been labeled "Schedule of Allowances." The term "overview" was used instead to emphasize the importance of looking at the big picture and the components of that picture. Thus, if we look at the summary section of the manufacturing costs listed in this exhibit—in the format of a monthly report—we see the magnitude of the various overhead categories as they relate to the total manufacturing cost (TMC). The operating statistics section shows these cost figures as percentages of the TMC.

Although material, at 44.9% of TMC, is the largest single item of cost and is not an overhead item, it was included to arrive at the TMC. Direct labor, although not an overhead item either, is also included. This item amounts to 14.5% of the TMC and is broken down by the individual production cost centers (departments) in the section of the report titled "Direct Labor."

The largest category in the overhead section is nonpayroll expenses—amounting to 21.5% of the TMC. Of the 25 items that make up this category, five make up 75% of the total cost. These are electricity, expendable tools, maintenance repair materials, tool maintenance, and equipment depreciation. These total $6,838,199 of the $9,078,857 in this category of overhead expense, $709,000 more than direct labor.

The overview being emphasized here calls attention to the importance of seeking greater accuracy in allocating these five costs to the production cost centers than the lowest five items, which total $129,646, or only 1.4% of the total nonpayroll expenses. Yet there are many who would spend a disproportionate amount of time allocating such items as subscriptions, travel expenses, and dues and memberships because the users of these services can be identified from cost records in the files. This "penny wise, pound foolish" approach can be illustrated by an actual example in which a corporate headquarters vice-president was given the responsibility for heading a cost reduction effort during a recessionary period. In one of the divisions he visited, he sat in the controller's office while the controller was making a long-distance phone call to another division. Upon completion of the call, the controller apologized for the delay. The visitor then pulled a stop watch from his pocket and exclaimed, "Do you realize that you were on that long-distance call for almost 20 minutes? Couldn't that have been handled by mail?" This is illustrative of poor overview, since telephone charges in a factory are relatively small. The vice-president spoke to the controller about his responsibility for carrying out a cost reduction program within the division but failed to tour the factory in order to become more familiar with the operations and other larger expenses that should be given greater emphasis than a 20-minute telephone call. Factory supplies in this division, for example, amounted to six times the telephone charges. Had this vice-president taken a proper approach, he would also have discussed the various other expenses that should

EXHIBIT 1
OVERVIEW REPORT
FOR
MANUFACTURING COST

MANUFACTURING COST REPORT

SUMMARY	Year to Date		Month	
	Actual	Allowance	Actual	Allowance
MATERIAL		18,979,950		
DIRECT LABOR		6,129,380		
PRIME COST		25,109,330		
INDIRECT LABOR - PROD'N DEPTS		2,128,125		
INDIRECT LABOR - SVCE. DEPTS.		4,152,750		
LABOR CONNECTED EXPENSES		1,802,483		
NON-PAYROLL EXPENSES		9,078,857		
TOTAL OVERHEAD		17,162,215		
TOTAL MANUFACTURING COST		42,271,545		

OPERATING STATISTICS	% OF TOTAL	% OF TOTAL	% OF TOTAL	% OF TOTAL
MATERIAL		44.9		
DIRECT LABOR		14.5		
PRIME COST		59.4		
INDIRECT LABOR - PROD'N DEPTS		5.0		
INDIRECT LABOR - SVCE. DEPTS.		9.8		
LABOR CONNECTED EXPENSES		4.3		
NON-PAYROLL EXPENSES		21.5		
TOTAL OVERHEAD		40.6		
TOTAL MANUFACTURING COST		100.0		

MATERIAL

Dept. No.		Year to Date		Month	
		Actual	Allowance	Actual	Allowance
	BRASS		12,014,308		
	NON-BRASS MATERIAL		6,965,642		
	TOTAL MATERIAL		18,979,950		

DIRECT LABOR

Dept. No.	Department	No. Emp.	Year to Date		Month	
			Actual	Allowance	Actual	Allowance
	MACHINE-PACED OPERATIONS					
	AUTOMATICS	50		1,121,677		
	HEADERS & PRESSES	28		471,960		
	SPECIAL AUTOMATICS	-0-		-0-		
	INGREDIENT MIXING MILL	11		251,305		
	MOLDING	46		1,041,995		
	LABOR-PACED OPERATIONS					
	SEMI-AUTOMATIC ASSEMBLY	38		766,173		
	HAND ASSEMBLY	48		1,305,558		
	PLATING	38		704,879		
	PACKING	28		465,833		
	TOTAL DIRECT LABOR	287		6,129,380		

INDIRECT LABOR-PRODUCTION DEPARTMENTS

Dept. No.	Department	No. Emp.	Year to Date		Month	
			Actual	Allowance	Actual	Allowance
	MACHINE-PACED OPERATIONS					
	AUTOMATICS	15		395,831		
	HEADERS & PRESSES	11		238,350		
	SPECIAL AUTOMATICS	18		487,341		
	INGREDIENT MIXING MILL	6		153,225		
	MOLDING	13		304,322		
	LABOR-PACED OPERATIONS					
	SEMI-AUTOMATIC ASSEMBLY	10		204,300		
	HAND ASSEMBLY	5		97,894		
	PLATING	7		140,456		
	PACKING	6		106,406		
	TOTAL INDIRECT LABOR-PROD'N DEPTS	91		2,128,125		

INDIRECT LABOR-SERVICE DEPARTMENTS

Dept. No.	Department	No. Emp.	Year to Date Actual	Year to Date Allowance	Month Actual	Month Allowance
	PLANT SUPERVISION	5		174,416		
	MANUFACTURING ENGINEERING	16		419,428		
	MATERIAL CONTROL	24		498,330		
	QUALITY CONTROL	18		394,511		
	PLANT ACCOUNTING	9		182,721		
	PERSONNEL	5		87,208		
	RECEIVING & RAW STORES	10		145,346		
	IN PROCESS STOCKROOM	7		107,972		
	INSPECTION	40		812,603		
	EQUIPMENT MAINTENANCE	25		639,524		
	TOOLROOM & MACHINE SHOP	26		690,691		
	TOTAL	185		4,152,750		

LABOR CONNECTED EXPENSES

Acct. No	Account Name		Year to Date Actual	Year to Date Allowance	Month Actual	Month Allowance
	OVERTIME & PREMIUM			237,928		
	SHIFT PREMIUM			57,679		
	VACATION EXPENSE			153,211		
	GROUP LIFE INSURANCE			70,297		
	HOSPITALIZATION			200,076		
	PENSION EXPENSE			243,335		
	COMPENSATION INSURANCE			146,001		
	UNEMPLOYMENT INSURANCE			167,631		
	PAYROLL TAXES			526,325		
	TOTAL			1,802,483		

NON-PAYROLL EXPENSES

Acct. No.	Account Name		Year to Date Actual	Year to Date Allowance	Month Actual	Month Allowance
	UTILITIES					
	WATER & SEWER CHARGES			59,104		
	GAS			61,010		
	ELECTRICITY			693,991		
	TELEPHONE			135,366		
	OTHER GASES			3,814		
				953,285		
	INDIRECT MATERIALS					
	EXPENDABLE TOOLS			556,083		
	MAINTENANCE REPAIR MATERIALS			1,757,221		
	LUBRICANTS & CHEMICALS			213,536		
	GAUGES			111,217		
	TOOL MAINTENANCE			1,570,375		
				4,208,432		
	FACILITIES					
	PROPERTY TAXES			142,938		
	DEPRECIATION - EQUIPMENT			2,260,529		
	DEPRECIATION - BUILDING			267,039		
	SECURITY			97,616		
	JANITORIAL			115,048		
	FUEL OIL			484,596		
	PURCHASED SERVICES			118,534		
				3,486,300		
	OFFICE EXPENSES					
	EMPLOYMENT EXPENSES			27,829		
	SUBSCRIPTIONS			2,668		
	DUES & MEMBERSHIPS			3,050		
	COMPUTER SERVICES			20,586		
	RENTAL OF OFFICE EQUIPMENT			62,140		
	TRAVEL EXPENSE			74,339		
	FORMS & STATIONERY			155,703		
	POSTAGE			84,525		
				430,840		
	TOTAL NON-PAYROLL EXPENSES			9,078,857		

be scrutinized—and would have discussed them with the plant manager as well as the controller.

Note, also, in the summary section of Exhibit 1 that indirect labor—service department costs are the second highest category of overhead, amounting to $4,152,750. This total, which broken down by department in another section of the exhibit, shows that six of the service departments—manufacturing engineering, material control, quality control, inspection, equipment maintenance, and toolroom and machine shop— amount to $3,455,087, or 83% of the total service department costs. This again points up the importance of placing major emphasis on major costs.

DETERMINE THE LEVEL OF ACTIVITY (STEP 2)

Once the sales forecast has been converted to a production budget, as reflected by the cost allowances shown in Exhibit 1, the second step is to establish the denominators by which the level of activity for the various production centers will be measured. These denominators will also be used as the base for calculating the costing rates.

Since this manufacturing operation consists of both machine-paced and labor-paced operations, it will be necessary to use machine hours for the former and direct labor hours for the latter. Exhibit 2 lists the machine-paced production cost centers (departments) in the upper half of the exhibit and the labor-paced centers in the lower half.

Machine-Paced Operations

Machine hours, which is the vehicle for applying overhead to the product, must also apply the direct labor cost. The exception is special automatics, which is in the robotics category, utilizing no direct labor. Exhibit 2 must therefore determine the annual direct labor cost as well as the machine hours. The overhead costs that apply to the machine-paced departments (cost centers) will be developed in the exhibits that follow. The key figures to be developed in this exhibit are the total annual direct labor cost, shown in column 7, and net machine hours, shown in column 10.

The annual direct labor cost is calculated for the automatics as follows:

Multiply 25 operators per shift by 2 shifts by 8 hours to arrive at the total available direct labor hours per day. This figure, multiplied by 242 days per year, shows the total available direct labor hours per year.

The calculations are: 25 operators × 2 shifts × 8 hours   = 400
400 hours per day × 242 days   = 96,800
96,800 hours per year × $11.59 per hour = $1,121,677

The net machine hours are calculated as follows:

Multiply 151 machines by 2 shifts by 8 hours by 242 days to arrive at the total available machine hours per year.

The above calculations are: 151 × 2 shifts × 8 hours × 242 days = 584,672
Adjusting the available machine hours by 65% to allow for such
unavoidable downtime as set-up and major maintenance   = 380,036

Labor-Paced Operations

The annual direct labor cost is calculated in the same manner as was done for the machine-paced operations. But since direct labor hours represent the vehicle for apply-

EXHIBIT 2
CALCULATION OF ANNUAL DIRECT LABOR COST AND NET MACHINE HOURS
MACHINE-PACED DEPARTMENTS

| | Number of Machines | Operators Per Shift | Shifts | Available Labor Hours | | Direct Labor Hrly. Rate | Direct Labor Cost/ Year | Available Machine Hours | Per Cent Machine Utilization | Net Machine Hours |
				8 Hour Day	242 Days					
	(1)	(2)	(3)	(4)	(5)	(6)	(7)	(8)	(9)	(10)
				(2) × (3) × 8	(4) × 242		(5) × (6)	(1) × (3) × 8 × 242		(8) × (9)
MACHINE-PACED OPNS.										
AUTOMATICS	151	25	2	400	96,800	$11.59	$1,121,677	584,672	65%	380,036
HEADERS AND PRESSES	71	28	1	224	54,208	8.71	471,960	137,456	60	82,473
SPECIAL AUTOMATICS	29	—	2.5	—	—	—	—	140,360	75	105,270
INGREDIENT MIXING MILL	12	12	1	96	23,232	10.82	251,305	23,232	85	19,747
MOLDING	35	23	2	368	89,056	11.70	1,041,995	135,520	70	94,864
							$2,886,937			

CALCULATION OF ANNUAL DIRECT LABOR COST AND NET DIRECT LABOR HOURS
LABOR-PACED DEPARTMENTS

| | Operators Per Shift | Shifts | Available Labor Hours | | Direct Labor Hrly. Rate | Direct Labor Cost/ Year | Direct Labor Utilization | Net Labor Hours |
			8 Hour Day	242 Days				
	(1)	(2)	(3)	(4)	(5)	(6)	(7)	(8)
			(1) × (2) × 8	(3) × 242		(4) × (5)		(4) × (7)
LABOR-PACED OPNS.								
SEMIAUTOMATIC ASSEMBLY	38	1	304	73,568	10.41	$ 766,173	64%	47,083
HAND ASSEMBLY	83	1	664	160,688	8.12	1,305,558	58	93,199
PLATING	25	1.5	300	72,600	9.71	704,879	62	45,012
PACKING	28	1	224	54,208	8.59	465,833	65	35,235
						$3,242,443		
						$6,129,380		

Notes: Small errors will be found in the direct labor cost/year because of rounding the direct labor hourly rate. Utilization percentages allow for such unavoidable downtime as setup and major maintenance.

ing overhead and direct labor to the product, the available labor hours must be factored by a direct labor utilization (efficiency) percentage. These calculations are demonstrated for the Semiautomatic Assembly Department.

The annual direct labor cost is calculated for the Semiautomatic Assembly Department as follows:

Multiply 38 operators per shift by 1 shift by 8 hours to arrive at the available direct labor hours per day. This figure, multiplied by 242 days per year, shows the total available direct labor hours per year.

The above calculations are: 38 operators × 1 shift × 8 hours   =   304
304 hours per day × 242 days   =   73,568
73,568 hours per year × $10.41/hr. = $766,173

The net annual labor hours are calculated as follows:
73,568 available labor hours × 64% =   47,083

The net machine hours for the machine-paced operations represent the standard level of activity for the individual production cost centers (referred to in the exhibit as "operations"). The same machine hours are used as the base for calculating the overhead plus direct labor costing rates.

The net labor hours, like the machine hours, represent the standard level of activity for the labor-paced production cost centers. These same labor hours are also used as the base for calculating the overhead plus direct labor costing rates.

Before the costing rates can be discussed, the overhead costs shown in Exhibit 1 must be allocated to the various production cost centers. This topic will be covered next.

Recap of Steps 1 and 2

At this point, we know the total allowable overhead for the level of activity at which the overhead costing rates are to be calculated. The overhead is summarized by category in Exhibit 1. We have also identified the machine-paced and labor-paced operations in Exhibit 2. This exhibit also shows the machine-hour base and the labor-hour base to be used in calculating the overhead costing rates.

IDENTIFY THE INDIRECT LABOR PERSONNEL REQUIREMENTS BY JOB TITLE AND NUMBER (STEP 3)

The annual indirect labor payroll cost in this company exceeds the direct labor cost—$6,280,875 for all indirect labor versus $6,129,380 for direct labor. The comparison

EXHIBIT 3
INDIRECT LABOR—PRODUCTION DEPARTMENTS'
BREAKDOWN OF PERSONNEL

	Total	Payroll
AUTOMATICS		
Foremen	2	
Group Leader A	1	
Group Leader B	1	
Tool and Die Setters	8	
Floormen	3	
Total Automatics	15	$ 395,831

EXHIBIT 3 (*Continued*)

	Total	Payroll
HEADERS AND PRESSES		
Foremen	1	
Group Leader B	2	
Tool and Die Setters	6	
Floormen	2	
Total Headers and Presses	11	238,350
SPECIAL AUTOMATICS		
Foremen	2	
Group Leader A	2	
Tool and Die Setters	8	
Maintenance Machinists	4	
Floormen	2	
Total Special Automatics	18	487,341
INGREDIENT MIXING MILL		
Foremen	2	
Group Leaders	3	
Floormen	1	
Total Ingredient Mixing Mill	6	153,225
MOLDING		
Foremen	2	
Group Leader A	2	
Group Leader B	2	
Tool and Die Setters	2	
Floormen	4	
Mold Cleaner	1	
Total Molding	13	304,322
SEMIAUTOMATIC ASSEMBLY		
Foremen	1	
Group Leaders	4	
Tool and Die Setter B	1	
Tool and Die Setter C	1	
Floormen	3	
Total Semiautomatic Assembly	10	204,300
HAND ASSEMBLY		
Foremen	1	
Group Leader A	1	
Group Leader B	2	
Floormen	1	
Total Hand Assembly	5	97,894
PLATING		
Foremen	1	
Group Leader B	2	
Stock Clerks	2	
Plater Mechanic	2	
Total Plating	7	140,456
PACKING		
Group Leader B	1	
Floormen	2	
Stock Dispatcher	1	
Printers	2	
Total Packing	6	106,406
TOTAL PAYROLL: INDIRECT LABOR—PRODUCTION DEPARTMENTS		$2,128,125

EXHIBIT 4
INDIRECT LABOR—SERVICE DEPARTMENTS'
BREAKDOWN OF PERSONNEL

	Total	Payroll
PLANT SUPERVISION		
General Manager	1	
Plant Superintendent	1	
Assistant Superintendent	1	
Secretary	1	
Clerk	1	
Total Plant Supervision	5	$ 174,416
MANUFACTURING ENGINEERING		
Manager	1	
Chief Industrial Engineer	1	
Industrial Engineer—Process	2	
Industrial Engineer—Methods	3	
Industrial Engineer—Standards	1	
Tool Designers	2	
Draftsmen	2	
Engineering Assistants	2	
Clerk-Stenographer	1	
Clerk-Typist	1	
Total Manufacturing Engineering	16	419,428
MATERIAL CONTROL		
Manager	1	
Purchasing Agent	1	
Buyer	1	
Expediter	1	
Clerk-Stenographer	1	
Production Control Supervisor	1	
Stockroom Foremen	5	
Central Planners	2	
Dispatch Planners	5	
Records Supervisor	1	
Office Clerks	2	
Factory Clerks	3	
Total Material Control	24	498,330
QUALITY CONTROL		
Manager	1	
Engineer	1	
Assistant Engineer	1	
Statisticians	2	
Metal Laboratory Foreman	1	
Tool and Gauge Foreman	1	
Tool Crib Attendants	5	
Tool Crib Inspectors	4	
Laboratory Technicians	2	
Total Quality Control	18	394,511
PLANT ACCOUNTING		
Plant Controller	1	
Cost Accountants	2	
Cost Clerk	1	
Machine and Labor Efficiency Clerks	3	
Payroll Clerk	1	
Typist	1	
Total Plant Accounting	9	182,721

EXHIBIT 4 (Continued)

	Total	Payroll
PERSONNEL		
Manager	1	
Clerks	2	
Industrial Nurse	1	
Switchboard Operator	1	
Total Personnel Department	5	87,208
RECEIVING AND RAW STORES		
Group Leader B	1	
Stock Assemblers	3	
Floormen	2	
Scrap Handler	1	
Traffic Clerk	1	
Mail Clerks	2	
Total Receiving and Raw Stores	10	145,346
IN-PROCESS STOCKROOM		
Group Leader C	1	
Stock Assemblers	5	
Stock Dispatcher	1	
Total In-Process Stockroom	7	107,972
INSPECTION		
In-Process Foremen	3	
Inspectors:		
Incoming Materials	6	
Returned Goods	1	
Headers and Presses	4	
Automatics	7	
Special Automatics	6	
Plating	1	
Assembly	2	
Molding	8	
Hand Assembly	1	
Statistician	1	
Total Inspection	40	812,603
EQUIPMENT MAINTENANCE		
Superintendent	1	
Group Leader A	2	
Group Leader B	1	
Electrician	4	
Electronic Maintenance	1	
Firemen	5	
Maintenance Mechanics	7	
Maintenance Helpers	4	
Total Equipment Maintenance	25	639,524
TOOL ROOM AND MACHINE SHOP		
Foreman	1	
Group Leader A	2	
Tool Maker A	7	
Tool Maker B	3	
Machinist A	4	
Machinist B	5	
Machinist C	2	
Tool Grinder A	1	
Tool Grinder C	1	
Total Tool Room and Machine Shop	26	690,691
TOTAL PAYROLL: INDIRECT LABOR—SERVICE DEPARTMENTS		$4,152,750

by head count is 276 for indirect labor and 287 for direct labor. Indirect labor costs of this relative magnitude, not readily controllable by standards as in the case of direct labor, should be identified not only by department, as shown in Exhibit 1, but by job title and number of incumbents in each job title. Such a breakdown is shown in Exhibits 3 and 4. Exhibit 3 lists, by department, the indirect labor in the production departments (cost centers). Exhibit 4 lists the indirect labor in the service departments. The analysis of indirect labor personnel shown in these two exhibits provides an important schedule that documents a large segment of overhead cost that affects the overhead costing rates.

The president of a company manufacturing knitwear products reviewed the documentation of an overhead costing rate study that was made for his company. In reviewing the indirect labor breakdown similar to Exhibits 3 and 4, several categories of jobs caught his eye. These are shown below, together with questions that he raised.

4 elevator operators	"What is the cost of automating?"
9 painters	"Why not contract out our painting?"
	"Seems like a lot of painters permanently on the payroll."
17 sweepers	"Wouldn't an automatic sweeping machine reduce this?"
24 box makers	"Seems like a lot of box makers. What can we do to reduce this?"

The questions were distributed to the appropriate managers for investigation, with a request that the results of their review and recommendations for cost reduction be presented at the next management meeting.

The responses to the questions raised by the president were as follows:

Automatic elevators There was no question as to the justification of automating; there would be a payback in less than four years. However, since two of the four elevators were being used for moving material, there was a fear that material handlers, by locking the elevator mechanism, could monopolize the elevators for long periods, leaving material handlers on other floors waiting for unreasonable lengths of time. The decision was made to automate the two passenger elevators and to continue operating the two freight elevators manually in order to ensure continual movement of materials on all floors.

Painters: Since there was enough of a certain type of painting that must be done year round, the decision was made to retain two full-time painters on the payroll. All other painting would be subcontracted. This would be advantageous because (1) painting would be done only when needed, without the necessity of keeping a crew of nine painters busy, and (2) contracted painting could be done on "off hours," without having to pay an overtime premium.

Sweepers: The recommendation was made to purchase an automatic sweeper to clean the large areas. This improved cleanliness because the vacuum action of the equipment sucked up the dust rather than agitating it. Because of corners and hard-to-reach areas between machines, it was necessary to maintain 11 employees who would continue to do the sweeping by hand.

Box makers: A saving of 35% was achieved in box making through a new design which permitted boxes to be assembled without having to insert tabs into slots in each of the four corners.

After the meeting, the president commented that there was obviously a serious weakness in the organization when it was necessary for the chief executive officer to review costs at this level to achieve cost reductions. He questioned how many other potential savings were going unnoticed because no one was monitoring the cost and operating controls. He criticized the accounting department for its academic approach to cost accounting but was particularly critical of his industrial engineers for letting so many inefficiencies go by.

DETERMINING THE APPROPRIATE ALLOCATION BASES (STEP 4)

Our present highly competitive business community requires that greater pains be taken in the methodology used to allocate overhead to products. The allocation method must be the result of a joint agreement between the cost accountant and the department head who is responsible for rendering the service. The individual responsible for rendering support services is familiar with the problem areas and his needs in order to perform his job efficiently.

The allocation of overhead for developing costing rates is done annually in most companies. It is conceivable that adjustments may be necessary in mid-year if an important change is made in a process or if labor-paced operations are converted to machine-paced operations. In such a circumstance, it would be necessary to revalue the inventory on the basis of revised rates. Although there is no standard formula that can be used in making allocations, the following illustrations can be used as guidelines.

Indirect labor—production departments	These indirect labor costs represent the payroll costs of those employees who are permanently assigned to the various production departments. Thus, there is no need to make any allocation of them. Exhibit 3 shows this breakdown. Total payroll = $2,128,125.

Indirect labor—service departments
 	
    Plant supervision
    Plant accounting
    Personnel
	In this company, it was felt that these functions should be allocated to the production centers on the basis of the number of direct and indirect employees. Among the factors considered were union relations, employee grievances, payroll preparation, production reporting, interviewing, and processing of new employees.

Industrial engineering	These costs were allocated on the basis of the number of labor and machine operations in the production departments. In the Assembly Department, there were two production lines performing similar tasks. Since the time studies of one of the production lines were applicable to the second, this was taken into

account to avoid doubling up the allocation of the time study personnel involved.

Material control

The allocation of this department was based on the number of different item types that had to be scheduled and monitored in the various production centers.

Quality control and inspection

Incoming inspection would be allocated according to the type of material being inspected and the production center using the material. In a company with a metallurgical laboratory, this cost would be allocated to the metal press production center. Any quality and inspection costs that can be identified with specific cost centers should be so allocated. The remaining quality office-type costs would be allocated on the basis of those that have been identified with the production cost centers.

Receiving, raw stores, and in-process stockroom

These costs should normally be allocated on the basis of the number of types of items handled. In receiving and raw stores, the size and weight of some of the items received may be a greater consideration than the number of types of items. In some companies in which the materials are fairly homogeneous, these costs can be allocated through a material overhead rate.

Maintenance labor, tool-room, and machine shop

Good records should be kept of these costs by individual project, with departmental foremen signing off on all hours charged to the production center. Such records would provide the basis for making charges to the various production centers, as well as providing controls for monitoring costs approximating $1,300,000 per year. In the absence of good records, the maintenance supervisors should estimate how their costs should be allocated among the various production centers.

Labor-connected expenses†

This group of costs is frequently referred to as "fringe benefits." Although some companies list these as part of the departmental payroll, it is preferable to show them in a separate grouping for use in union negotiations. Some companies also include such costs as cafeteria subsidies and uniforms furnished by the company for sports activities.

The overtime and shift premiums can be identified by production cost center. The portion applicable to the indirect labor service departments would be allocable to production centers in the same proportion as the basic salaries and wages are allocated.

---

† The breakdown of labor connected expenses is shown in Exhibit 1; the total annual figure amounts to $1,-802,483.

The balance of the items could be allocated on the same basis as the salaries and wages are allocated.

Nonpayroll expenses‡

Water and sewer charges
This is not usually a large charge unless water is used in the manufacturing process. An estimate should be obtained from the plant engineer.

Gas
If gas is used for heating, the applicable portion should be allocated on the basis of the floor space occupied by the production centers. The amount used in the production process should be estimated by the plant engineer. Some plant engineers determine usage by attaching a flow meter to the equipment and extending the flow per hour by the number of hours that the equipment is in use.

Electricity
The plant electrician would be the logical individual to determine the allocation of this item of cost. Most electricians would determine the connected load and extend this by the hours of usage of the equipment to arrive at the amount to be allocated to the various production centers.

Telephone
This is not usually a large item in a factory. The majority of the usage stems from the purchasing department and the general manager's office. This cost, then, could be allocated to the production centers on the basis of the allocation used for purchasing and the general manager.

Other gases
This is a small item used by the maintenance department in this company. It could be allocated on the same basis as the maintenance department.

Expendable tools
This cost allocation could be made on the basis of the number of direct labor employees in the various production centers if records of issues are not available.

Maintenance and repair materials
Maintenance project costs should include usage by production center. If such records are not available, the maintenance supervisor's best estimate should be used.

Lubricants and chemicals
Allocation would be based on the maintenance supervisor's estimate.

Gauges
This allocation would be estimated by the tool crib attendant who issues the gauges.

Tool maintenance
In this company, a good deal of the tool maintenance work is done on the outside. This cost can be identified by the production center in which the tools are used.

---

‡ The nonpayroll items discussed above are shown in Exhibit 1. The total annual cost, as pointed out earlier, is $9,078,857, with maintenance repair materials, tool maintenance, and equipment depreciation accounting for more than half of the nonpayroll expenses. This is frequently the case in companies that are highly machine paced.

Property taxes Depreciation—building Security Janitorial Fuel oil	These items, which are rent-equivalent costs, were allocated on the basis of the floor space occupied. Because stockrooms occupy 44% of the floor space, these costs were allocated to the stockrooms and then reallocated to the production centers on the basis of the stockroom space required to service the various centers.
Depreciation—equipment	The asset records should be the source of depreciation charges assignable to the various production centers. In many companies, however, the records are not kept up-to-date. Equipment is transferred to other plants within the company without paperwork, and machines are cannibalized to obtain spare parts. In such instances in which the asset records are not correct, the allocation can be determined by inventorying the major pieces of equipment by production center and then allocating the small miscellaneous items on the basis of the major items.
Purchased services	This could represent such outside services as painting, rigging, or even rental of certain equipment. The purchasing department usually has records in the form of purchase orders, and the accounting department has invoices in its accounts payable file. Either the purchasing department or accounting files could provide information to identify the types of services purchased and thus help determine how these costs should be allocated.

Office expenses
  Employment expenses
  Subscriptions
  Dues and memberships
  Computer services
  Rental of office equipment
  Travel expense
  Forms and stationery
  Postage
	This is the smallest category of expense in nonpayroll items. It is ironic that the documentation available for the smallest category is the greatest. Unfortunately, there are many who concentrate heavily on these items in determining allocations (and cost reductions) and overlook many of the larger expenses that warrant greater effort because of their size.

The foregoing procedures, relative to determining appropriate allocation bases for the various expenses making up the $17,162,215 in overhead, illustrate two potential benefits:

- The key manufacturing-oriented personnel, with familiarity in the cost behavior of the particular expense being allocated, participate in the determination of the most appropriate method for allocating the expense.
- The accountant, in his discussions with such personnel, will become more intimately familiar with the manufacturing operations and less likely to seek arbitrary methods for allocating overhead costs to production centers.

Allocations Can Be Quite Controversial

The methods of allocating costs can be quite controversial, particularly when products made in one division of a company are sold to another. It is natural for the supplier division to challenge costs allocated to it. It is also natural for the purchasing division to dispute transfer prices of the products it purchases from another division.

The financial executive of one company, whose department was responsible for developing overhead costing rates for the various divisions, related the following story:

> The vice-president of our CRT division called me into his office one day and began chewing me out because of the excess charges he felt he was being assessed for his shipping warehouse. He challenged our costing allocation for electricity. He argued that warehouses have only a few lights, so they shouldn't receive such exorbitant charges for electricity.
>
> Having recently been through the warehouse with the chief electrician, I was prepared for this question. I explained that the electrician said that the same wattage per square foot is used in the warehouse for lighting as is required in the office areas. However, because the ceiling height in the warehouse is double that of the offices, the warehouse appears to be dimly lit. I also called attention to other uses that his warehouse was making of electricity that far exceeded the lighting. These included a coating operation on the outside of the finished CRT, which called for spraying. This meant special exhaust equipment to carry out the fumes, a conveyorized line, and a battery of heat lamps to dry the finish. Additionally, there were eight lift trucks run by batteries that required overnight charging.
>
> The connected load for all these facilities was multiplied by the hours of usage to obtain the amount of electricity to be charged to the warehouse. When I listed these other factors, the vice-president quickly changed the subject.

Controversy is to be expected when costs are being allocated. It is therefore important that the individual responsible for making the allocation be thoroughly knowledgeable about the operations and that he consult those who know the most about the cost to be allocated. In this case, it was the electrician.

Recap of Steps 3 and 4

With the machine-hour and labor-hour bases established in step 2, we are ready in step 3 to identify the indirect labor personnel by job title, by head count, and by the total payroll cost in each department. Step 4 summarized the guidelines to be followed in allocating the indirect labor payroll as well as the nonlabor indirect expenses.

CALCULATE THE OVERHEAD COSTING RATES (STEP 5)

With the level of activity established in Exhibit 2, indirect labor personnel requirements determined by job title and number of employees in Exhibits 3 and 4, and allocation bases determined for the various overhead expenses in the preceding section, we are now ready to calculate the overhead costing rates for both the machine-paced and labor-paced operations.

This has been done in Exhibit 5. The five machine-paced and four labor-paced production centers are listed horizontally across the exhibit. The major overhead categories, as shown in the summary section of Exhibit 1, are listed vertically.

Since direct labor will be included in the costing rates, the breakdown of direct labor by production centers is also shown and is added to the total overhead in arriving at the total of both elements of cost for each production center.

The first line in the lower section of Exhibit 5 shows the net machine hours for the five machine-paced production centers. The second line shows the overhead costing rate of $25.11, which was obtained by dividing the total overhead of $2,071,073 in the headers and presses production center by the net machine hours of 82,473. The third line indicates the direct labor costing rate to be $5.72. This was obtained by dividing the direct labor cost for headers and presses of $471,960 by the net machine hours of 82,473. The total costing rate, including overhead and direct labor, is $30.83. The same procedure is followed for the labor-paced departments.

The availability of costing rates for each production center does not necessarily ensure good product costing. This is particularly true when a production center includes a highly sophisticated machine whose hourly cost of operation may be well above the rate calculated for the center. The next section will deal with this topic.

Breaking Down the Costing Rates Within the Production Center

Production centers (more frequently referred to as "production departments") provide a natural pool of costs from which departmental costing rates are developed.

If the production center includes a computerized machine, for example, that is costlier and requires greater support services than the other machines, it is necessary to establish a separate costing rate for such equipment. This can be accomplished by making adjustments to the production center rate rather than reallocating every single cost. The procedure to follow is described in the following steps.

Step A: Identify the differential costs. "Differential" refers to major machine-related costs that vary from machine to machine. Based on the terminology used in this company, examples are equipment maintenance, toolroom and machine shop, maintenance repair materials, tool maintenance, equipment depreciation, and direct labor.

Step B: Calculate the basic overhead costing rate. The basic overhead costing rate is the total overhead rate reduced by the differential overhead items listed in step A. This basic rate would apply to all equipment in the production center, whether sophisticated or not. The differential costs would be allocated between the sophisticated machine and the remaining machines, and a differential costing rate would be calculated for each of these two categories.

Step C: Make the calculations. The total overhead for the headers and presses production center is $2,071,073 (see Exhibit 5). This includes the following differential overhead items:

Equipment maintenance	$ 65,043
Toolroom and machine shop	141,124
Maintenance repair materials	193,294
Tool maintenance	204,148
Depreciation—equipment	221,146
	$824,755

Subtracting the total differential overhead of $824,755 from the total overhead of $2,071,073 leaves a total basic overhead of $1,246,318. Dividing this figure by the total net machine hours of 82,473, shown in Exhibit 5, we obtain a basic overhead

EXHIBIT 5
BREAKDOWN OF OVERHEAD AND DIRECT LABOR BY DEPARTMENTS

	Machine-Paced Departments					Labor-Paced Departments				Total All Departments
	Automatics	Headers & Presses	Special Automatics	Ingredient Mixing Mill	Molding	Semi-Automatic Assembly	Hand Assembly	Plating	Packing	
INDIRECT LABOR:										
PRODUCTION DEPARTMENTS	$ 395,831	238,350	487,341	153,225	304,322	204,300	97,894	140,456	106,406	2,128,125
SERVICE DEPARTMENT	1,022,837	543,812	785,125	98,702	413,312	348,845	509,825	269,404	160,888	4,152,750
PAYROLL-RELATED EXPENSES	310,027	185,656	86,519	81,112	281,188	228,915	252,348	214,495	162,223	1,802,483
NONLABOR EXPENSES	2,082,630	1,103,255	2,273,983	264,014	767,626	630,166	617,100	988,015	352,068	9,078,857
TOTAL OVERHEAD	$3,811,325	2,071,073	3,632,968	597,053	1,766,448	1,412,226	1,477,167	1,612,370	781,585	17,162,215
TOTAL DIRECT LABOR	$1,121,677	471,960	–0–	251,305	1,041,995	766,173	1,305,558	704,879	465,833	6,129,380
TOTAL OVERHEAD AND DIRECT LABOR	$4,933,002	2,543,033	3,632,968	848,358	2,808,443	2,178,399	2,782,725	2,317,249	1,247,418	23,291,595

CALCULATION OF OVERHEAD AND DIRECT LABOR COSTING RATES

	Automatics	Headers & Presses	Special Automatics	Ingredient Mixing Mill	Molding	Semi-Automatic Assembly	Hand Assembly	Plating	Packing
NET MACHINE HOURS (Note 1)	380,036	82,473	105,270	19,747	94,864				
OVERHEAD COSTING RATE	$10.03	25.11	34.51	30.23	18.62				
DIRECT LABOR COSTING RATE	2.95	5.72	–	12.73	10.98				
TOTAL COSTING RATE	12.98	30.83	34.51	42.96	29.60				
NET DIRECT LABOR HOURS (Note 2)						47,083	93,199	45,012	35,235
OVERHEAD COSTING RATE						$30.00	15.85	35.82	22.18
DIRECT LABOR COSTING RATE						16.27	14.01	15.66	13.22
TOTAL COSTING RATE						$46.27	29.86	51.48	35.40

Note 1: Source: Exhibit 2, Machine-paced operations—Column 10
Note 2: Source: Exhibit 2, Labor-paced operations—Column 8

rate of $15.11. This basic rate applies to all equipment in the headers and presses production center, whether sophisticated or not.

Step D: Calculate the differential rates. A differential rate would be calculated for the more sophisticated machine (or machines, if there are more than one) and another for the remaining equipment. This requires that the differential costs shown in step C, as well as the direct labor, be split as follows:

	TOTAL HEADERS & PRESSES	COMPUTERIZED MACHINE	REMAINING EQUIPMENT
Equipment maintenance	$ 65,043	6,500	58,543
Toolroom and machine shop	141,124	13,150	127,974
Maintenance repair material	193,294	11,100	182,194
Tool maintenance	204,148	9,500	194,648
Depreciation—equipment	221,146	25,400	195,746
Total differential overhead	$ 824,755	65,650	759,105
Total direct labor	471,960	40,274	431,686
	$1,296,715	105,924	1,190,791
Net machine hours	82,473	4,643	77,830
Differential overhead costing rate	$10.00	14.14	9.75
Differential direct labor rate	5.72	8.67	5.54
Total differential costing rate	$15.72	22.81	15.29
Basic overhead rate (from steps B and C)	15.11	15.11	15.11
Total overhead and direct labor rate	$30.83	37.92	30.40

The definition of differential costs is flexible. If, for example, the more sophisticated equipment in a department requires substantially more floor space than the other machines, the differential costs may have to include such items as real estate taxes/rent, security, and janitorial services, in addition to the items referred to earlier as differential costs. A heat-treating operation might require the inclusion of energy costs in the differential category. Some computer-controlled machines require high electronic maintenance costs rather than the conventional types of mechanical and electrical maintenance.

GUIDELINES FOR CALCULATING OVERHEAD COSTING RATES

The intent of this chapter has been to provide the reader with a guide that can be used in developing overhead costing rates for a fairly sophisticated manufacturing operation. Although the procedures may appear to be complex, they are relatively simple if taken step by step. The guidelines can be summarized as follows:

1. Prepare a breakdown of all manufacturing costs by category similar to Exhibit 1. This will provide an overview that will also furnish the overhead cost detail needed to calculate the costing rates.
2. Remember that available machine hours and available direct labor hours must be adjusted downward to allow for unavoidable downtime (see Exhibit 2). This step cannot be glossed over because it can greatly influence the costing rates.
3. Since indirect labor in Exhibits 3 and 4 (plus labor-connected costs) represents almost half of the total overhead, it is important that this large cost be broken down by job title to facilitate proper allocation. This information will be helpful

in ensuring that all costs are considered when reviewing the allocations with the department heads.

4. Department heads should be involved in determining the best allocation basis for the overhead costs under their jurisdiction. The accountant responsible for making the allocations must know the rationale behind them in the event that costing rates are challenged.

5. When the various overhead costs referred to in guideline 1 have been allocated, the calculation of the overhead rates consists of an assembly of the figures and the arithmetic required to make the necessary calculations of the rates. Note in Exhibit 5 that all costing rates are broken down to show the direct labor rates as well as the overhead portion. The exception is special automatics, which does not require direct labor.

6. Departmental costing rates may have to be broken down further to recognize one or more high-cost operations. This can be accomplished with relative ease. See the section "Breaking Down the Costing Rates within the Production Center." This section discusses differential costs and differential costing rates for both direct labor and overhead.

7. Upon completion of the costing rates, have the various schedules typed and "packaged" for distribution to key executives—as many companies do with the annual budget.

3
Importance of Integrating Costing and Cost Controls

A surprising number of companies develop budgets from figures that are different from those used for calculating overhead costing rates. In some cases, this is due to the use of different time frames. Another reason is that the individual responsible for planning and budgeting may work independently of the accounting function. Failure to work from the same set of figures weakens controls because inventory values and product costs are developed from one set of figures while measurements of overhead variances and breakeven analyses are developed from another set. Printing-Binding, Inc., a company used as a case example in this chapter, illustrates the integrated approach.

Chapter 2 concentrated on the steps involved in developing machine-hour and labor-hour costing rates for overhead and for direct labor in a company with production departments. As in Chapter 1, emphasis was placed on the importance of separating labor-paced and machine-paced operations when developing overhead and direct labor costing rates. Chapter 2 also illustrated how production center costing rates could be broken down further to reflect cost differences in manufacturing equipment within a production center. The use of the differential cost technique provides a simplified approach to more definitive product costing—an important consideration in this age of high technology.

This chapter goes a step further. It not only develops machine and labor-hour costing rates for a printing firm; it illustrates how the costing rates are used in making up a job cost estimate, how the overhead costs are broken down into their fixed and variable components to facilitate the development of flexible budgets, and how the breakdown of fixed and variable costs can be used in developing a breakeven analysis. This "full-service" concept provides a system of checks and balances wherein the costing rates used in job cost estimates, flexible budgets, and breakeven analyses are all developed from a common data base. A short history of the company used for illustrative purposes follows.

PRINTING-BINDING, INC.—A SHORT HISTORY

This company started in the days when linotype machines were used to cast type one line at a time. This was a vast improvement over the previous method, by which typographers set movable type by hand. Both of these methods of typesetting have been almost completely replaced by newer technologies—first, photocomposition and, more recently, electronic typesetting systems. Now word processors are used to produce electronic manuscripts copied onto floppy disks or magnetic tapes or transmitted by telecommunications. Such media, with proper interfacing techniques and along with additional type-specification instructions, are processed through electronic typesetting equipment. The end product is high-quality type (reproduction proofs) in galleys or pages. Proofreading, correction work, and paste-up complete the preparation of the finished copy. The work is then ready for the camera to make negatives which are used in exposing the offset plates. These plates are sent to companies like Printing-Binding, Inc., to print and bind the book.

Folding

Commonly at Printing-Binding, Inc., the offset plates used in the printing process provide for 16 pages to be printed on both sides of 36 × 48-inch sheets shown in the cost estimate later in this chapter. The sheets are printed on both sides. The folding process consists of folding these sheets in a predetermined pattern so that the 32 pages in the folded packet are arranged in numerical sequence. A 256-page book would require eight packets (called "signatures"). As the folding is done, the signatures are bundled and the process continues until the edition is complete. The bundles of signatures are then ready for the binding operations.

Binding

After folding is completed, the signatures are gathered in proper sequence, bringing all the pages for each book together. Then, depending upon the style of binding, the book may be either sewn or bound by the use of adhesives. If the book is sewn, the signatures are stitched together in sequence. Each book is held together by the sewing on the back edge or the spine. Adhesive binding holds the pages together by milling off the closed back edge of the spine and applying an adhesive.

Once the semifinished book is sewn or bound by an adhesive, it may be encased in either a hard or a soft cover.

The hardcover binding is more expensive and requires additional operations and materials. Cases are made of boards and covering material, and then are stamped with the title or design. Endpapers are used to connect the front and back covers to the first and last signatures of the book. In hardcover binding, the endpapers together with the book pages are trimmed on the three outside edges. This becomes the "book block"; it is finally brought together with the cover as it is "cased in."

Papercover binding is much simpler and involves a preprinted cover to be glued to the spine of the book block. Then the cover and the book receive a final trim of the three outside edges.

Need for Changes in Costing Practices

Prior to the introduction of electronic typesetting, Printing Binding, Inc., did its own typesetting. It used letterpress rather than offset printing, so plant operations were essentially labor paced. The company was satisfied with the use of a single plantwide direct-labor costing rate. But with the substitution of the more expensive offset presses for letterpress printing, management recognized the need for more sophisticated costing. Accordingly, the decision was made to establish the following four cost centers:

Color presses: Color presses, being larger and more complex than black and white presses, required a greater amount of maintenance, depreciation, floor space, supplies, and the like.

Black and white presses: These were set up as a separate cost center to distinguish between the higher overhead machine hour costs of the color and black and white presses.

Folding: This includes the folding operation and the bundling of the signatures as described earlier.

Binding: Binding includes the gathering of signatures in the proper sequence, the sewing or application of adhesives, forming the book block, and casing in the binder, as described earlier.

The balance of this chapter will discuss the seven steps required to provide the management of this company with full-service overhead analysis. The exhibits illustrating these steps are:

1. Projected Level of Activity: Direct Labor and Machine Hours
2. Overhead Requirements
3. Allocation of Overhead to Production Centers
4. Calculation of Hourly Costing Rates
5. Job Cost Estimate
6. Development of the Flexible Budget Formula
7. Breakeven Analysis

PROJECTED LEVEL OF ACTIVITY: DIRECT LABOR AND MACHINE HOURS

Exhibit 1 sets forth the level of activity at which the business is expected to operate in the coming year. It takes into consideration that this will also be the level at which the fixed costs of the business are fully absorbed and the business yields an acceptable return on investment.

A number of financial executives who were interviewed about their practices in establishing the level of activity were found to favor forecasts of what was anticipated in the coming year. Others based the level on what they referred to as normal, or the expectation based on the past history.

These approaches are only partly correct. The important factor that must be taken into account is the economics of the business. Depending on the nature of the business,

EXHIBIT 1
PROJECTED LEVEL OF ACTIVITY:
DIRECT LABOR AND MACHINE HOURS

	Shifts	Direct Labor Dollars	Direct Labor Hours	Machine Hours
LABOR-PACED OPERATIONS				
Folding				
6 Operators	1	$ 86,400	11,664	
Binding				
5 Sewing Machine Operators	1	67,000		
3 Binders	1	40,500		
Total Sewing and Binding		107,500	15,550	
Total Labor-Paced Operations		$193,900	27,214	
MACHINE-PACED OPERATIONS				
Color Presses				
4 Pressmen	2	$ 90,800		
4 Helpers	2	55,200		
Total Color Presses		$146,000		6,800
Black and White Presses				
4 Pressmen	2	89,200		
3 Helpers	2	53,600		
Total Black and White Presses		142,800		7,760
Total Machine-Paced Operations		$288,800		14,560
TOTAL LABOR AND MACHINE-PACED OPERATIONS		$482,700		

economic considerations normally dictate that labor-paced operations would be carried on a single-shift basis, while machine-paced operations would be performed on a two- or three-shift basis, depending on the amount of capital investment in equipment. In Printing-Binding, Inc., the labor-paced operations are done on a single shift, with some second-shift work during peak periods. The presses are operated on a two-shift schedule, with the possibility of some third-shift operations in peak periods. Exhibit 1 identifies the labor-paced and machine-paced operations and lists the number of employees in each production center, the job title, payroll, direct labor hours, and machine hours. It should be noted that the costs and hours reflect what might be termed "gross" costs and hours. The more important factor is the level of utilization of labor hours and machine hours. This will be covered in Exhibit 4, which deals with the calculation of the hourly costing rates.

The 27,214 direct labor hours and 14,560 machine hours are the available hours. The adjustment for unavoidable downtime is made in Exhibit 4. In the previous chapter, the available hours and the net hours, after application of the utilization factor, were calculated at the same time. This is a matter of choice.

OVERHEAD REQUIREMENTS

The overhead requirements listed in Exhibit 2 consist of the indirect employees identifiable with the production and service departments. The nonlabor category includes

EXHIBIT 2
OVERHEAD REQUIREMENTS

	Annual Payroll	
INDIRECT LABOR—PRODUCTION DEPARTMENTS		
1 Factory Superintendent	$ 33,500	
1 Steno-Clerk	15,200	
2 General Maintenance	26,700	$ 75,400
INDIRECT LABOR—SERVICE DEPARTMENTS		
Accounting		
1 Accountant	$ 21,650	
2 Cost Clerks	23,750	$ 45,400
Production Control		
1 Production Scheduler/Estimator	$ 19,500	
3 Expediters	42,000	$ 61,500
TOTAL INDIRECT LABOR PAYROLL		$182,300
NONLABOR OVERHEAD		
Fringe Benefits	$131,590	
Ink	28,700	
Freight	950	
Rollers	10,300	
Replacement Parts	8,200	
Oil Wipers	3,300	
Electricity	22,400	
Chemicals	7,200	
Depreciation-Equipment	32,300	
Depreciation-Building	14,500	
Real Estate Taxes	17,960	
Property Taxes	4,200	$281,600
TOTAL NONLABOR OVERHEAD		
TOTAL ALL OVERHEAD REQUIREMENTS		$463,900

the fringe benefits for direct as well as indirect labor employees. It also includes all items that do not fit in the direct material category, as well as other support costs such as occupancy-related costs, depreciation, and utilities. Note that the indirect labor payroll of $182,300 plus the fringe benefits of $131,590 account for two-thirds of the overhead of $463,900.

ALLOCATION OF OVERHEAD TO PRODUCTION CENTERS

The allocation of overhead is shown in Exhibit 3. The column called "Overhead Requirements" presents the same information as that shown in Exhibit 2. The columns to the right show the basis of allocations and the dollar values of each item distributed to the four production centers on the basis indicated. The rationale used in determining the most appropriate bases for distributing the individual items is shown below.

Superintendent's estimate:	The factory superintendent felt that, from past experience, his time and that of his stenographer-clerk was provided on a "readiness to serve" basis. He therefore estimated that their payroll allocations should be made on the basis of one-third to the two labor-paced operations (split 50/50 between the two), one-third to the color presses, and one-third to the black and white presses. However, because there were more presses of the black and white type, and many troublesome short runs which frequently required his attention, he increased the amount allocated to this group.
General maintenance	The factory superintendent required all maintenance work to be recorded on job cards showing the time spent and the material used. Upon completion of such work, the time started and time finished were to be approved by the responsible individual in each production center. The allocations were based on an analysis of job cards after adjustment for certain unusual, nonrecurring costs.
Accountant	The accountant's services were considered to be on a "readiness to serve" basis. His payroll was therefore allocated in the same manner as the factory superintendent's.
Cost clerks Fringe benefits	Since these clerks made up the payroll, maintained the quarterly records, and performed duties normally done by a personnel department, their time was allocated on the basis of the number of direct and indirect employees. The fringe benefits were likewise distributed on the basis of the direct and indirect payroll of each department, except that number of employees was used in the first case and payroll dollars in the latter.
Production scheduler/estimator and expediters	The effort of this group is influenced by the number of jobs in the shop. This was used as the basis for distribution.

EXHIBIT 3
ALLOCATION OF OVERHEAD TO PRODUCTION CENTERS

Overhead Requirements	Amount	Basis of Allocation	Labor-Paced Operations		Machine-Paced Operations	
			Folding	Binding	Color Presses	Black & White Presses
INDIRECT LABOR—PRODUCTION DEPTS.						
1 Factory Superintendent	$ 33,500	Superintendent's Estimate	5,025	5,025	10,050	13,400
1 Steno-Clerk	15,200	Superintendent's Estimate	2,280	2,280	4,560	6,080
2 General Maintenance	26,700	Job Card Analysis	4,806	4,005	11,748	6,141
Total	$ 75,400		12,111	11,310	26,358	25,621
INDIRECT LABOR—SERVICE DEPTS.						
Accounting						
1 Accountant	$ 21,650	Accountant's Estimate	3,247	3,248	6,495	8,660
2 Cost Clerks	23,750	Direct and Indirect Employees	6,650	8,787	3,800	4,513
Total	$ 45,400		9,897	12,035	10,295	13,173
Production Control						
1 Production Scheduler/Estimator	$ 19,500	Number of Jobs in Process	3,900	4,875	4,875	5,850
3 Expediters	42,000	Number of Jobs in Process	8,400	10,500	10,500	12,600
Total	$ 61,500		12,300	15,375	15,375	18,450
TOTAL INDIRECT LABOR PAYROLL	$182,300		34,308	38,720	52,028	57,244
NONLABOR OVERHEAD						
Fringe Benefits	$131,590	Direct and Indirect Labor Payroll	23,686	28,950	39,477	39,477
Ink	28,700	Number of Impressions	—	—	17,220	11,480
Freight	950	Number of Impressions	—	—	570	380
Rollers	10,300	Number of Impressions	—	—	6,180	4,120
Replacement parts	8,200	Job Card Analysis	1,230	656	3,608	2,706
Oil Wipers	3,300	Number of Impressions	—	—	1,980	1,320
Electricity	22,400	Connected Load × Hours of Usage	3,584	2,688	10,080	6,048
Chemicals	7,200	Production Control's Estimate	—	—	4,104	3,096
Depreciation—Equipment	32,300	Fixed Asset Ledger	5,491	5,168	12,274	9,367
Depreciation—Building	14,500	Floor Space Occupied	2,610	2,175	6,380	3,335
Real Estate Taxes	17,960	Floor Space Occupied	3,233	2,694	7,902	4,131
Property Taxes	4,200	Floor Space Occupied	756	630	1,848	966
TOTAL NONLABOR OVERHEAD	$281,600		40,590	42,961	111,623	86,426
TOTAL OVERHEAD REQUIREMENTS	$463,900		74,898	81,681	163,651	143,670

Ink, freight, rollers, oil wipers	These items are all influenced by the number of impressions made by the various printing presses. The color presses took about 50% more of the cost allocation for these items, since there were more rollers on these presses because of the additional colors.
Electricity	The determination of this allocation was based on the connected load in each production center multiplied by the hours of operation. While electricity was also used by the office area, no attempt was made to charge these departments and then to reallocate the costs to the production centers. Such recirculation of costs was not considered to be worth the effort.
Chemicals	Chemical usage, which was confined to the presses, was estimated by the production control scheduler/estimator.
Depreciation—equipment	This item was taken from the asset ledger, which recorded the purchase price of the equipment as well as the amount of depreciation.
Depreciation—building, real estate and property taxes	These items were allocated on the basis of the floor space occupied. To avoid recirculation of costs into the offices, these expenses were charged directly to the four production service departments on the basis of the floor space occupied.

Exhibit 3, in addition to showing the amount of allocation of each overhead item, shows the total for each of the four production centers. These totals are shown in Exhibit 4, in which the hourly costing rates are calculated.

EXHIBIT 4
CALCULATION OF HOURLY COSTING RATES

				Machine-Paced	
		Labor-Paced		Color	Black & White
	Amount	Folding	Binding	Presses	Presses
ACTIVITY BASE:					
Direct Labor Hours Available	27,214	11,664	15,550	—	—
Direct Labor Hours Utilized—85%	22,548	9,331	13,217	—	—
Machine Hours Available	14,560	—	—	6,800	7,760
Machine Hours Utilized: Color, 70%; B/W, 80%	10,968			4,760	6,208
TOTAL OVERHEAD AND DIRECT LABOR:					
Total Overhead	$463,900	74,898	81,681	163,651	143,670
Total Direct Labor	482,700	86,400	107,500	146,000	142,800
Total Overhead and Direct Labor	$946,600	161,298	189,181	309,651	286,470
HOURLY COSTING RATES:					
Overhead Cost Per Hour		$ 8.03	6.18	34.38	23.14
Direct Labor Cost Per Hour		9.26	8.13	30.67	23.00
Total Costing Rate		$17.29	14.31	65.05	46.14

CALCULATION OF HOURLY COSTING RATES

The elements used in making the calculations of the hourly costing rates, shown in Exhibit 4, are taken directly from the figures in Exhibits 1, 2, and 3. The section headed "Activity Base" in Exhibit 4 shows the available direct labor hours and the available machine (press) hours as presented in Exhibit 1. However, these figures are reduced by a utilization percentage to take into account such delays as unavoidable downtime due to changeovers from one job to another.

In the case of direct labor hours, the utilization factor is 85%. For machine hours, this percentage is 70% for color presses and 80% for black and white presses.

The second element in making the calculation of the costing rates shows the total overhead after allocation. This is taken from Exhibit 3. The direct labor dollars, which are broken down by the production centers in Exhibit 1, appear on the line below the overhead.

The third element, showing the overhead cost per machine hour and per direct labor hour, is obtained by dividing the direct labor and the overhead costs in each production center by the direct labor hours and machine hours after reduction by the utilization percentage. The downtime and other unavoidable delays provided by the utilization percentage are thus accounted for in the costing rates because the rates will be higher due to the use of the lower labor hours and machine hours.

JOB COST ESTIMATE

The job cost estimate shown in Exhibit 5 was prepared for a job that was printed on the black and white press. The materials are made up of the cost of paper plus a 10% spoilage allowance and bindery materials. These add up to $637.81.

Although the labor costing rates and overhead rates were calculated separately, the combined rate was used in costing the labor and overhead operations. These are the same rates that appear in Exhibit 4. The direct labor and overhead costs add up to $1,673.87.

The company uses a standard markup of 35% applied to the total job cost. This

EXHIBIT 5
JOB COST ESTIMATE

MATERIALS:			
Paper—36″ × 48″ Sheets		$ 332.63	
10% Spoilage		33.26	
Bindery Materials		271.91	$ 637.81
DIRECT LABOR AND OVERHEAD:			
Folding	14.0 Hrs. @ $17.29	242.06	
Binding			
Gathering	1.7 Hrs.		
Sewing	4.9 Hrs.		
Trimming	1.0 Hrs.		
Case-In	5.4 Hrs.		
Total	13.0 Hrs @ $14.31	186.03	
Black & White Press 27.0 Hrs. @ 46.14		1,245.78	1,673.87
TOTAL JOB COST			2,311.68
Markup—35% on Cost (26% on Sales Price)			809.09
SELLING PRICE			$3,120.77

becomes the selling price of the job. The 35% allows not only for the profit but for the selling and administrative expenses not shown in the overhead category.

Although the total direct labor and overhead costing rate was used in this job cost estimate, there are occasions when a job requires a larger crew on the press. In such a case, the labor costing rate would be increased and then added to the overhead costing rate.

DEVELOPMENT OF THE FLEXIBLE BUDGET FORMULA

The flexible budget formula is a recasting of the same overhead figures used to obtain the overhead costing rates. The breakdown, instead of being made by production centers, is made by those costs that are considered to be fixed and those that vary with the changes in the level of activity. This determination must be based on what is considered to be normal (optimum) in the determination of costing rates. The range selected as normal, in this case, was from 20% below to 20% above the normal level of activity.

The guide to use in deciding how much of each overhead item is fixed and how much is variable might be stated as follows:

If the activity level drops by 20% on a sustained basis, those overhead items that can be reduced by 20% are considered to be in the variable category. Example: the steno-clerk working for the factory superintendent at an annual salary of $15,200 was categorized as being 50% fixed and 50% variable. In terms of dollars, this would mean $7,600 fixed and $7,600 variable. If the level of activity dropped by 20%, the variable allowance would be 80% of the $7,600 or $6,080—a reduction of $1,520. The total budget allowance would be:

$$\begin{array}{r} \$\ 7,600 \text{ fixed} \\ \underline{6,080 \text{ variable}} \\ \$13,680 \text{ total} \end{array}$$

If the low level persists, the reduction of $1,520 (10% of the total salary) could be made in the form of a reduction in pay of 10%, with or without a corresponding reduction in the number of hours worked. This would depend on management policy.

Normally, in calculating the variable allowances, labor hours would be used as the base for labor-paced operations and machine hours for machine-paced operations. In Exhibit 6, rollers are used exclusively in the machine-paced operations. Therefore, this variable cost is expressed as $0.94 per machine hour. Thus, if the total machine hours of 10,968 were reduced by 20% to 8,774 hours, the allowance for rollers would be $0.94 × 8,774, or $8,248. It would be more accurate to calculate a separate allowance for rollers and other press-related overhead for the color and black and white presses because color presses use a greater quantity. But since the activity fluctuations for the two types of presses are about the same, the simpler approach illustrated above has been used.

Some of the overhead items—freight and electricity, for example—are used in the labor-paced operations, but their variability is not applied to the labor hour activity in cutting/folding or sewing/binding. This, too, would be more accurate. But since the labor hour activity in these production centers is gaited by the machine hour

EXHIBIT 6
DEVELOPMENT OF THE FLEXIBLE BUDGET FORMULA

	Annual Overhead Cost			Variable	
	Total	Fixed	Variable	Rate Per Sales $	Rate Per Machine Hour
INDIRECT LABOR-PRODUCTION DEPARTMENTS					
1 Factory Superintendent	$ 33,500	33,500	—	—	—
1 Steno-Clerk	15,200	7,600	7,600	.0032	—
2 General Maintenance	26,700	17,900	8,800	.0037	—
Total	$ 75,400	59,000	16,400	.0069	
INDIRECT LABOR-SERVICE DEPARTMENTS					
Accounting					
1 Accountant	$ 21,650	21,650	—	—	—
2 Cost Clerks	23,750	15,850	7,900	.0033	—
Total	$ 45,400	37,500	7,900	.0033	
Production Control					
1 Scheduler/estimator	$ 19,500	19,500	—	—	—
3 Expediters	42,000	28,000	14,000	.0058	—
Total	$ 61,500	47,500	14,000	.0058	—
TOTAL INDIRECT LABOR	$182,300	144,000	38,300	.0160	—
NONLABOR OVERHEAD					
Payroll Fringes	$131,590	28,950	102,640	.0428	—
Ink	28,700	—	28,700	—	2.62
Freight	950	—	950	—	.09
Rollers	10,300	—	10,300	—	.94
Replacement Parts	8,200	—	8,200	—	.75
Oil Wipers	3,300	—	3,300	—	.30
Electricity	22,400	—	22,400	—	2.04
Chemicals	7,200	—	7,200	—	.66
Depreciation-Equipment	32,300	32,300	—	—	—
Depreciation-Building	14,500	14,500	—	—	—
Real Estate Taxes	17,960	17,960	—	—	—
Property Taxes	4,200	4,200	—	—	—
TOTAL NONLABOR OVERHEAD	$281,600	97,910	183,690	.0428	7.40
TOTAL ALL OVERHEAD	$463,900	241,910	221,990	.0588	7.40

activity of the presses, the machine hours were used for these expenses rather than splitting them by labor hours and by machine hours.

Sales Not Normally Used as a Base for the Flexible Budget Formula

Normally, the bases for the flexible budget would be the same as those used for calculating the costing rates. In this case, management preferred to relate the indirect labor control to sales because each month's sales volume was known sooner than the labor hours and machine hours. Accordingly, the indirect labor (and payroll fringes) in Exhibit 6 show the variable allowances as so many cents per sales dollar.

EXHIBIT 7
BREAKEVEN ANALYSIS

		Projected Volume	Percent	Breakeven Volume	Volume Above Breakeven
SALES		$2,400,000	100.00	1,435,556	964,444
Variable Costs					
Material	$750,000				
Direct Labor	482,700				
Variable Overhead	221,990				
Sales Commission	240,000	1,694,690	70.61	1,013,646	681,044
CONTRIBUTION TO PROFIT		705,310	29.39	421,910	283,400
Fixed Costs					
Manufacturing Fixed Cost	241,910				
General & Administrative	180,000	421,910		421,910	—
PRETAX PROFIT		$ 283,400		–0–	283,400
Pretax Profit Percent		11.81%			29.39%

$$\text{BREAKEVEN CALCULATION} = \frac{\text{Fixed Costs}}{\text{Contribution to Profit Percent}} = \frac{\$421,910}{29.39\%} = \$1,435,556$$

Going back to the illustration of the steno-clerk used earlier, the variable allowance is shown as $0.0032 per sales dollar. If sales dropped 20% to $1,920,000, the variable budget allowance for this item would be $.0032* × $1,920,000 or $6,080. Since fixed costs are also part of the flexible budget formula, the fixed cost of $7,600 would be added to the variable cost of $6,080 to arrive at a total allowance of $13,680, which is the same figure arrived at earlier using a different approach.

The example shown here was calculated on an annual basis. For use on a monthly basis, the fixed costs would be $\frac{1}{12}$th of the amount shown in Exhibit 6, but the variable rate would remain the same.

BREAKEVEN ANALYSIS

Exhibit 7 demonstrates the calculation of the breakeven analysis. The sales volume of $2,400,000, which was the basis for determining the activity level for the studies in this chapter, is also the starting point in the breakeven analysis.

Variable costs: The direct labor of $482,700 required to generate this level of sales was taken from Exhibit 1. The total variable overhead cost of $221,990 was taken from Exhibit 6. The material cost of $750,000 is the amount of paper and bindery material used to achieve a sales level of $2,400,000. Commissions paid to salesmen are 10% of the dollar volume sold and therefore amount to $240,000. All variable costs add up to $1,694,690 or 70.61% of sales. Subtracting this from the total sales of $2,400,000 gives a contribution to profit of $705,310 or 29.39% of sales.

Fixed costs: The manufacturing fixed costs of $241,910 were taken from Exhibit 6. To this was added $180,000 to cover the general and administrative (G&A) costs. These include the owner of the business and a small staff. These two fixed

* Actually $0.00317.

costs, totaling $421,910, when subtracted from the contribution to profit of $705,310, leave a pretax profit of $283,400 or 11.81% of sales.

Breakeven volume calculation: This calculation requires only two figures:

1. Total fixed costs
2. The percentage that the contribution to profit is to total sales.

To arrive at the breakeven volume, the fixed costs are divided by the percent contribution to profit. This is shown in the lower part of the exhibit.

Profits Can Only Be Made from Sales Above the Breakeven Point

Since "breakeven" means no profit and no loss, a profit can only be made on the sales above the breakeven level. This is illustrated in the last two columns of Exhibit 7.

In the column headed "Breakeven Volume," the breakeven sales of $1,435,556 are multiplied by the variable percentage of 70.61—showing that the variable costs at the breakeven volume amount to $1,013,646. When this figure is subtracted from breakeven sales, the contribution to profit equals the fixed costs—leaving no profit.

The "Volume Above Breakeven" (last column) amounts to $964,444. This is obviously the portion of the sales from which the profit is derived. To verify this, the $964,444 was multiplied by 70.61% to determine the amount of the variable cost, which is shown as $681,044. Subtracting this from $964,444, we obtain a contribution to profit in the amount of $283,400. Inasmuch as the fixed costs have already been accounted for in the breakeven sales, the contribution to profit in this column is actually the pretax profit shown in the first column. The pretax profit, then, is not 11.81% of total sales; it is 29.39% of the sales above breakeven.

GUIDELINES TO FULL-SERVICE OVERHEAD ANALYSIS AND CONTROL

Overhead is probably the most discussed and least understood of the three elements of manufacturing cost. Many think of it in terms of a rate—the percentage applied to the labor cost to recover this "mixed bag" of costs that cannot be directly identified with specific products. It is for this reason that several chapters have been devoted to this subject. If a set of guidelines were to be proposed, they would include the following:

1. Determine which production centers are in the labor-paced and which in the machine-paced category. This will result in more meaningful costing rates.
2. Separate the direct labor costing rate from the overhead costing rates for convenience in adjusting the direct labor rate when the number of operators at a machine varies because of differences in the products processed at that machine.
3. Discuss allocation bases with those who are most familiar with each of the overhead expenses. This will result in more accurate cost allocations and will preclude the use of arbitrary methods of assigning costs to products.
4. Many companies develop a single costing rate for each production center even if the center contains high-cost equipment. Separate costing rates can be developed through analysis of differential costs and adjustment of the departmental rate by the amount of such differences. This is explained in Chapter 2.

5. When costing rates are being developed, extend the study to include a flexible budget formula and a breakeven analysis tied in with the same overhead figures used for the costing rates.

6. When the study is completed, prepare formalized schedules for distribution to interested parties. This will not only be of educational value, it will also add credibility to the cost accounting system.

4
How a Standard Cost System Can Distort the Cost of Highly Engineered Products

Manufactured components for highly engineered products can look exactly the same as their industrial (commercial) counterparts. The difference is in the specifications to which they are manufactured. Such items as packaging, gaskets, bolts, welding material, and rework, for example, are normally considered as overhead for industrial products. But the same items used for highly engineered products can become so costly because of tighter specifications that they must be accounted for as direct labor or direct material rather than overhead. If both types of products are manufactured under the same roof, two different cost systems must be used to assure proper costing.

This applies to many products used for defense, space exploration, and nuclear applications. A product used in nuclear applications has been selected for illustrative purposes in this chapter.

With the start of the nuclear age in the 1940s, it was generally expected that interest in harnessing atomic energy for peaceful uses would eventually develop. Within two decades, a number of industries were engaged in the production of components for various nuclear applications.

Coal promised a quick but temporary solution to our energy needs—and an endless struggle with environmentalists. Geothermal and solar energy sources offer great possibilities but are potential sources only; their application on a large scale is a long way off. Nuclear power represents the only suitable technology that can be brought into production. But this industry has encountered fierce citizen resistance because of the fear of nuclear disaster.

Early components of nuclear power plants were built to existing specifications which were used for valves (and other nuclear components) employed for commercial* applications. Although some of these specifications were tightened for nuclear components, the Atomic Energy Commission (AEC) was not satisfied. Its concern was to satisfy the developing fears of the public about radioactivity and possible disasters from nuclear power plants. As a result, the AEC pressed all manufacturers of nuclear components to come up with specifications that would guard against any remote possibility of serious accidents. This pressure ultimately resulted in an expanded Section III of the American Society of Mechanical Engineers (ASME) Code. Before the expansion, only vessels had been covered. Certificates of authorization are now required of manufacturers of such nuclear components as valves, pumps, pressure vessels, reactor vessels, safety valves, and piping.

The advent of these stricter requirements has, naturally, had a great impact on the amount of inspection, quality assurance effort, engineering, contract administration, and rework. Additionally, the manufacturing cycle is greatly lengthened because of many interruptions for inspection and the need for rework to meet code requirements.

---

* The terms "commercial" and "industrial" used interchangeably.

Yet the manufacturers of these valves, pumps, piping, and safety vessels are mainly commercial suppliers, the bulk of whose products require no such care in manufacture. Nuclear components pose all the problems of manufacturing to extremely close tolerances, whereas the manufacturers are accustomed to dealing with relatively loose tolerances—their business methods being built on these practices.

As more and more emphasis is put on nuclear applications, we can expect to see more and more costing problems arising among a number of manufacturers.

IMPACT OF TIGHTER SPECIFICATIONS

The cost system that covers the carefully monitored manufacture of nuclear power components differs from one that accounts for the manufacture of the same parts used for nonnuclear applications. The reason for the differences warrants further discussion.

Inspection

The cost of inspection for nuclear valves is more than double that required for industrial-type valves. There can be as many as 900 inspection, hold, verification, and approval points, as illustrated in Exhibit 1. This exhibit summarizes the requirements of a large customer of one of the valve manufacturing companies.

Manufacturing Interruption

The impact of increased inspection, not only by the manufacturer's personnel, but by the customer representatives and third-party inspectors, results in production delays and consequently a much longer manufacturing cycle during which costs keep increasing and investment is tied up.

Quality Assurance

In the manufacture of industrial-type valves, the quality assurance function does not go much beyond the inspection stage. With the more demanding requirement for Code adherence in making nuclear valves, the quality assurance function must relate to the total controlled manufacturing system. To do this, quality assurance must take responsibility for:

- Auditing and control of suppliers to assure conformance to Code and contract requirements.
- Internal training of inspection personnel.
- Auditing and control of internal departments for conformance to Code and contract requirements.
- Control of internal quality standards.
- Development and monitoring of programs for calibration of measuring equipment.
- Control of quality documentation.

The opinion expressed by several valve manufacturers is that assuring conformance can more than triple the cost of the quality function.

EXHIBIT 1
INSPECTION, HOLD, VERIFICATION AND APPROVAL POINTS CODE CLASS I STAINLESS STEEL VALVE

	Manufacturer	Customer	Code	Total
Review of Procedures/Drawings	100	55		155
Purchase Orders	15			15
Certifications (Chemical and Physical Characteristics)				
Body	35	35	35	105
Bonnet	35	35	35	105
Disc	25	25	25	75
Seats	15	15		30
Bushing	10	10		20
Bolting	15	15	15	45
Other	30	30		60
	165	165	110	440
Data Book	1	1	1	3
Inspection at Vendor				
Body	8	8		16
Bonnet	8	8		16
Disc	16	16		32
Seats	16	16		32
Bolting	5	5		10
Other	2	2		4
	55	55		110
Inspection in Process				
Body	22	21	16	59
Bonnet	17	16	11	44
Disc	9	8	4	21
Seats	7	6		13
Bushing	4	3		7
Other	30	1	1	32
	89	55	32	176
GRAND TOTAL	425	331	143	899

Notes
  • Utility has option to review, witness, verify and approve any of the above categories
  • Figures do not include waivers or rejected material notices

Engineering

Engineering must also expand its role. It must go far beyond the relatively simple requirements of industrial-type valves. In industrial types the customer can order by a simple designation such as catalog number. But when nuclear valves are being ordered, the customer must provide a design specification along with his order for each different type valve. Accordingly, for every contract, engineering must:

  • Design the end product according to the design specifications that were furnished.
  • Certify that the design meets Code and contract requirements.
  • Spell out specifications for the purchase of material by customer order.

- Make detailed drawings for the shop based on customer design specifications and write instructions.
- Write test procedures.
- Coordinate customer requirements with manufacturing procedures.

According to industry engineers, engineering costs in a nuclear valve can be expected to be double or triple the cost of the industrial valve.

Contract Administration

In any product in which manufacturing procedures are spelled out in great detail and documentation for each step is required, close liaison must be maintained between the manufacturer and the customer. This liaison goes much further than the conventional customer service function. It is called "contract administration" and has the following requirements:

- Act as contact with the customer—providing the necessary liaison on all matters relating to the contract.
- Monitor the status of the job and prepare progress reports.
- Review all correspondence relating to the contract.
- Furnish the customer with any information required by him.
- Monitor witness inspection dates.
- Close out orders and finalize documentation.

Rework

In an industrial-type valve, rework would normally be considered as overhead. In many cases, the parts would be scrapped rather than investing additional labor and overhead in salvage. In nuclear valves, rework is an unavoidable cost and should be considered as a direct cost rather than overhead.

Mixed Production

Companies manufacturing industrial-type valves in the same facility that is used for making nuclear valves can expect to find the costs of the industrial type increasing. This is due to the normal tendency to upgrade lower-graded products when two disparate types are being manufactured.

The foregoing are some of the factors that will greatly affect the need for more definitive costs, particularly when industrial and nuclear-type valves are being made in the same facility. Costs that have traditionally been classified as indirect must now be considered direct. The traditional definition of what is direct and what is indirect must be abandoned in favor of a definition that will recognize costs that are identifiable and supportable as direct charges to each contract. What these costs are and how they should be measured are the subject of the sections that follow.

IDENTIFYING COSTS DIRECTLY WITH THE CONTRACT

It has been traditional in some valve manufacturing companies to consider as overhead such items as packing, gaskets, bolting, welding material, purchased services, incoming freight, shipping preparation, engineering/drafting, rework, and other costs. In light of the more demanding requirements in nuclear work, these costs have increased greatly in magnitude. They can also vary radically from one contract to another. Because of such variations, inclusion of these costs in the overhead rate could result in allocations to contracts that are quite different from reality. The following examples are illustrative.

One executive had strong feelings against treating purchased services as an overhead expense. He felt that purchased services, particularly as they related to the castings, should be considered as material cost. His comment was:

Material costs are appreciably higher due primarily to the software or documentation that must be provided for the nuclear class material. Not only is more nondestructive testing (NDT) required, but also the documentation to substantiate it is extensive. A foundry, for example, must provide heat treatment procedures of how castings will be processed; charts of the temperature and time of heat treatment are required; calibration records of the temperature recording equipment must be furnished; complete radiographic procedures, qualifications, and film packages are called for, and other procedures or certifications of additional nondestructive testing, such as magnetic particle, or ultrasonic testing, are required.

Another executive who observed that the cost of a nuclear valve can be as much as four times that of the same type valve for commercial applications made the following comment:†

A large difference occurs during final assembly, test, inspection, and preparation for shipment. We found that over 30 additional hours were spent in completing the nuclear valves. The extra time went into such items as additional particle test inspection of finished surfaces for a customer's inspector, additional time required by the Quality Assurance Department to prepare a "Record Package" for the customer, special cleaning, packaging and preparation for shipment, and more complex test and inspection requirements. Many of these extras are in cost areas that may be concealed in a general overhead account, but when they are identified and studied, they show a substantial number of extra hours which we feel should be charged directly against a nuclear order.

A discussion of the various costs that should be identified more specifically follows:

Supply Type Items

In most accounting systems, items of relatively small value are expensed at the time of purchase and charged to an overhead account. An allowance is provided for these items through application of the overhead rate.

This is an acceptable expedient when items like a bolt cost only $0.10 each, gasket material only a few cents per sheet, and welding material so little that it can be practically ignored. Since the aggregate cost of supply-type expenses like the foregoing can amount to more than $1,500 for a nuclear valve, it is highly desirable that such items be considered direct material and charged directly to the valve on which used.

Incoming Freight

In some companies, incoming freight is treated as an overhead expense. When valve manufacturers were, by and large, making castings in their own foundries, incoming

---

† Depending upon the type, a nuclear valve can cost 2 to 10 times as much as its industrial counterpart.

EXHIBIT 2
COST COMPARISON
LABOR/OVERHEAD CONTENT VERSUS BASE MATERIAL FOR THE 600# CS
PRESSURE SEAL VALVES
COST PER UNIT

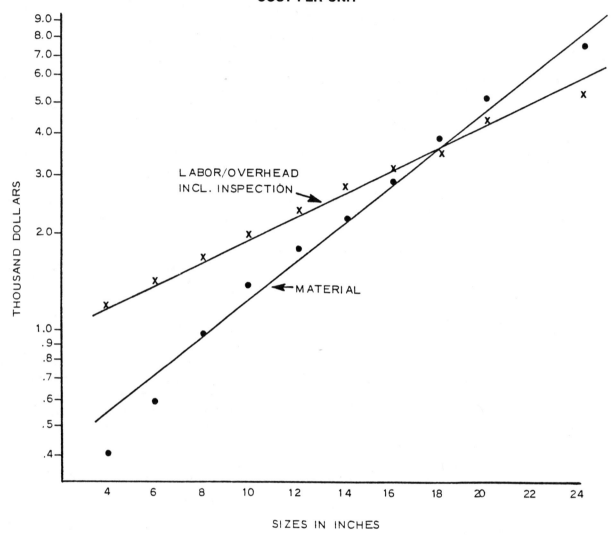

freight was not as substantial an item as it is now when many companies purchase their castings from outside foundries. If these higher costs are included in overhead, as in the past, and allocated to the various valves on the basis of an overhead rate applied to direct labor, the amount charged to individual valves could be greatly distorted. This distortion occurs because the labor content in a valve does not correctly reflect the material content. Note in Exhibit 2 that the line representing material cost in the various sizes is quite different in slope than the line representing labor cost.‡

A more accurate approach would be to identify the amount of incoming freight actually incurred for each casting and to add this amount to the cost of the casting as material.

---

‡ The plottings in Exhibit 2 are made to a semilogarithmic scale. A line on such a scale reflects percentage rather than absolute dollar changes.

Rework

The requirement for nondestructive examinations means that certain additional operations will need to be performed when defects are found. These are:

- Gouging
- Welding
- Grinding
- Hand dressing
- X-ray (if rejects still present, cycle starts again)
- Heat treat
- Remachining
- Inspection

Companies that include rework as part of overhead are allocating such costs to the various valves on the basis of the amount of direct labor required to make the valve. Obviously, when the rework operations can be specifically identified with the valve on which they are being performed, it would be more accurate to have the individuals doing the work charge their time to the specific valve and charge it as direct labor.

Special Tooling, Fixtures, and Patterns

The cost of these items could have a wide range. Special tooling could cost in excess of $18,000, and patterns and fixtures could cost in excess of $5,000. Since these items are usually made for a specific valve, the cost should, like material, be charged directly to that valve rather than being spread through an overhead rate. It is conceivable that fixtures, tooling, and patterns could be used for a subsequent order. The method of amortizing such costs against orders is a separate matter, the treatment of which depends upon the negotiations with the customer.

Shipping Costs

Traditionally, some companies consider shipping to be part of the selling expenses rather than part of the manufacturing cost. Before the advent of the nuclear valve, the industrial types could be loaded on trucks with little or no protective packing, so that the shipping cost was merely a handling expense.

This is no longer the case with nuclear valves, which must be crated to protect the weld end and the operating mechanisms. The crating and bagging of a large valve could amount to as much as $3,000. The operations required to prepare the valve for shipment should be identified as direct labor and charged to the specific valve.

Engineering/Drafting

The concept of product engineering has been expanded greatly with the introduction of nuclear valves. The function now includes designing, writing instructions to the shop and the purchasing department, preparing detail drawings, writing test procedures and coordinating with the customer. Engineering/drafting efforts can start as much as a year before the shop begins to build the valve.

Because of the foregoing factors, and in the interest of matching costs with revenues, engineering—as well as other related items—must be charged as direct costs when incurred. Application of such costs through a manufacturing overhead rate (or a G&A rate), rather than a direct charge, will not yield correct product costs. Take the case of a customer ordering two or more valves of the same type, while another customer orders the same number of valves but each of a different type. Application of this cost through an overhead rate would overstate the cost of engineering/drafting to the first customer and understate the cost to the second one.

The proper way of charging this function to the product is to identify the charges as direct costs to the specific product. Engineering/drafting, then, would become direct labor to which the engineering overhead rate would be applied. The same principal would apply to quality assurance.

Contracts Administration

Contract administration is a liaison function in which the administrator or project manager acts as a coordinator between the customer and the company. He must review all correspondence, monitor the status of the job, advise the customer of witness inspection dates, close out the orders, and finalize the documentation.

The effort required for each contract is not likely to vary with the amount of shop labor required to make the product, so this expense should not be allocated through an overhead rate. It should be considered as a direct charge supported by time charges.

Those nuclear component manufacturing companies that do not have a contracts administration group must perform the function nonetheless. Undoubtedly the work is being performed by several individuals in such departments as production control, purchasing, accounting, or some other service department. If so, then the cost of the function is most likely being included in the product through application of the overhead or G&A rate—causing distortions. The contracts administration function, whether a separate department or not, must identify the amount of cost incurred against each contract.

WHICH COST SYSTEM IS CORRECT?

There is no pat answer to this question. The accounting system must adapt to the state of technology. When a product is new, unit volume small, and changes frequent, a job cost system is the most appropriate. It provides the means for identifying each cost as it relates to the specific job.

Standard Versus Custom Engineered Valves

As certain valves became standardized in past years, those companies that specialized in these types correctly adopted a standard cost system of accounting. Standard costs were predetermined. These became the cost of production and the inventory values from which variances were calculated.

Predetermined Standard Costs Versus Job Costing

However, when the complexity and proliferation of specifications expands, as it did for nuclear plant requirements, the valve and other components can no longer be

EXHIBIT 3
ABBREVIATED INCOME STATEMENT

	Example 1 Standard Costing Used for Both Industrial and Nuclear Valves			Example 2 Standard Costing Used for Industrial and Job Costing Used for Nuclear Valves		
	Total	Industrial	Nuclear	Total	Industrial	Nuclear
SALES	$605,100	323,515	281,585	$605,100	323,515	281,585
MANUFACTURING COSTS						
MATERIAL	206,300	103,349	102,951	218,850	102,827	116,023
DIRECT LABOR	92,100	51,167	40,933	170,400	65,767	104,633
OVERHEAD	240,300	133,498	106,802	149,450	83,026	66,424
TOTAL	538,700	288,014	250,686	538,700	251,620	287,080
GROSS PROFIT	$ 66,400	35,501	30,899	$ 66,400	71,895	(5,495)

Note: The terms "industrial" and "commercial" are used interchangeably.

considered standard. Each one can be quite different in its specifications; each customer buying the same valve can have different requirements for the same valve. Also, purchases are low in terms of the number of units purchased. Since the nuclear valve is not a standardized product, standard costs cannot be used; a job costing system accumulating actual costs is mandatory. It is entirely possible that as nuclear plant production becomes standardized, nuclear components too will achieve a greater degree of standardization.

Companies making standard components which then add some nuclear components to their line are in the most vulnerable position when it comes to proper costing; they are not likely to change their cost system to accommodate the few nuclear items that have just been added to the line. Such costs as engineering, quality assurance, and contract administration, which are substantially larger for nuclear products, are likely to be included in the overhead rate and allocated on the basis of direct labor or in the G&A rate.

Thus, if nuclear items make up only 10% of the business, the additional costs applicable to this 10% will be spread over all products. The excess costs charged to the industrial items will probably not be noticed, but the cost of the nuclear ones will appear to be substantially lower than the true cost. Because the undercosted nuclear components will appear to be highly profitable, management will be encouraged to bring in more such business. As the proportion of nuclear business increases, the inadequacies of the standard cost system will become evident as the overcosted industrial types indicate lower and lower profitability (see Exhibit 3). Exhibit 3 illustrates how the costs assignable to the industrial and nuclear valves can differ depending on whether standard costing is used for both, as in Example 1, or for the industrial valves only, and job costing is used for the nuclear valves. Contract administration, which may be classified as G&A (or marketing) in some companies, was included in overhead in examples 1 and 2. This situation bears out the observation made by one executive who states:

We continued to use standard costs to value our castings after we sold out our standard line. When nondestructive examinations became a larger and larger factor in nuclear castings, our variances from standard became correspondingly larger. The variances identified the excess cost all right, but they didn't tell us what product the variances should be charged to. We considered building the nondestructive examination costs into the standards, since we recognized this was part of the material cost, but gave up the idea because of the infinite number of standards we would have had to keep in file.

After this experience, we gave up on standard costing of nuclear valves and went to job costing.

Another company executive had this to say:

A custom-engineered product produced in a manufacturing system designed for standardized volume production creates costing problems which need far more attention than management generally gives.

Format for Accumulating Job Costs

The conventional job order cost system used by many companies accumulates three categories of cost. These are:

Material
Direct Labor
Overhead (usually applied on direct labor)

Under this conventional format, such costs as engineering/drafting, quality assurance, and rework would be included in overhead. Since overhead is usually applied to products through a departmental overhead rate based on direct labor, these costs are distributed in proportion to the amount of labor contained in the various products.

When custom-engineered products such as nuclear components are made in the same facilities as standard products, use of this conventional format will result in the spreading of too much overhead to the standard products which properly belongs with the custom-engineered items.

More and more companies dealing in government contract work have added an additional category called "direct charges" to identify such costs as special tooling or special equipment purchased for a specific job. This does not, however, provide for specific direct charging of such costs as engineering/drafting and quality assurance if these are left in the overhead category.

A more appropriate format would be one that recognizes as direct cost items like the following:

Engineering/drafting
Quality assurance
Rework

An example of such a format in use by a company making both nuclear and high specification special valves is shown below:

	BREAKDOWN OF HOURS			BREAKDOWN OF DOLLARS		
	BUDGETED HOURS	ACTUAL HOURS TO DATE	ESTIMATED HOURS TO COMPLETE	BUDGETED DOLLARS	ACTUAL DOLLARS TO DATE	ESTIMTED DOLLARS TO COMPLETE
Labor and Overhead	1,655	—	1,655	$ 27,608	$ —	$ 27,608
Rework	279	—	279	4,655	—	4,655
Material	—	—	—	110,190	—	110,190
Engineering	264	214	50	1,588	3,110	—
Drafting	250	293	—	1,504	2,819	—
Direct Charges	—	—	—	12,875	23,108	—
TOTAL	2,448	507	1,984	$158,420	$29,037	$142,453

Estimate to Complete

The budgeted hours and budgeted dollars are synonymous with "estimated," the budget being based on the original estimate used to establish the selling price. The estimated hours and estimated dollars to complete represent updated estimates.

In the event that a customer requests a change after negotiations have been completed, the new estimated hours and dollars would be added (or subtracted) to arrive at an updated estimate. Performance against this latest estimate is an important measure and should be monitored closely. It is not enough simply to compare actual costs with the estimate because mere incurrence of costs does not assure accomplishment. What is needed is an estimate of the hours and dollars required to complete the job. This "estimate to complete" should be added to the costs incurred to date. The resulting total should then be compared with the estimate to determine whether the job will be completed within budget or if there will be an overrun.

This should be a monthly procedure. On critical jobs it may be necessary to do this weekly.

Labor and Overhead

Although many companies prefer to record direct labor separately from overhead, some companies prefer to combine these two elements of cost. Either approach is acceptable. Inspection is included as direct labor, and overhead is applied in the same manner as it is for all other direct labor operations. Overhead rates are established separately for the machining, welding, and assembly and test operations.

Rework

Rework, which in a standard product would normally be considered an overhead item, is properly recorded as a direct cost chargeable with overhead directly to the specific job.

Material

This includes not only the cost of castings, operators, bolting, and stellite, but also the incoming freight and the cost of upgrading.

Engineering and Drafting

These two categories of cost go hand in hand, since drafting supports engineering. A review of job cost records for nuclear components will show a fair-sized expenditure for engineering and drafting even before any actual production has begun. This is a realistic expectation, and it shows that this type of expenditure is incurred before any labor operations have been performed. It also points up the fallacy of including engineering/drafting in the overhead rate, since there would then be no such cost charged against the job until labor operations have been performed on the product. In the event of a customer cancellation in the early stages of a job, there would be no data to support these early charges.

Some companies include quality assurance costs in the engineering category. The engineering/drafting and quality assurance costs also include overhead of these functions, as well as the directly identifiable charges.

Direct Charges

These include such items of cost as tooling, patterns, and other special equipment, as well as contracts administration.

REASONS FOR DEFICIENT COST ESTIMATES

The importance of good product costing for custom-engineered products cannot be overemphasized. Some of the reasons for deficient cost estimates are:

- Arbitrary costing through use of predetermined standards.
- Failure to take into account cost escalation factors.
- Requests for changes.
- Hasty estimating.

Arbitrary Costing

Standardized products can be costed at predetermined standards with a reasonable degree of accuracy. Customer-engineered items such as nuclear components cannot be so costed because of the many variations and differences in customer requirements that make it impractical to establish individual standards for all the possible combinations. Nor does the answer lie in "guesstimated token adders" that are used to adjust a predetermined standard to arrive at an actual cost. (If adders are used, there must be assurance that the costs they represent will be fully absorbed.) Consequently, custom-engineered products must be costed through a system that will identify the actual costs, as well as the budget, for each job. Availability of the actual costs, correctly compiled, will provide a basis for monitoring performance as well as providing feedback on the correctness of the estimates.

Cost Escalation on Future Commitments

Cost estimates that may be correct at the time they are prepared could become very inaccurate if escalation factors are not taken into account to provide for cost increases with the passage of time. This is important when one considers how many commitments are made for delivery a year or more hence.

Requests for Changes

Requests for changes are frequently accepted from the customer with insufficient consideration of the impact of such a change in terms of additional out-of-pocket costs or the extended time during which inventory investment is tied up. Requests for changes should be handled in the same manner followed in making all cost estimates. The amount of additional cost required to comply with the change should be known to management as soon after receipt of the request as possible.

Hasty Estimating

There is no better way to assure faulty cost estimates than to make them in haste to meet an unrealistic deadline. One way to assure better utilization of a limited time allowance (though every effort should be made to obtain a reasonable amount of time) is to make available extra copies of the customer's order for purposes of obtaining, simultaneously, the various kinds of information required in putting together an estimate. Availability of a reliable history of past jobs can also be very helpful in cutting time requirements for making cost estimates.

VERIFICATION OF PRODUCT COST ESTIMATES—BUILDING THE HISTORY

A cost system provides the basis for regular accumulation of costs. In the accumulation process, the system must correctly reflect actual product costs that can be used to verify the correctness of the cost estimates. These can be summarized in two basic reports illustrated in Exhibit 4:

- Unit costs of orders shipped.
- Cost history record.

These reports include the following data:

Unit Costs of Orders Shipped

This is a unit cost breakdown by individual valves that have been sold during the period. The various elements of material, labor and overhead cost, tooling, and non-manufacturing direct charges are shown on a per unit basis. Each of these costs is compared with the original estimate that was made at the time the item was quoted to the customer. A comparison is also made of the total manufacturing cost with the selling price. This report also provides clues as to where further analysis is required. Illustrative of this is the 12-inch 900# carbon steel valve for which the actual cost of the body was $3,123, while the original estimate called for $2,138. The difference of $985 in excess costs is explained as follows:

	ESTIMATE	ACTUAL	EXCESS COSTS
Body weight	1450#	1810#	
Cost of body	$1,888	$2,444	$556
Heat charts	—	15	15
Charpy tests	—	45	45
Film	200	455	255
Rough machine	50	164	114
Total	$2,138	$3,123	$985

The estimate, which was incorrectly made, assumed that an elliptically shaped body would be used. Since a round shape was called for, more pounds of material were required. These were purchased at a higher cost per pound than was estimated. In addition, certain other costs listed above were not recognized or were understated.

Companies that fail to compare actual costs with the original estimate are missing an important step in the process of management control.

Cost History Record

This is also a unit cost analysis which embodies most of the elements shown above. There are two differences, however.

- This history record recasts the actual valve costs to show the cost history of all similar items on a single document.
- In place of the labor and overhead costs, which are shown as the unit costs of orders shipped, this record shows the labor hours in the various departments. Hours are preferable in making comparisons of jobs at different periods of time because they eliminate the inflationary effects of cost increases.

EXHIBIT 4
COST HISTORY RECORD
ALTERNATIVE 1

UNIT COSTS OF ORDERS SHIPPED

| | ORDER NO. | QUAN. | TOTAL MATERIAL COST | | | | | | TOOLING AND PATTERNS | TOTAL LABOR AND OVERHEAD | | | | TOTAL MFG. COST | SELLING PRICE | GROSS PROFIT % | NON-MFG. DIRECT CHARGES |
			BODY	BONNET	DISC.	OPERATOR	OTHER	TOTAL		MACHINING	WELDING	ASSEMBLY AND TEST	TOTAL				
4" 300# S.S.																	
ACTUAL	22113-11	2	$ 327	$268	$ 54	$ 966	$ 235	$1,850	$ 24	$ 617	$ 318	$ 299	$1,234	$ 3,108	$ 5,044	38.4%	$ 410
ESTIMATE		2	620	460	35	834	213	2,162	—	721	350	371	1,442	3,604	5,044	28.5	580
12" 900# Ca. St.																	
ACTUAL	26126-12	1	3,123	991	165	3,904	1,341	9,524	2,140	3,174	1,597	1,578	6,349	18,013	16,602	(8.5)	1,040
ESTIMATE		1	2,138	874	126	2,004	1,027	6,169	2,515	2,056	1,019	1,037	4,112	12,796	16,602	22.9	796
20" 150# Ca. St.																	
ACTUAL	23957-15	2	1,288	154	229	—	376	2,047	15	682	362	320	1,364	3,426	5,910	42.0	804
ESTIMATE		5	1,015	148	297	—	260	1,720	—	607	365	342	1,314	3,034	5,910	48.7	760
30" 150# Ca. St.																	
ACTUAL	24628-16	2	2,943	349	441	—	688	4,421	—	1,474	716	757	2,947	7,368	20,200	63.5	1,149
ESTIMATE		2	4,984	300	501	—	861	6,646	5,028	2,215	1,097	1,119	4,431	16,105	20,200	20.3	1,296

COST HISTORY RECORD
UNIT COST

PRODUCT ____20" 150# GATE VALVE____

| SHOP ORDER # | QUAN. | MATERIAL COST | | | | | | HOURS | | | | | TOTAL MFG. COST | SALES PRICE | GROSS PROFIT | NON-MFG. DIRECT CHARGES |
		BODY	BONNET	DISC.	OPERATOR	OTHER	TOTAL MATERIAL	UPGRADE	MACHINE SHOP	WELD	ASSEMBLY	TOTAL HOURS				
21428-16	3	$1,285	$163	$246	—	$346	$2,040	3	57	14	21	95	$3,521	$5,910	$2,389	$1,519
21585-17	2	1,273	162	241	—	345	2,0.1	4	58	12	18	92	3,502	5,910	2,408	1,307
23561-14	2	1,311	189	220	—	298	2,018	5	71	29	22	127	3,982	5,910	1,928	1,275
23957-15	5	1,288	154	229	—	376	2,047	4	63	16	21	104	3,426	5,910	2,484	804

EXHIBIT 5
COST HISTORY RECORD
ALTERNATIVE 2

SUMMARY

DESCRIPTION: 20" GATE VALVE

DATE MO	YEAR	ORDER NO	CUSTOMER	UNIT PRICE STANDARD	UNIT PRICE ACTUAL	UNIT SELLING PRICE
9	7X	27327-18	J C P EL.		49,600 00	56,718.00
9	7X	27327-19	"		51,241 80	56,718.00
10	7X	26499-31	"		44,369 67	56,718.00
12	7X	29320-32	"		50,394 92	56,718.00
12	7X	29320-33	"		51,271 31	56,718.00

COST HISTORY RECORD — ALL OTHER

DATE	ORDER NO.	QUAN. MADE	QUAN.	ALLOY	MATERIAL	DIRECT LABOR	BURDEN	TOTAL COST
						1,142 62	9,434 23

COST HISTORY RECORD — STEMS

DATE	ORDER NO.	QUAN. MADE	QUAN.	ALLOY	MATERIAL	DIRECT LABOR	BURDEN	TOTAL COST
				CP	202 80	150 83	504 37	958 00
				CP				

COST HISTORY RECORD — DISCS

DATE	ORDER NO.	QUAN. MADE	QUAN.	ALLOY	MATERIAL	DIRECT LABOR	BURDEN	TOTAL COST
9-7X	27327-18	1		CP	2,354 16	656 03	2,133 10	5,143 29
9-7X	27327-19	1		CP	2,324 75	345 75	1,138 61	3,808 41

COST HISTORY RECORD — BONNETS

DATE	ORDER NO.	QUAN. MADE	QUAN.	ALLOY	MATERIAL	DIRECT LABOR	BURDEN	TOTAL COST
9-7X	27327-18	1		CP	6,255 06	391 74	1,235 20	7,882 00
9-7X	27327-19	1		CP	6,262 43	446 53	1,418 73	8,127 69

COST HISTORY RECORD — BODY ASSEMBLIES

DATE	ORDER NO.	QUAN. MADE	QUAN.	ALLOY	MATERIAL	DIRECT LABOR	BURDEN	TOTAL COST
9-7X	27327-18	1		CP	22,702 97	853 79	2,625 72	26,182 48
9-7X	27327-19	1		CP	22,721 04	1,018 53	3,045 35	26,784 92
10-7X	28499-31	1		CP	21,991 74	1,562 40	5,374 07	28,928 21
12-7X	29320-32	1		CP	22,001 64	1,616 66	5,639 88	29,258 18
12-7X	29320-33	1		CP	24,918 06	821 59	2,827 44	28,567 09

The cost history record illustrated in Exhibit 4 summarizes the elements of cost on a single sheet for an entire valve. There is also an alternative method that breaks down the elements for each of the major parts making up a valve. For example, the material, labor, and overhead are broken down for each of the major parts, such as the body, bonnet, and disc. This is illustrated in Exhibit 5. Either method provides the kind of information required to verify the accuracy of estimates. In addition to this verification, there are other advantages.

1. Future estimating will be improved.
2. These records develop a history which will provide a useful basis for making estimates.
3. Visibility is given to the profitability of different jobs. Profitability trends as well as cost trends will be more clearly evident.

SUMMARY

Costs such as those for engineering, quality assurance, and rework, which are normally part of overhead and applied through an overhead rate based on direct labor, cannot be allocated in the conventional manner when nuclear components are being made. Costs of this type that are substantially greater for nuclear components must be excluded from the overhead rate and applied to the jobs on a direct-charge basis in much the same manner as material is identified by job. Companies with sophisticated systems in which predetermined standards are used are particularly vulnerable to cost distortion.

When improper accounting procedures are being followed, it is likely that these deficiencies will be carried over into the estimating process. For this reason, the following basic guidelines should be followed:

1. The cost system must provide for direct charging of major costs that are identifiable with a job.
2. When adders are used to adjust for differences among jobs because direct charging is impractical, they must be tested to assure that they will be recovered in the normal volume of business.
3. Estimates must provide for inflationary factors. The time phasing of such escalation must be explicitly stated and firmly enforced.
4. The cost impact of all engineering changes must be estimated in the same manner as if a new job were being estimated.
5. The cost system must go "full circle" to provide feedback through a comparison of actual costs with the original cost estimate used for quoting the job.

The tighter specifications called for in highly engineered components, the rigid documentation requirements, and the multiplicity of specifications for the same product ordered by different companies and agencies of the government add up to substantially higher costs than for their industrial counterparts. The adequacy of a cost system is not measured by its degree of sophistication but by its ability to identify these product cost differences and relate them to the cost estimate.

5
Present Methods of Accounting for SG&A Costs: A Distortion of Product Line Profitability

The first two chapters in this book emphasized the importance of recognizing changes due to automation and the use of other high-technology equipment when establishing manufacturing overhead costing rates.

Nonmanufacturing overhead such as selling, general, and administrative (SG&A) expenses has grown substantially in many industries. Frequently, these expenses far exceed the size of manufacturing overhead. The methods followed in allocating such expenses to product lines warrant just as much, if not more, attention than is being given to the manufacturing overhead.

Executives with responsibility for profitable operations frequently find themselves at a competitive disadvantage because of incorrect procedures being followed in the allocation of burgeoning, SG&A expenses to the various product lines. As a result, the true profitability of the product lines is obscured. This problem could result in the dropping of product lines that are actually profitable and the promotion of others that are only marginal.

One of the reasons for such distortions in product line profitability is the practice of using arbitrary allocation methods such as sales and cost of sales in the interest of simplicity.

Use of such arbitrary across-the-board allocations often ignores SG&A differences by market segments such as the Original Equipment Manufacturers (OEM), replacement, and distributor markets. This overlooks the fact that the SG&A cost for the same product can be quite different in one market than in another—as will be demonstrated in this chapter.

Use of percent return on sales to the exclusion of percent return on investment is another factor that can mislead management. This chapter explains in some detail how sales in the OEM market, for example, can show the lowest percent return on sales but the highest return on investment when the investment turnover is taken into account.

In addition to distortions in product line profitability, there are inconsistencies between the method of allowing for SG&A on customer requests for quotation and the method used in allocating SG&A on product line profitability statements.

SG&A IS A "GROWTH INDUSTRY"

With the maturation of the Industrial Revolution, the concurrent improvements in communications and transportation expanded the potential marketing areas and fostered large-scale production and distribution. This, in turn, resulted in an explosive increase in the number of mergers and acquisitions.

The consequent consolidation of many small companies into giant corporations resulted in centralization of services that were previously performed locally. It also resulted in the creation of new services. This classification at the corporate level became known as "selling, general and administrative (SG&A)" expenses.

The survival of a free-enterprise system is dependent upon the ability to respond to market demand and to compete successfully. The capacity to compete, in turn, is tempered by the ability to contend with dramatic changes in the marketplace caused by changing customer demands, government regulations, and new sources of competition.

In contrast to the past, when companies could "coast" comfortably, year after year, on stable product lines, the life cycle of many products has become increasingly short because of changes in taste and rapid advances in technology. Adhering to the status quo is no longer a viable strategy.

Sales messages, once delivered by the printed word, are now relying extensively on the air waves. Manufacturers have found themselves in "show business"—entertaining audiences numbering in the millions. The Marketing Department has virtually become a co-producer of shows to induce the public to buy its company's products.

As a result of such increased costs as selling, advertising, promotion, warehousing, packing, and freight, many companies are finding that their SG&A costs are approaching, and in some cases exceeding, their manufacturing costs. A study of 1984 annual reports showed that Pfizer's SG&A expenses approximated 82% of the cost of its products sold while Warner-Lambert's amounted to 115%. For Xerox, the SG&A expenses amounted to 74% of the cost of products and services sold and for IBM, its percentage amounted to 61% of products and services sold.

On the subject of rising SG&A expenses, one pharmaceutical company commented as follows in its annual report:

> Our marketing expenditures increased at a faster rate than sales as a result of management's decisions to accelerate spending levels in support of existing business and to provide for an expanded flow of new products. Advertising and promotional outlays, a chief component of marketing expenses, increased by 13%.

The chairman of another company, producing electronics information processing systems, commented as follows:

> Major reorganization of our field sales organization in the United States—the first since 1968—has created a separate selling staff to concentrate on the small office and single machine user. At the same time, in the United States and other countries, as well, we are experimenting with new marketing channels ranging from dealers and direct mail to free-standing stores. Our criteria are convenience and service to potential customers.

Many companies rise to the challenges in the marketplace, as noted in the preceding quotations. Unfortunately, there are unintended distortions in reflecting the results of such changes in product profitability statements and in price quotations made to customers. Admittedly, the marketplace often dictates selling prices. However, management must know the true relationship of product costs to selling prices on an ongoing basis—not merely in a total company figure, but by major product lines and by the markets in which they are sold. For this reason, SG&A expenses can no longer be allocated in broad aggregates.

ALLOCATION METHODS ARE TOO MECHANICAL

The allocation of SG&A costs to the various product lines is usually the responsibility of the Accounting Department. Because this group is under pressure to meet deadlines for issuing financial statements, the accounting procedures take on the characteristics of a production line. Since allocation of SG&A becomes part of the production line process, the basis for making the allocations to the various product lines tends to become overly mechanical.

Allocations Must Be Sensitive to Differences in Cost Makeup

The allocation method utilized at Sewing Notions, Inc. (name disguised), is illustrative of the results of mechanical methods that do not take the cost behavior of the various items in SG&A into account. The president of this company recognized the inadequacy of using sales as the basis for allocating SG&A in his company. He commented as follows: "Wool has a high material cost and a low gross margin. Sales have been increasing steadily but as sales increase, so do the losses."

The comptroller, in seeking to change the allocation procedure, acknowledged that a product line should not be penalized because its per pound cost happens to be higher than that of another product line. Nor should gross profit enter into SG&A absorption into the product lines. He therefore eliminated raw material and gross profit from the base in making the allocation. Stated another way, sales by product line were reduced to "conversion costs" (direct labor plus manufacturing overhead). The conversion costs of the various product lines were divided by the total company conversion cost. The resulting ratios were used as the basis for allocating the SG&A expenses. This change in method took wool out of its loss position. While the profitability of other product lines was reduced, the reduction was anticipated because the president felt that some of the profits were artificially high.

Although the use of conversion costs as the basis for allocation served as a "quick fix" in this company, it cannot be adopted arbitrarily because other factors must be taken into account. As an example, some companies buy finished products on the outside and therefore incur little or no conversion cost on such items because the entire purchase price is considered to be a material cost. Use of conversion costs as an allocation base would therefore overstate the profitability of such purchases for resale because little or no SG&A charges would be levied against them even though sales effort, advertising, and other costs had been incurred. SG&A is too significant a cost in many companies to be allocated on an across-the-board basis through the use of a single allocation base such as sales or conversion costs. A more analytical approach must be taken wherein the cost behavior of the major cost items is reflected in the allocation. The accountant must therefore work in conjunction with the Marketing Department to determine the cost behavior of the various items to be allocated.

Allocation Problems with SG&A Similar to Those of Manufacturing Overhead

In allocating manufacturing overhead, the key manufacturing operations are identified as production departments or cost centers. The various overhead costs associated with the manufacturing process are then allocated to the various production departments based on the cost behavior of each overhead item. It is only logical that a similar approach be followed in allocating the SG&A expenses. The product lines should be identified by families and the various components of SG&A allocated to each family. Pfizer, in the "Review of Operations" section of its annual report illustrates such a breakdown:

Health care
   Pharmaceuticals
   Hospital products
Agriculture (animal health and feed supplements)

Specialty chemicals (used in making pharmaceuticals)
Materials science
   Minerals, pigments, and metals
   Refractory products
Consumer (nonprescription items)

Note that health care is broken down by pharmaceuticals and hospital products. The latter is identified separately to show the sales of such items as orthopedic reconstruction devices, heart-lung pumps, heart valves, and the like. A similar breakdown is shown within the materials science product line.

SG&A COSTS MUST RECOGNIZE COST DIFFERENCES BY MARKET

It rarely occurs to the accountant processing large amounts of paperwork that packing costs, for example, can be quite different for the same product sold in two different markets. Too few companies, in their allocation of SG&A expenses to product lines, recognize differences in the markets in which the products are sold. Exhibit 1 demonstrates how the Electro Company (name disguised) allocates its SG&A items by the three markets in which its products are sold. Electro contains the following cost components in its SG&A:

Selling expenses
Warehousing
Packing
Advertising and promotion
Freight
Administration

The costs included in administration are the residual costs left after direct charges have been made to the various manufacturing units. The direct charges include such services to payroll, billing, accounts payable, and any other corporate charges that can be specifically identified by location. These represent costs that would have been incurred by the individual plants as manufacturing overhead if they had been completely decentralized.

The most common markets in which industrial manufacturers sell their products and component parts are:

Original Equipment Manufacturers (OEM)
Replacement market
Distributors

The Electro Company was selected for this illustrative example because it sells to all three markets.

1. *Equipment manufacturers.* The equipment manufacturers supplied by the Electro Company make table lamps, floor lamps, and other electric lighting fixtures found in the home. These fall into the category of customized products because of the assortment of end products made to satisfy the variety of customer tastes. The types of products sold in this market are labor intensive, requiring a good

deal of manual assembly. The highly labor-intensive nature of the manufacturing process in making these items results in a lower gross profit. However, since these products are shipped in bulk, the packing and freight costs are lower, partly offsetting the lower gross profit.

2. *Replacement market.* In contrast to the equipment market, a broad line of components is sold to the replacement market, which is made up of such retailers as hardware stores and home building center stores. Packing costs are higher because these parts are packed in smaller cartons rather than being shipped in bulk. Some of the items are blister packed, thus adding even more to the packing expenses and freight costs. Blister packing might technically be considered a manufacturing cost, but this company treats it as SG&A.

3. *Distributors.* This market, like the replacement market, also purchases a broader line of parts, which are sold to building contractors for use in construction and maintenance. Packing and freight costs are lower than those of the replacement market because of the bulk method of shipping.

Packing and freight costs were used above as illustrative examples to demonstrate the rationale followed in identifying differences in SG&A costs in the three markets. The same applies to the other items contained in SG&A:

1. Selling expenses are lower in the OEM market because there are fewer calls to make than in the other markets.
2. Warehousing costs for the equipment manufacturers (OEM) are about 44% of those in the replacement market and 57% of those of the distributors. The allocation of this charge is based on the approximate warehousing space required to supply these three markets. The floor space figures were furnished by the Production Control Department, to which the various warehouse managers report.
3. Advertising and Promotion considers the markets to which it sells, as well as the number of families of products that are sold to each of the markets. Some may argue that orders placed by the equipment manufacturers are not influenced by the amount of advertising. Electro's marketing manager advised that manufacturers are more likely to purchase from suppliers whose names are known. The advertising cost charged to the equipment market was substantially lower than that charged to the other two, however. The estimates for the three markets were based largely on the number of different products sold to each market.
4. Bad debts are considered to be part of the administrative costs by most companies. Electro, however, felt that because the bad debt expenses had been running over $100,000 annually, they should be identified separately by market.
5. Administration was divided about equally among the three markets because it was looked upon as a "readiness-to-serve" expense. As explained earlier, the administrative costs were the residual amount after all corporate service costs rendered to the factory locations were distributed.

Exhibit 1 shows that the total SG&A expenses are 11.6% of sales in the OEM market, 19.2% in the replacement market, and 16.7% in the distributor market. (These three percentages are broken down by the individual items in Exhibit 2.) The resulting net pretax profit for the three markets, shown in Exhibit 1, is 4.5%, 4.8%, and 5.4%, respectively.

EXHIBIT 1
BREAKDOWN OF INCOME STATEMENT BY MARKET

	Equipment Manufacturers		Replacement Market		Distributors		Total	
Net Sales	$8,295,690	100.0%	9,608,300	100.0%	8,269,400	100.0%	$26,173,390	100.0%
Cost of Sales	6,960,080	83.9	7,302,314	76.0	6,441,860	77.9	20,704,254	79.1
Gross Profit	1,335,610	16.1	2,305,986	24.0	1,827,540	22.1	5,469,136	20.9
SG&A								
Selling Expenses	258,400		413,440		361,760		1,033,600	
Warehousing	112,990		254,200		197,730		564,920	
Packing	136,420		341,040		204,630		682,090	
Advertising and Promotion	150,645		338,950		263,635		753,230	
Bad Debts	11,720		82,020		23,430		117,170	
Freight	75,320		188,310		112,985		376,615	
Administration	216,805		223,370		216,805		656,980	
Total SG&A	962,300	11.6	1,841,330	19.2	1,380,975	16.7	4,184,605	16.0
Net Profit	$ 373,310	4.5%	464,656	4.8%	446,565	5.4%	$ 1,284,531	4.9%
Markup factors for use in price quotations: see page 81	19.2%		31.6%		28.4%			

EXHIBIT 2
PERCENT BREAKDOWN OF SG&A EXPENSES BY MARKET*

	Equipment Manufacturers	Replacement Market	Distributors	Total
Selling Expenses	3.1%	4.3%	4.4%	3.9%
Warehousing	1.4	2.7	2.4	2.2
Packing	1.7	3.5	2.5	2.6
Advertising and Promotion	1.8	3.5	3.2	2.9
Bad Debts	.1	.9	.3	.5
Freight	.9	2.0	1.3	1.4
Administration	2.6	2.3	2.6	2.5
SG&A % of Sales	11.6%	19.2%	16.7%	16.0%

* Percentages based on the sales in each market.

RETURN ON INVESTMENT IS MORE MEANINGFUL THAN RETURN ON SALES

Top-level executives in many companies are too prone to accept the return on sales as an infallible indicator of profitability—forgetting the significance of return on investment.

When money is invested in a business, the investors are more interested in the return on their investment than on the percentage on sales. This makes sense when one considers that the return on sales compares revenues with costs but does not take into account the amount of invested capital and the turns per year of that capital. If return on investment is such an important factor for the owners of the business, then it must be just as important to follow the same reasoning when evaluating the profitability of different markets in which the company does business.

To demonstrate the impact that the amount of investment and the annual turns of that investment can have on the individual profitability of Electro's three markets, the income statement in Exhibit 1 has been expanded in Exhibit 3 to show the return on investment.

EXHIBIT 3
CALCULATION OF RETURN ON INVESTMENT BY MARKET

	Equipment Manufacturers	Replacement Market	Distributors	Total
Net Sales	$8,295,690	9,608,300	8,269,400	$26,173,390
Factory Investment				
Inventory	795,043	1,788,848	1,391,326	3,975,217
Net Fixed Assets	1,076,621	1,722,594	1,507,270	4,306,485
Total	$1,871,664	3,511,442	2,898,596	$ 8,281,702
Investment Turns/year*	4.4X	2.7X	2.8X	3.2X
Return on Sales per Exhibit 1	4.5%	4.8%	5.4%	4.9%
Return on Investment†	19.8%	13.0%	15.1%	15.7%

* Investment Turns/Year = Net Sales divided by total Factory Investment.
† Return on Investment = Investment Turns/Year X Return on Sales per Exhibit 1. This can also be calculated by dividing Net Profit in Exhibit 1 by Total Factory Investment. There will be small differences in the return on investment percentage because of rounding.

Breaking Down the Investment by the Three Markets

Exhibit 3 shows the factory investment by market. Although there are items other than inventory and fixed assets that could be included as investments, these were found to be so small that they were eliminated from consideration. Accounts receivable could have been, but was not, included as part of the investment because there is some offset of receivables by payables. In the interest of simplicity, only inventory and fixed assets were included.

1. *Inventory.* The allocation of inventory by markets was determined by breaking down the inventory by major product lines and making the allocation of each of these product lines on the basis of the units sold to each of the three markets. The units were then valued at the standard cost to arrive at the amount of investment in the inventory required to support the three markets. The unit figures, before costing, were used to allocate the warehousing costs in the three markets.
2. *Fixed assets.* The allocation of fixed assets was based on the percentage of machine hours required to produce the quantities of the product lines sold in each of the three markets. The machine hours represented the fixed assets that were used for the machine-paced operations. For the labor-intensive products, the percentage breakdown was based on the direct labor hours applicable to the less expensive nonautomatic equipment.

Calculating the Return on Investment

This calculation was made in the following two steps:

- The investment turns per year were calculated by dividing the total factory investment in each market into the sales for each market.
- The investment turns per year were then multiplied by the percentage profit on sales shown in Exhibit 1. This calculation could also have been made by dividing the dollars of profit shown in Exhibit 1 by the total factory investment shown in Exhibit 3.

The comparison of the percentage return on sales is compared with the percentage return on factory investment below:

	OEM MARKET	REPLACEMENT MARKET	DISTRIBUTOR MARKET	TOTAL
Return on sales	4.5%	4.8%	5.4%	4.9%
Return on investment	19.8%	13.0%	15.1%	15.7%

Note that the percentage return on sales shows profitability in the OEM market to be the lowest of the three and sales to the distributor market to be the highest—4.5% versus 5.4%.

The return on investment, however, shows the OEM market to be the most profitable of the three and the replacement market to be the least profitable—19.8% versus 13.0%.

Why the OEM Market, with the Lowest Return on Sales, Has the Highest Return on Investment

The "turnaround" for the OEM market from the least to the most profitable is not a freak of mathematics. It is due to two factors:

- The level of inventory required to supply the OEM market is lower because fewer items are sold in greater volumes. In short, sales to the OEM market make up about 32% of total sales but require only 20% of the total inventory—resulting in a greater number of inventory turns.
- The assembly of the products sold to OEM is more difficult to automate. Therefore, the amount of investment in fixed assets is only 25% of the total—the balance of 75% is required for the other two markets. The sales are roughly one-third for each of the three markets.

When seeking to eliminate unprofitable business, executives with profit responsibility sometimes question the desirability of OEM business because of the lower selling prices and tighter product specifications.

The decision on whether or not to accept such business should be based on the return on investment rather than the return on sales. True, the tighter specifications will result in a greater number of production rejects. However, it is likely that the looser specification requirements in the other markets will permit most of the OEM rejects to be sold in the other markets at higher prices.

In some types of government business, the major material, and sometimes equipment, are government furnished. Here, again, because the size of the investment will be lower, return on investment will reflect the more meaningful measure of profitability.

SPECIAL ATTENTION MUST BE GIVEN TO LOW-VOLUME PRODUCTS

This section deals with the distorting effect of small allocation errors on low-volume products. The subject could have been discussed in the section "Allocation Methods Are Too Mechanical." It was felt, however, that this subject might have been considered to be a refinement and may not have been given the attention it warrants.

Any allocation method that uses a percentage breakdown contains a built-in flaw. The resulting inaccuracy has a greater impact on products with a small volume than on those with a higher volume of sales. Take, for example, the simplified example of a company with only two product lines—jewelry and porcelain figurines. Assume that the figures shown below represent the current month's sales:

	CURRENT MONTH'S SALES	
	DOLLARS	PERCENT
Jewelry	$421,750	94.5%
Porcelain figurines	24,546	5.5%
Total	$446,296	100.0%

Assume further that the selling expense to be allocated to these two products is $96,650. The breakdown of this allocation based on the percentages shown above is 94.5% and 5.5%, respectively. The results are as follows:

| | SELLING EXPENSE | |
	DOLLARS	PERCENT
Jewelry	$91,334	94.5%
Porcelain figurines	5,316	5.5
Total	$96,650	100.0%

Although allocation percentages can have a margin of error that could approach, and even exceed, several percentage points, let us assume in this illustrative example that the margin of error would be the result of rounding off the percentages to 94% and 6%, respectively. The resulting difference is as follows:

| | SELLING EXPENSE | | % OF |
	DOLLARS	DIFFERENCE	SALES
Jewelry	$90,851	−483	.1%
Porcelain figurines	5,799	+483	2.0
	$96,650	–0–	–0–

Note how the small rounding difference of 0.5% increased the selling expense charged to the figurines by $483, or 2.0% of the figurine sales. The offsetting reduction of $483 allocated to jewelry amounted to only 0.1% of jewelry sales. The difference in rounding the percentages was enough to put the figurines into a low-profit position. The impact on the jewelry of 0.1% was insignificant. The alternative to the use of a percentage allocation to a product with low volume is illustrated in the following case example:

The CEO of a company that manufactures sunglasses realized that his molding presses had sufficient capacity to make combs during periods when the molding of sunglasses was low—thus obtaining greater utilization of equipment. The same sales people who sold the sunglasses could easily handle the combs, thereby adding no additional selling costs. The CEO nonetheless insisted that the selling expenses, as well as the other items in SG&A, be charged to the combs as if they were a separate business. He left it to his controller to determine how the SG&A should be allocated between the sunglasses and the combs. The controller instructed his department to use sales as the basis for making the allocation to the two products.

Since the combs sold at a low unit price, compared with sunglasses, the sales volume was only 15% of that of the sunglasses. As a result, small fluctuations in the percentage allocations made to the combs caused wide fluctuations in the reported profits. During periods in which the production of sunglasses was low, the percentage allocations to combs were much larger—with the result that this product showed large losses.

The CEO was disturbed by the erratic behavior of profits (and losses) resulting from the combs and inquired about a more reliable method for making the allocations. He was advised to establish a fixed SG&A readiness-to-serve charge for combs rather than using an allocation based on percentages of sales volume. This minimized the fluctuations in reported profits for the combs because the reduced production of sunglasses no longer penalized the product with the smaller volume. The impact on sunglasses, as illustrated for jewelry in the preceding example, was small. This solution minimized distortions to the porcelain figurines in the earlier example as well.

ASSURING CONSISTENCY BETWEEN CUSTOMER QUOTATIONS AND PRODUCT PROFITABILITY STATEMENT PREPARATION

Exhibit 1 provides a convenient method for illustrating how the markup factor was developed for the Electro Company's products sold in the OEM market. This exhibit was discussed earlier, except for the last line of figures, identified as "Markup factors for use in price quotations." The markup factors for three markets were obtained by dividing the budgeted gross profit by the budgeted cost of sales (manufacturing cost). In the first column, for example, the gross profit of $1,335,610 was divided by the cost of sales of $6,960,080 to arrive at the markup factor of 19.2% on manufacturing costs. The selling price is then calculated by multiplying the manufacturing cost shown on the quotation by 119.2%. This price will provide for recovery of 11.6% of the selling price for SG&A and a net profit of 4.5% of the selling price— which should mean a 19.8% return on investment. Thus, if the manufacturing cost per 1,000 on a quotation amounted to $69.60, it would be multiplied by 119.2% to arrive at a selling price of $82.95 per 1,000. The use of this markup factoring method for sales in the OEM market would be in consonance with the method used for calculating the product line profitability statements each month.

BASES FOR ALLOCATING SG&A CANNOT BE USED AD INFINITUM

When studies for determining proper SG&A allocation bases and markup factors by market have been completed, some companies tend to assume that the original study will suffice until a product line is dropped or a new one added. This is a false premise.

Even if a company retains the same products, there can be shifts in sales volume that could alter the ground rules for allocating SG&A. Take, for example, the product line breakdown for the five-year period between 1978 to 1982 for Talley Industries. The annual reports showed the following percentage breakdown of the five product lines for the first and fifth years of the five-year period.

	1978	1982
Clocks and timing products	40%	38%
Specialty products	13	13
Apparel	32	24
Government and technical	13	23
Realty	2	2
Total	100%	100%

Apparel sales showed a steady reduction from 32% of total sales in 1978 to 24% in 1982, while government and technical sales increased from 13% of total sales in 1978 to 23% in 1982.

If the type of work being done for the government is such that selling and advertising are disallowed, the increase in government sales would not increase the absorption base for selling and advertising. And in view of the 8% reduction in apparel sales, management would probably look for some reduction in SG&A—not only in selling and advertising but in some of the other SG&A costs as well. This points up the importance of recalculating the allocation factors as well as the markup factors for the different markets in which the products are sold. These features should be part of the annual financial plan.

SG&A EXPENSES TOO LARGE TO BE ALLOCATED ARBITRARILY

The production line approach to accounting can serve a highly useful purpose in handling a large volume of repetitive transactions. But it is important to know where to draw the line when selecting allocation methods. The key term is "cost behavior." This requires the involvement of the individual(s) most familiar with the cost behavior of the elements that make up SG&A. Those responsible for preparation of the product line profitability statements will thus become more knowledgeable about the operations behind the figures.

The implementation of better methods of accounting for SG&A costs must start with the annual financial plan. The procedures outlined in this chapter should be incorporated into the plan. The percentage breakdown of the individual SG&A expenses, as shown by market in Exhibit 2, would represent the standard percentages to be used for the year. Obviously, any major changes that occur during the year would require adjustment of these standards.

The markup factors by market shown in Exhibit 1 would likewise represent the standard percentages to be applied to the estimated manufacturing costs in requests for customer quotations to arrive at desired selling prices. SG&A expenses may continue to be referred to as "below-the-line" costs, as they are in many companies, but by following the recommended procedures, they will be accorded the same treatment given to the "above-the-line" costs.

SECTION 2
INVENTORY MANAGEMENT AND MISMANAGEMENT

The first chapter in this section is titled "Common Pitfalls in Accounting for inventory." This chapter deals with the yearend inventory shortage trauma experienced by many executives with profit responsibility. It explains the various reasons why large discrepancies between the yearend physical and book values occur—sometimes turning an eleven month profit into a loss. It also discusses measures for greatly minimizing such differences.

Chapter 7 points out that it is characteristic of an industrial society to first automate those operations that are the simplest and most voluminous. This applies to processing data as much as it does to performing manufacturing operations. It is only natural in the computerization of inventory that primary emphasis is placed on processing the many thousands of routine transactions that occur each month—leaving some of the more complex and less routine transactions to be performed manually. This chapter, titled, "Computerized Inventory Management: Its Strengths and Weaknesses," points out that these manually performed transactions introduce a time lag between the routine and the manually performed operations. This throws the inventory management process "out of sync"—resulting in errors in the status reports used for control purposes. The chapter emphasizes the need for programming an exception audit procedure with the ability to flag the discrepancies and correct them before they appear on the status reports.

Transaction reporting of the physical units for inventory management purposes also provides the cost department with the basis for determining the value of the inventory carried on the books. Chapter 8, "Interface of Inventory Management and the Cost Accounting System," shows how the physical units are costed at various stages of production and processed through the cost accounting system.

Many computerized cost systems accumulate the material, direct labor and overhead costs for each department and transfer the total to the next department as material. Chapter 9 points out other costing applications that require the three elements of manufacturing cost to remain "pure" throughout the system to provide management control reports. Illustrative examples of such reports are included in this chapter.

Chapter 10, "Inventory Valuation in an Inflation Economy," describes the various LIFO costing methods. Many companies use standard costs. In such instances, the adjustments to LIFO are made by charging or crediting variances to cost of sales. Changes in the dollar value of inventory prices at standard cost represent changes in the inventory levels (i.e., an increment or decrement).

6
Common Pitfalls in Accounting for Inventory

Companies with process costing systems (repetitive production) are more vulnerable than those using job costing systems to year-end differences between the value of the physical inventory and the value carried on the books.

Although differences can occur in companies using job costing systems, they occur less often because the inventories are broken down by individual jobs and are closed out as each order is completed.

This chapter describes how discrepancies occur. It also explains how such differences can be monitored during the year before they become too large.

The number of companies in which the annual physical inventory reveals a large difference between physical and book values is much greater than many realize.

When an inventory adjustment causes a substantial change in the year's profits, everyone wants an immediate explanation. This includes the financial analysts, who, after studying the results of the first three quarters, accept the validity of the company's fourth quarter and total-year profit projections. Investors who purchased the company's stock on the basis of such projections can naturally be expected to demand an explanation from their brokers or financial advisors.

Those who are already shareholders are likewise disappointed because the momentum of the first three quarters has suffered an unexplained reversal. A member of the board of directors of a medium-sized company who had a large investment in the company threatened legal action when the company found a $410,000 unfavorable difference between the physical and book inventories. This discrepancy was due to a programming error in the newly computerized cost accounting system. The programmer had coded the overtime premium and the shift premium as direct labor, not realizing that these items were already included in the overhead rates. The result was a doubling of these costs in inventory.

Usually the shortages are not real losses. The discrepancy is the result of a poor cost system that overstates inventories during the year, requiring adjustment at year-end. This raises the following questions:

1. Why is correct inventory valuation so important?
2. How do the discrepancies occur?
3. Is realistic cost flow the key?

WHY IS CORRECT INVENTORY VALUATION SO IMPORTANT?

Good inventory accountability is necessary to assure correct reporting of profits during the interim periods as well as at year-end. There is nothing more disconcerting to the executive responsible for the profit goals of his operation than to go along for 11 months of the year under the illusion that he is meeting his business plan, only to find in the 12th month that a large inventory difference between physical and book inventories has wiped out a large part of the profit.

Sometimes a defensive stance is taken, wherein it is argued that the inventory discrepancy between physical and book inventories is only, say, 1% of the total throughput (flow of production). The implied question is, "How much more accuracy can you expect with the massive movement of material and parts that takes place in the course of a year?"

While it seems logical to equate the magnitude of the discrepancy with the volume of throughput, the more frequently used measure in the real world of business is the impact on profits. The difference is demonstrated in this illustration of company A and company B:

	COMPANY A	COMPANY B
Annual production	$20,000,000	20,000,000
Inventory difference	200,000	200,000
Percent of production	1%	1%
Pretax profit	2,000,000	400,000
Percent inventory difference in profit	10%	50%

Obviously, a greater unfavorable reaction can be expected from company B's management and stockholders than from company A's even though the amount of inventory difference and the throughput are exactly the same.

Another reason for the need for proper inventory accountability is the requirement for quarterly submission to the Securities and Exchange Commission. A company whose inventory is overstated on its books may show overstated profits in the first three quarters and a relatively poor performance for the fourth quarter. This does not constitute acceptable reporting.

Stock analysts who make recommendations to their clients on the basis of reported earnings can be greatly misled by incorrect profits resulting from overstated earnings. This can work to the detriment of a company seeking to raise capital.

HOW DO THE DISCREPANCIES OCCUR?

Inventory adjustments or discrepancies are of two general types:

1. Disappearance through theft.
2. Improper accounting.

Discrepancies due to disappearance are generally smaller than those due to improper accounting. However, disappearance through theft is a true loss, while improper accounting results in the mismatching of revenues with costs during the year, with a large correcting adjustment at year-end.

Disappearance Through Theft

Detecting inventory theft losses through the accounting records is usually difficult because of the many different types of transactions, normal errors in identification, and possibly incomplete paperwork. Prevention, rather than after-the-fact bookkeeping, should therefore be the approach to take in preventing inventory theft losses.

Case example: One manufacturer of small automotive accessories dismissed the possibility of employee theft on a large scale because the plant and its employees were all new—presumably too new to make the proper connections needed to dispose of stolen inventory. It was no small surprise to the company officials when the Highway Patrol found employees on the night shift passing cartons over the fence and loading a car. The average-sized car could hold $5,000 worth of merchandise. The annual loss based on losing one carload each week could total as much as a quarter of a million dollars. As a result of this experience, the company realized that while the accounting records would certainly reflect the loss, more direct preventive measures were required.

Laxity of internal control is the primary factor that invites employee dishonesty. The AGO kitchen and bathroom hardware company (name disguised) was advised by its accounting firm that the finished stock storeroom should be fenced in. This storeroom was located within 50 feet of the shipping dock—a tempting target. The president was reluctant to spend the money. The inevitable happened. The shipping room employees, who had free access to the stock stored in the open area near the dock, would add several cartons over and above the number authorized by the shipping papers. One of the truckers would sell the stock to a fence and share the receipts with the shipping clerks—until discovered. The estimated loss was found to be substantially more than the cost of enclosing the stockroom and maintaining a perpetual inventory of its contents.

Improper Accounting

Improper accounting, which can result in large, usually unfavorable differences between physical and book inventories, can be grouped into two basic categories:

- Overstatement of input (i.e., amounts put into inventory)
- Understatement of relief (i.e., amounts taken out of inventory)

Overstatement of Input

Input can be overstated from such factors as overcosting of production, improper handling of customer returns, and improper coding.

Overcosting of production: When products or components prove to be defective, they are frequently reprocessed to correct the defect. If not properly accounted for, such rework might be counted as good production twice—with the result that the book value of inventory will be overstated when compared with the value of the year-end physical inventory.

Case example: The Rago Company (name disguised) had well-written procedures for handling defective units. A rework tag was attached to the batch of units requiring reprocessing. Upon completion of the rework, the batch was moved back into the stream of production. The rework tag was the signal that the batch had already been counted as production at that operation. It was found, however, that employees were sometimes destroying tags as the parts entered the line. The result was that many of the reworked items did not have tags and were therefore counted as good production a second time. Because of this, the year-end inventory discrepancy amounted to $190,000.

While the procedures were fine as far as they went, they lacked an important control feature which was readily available. Although the rework tags were prenumbered, no effort was being made to assure that all tags had been accounted for. As a result of the large inventory discrepancy, the procedure was changed so that all tag numbers were logged when issued and checked when they were returned from the production line. Thus, if a tag was improperly detached in the rework process (so that the goods were counted twice), the missing number would be brought to the attention of the accounting personnel and the amount represented by the missing tag would be subtracted from the reported production for that period.

Improper handling of customer returns: If sales returns are not handled properly, it is possible to have duplicate inventory input entries, which can produce substantial distortions.

Case example: The Hydraulic Valve Corporation (name disguised) experienced a substantial jump in customer returns due to the incorrect design of a new product. Each month an inventory of all items returned during the month was taken, and these totals were added to the book inventory. But as these defective units were processed, credits were issued to the customers. These credits resulted in an automatic entry into inventory a second time, causing a duplication totaling $90,000.

The procedure was changed so that items were added to inventory only upon issuance of the credit to the customer. This was more logical, since the units were not the property of the company until a credit was actually issued.

Improper coding: Poor communication of a policy change resulted in a coding error at the KGO Company (name disguised)—causing a doubling up of freight costs on incoming material.

Case example: The cost manager decided that freight on steel, the principal material used, would be better treated as part of the standard cost of steel. The advantage of including freight as part of the standard cost is that the freight would be more equitably charged to production. The existing practice of inclusion in overhead charges on the basis of an overhead rate had little relevance to the usage of steel. All other smaller items of freight would continue to be included in overhead. This procedure, with the approval of the controller, was implemented. However, the accounts payable department, which coded all invoices, was not notified of the change. As a result, freight on steel, not a small number, was double-charged—once in the standard cost of steel that was issued and again in the overhead rate. Fortunately, the error was discovered when the first-quarter results for the new year was issued. This demonstrated the importance of good communications whenever changes are made.

Understatement of Relief

Understatement of relief is another way in which inventory shortages can develop. Inventories can be overstated if the company costs its shipments as a percentage of sales and this percentage is too low, or if losses in production are not accounted for.

Incorrect cost of sales: Companies that have thousands of items in inventory, but lack the capability to cost each item, frequently use a percentage that is applied to the month's sales. This percentage is determined from historical experience. It may be an overall percentage applied to total sales or it may be separate percentages for each major product line.

This percentage method might work well for a time. Some firms even add contingency factors to the percentages to assure that if an error does occur, it will be on the favorable side.

The problem with this method is that the factors affecting the percentage are subject to change, and the effects of such changes cannot be measured with precision at interim dates.

Case example: The JTC Company, using this percentage-of-sales method, found that its mix of sales had changed—as had the percentage of the cost of sales to sales. Although the change appeared to be imperceptible, it resulted in a percentage-of-sales increase from 58% in the previous year to 62% in the current year. Because 58% was used in the current year, the relief to inventory was so understated that an 11-month profit of $1,650,000 actually turned out to be only $375,000 at year-end. There was no easy remedy because the inventory consisted of some 14,000 different items. The solution was a long-term program to computerize the cost system so that individual items could be costed without resort to percentages based on a past history. The resulting cost system is similar to the one described in Chapter 8.

Losses in production not accounted for: Companies whose input into inventory is based on standards applied to production must rely on accurate reporting of production losses to adjust the inventory as these production losses are reported. These losses are made up of costs such as the following:

- Excess usage of raw materials—the amount of material in excess of normal requirements that is spoiled during the manufacturing operation.
- Yield loss—the material and conversion costs that are lost because the quantity of good production is less than can normally be expected from the input quantity.
- Manufacturing defects—parts that do not meet the inspection requirements and cannot be reworked.

Rare is the company that can attest to the accuracy of its reporting of production losses. A company that can account for two-thirds of such losses is doing well. The reason is economics. In many instances, the unit cost of the items produced is so small that the cost of an accurate reporting system would be prohibitive.

The answer, when economics permits, is a "shop order" system whereby the production control department monitors physical quantities through work-in-process. Under this method, production quantities are recorded by operation. To account for all the losses, the number of units accepted into stock is subtracted from the initial number. This shows the total number of rejects. Subtracting the reported rejects from this figure will show the unaccounted-for losses that must be relieved from inventory. This shop order system is illustrated in Exhibit 1.

The total units placed in production were 75,500, while the number of units actually accepted into the stockroom were 65,000, a loss of 10,500 units. Of this 10,500, 6,300 units were reported to the accounting department and were relieved from inventory. The unaccounted-for loss of 4,200 units that still remain in the book inventory must be removed, or there will be a discrepancy between physical and book inventories at year-end.

EXHIBIT 1
A SYSTEM FOR MONITORING INVENTORY LOSSES
SHOP ORDER #720568

Cost Center	Operation	Started	Completed	Reported Rejects	Unaccounted-for Losses
20	1	75,500*	74,800	300	400
21	2	74,800	67,600	4,500	2,700
23	3	67,600	65,000	1,500	1,100
26	To Stock	65,000			
				6,300	4,200

* Starting quantity

IS REALISTIC COST FLOW THE KEY?

The key to good inventory accounting procedures is a realistic cost flow, which in turn should be based on the actual production flow. The production flow should depend upon the type of product or service involved. When the product or service is unique and its specific cost must be known, as in the case of a custom-made product, the job cost system is mandatory. On the other hand, in a process-type business in which standardized products are built to stock rather than to order, a process cost system is more suitable (see Exhibit 2). Where a company makes custom products from standard components which are interchangeable, the production flow to make the components can be the same as that used in making the standard components. The operations in which these components are assembled into custom products would follow the job costing procedures. However, for purposes of this discussion, we will disregard this hybrid but perfectly valid type of production flow.

Job costing: The production flow in a job cost system focuses on a specific product for a specific customer. The flow of material, labor, and overhead is designed to satisfy the requirements for making that particular product. When completed, the product is shipped to the customer out of work-in-process.

A job costing system utilizes two basic inventory accounts:

- Raw material.
- Work-in-process (or jobs in process).

There is usually no finished goods inventory unless one prefers to run shipments through a finished goods account as a means of tracking. In some instances, when only part of a completed lot is retained for later shipment, use of the finished goods account will provide a "resting place" for the completed but unshipped balance.

While purchases are normally directed into the raw material inventory account and then issued to jobs as needed, this is not always the case; material purchased specifically for a job can bypass the raw material inventory account and be charged directly to work-in-process. Direct labor is charged directly against the job on which the work is performed, as is overhead.

Inventory accountability under job costing has the advantage of being relatively easy. As each job is completed, all accumulated costs that were charged to that job are cleared out of inventory, leaving no unaccounted-for residual quantities. However, there is also a disadvantage to the job costing method: it requires substantially more work than a process costing system. As an example, a company with annual sales

EXHIBIT 2
TWO BASIC COST FLOWS

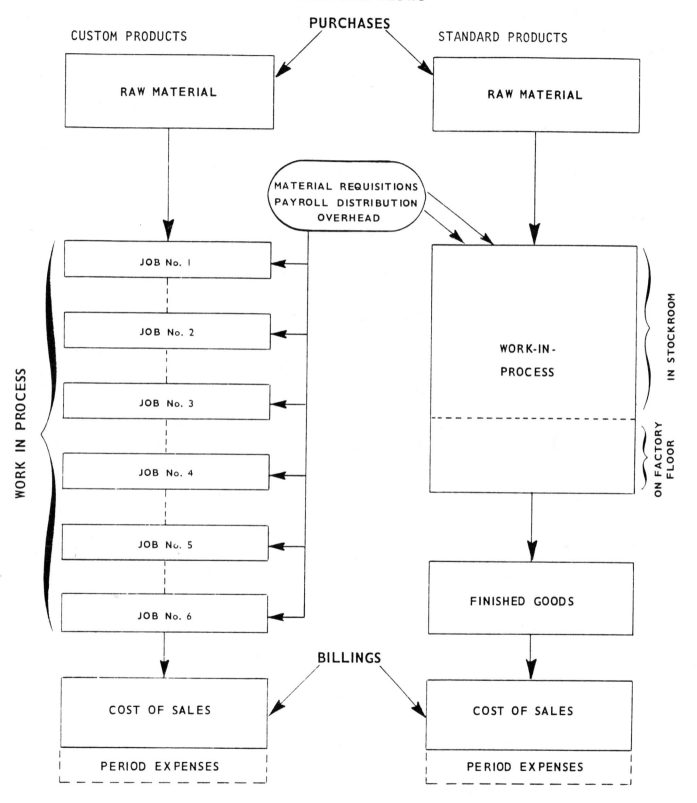

of less than $10,000,000 might have as many as 500 or more shop orders in process. Another disadvantage is the tendency in job shops to "borrow" from one job in order to meet the priority requirements of another job. When such borrowing is done without paperwork documentation, the accuracy of the inventory accounting becomes questionable.

Process costing: The production flow in a process costing system can be pictured as a steady stream of material, labor, and overhead flowing into work-in-process through the various operations. From work-in-process, the flow is to the finished goods inventory, out of which shipments are made.

In a process-type business, the three basic inventory accounts are raw material, work-in-process, and finished goods. The work-in-process account should be further broken down into a component parts stockroom (parts fabricated in advance for use in later assembly operations, which are held in the stockroom until needed) and factory floor inventory (work-in-process around work areas).

Although the production control department segregates these two types of work-in-process in monitoring progress in production, most accounting departments do not do so in their records. While the balance sheet would not reflect this breakdown of work-in-process, the supplementary inventory records should.

Basing Inventory on Production Flow

Accounting systems in which no breakdown is made between raw material, work-in-process, and finished goods inventories are most vulnerable to year-end discrepancies between physical and book inventories. The reason is that input is made into a large pool of costs with little or no accountability until the inventory is relieved by shipments. If a breakdown of inventory is maintained by segments, as illustrated in Exhibit 2, the costs as they apply to the individual segments can be tracked and verified with greater accuracy.

Further, as noted earlier, the relief values in such instances are estimates based on broad averages, such as percentages applied to sales to arrive at the inventory value of shipments. There are many instances in which there is no other approach short of a long-term program to establish a computerized cost system in which individual items are costed through the use of standards. Such a program would divide the single inventory account into its three natural segments: raw material, work-in-process, and finished goods. Each of these can then be monitored individually.

Many companies that have computerized their cost system—and have greatly improved the credibility of their financial statements—are still vulnerable to year-end discrepancies because of incipient problems which are not reflected in the paperwork that documents the various transactions affecting the inventory. Such discrepancies might stem from the following:

- Overcosting of production, such as when reworked items are counted a second time and when returns from customers are erroneously added to inventory while the product is still the property of the customer.
- Excessive use of material that is unreported, such as when material is taken out of stockrooms by unauthorized personnel without accounting for it.
- Unaccounted-for rejects, such as when losses in production are not reported in their entirety.

Most of the foregoing problems that result in underrelief of inventory occur in the work-in-process inventory account. Efforts to correct costing frequently become highly frustrating because the cost of the cure often far exceeds the benefits. This is particularly true when low unit values are involved. What, then, is the answer?

Breaking Out Work-in-Process

The answer, stated briefly, is to correlate the cost flow with the production flow— that is, to break out work-in-process in order to identify the fabricated parts (components) stockroom inventory separately from the floor inventory and to account for each separately.

Fabricated parts (components) stockroom inventory: When the shop order controls needed to identify production losses are not available, an alternative method can be used. Rather than input the labor and overhead costs into inventory on an operation-by-operation basis (and then be concerned with the problem of reducing input by losses that are difficult to account for), it is far better to record transfers into inventory only when the completed components are accepted into the components stockroom. Then the number of good units accepted into stock multiplied by the standard labor and standard overhead would determine the proper input value into inventory of these two elements. The same would, of course, apply to the material content of the items accepted into the stockroom as well. This would conform to normal production control procedures in which perpetual inventories would be maintained for each stockroom. The same paperwork that supports the physical units being accepted into stockrooms would be used to support the input into the books of account.

Floor inventory: The floor inventory, which is usually a relatively small segment of total work-in-process, would be accounted for separately. Many production control departments maintain a complete list of the balances of the various items in process. These balances, reflecting the latest operation, extended by the standard cost, would provide the book value of this segment of work-in-process. Each month the prior month's entry would be reversed and the new floor inventory balance recorded.

In the event that this type of control of floor inventory is not being maintained, two alternatives are available:

- Establish a constant value if the floor inventory is represented by a type of pipeline inventory which remains fairly constant irrespective of changes in the volume of production.
- Take a monthly physical inventory if inventories are accumulated at various points on the factory floor as reservoirs for subsequent operations, since using a constant value on the books will result in distortions on the financial statements. The physical inventory can often be limited to those areas in which fluctuations over and above the pipeline equivalent occur.

MONITORING THE INVENTORY COST FLOW

We have discussed some of the major weaknesses in costing procedures that result in physical to book inventory discrepancies. We have also emphasized the importance of correlating the accounting cost flow with the physical movement of production through the inventory accounts. Although these cover the essentials of sound inventory control in minimizing the differences between physical and book inventory values, it is not enough merely to implement these new procedures and put the system on "automatic pilot." The old saying that "there's nothing as certain as death and taxes" should be expanded to include "change." Change is a real fact of life that can render obsolete the best-conceived procedures. In our high-technology economy, the rate of change is accelerating rapidly—requiring constant vigilance over all procedures, however soundly conceived they may be.

There is no "fail-safe" method for guarding against the buildup of differences between book and physical inventories. There is, however, a relatively simple method for determining the extent to which the cost of production on a cumulative (year-to-date) basis is in excess of or less than the cumulative cost of sales. If such a comparison shows a continuous excess in the cost of production on a year-to-date basis, it means that the book inventory is rising faster than the rate of shipments.

Exhibit 3 illustrates an after-the-fact case example of this situation. The first group of figures, "Production Costs," are shown month by month, broken down by the three elements of manufacturing cost for the months January through December. These monthly figures are then accumulated to arrive at year-to-date totals, as shown on the line "Cumulative cost of production." The next line of totals, "Cumulative cost of sales," shows the year-to-date totals for the cost of sales without indicating the amount in each month. The line "Cumulative cost of production in excess of (or less than) the cumulative cost of sales" shows the difference between the year-to-date cost of production and the year-to-date cost of sales.

Since the cost of production is in excess throughout the year, it is apparent that the value of the inventory built up on the books exceeds the amount being shipped. This excess amounts to an average of 7.4% of the cost of sales. The physical-to-book difference showed an excess booked inventory of $117,501. This adjustment was used in reducing the overstated inventory and increasing the December cost of sales. After adjustment, this left the December cumulative cost of production only $8,912 higher than the adjusted December year-to-date cost of sales.

Although the use of this method for monitoring a possible buildup of inventory provides a good "early warning signal" when the cumulative cost of production indicates a buildup of inventory, two suggested actions are indicated:

1. Determine the extent to which a buildup of inventory may have been authorized by the materials management group.
2. If it has been determined that the excess of the cost of production over the cost of sales exceeds any planned buildup of inventory, an investigation should be made to find why this "phantom" inventory is growing.

In the case example illustrated by Exhibit 3, the investigation included, in addition to a detailed plant tour of every operation, an analysis of the paperwork on which the production figures were reported.

Production Flow

The manufacturing operations in this plant started with die casting in which parts were molded with zamac in much the same manner in which plastic parts are made.

EXHIBIT 3
COMPARISON OF CUMULATIVE COSTS BOOKED INTO INVENTORY
WITH CUMULATIVE COST OF SALES

	January	February	March	April	May	June	July	August	September	October	November	December
Production costs												
Material	$147,628	142,406	148,192	130,206	135,401	142,263	96,048	143,565	142,488	148,941	128,625	132,409
Direct labor	11,672	12,241	7,410	6,530	7,880	7,065	4,771	8,278	7,215	7,347	7,428	7,942
Overhead	30,016	34,681	19,620	18,655	21,061	18,782	15,489	22,781	21,203	21,276	19,984	21,630
Total cost of production	189,316	189,328	175,222	155,391	164,342	168,110	116,308	174,624	170,906	177,564	156,037	161,981
Cumulative cost of production	$189,316	378,644	553,866	709,257	873,599	1,041,709	1,158,017	1,332,641	1,503,547	1,681,111	1,837,148	1,999,129
Cumulative cost of sales	$171,214	350,467	513,926	650,491	813,596	962,164	1,079,867	1,248,239	1,417,061	1,558,693	1,710,735	1,990,217*
Cumulative cost of production in excess of (or less than) cumulative cost of sales	$ 18,102	28,177	39,940	58,766	60,003	79,545	78,150	84,402	86,486	122,418	126,413	8,912*
Percent excess to cost of sales	10.5%	8.0%	7.8%	9.0%	7.4%	8.3%	7.2%	6.8%	6.1%	7.9%	7.4%	0.4%

* Inventory and cost of sales adjusted for excessive amounts booked into inventory.

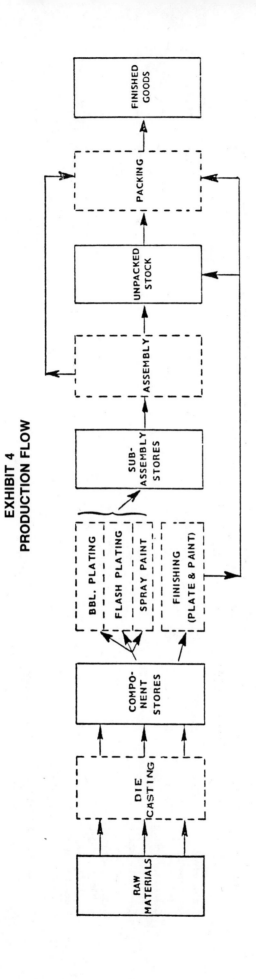

EXHIBIT 4
PRODUCTION FLOW

RAW MATERIALS

DIE CASTING

COMPONENT STORES

BBL. PLATING
FLASH PLATING
SPRAY PAINT

FINISHING (PLATE & PAINT)

SUB-ASSEMBLY STORES

ASSEMBLY

UNPACKED STOCK

PACKING

FINISHED GOODS

SOLID LINES — CONTROLLED STORES
DOTTED LINES — FLOOR WORK-IN-PROCESS (FLOAT)

Holes were drilled and tapped in the cast parts, which were then moved into Component Stores, a controlled stockroom. The parts were then withdrawn from Component Stores and moved through one of the plating/painting operations. Some of these moved into Subassembly Stores, another controlled stockroom. Others, such as knobs, were transferred to the Unpacked Stock Storeroom, to await packing. Those parts that required assembly were transferred as needed into the assembly department and then into packing.

Die casting—deficiencies in reporting production

A review of the die casting operation revealed that production reporting left much to be desired. This became immediately obvious when the operation was studied.

- The die casting operation consisted of a battery of die casting machines, each of which contained a counting mechanism that indicated the number of times the machine cycled and released a mold with completed castings. The production count was obtained by multiplying the number of cavities in the mold by the number of cycles completed during the shift.
- The completed castings were then drilled and tapped prior to being moved into Component Stores.

The production count was incorrect for two reasons:

1. Every cavity in the mold did not produce a good part.
2. Rejects were also produced in the drilling and tapping operation which was part of the casting department, but these were not being reported.

The result was that production was really being reported in terms of the number of cavities in the molds run through the casting machines, whether they produced good parts or not. Further, no accounting was being made of rejects in the drilling and tapping operation. The corrective action taken was to recognize only good production accepted into Component Stores. Improperly molded castings and castings that were not correctly drilled/tapped were automatically excluded. The same procedure of booking production counts only when they have been accepted by a controlled stockroom was recommended for all other operations.

The quantities received and issued by each of the controlled stockrooms are the basis for maintaining current on-hand figures on the perpetual inventory status report for each of the stockrooms (see Chapter 7). The same paperwork used for maintaining current on-hand figures should be the basis for input into inventory on the books.

GUIDELINES FOR MINIMIZING PHYSICAL-TO-BOOK DIFFERENCES

These guidelines for minimizing inventory discrepancies summarize the major causes of overstatement of input and understatement of relief of inventories. Also shown are corrective measures that can be taken to minimize discrepancies between physical and book inventories.

CAUSES OF DIFFERENCES

MINIMIZING DIFFERENCES

Theft

Enclose and keep all stockroom areas locked when unattended by authorized personnel.

Returns from customers. Adding returns to inventory while they are still the property of the customer.

Use the credit memo, when issued to customers, as the vehicle for adding back the returns to inventory.

Molded parts and die casting. Counting production by multiplying the number of cavities in the mold by the number of cycles.

Input into inventory should be based on production counts made after inspection.

Metal stampings. Material widths and thicknesses greater than called for in the specifications.

Add the weight of scrapped metal to the weight of finished stampings and subtract this from the weight of the metal issued. The difference represents the adjustment to inventory.

Understatement of the cost of sales. Cost of sales understated when historical percentages of cost of sales to sales used for relieving shipments are too low.

Establish standard costs for valuing production and inventory. Input into inventory and cost of sales relief must be consistently valued. Chapter 8 illustrates this process.

Understatement of production reject reports. Production rejects are understated—a common occurrence.

Don't input production into inventory at every operation. Record input only when finished parts, assemblies, and finished products are accepted into a controlled stockroom. Chapter 8 illustrates this procedure.

Many (probably most) companies do not maintain a running control that alerts them when differences between physical and book inventories are becoming excessive. Such a control can be established by comparing the year-to-date cost of production with the year-to-date cost of sales (see Exhibit 3).

7
Computerized Inventory Management: Strengths and Weaknesses

Computer programming in most companies concentrates on routine transactions, leaving less routine adjustments to be processed manually. This chapter shows that many such adjustments do not readily lend themselves to treatment on an automatic basis and therefore require manual input. Manual adjustments take more time, so that a lag can often result in material being received for canceled customer orders before the cancellation has been processed through the system. The detection of this and other types of weaknesses through computerized exception audits is discussed in this chapter. The next chapter illustrates actual reports showing the steps followed in developing the computer programming for interfacing inventory management with a computerized cost accounting system.

The importance of sound inventory management was recognized soon after factory labor replaced work done at home—a common practice prior to the Industrial Revolution. By the mid-1800s, many companies were using card files which were broken down by raw material, work-in-process, and finished goods. One practice followed by some companies was to record receipts in the raw material category when the material was received and to reduce the balance when material was issued to the factory floor. The receipts of such material in the factory were treated as additions to work-in-process. These, in turn, were reduced by transfers to finished goods as products were completed. When the finished items were shipped, the finished goods category was reduced. The balances shown on the individual cards for all three categories represented perpetual inventory figures that were checked periodically by taking a physical count. The assignment of values to these perpetual figures provided a logical means of determining inventory values for balance sheet purposes—so long as the number of cards to be costed was not prohibitively large.

IMPACT OF INCREASING COMPLEXITY AND INCREASING NUMBER OF PRODUCTS

The use of card files was an effective means of managing inventory when the products were simple in construction and few in number. But as the Industrial Revolution progressed and society became more and more affluent, the demand for more conveniences and creature comforts greatly increased the number of items and multiplied the problems associated with managing inventory by manually posted cards. The automobile, for example, required a substantially greater number of parts than its predecessor, the horse-drawn carriage, even though the early cars were quite primitive and lacking in the conveniences of today's automobile. The Chevrolet by the 1920s required some 5,500 parts. By 1930, this number had risen to 6,800. The present Chevrolet contains about 15,000 parts.

This increase in the size of the inventory not only affects the auto manufacturers (and other industries); it also affects the many suppliers who sell components to them. The companies that produce tire valves, for example, make them not only for passenger cars but for trucks, tractors, bicycles, motorcycles, and airplane tires as well. The tire valves, along with related products such as tire pressure gauges and parts used on air hoses, require the inventory of a substantial number of items. A study of one such manufacturer shows an inventory of approximately 18,500 parts. This total was broken into the following three categories:

Raw material	500	2.7%
Work-in-process	13,500	73.0
Finished goods	4,500	24.3
Total	18,500	100.0%

Note that almost 75% of the inventory is made up of fabricated parts that are inventoried and then reissued for later assembly into finished products.

INVENTORY MANAGEMENT OUTGROWS MANUAL (AND PUNCHED) CARD SYSTEMS

The auto industry and its suppliers were not alone in recognizing the increased difficulty of managing inventories effectively. Practically all industries and their suppliers were similarly affected by the exponential growth in the number of parts being carried in inventory. One progressive general manager, who believed in standardization of the parts used in his products, summarized the problem in this manner:

> I told my chief engineer that we must continually reduce costs by standardizing as many components as possible. In their preliminary study, they found that one component could be standardized for use in 749 of the 5,600 end products in our line. Our Production Control Department has no logical method for keeping up with such improvements made by Engineering. They continue to forecast every component individually on its own economic order quantity, irrespective of the number of end products on which the item is used. What we gain in standardization we seem to lose because of excess inventories that must later be written off because of obsolescence.

This was a case in which the computer merely transferred existing manual procedures to the computer, with no research to determine first whether improvements could be made before automating. The materials manager of another company reacted strongly to a similar situation in his company. His comment was substantially as follows:

> When the systems analyst from our corporate office and one of his programmers looked over the manual procedures being used to control our inventory, they assured me that they would greatly improve the procedures. When they finished, months later, I found that all they had done was to mechanize what had been done manually. The printouts were voluminous and, even worse, were always late. We would have been better off with the manual system because we would at least have retained the judgment factors exercised by the people who posted the cards manually.

What the systems analyst should have done was to develop a materials requirements planning system (MRP) in which:

1. A product structure capability was built into the program.
2. With this product structuring feature, a production forecast would be made

EXHIBIT 1

End Product Code: 01-02608 Suffix: 172-2

Machine Code: 5036

FORECASTED UNITS FOR JAN–JUNE AND MATERIAL REQUIREMENTS

Revised

1	2	3	B/M LEVEL	4	5	6	7	8	9	10	11
PART #	COST CENTER	OPERATION NUMBER	B/M LEVEL	Lbs. of Material/ 1000 Units	JAN 21,000 Units	FEB 19,000 Units	MAR 23,000 Units	APR 21,000 Units	MAY 21,000 Units	JUN 22,000 Units	TOTAL 127,000 Units
5036	1369	010	01	(1)							
5036		010	01	(1)							
5036	1369	020	01	(1)							
0537	0267	010	02	—							
0537	0267	020	02	—							
0005	0568	010	03	—							
0005	0981	020	03	—							
0008	0447	010	04	37.800	793.800	718.200	869.400	793.800	793.800	831.600	4,800.600
0008	0450	020	04	—							
0008	0761	030	04	—							
0008	0568	050	04	—							
0002	1294	010	04	—							
9562-0000	1291	010	05	3.472	72.912	65.968	79.856	72.912	72.912	76.384	440.944
5401-0000		010	05	.174	3.654	3.306	4.002	3.654	3.654	3.828	22.098
1202-0000		010	05	.038	.798	.722	.874	.798	.798	.836	4.826
8110-0000		010	05	.045	.945	.855	1.035	.945	.945	.990	5.715
7326-0000		010	05	.070	1.470	1.330	1.610	1.470	1.470	1.540	8.890
4202-0000		010	05	.347	7.287	6.593	7.981	7.287	7.287	7.634	44.069
7320-0000		010	05	.868	18.228	16.492	19.964	18.228	18.228	19.096	110.236
5407-0000		010	05	.858	18.018	16.302	19.734	18.018	18.018	18.876	108.966
7315-0000		010	05	.035	.735	.665	.805	.735	.735	.770	4.445
9536-0000		010	05	.694	14.574	13.186	15.962	14.574	14.574	15.268	88.138
9537-0000		010	05	2.222	46.662	42.218	51.106	46.662	46.662	48.884	282.194
1214-0000		010	05	.208	4.368	3.952	4.784	4.368	4.368	4.576	26.416
4213-0000		010	05	.868	18.228	16.492	19.964	18.228	18.228	19.096	110.236
TOTAL 97-00019-0000				9.899	207.879	188.081	227.677	207.879	207.879	217.778	1,257.173

(1) Packing material and labels purchased in bulk for all products

for end products only (about one-fourth to one-fifth of the total items in inventory).

3. Once the forecasted production schedule for the end products was completed, the computer would explode these products into the production requirements of the thousands of components used (see Exhibit 1).
4. The computer program would then prepare production schedules for the components based on the lead time required for manufacturing.

At a later time, the basic computerized system could be enlarged to:

1. Provide automatic "pick lists." These pick lists would also be treated as requisitions that would simultaneously relieve the appropriate stockrooms and update the stock status reports.
2. Serve as a vehicle for shop floor controls.
3. Cost all transactions at the various operations as the components were being processed.

This chapter will deal with the MRP portion of inventory management, concentrating on the strengths and weaknesses of many MRP installations.

STRENGTHS OF COMPUTERIZED INVENTORY MANAGEMENT

A major strength of MRP is the great reduction in time and effort needed to determine and schedule material requirements. In the earlier example of the tire valve manufacturer, the manual card system required a determination of the material requirements for every one of the 18,500 items in inventory. Under MRP, a forecast and production schedule would be made for the 4,500 end products. The computer would then convert these 4,500 items into requirements for every part in the bill of material making up the end products. This means that effort would need to be expended only in forecasting production requirements for 24% of the items in inventory; the computer would quickly break down the requirements for the remaining 76%.

Adjusting Requirements for Customer Order Changes, Cancellations, Machine Breakdowns, and Other Delaying Factors

These factors, which require numerous changes in the production schedule, can be implemented in a fraction of the time it would take under manual procedures. In our highly competitive economy, the frequency of such changes is the rule rather than the exception.

Adding New Products to the Line

When new products are frequently introduced into the line or old products are redesigned, the material requirements are quickly ascertainable. Production schedules can be rearranged simultaneously to permit timely introduction of the new or redesigned product into the marketplace.

Reducing Lead Times

MRP correlates the requirements for parts with the related end products for which the parts will be used. Production schedules for fabricating the parts to be used for assembly can likewise be correlated with the needs of the assembly operation, thus reducing the time required to produce the various end products.

Reducing Inventories

Here, again, since determination of the requirement for parts is geared to the requirement for end products to be produced, inventories are more likely to be balanced with actual needs rather than being based on a theoretical reorder point which usually provides for safety stock in addition to the estimated needs.

Stock Status Reports

In pre-MRP days, when inventory management was limited to manually posted card files, these were maintained in the Production Control Department. There was no inventory status report published regularly for use by personnel who could benefit by such information. Inventory values carried on the account books were estimates at best. The accuracy of these values could be verified only when a physical inventory was taken—usually once a year. Although physical counts continue to be made even in companies that use MRP, many stock status reports such as the type illustrated later in Exhibit 5, provide a column for valuing the on-hand balance of each item. This is helpful because it provides useful backup information to support the figures carried on the books.

Other Applications of the Mechanics of Computerized Inventory Management

In precomputer days, when punched cards and tabulating equipment were in use, a rule-of-thumb guide indicated that a punched card must be used for at least three applications to justify its cost. Although the mechanics of computerized inventory management more than justify its cost in better inventory control capability, they are also readily adaptable for other important management uses. These include (1) determination of production hour requirements and (2) shop floor control.

Production hour requirements (capacity utilization): Exhibit 2 follows a format quite similar to that used in Exhibit 1 for forecasting material requirements. Note that the same levels, cost centers, and operations are shown. The advantage of this type of information is that it not only shows the production hour requirements, it can also be used to determine whether there is sufficient capacity at certain machines to fulfill schedule needs, as well as pointing out areas of underutilization of equipment.

Shop floor control: Exhibit 3 illustrates a type of shop floor control used by the plant manager of one company. This report breaks down the units produced each week, showing cumulative totals as well (upper half of the exhibit). The figures are broken down by levels, each of which represents completed components.

The measure of performance (lower half) compares the actual number of units produced for the month by level. This total is then compared with the amount scheduled. The control allows a variation of 2.5%. It should be noted that levels 05, 04, and 03 exceeded this maximum, while levels 02 and 01 were within the acceptable range. Level 01 represents packed production in which the counts are accurate. However, the levels below 01 are weigh counted and can therefore be less accurate than the count of the finished packed product.

EXHIBIT 2

FORECASTED UNITS FOR JAN–JUNE AND REQUIRED HOURS OF PRODUCTION

End Product Code: 01-02608 Suffix: 172-2
Machine Code: 5036 Revised

1	2	3	4		5	6	7	8	9	10	11
PART #	COST CENTER	OPERATION NUMBER	B/M LEVEL	HOURS PER 1,000 Units	JAN 21,000 Units	FEB 19,000 Units	MAR 23,000 Units	APR 21,000 Units	MAY 21,000 Units	JUN 22,000 Units	TOTAL 127,000 Units
5036	1369	010	01	.02	.420	.380	.460	.420	.420	.440	2.540
5036		010	01								
5036	1369	020	01	.05	1.050	.950	1.150	1.050	1.050	1.100	6.350
			TOTAL 01		1.470	1.330	1.610	1.470	1.470	1.540	8.890
0537	0267	010	02	1.67	35.070	31.730	38.410	35.070	35.070	36.740	212.090
0537	0267	020	02	1.18	24.780	22.420	27.140	24.780	24.780	25.960	149.860
			TOTAL 02		59.850	54.150	65.550	59.850	59.850	62.700	361.950
0005	0568	010	03	.05	1.050	.950	1.150	1.050	1.050	1.100	6.350
0005	0981	020	03	1.16	24.360	22.040	26.680	24.360	24.360	25.520	147.320
			TOTAL 03		25.410	22.990	27.830	25.410	25.410	26.620	153.670
0008	0447	010	04	.15	3.150	2.850	3.450	3.150	3.150	3.300	19.050
0008	0450	020	04	.50	10.500	9.500	11.500	10.500	10.500	11.000	63.500
0008	0761	030	04	.81	17.010	15.390	18.630	17.010	17.010	17.820	102.870
0008	0568	050	04	.07	1.470	1.330	1.610	1.470	1.470	1.540	8.890
0002	1294	010	04	.08	1.680	1.520	1.840	1.680	1.680	1.760	10.160
			TOTAL 04		33.810	30.590	37.030	33.810	33.810	35.420	204.470
9562-0000	1291	010	05								
5401-0000		010	05								
1202-0000		010	05								
8110-0000		010	05								
7326-0000		010	05								
4202-0000		010	05								
7320-0000		010	05								
5407-000		010	05								
7315-0000		010	05								
9536-0000		010	05								
9537-0000		010	05								
1214-0000		010	05								
4213-0000		010	05								
TOTAL 0000			TOTAL 05	4.65	97.650	88.350	106.950	97.650	97.650	102.300	590.550
					97.650	88.350	106.950	97.650	97.650	102.300	590.550
TOTAL ALL COST CENTERS					218.190	197.410	238.970	218.190	218.190	228.580	1,319.530

EXHIBIT 3
SHOP FLOOR CONTROL
PERFORMANCE SUMMARY

End product Code: 01–02–02608 Suffix 172.2
Machine Code: 5036

	Level 05 Weight & Mix Ingredients	Level 04 Make Brass Stem Make Disc	Level 03 Mold Disc to Stem	Level 02 Drill & Ream Combined Unit	Level 01 Carton, Label & Pack
	BREAKDOWN OF UNITS PRODUCED				
	(1)				
First Week	5,980	5,860	5,590	5,530	5,480
Second Week	5,060	4,952	4,840	4,381	4,490
Cumulative	11,040	10,812	10,430	9,911	9,970
Third Week	5,380	5,360	4,765	5,106	5,272
Cumulative	16,420	16,172	15,195	15,017	15,242
Fourth Week	6,428	6,355	6,016	5,680	5,259
Cumulative	22,848	22,527	21,211	20,697	20,501
January 31st	1,286	1,247	1,203	1,171	1,052
Cumulative	24,134	23,774	22,414	21,868	21,553

(1) Batch weights converted to units.

	MEASUREMENT OF PERFORMANCE				
	Actual versus Scheduled				
Total Actual Production	24,134	23,774	22,414	21,868	21,553
Total Scheduled Production	23,050	22,840	21,835	21,330	21,000
Actual Above (or Below) Schedule	1,084	934	579	538	553
Percent Above (or Below)	4.7%	4.1%	2.7%	2.5%	2.6%
	Actual Hrs/M Units Versus Standard				
Actual Production Hours	119.5	39.8	24.7	67.1	1.5
Actual Hours per M/ units	5.0	1.7	1.1	3.1	0.07
Scheduled Production Hours (Std. Hrs.)	97.7	33.8	25.4	59.9	1.5
Standard Hours per M/ units	4.2	1.5	1.2	2.8	0.07

This report also compares the actual hours expended during the month with the scheduled hours to determine how many excess hours were expended over those that were scheduled. Additionally, the actual hours per 1,000 units are compared with the standard hours per 1,000 units scheduled. The plant manager, who was a party to the development of the format illustrated in Exhibit 3, had rather strong opinions on the types of efficiency measures he wanted. His comment was: "We measure things to death around here and get little in return for our investment in figures for every operation in the place for every employee for each shift. By the time each foreman receives his 2 to 3-inch stack of printouts, he can't remember why there was a drop in efficiency the day before. The foremen know which ones lay back and which ones produce. That's why they have their desks out on the production floor rather than in some secluded office. I want the controls by individual shop order because I consider each one a job that must make a profit."

Cost accounting: Since the cost accounting department must assign values to the various inventory categories for statement purposes, the mechanics of computerization used for MRP can serve a double purpose—recording the costs of the various items as well as the quantities in stock. The various transactions through each operation within each level of the product structure can be costed, not only to arrive at raw material, work-in-process, and finished goods values but also to provide information on the material, direct labor, and overhead expenditures during the month as well as the cost of products sold.

There is little doubt that computer technology has lifted inventory management out of the horse and buggy age and provided management with infinitely better controls of an asset that bulks large in manufacturing companies. However, in spite of the many improvements, numerous MRP systems are fraught with weaknesses that must be corrected. What these weaknesses are and how they occur will be covered next.

WEAKNESSES OF COMPUTERIZED INVENTORY MANAGEMENT

A study of MRP systems in a number of companies reveals the most of the installations are highly transaction oriented but lack the ability to make analytical exception reports that point out the inconsistencies and errors, which under a manual system would be monitored by the inventory clerks. Before becoming specific, it might be well to show the stock status report format (which varies from company to company) used in this study. Such a format is illustrated in Exhibit 4. Each of the 12 columns contains an explanation on the exhibit. Note that columns 4, 5, and 6 show the requirements that are produced by the MRP system. Columns 7, 8, and 9 indicate the open orders required to fulfill the requirements. The average usage per month is shown in column 11, and the inventory value of the on hand balance in column 3 is shown in column 12.

Exhibit 5 uses the same stock status report format and shows a listing of 13 different inventory items, which will be referred to in later exhibits to illustrate the weaknesses that occur because of the absence of analytical features. Examples of some of the weaknesses that were found are as follows:

- Numerous on-hand balances showing negative quantities.
- Outstanding (open) orders with suppliers that exceed the requirements called for by MRP.
- Large differences between the quantities called for by the projected requirements and the open orders.

Numerous On-Hand Balances Showing Negative Quantities

Items showing negative balances were valued by the computer at zero. The controller, who concurred in what he considered a conservative approach, overlooked the fact that use of a zero dollar value for negative quantities can represent a writeup of the inventory, thus creating a "phantom" inventory that results in a discrepancy between book and physical values.

EXHIBIT 4
EXPLANATION OF COLUMNS IN STOCK STATUS REPORT

#	Column	Explanation
1	Part Number	Part number used by computer. In some companies, precomputer part numbers are included in printouts as a suffix since many employees accustomed to the old part numbers are not likely to relearn thousands of new identifying numbers.
2	Part Name	Part name should correspond with supplier's nomenclature to the extent possible to minimize errors.
3	On Hand	Units on hand include items in stockrooms as well as items in staging area prior to fabrication into a component or into an assembly making up the end product.
4, 5, 6	Reqmt. Overdue / Reqmt. 1st 3 Months / Reqmt. Next 9 Months	Total material needed per MRP (material requirements planning), broken down into the amount overdue as of the date of the report, the first-three month horizon forward from the date of the report, and the next nine-month horizon.
7, 8, 9	Open Orders Overdue / Open Orders 1st 3 Months / Open Orders Next 9 Months	Items on order: column 7 represents orders overdue as of the date of the report; column 8, orders due within three months of the date of the report; and column 9, orders due in the following nine months. Under MRP procedures, every requirement will generate either a shop order for fabricating or a purchase order to buy—unless the item is flagged for manual ordering.
10	Reqmt. Total	This is the total of the requirements broken down in columns 4, 5, and 6.
11	Avg. Usage per Month	Average usage per month calculated by dividing the most recent six months' usage by six. This explains the fractional quantities.
12	Invty. Value	Units in stock usually valued at standard cost. In customized work, actual costs are frequently used.

EXHIBIT 5
STOCK STATUS REPORT

1 Part Number	2 Part Name	3 On Hand	4 Reqmt. Over-due	5 Reqmt. 1st 3 Months	6 Reqmt. Next 9 Months	7 Open Orders Over-due	8 Open Orders 1st 3 Months	9 Open Orders Next 9 Months	10 Reqmt. Total	11 Avg. Usage per Month	12 Invty. Value
17234	RING	41	22	93	93	–0–	49	–0–	208	21.2	$1,133
20611	BASE	451	–0–	1	148	–0–	–0–	500	149	5.2	182
44820	BRACKET	–4	15	–0–	142	197	–0–	–0–	157	62.3	–0–
90120	SHAFT	9	–0–	–0–	1	–0–	–0–	2	1	.3	2,369
49054	SHAFT	–0–	67	28	14	90	9	–0–	109	16.7	–0–
60841	COLLAR	13	–0–	–0–	–0–	–0–	–0–	–0–	–0–	–0–	620
62334	BOLT	28	–0–	2	1	–0–	–0–	4	3	–0–	6,777
32761	CAM	–15	49	–0–	–0–	200	–0–	–0–	49	21.3	–0–
42367	SUPPORT	–40	168	–0–	–0–	397	–0–	–0–	168	3.5	–0–
70300	ROLL	–0–	220	150	150	525	–0–	–0–	520	40.2	–0–
77140	GEAR	–0–	111	78	–0–	924	–0–	–0–	189	–0–	–0–
71655	ROLL	–0–	–0–	–0–	–0–	–0–	–0–	274	–0–	–0–	–0–
71655–1	ROLL	–0–	–0–	–0–	–0–	–0–	–0–	274	–0–	–0–	–0–

NOTES: Columns 3 through 11 are expressed in units; column 12 in dollars. Part Number 71655–1 is a companion roll to Part Number 71655

Outstanding (Open) Orders with Suppliers Exceeding Actual Requirements as Indicated by MRP

In several companies, when orders were canceled by customers, there was no procedure advising the purchasing department to cancel or reduce the outstanding orders relating to the products canceled by the customer. The obvious result was that excess inventory was built up.

Large Differences between the Quantities Called for by the Projected Quantities and the Open Orders

In some companies whose forecasting method for determining material requirements was questioned, the validity of the material requirements was checked against the actual usage. In such cases, the usage history did not agree with the projected requirements; instead, there was a wide divergence. The result was a complete loss of confidence in the MRP system and concern on the part of management about its ability to maintain good service levels in filling customer orders.

It is obvious from these examples that a judgmental factor had to be provided to supply the monitoring effort.

A common error in inventory management is negative and overstated balances. Column 3 in Exhibit 6 illustrates negative figures taken from a company that makes large equipment. Negative and overstated balances can occur when:

1. Material on the "hot list" is issued to the factory floor before the stockroom has had an opportunity to record the receipt.
2. Later shifts draw stock from an unattended stockroom without submitting a requisition. Stockrooms are better controlled on the first shift because of the presence of a full stockroom staff, which usually enforces paperwork procedures. Although attempts are made to anticipate the needs of the second and third shifts by issuing a sufficient amount of stock in advance, excess spoilage of production can result in shortages on the factory floor. In many such cases, the foreman, who has access to the stockroom, may obtain additional stock without accounting for what has been taken. When production losses are high, failure to account for what has been withdrawn from stock serves as a cover-up for poor performance.
3. The wrong number (or incorrect quantity) has been used for the parts that have been issued. This type of error can have a double-barreled effect:
   a. When the wrong number or (incorrect quantity) has been shown for the parts actually issued, the on-hand balance of such parts is misstated.
   b. When the wrong part number has been used, the on-hand balance of one is understated and that of another overstated. While the parts actually issued are given visibility by the minus sign shown in column 3, the overstated balances are not readily discernible. This is what is referred to above as a "double-barreled effect."

Use of the wrong part number or incorrect quantity for parts that have been issued does not always result in a negative on-hand balance. The reason is that the quantity withdrawn may be smaller than the amount on hand. It is also possible that replenishment of the item may obscure the negative balance that would otherwise be shown.

EXHIBIT 6
COMMON ERRORS IN INVENTORY MANAGEMENT

1	2	3	4	5	6	7	8	9	10	11	12
Part Number	Part Name	On Hand	Reqmt. Over-due	Reqmt. 1st 3 Months	Reqmt. Next 9 Months	Open Orders Over-due	Open Orders 1st 3 Months	Open Orders Next 9 Months	Reqmt. Total	Avg. Usage per Month	Invty. Value
44820	BRACKET	−4	15	0	142	197	0	0	157	62.3	0
32761	CAM	−15	49	0	0	200	0	0	49	21.3	0
42367	SUPPORT	−40	168	0	0	397	0	0	168	3.5	0

Note: Columns 3 through 11 are expressed in units; column 12, in dollars.

Whether or not the on-hand figure becomes low enough to show a negative balance, the factors that cause these minus figures result in overordering to replace the "missing" parts and underordering the parts that have been overstated.

Note also that in Exhibit 6, where the negative on hand balances are shown, inventory values in column 12 have been programmed by the computer to reflect zero values. This seems to be perfectly logical, since the concept of negative inventory values appears to be unrealistic. However, if the negative balance has resulted from misidentification of part numbers, the assignment of zero values is tantamount to a writeup of inventory values. Technically, the inventory value carried on the accounting books should be reduced by the minus value because the value of another part number has been overstated.

Setting the Record Straight

The annual physical inventory sets the record straight once a year. At this time, negative balances caused by misidentification, as well as the matching overstated balances, are all corrected. In fact, all balances—regardless of the cause of errors—are corrected. As the year progresses, errors start the cycle all over again—increasing month by month until another physical inventory sets the record straight again. This unfortunate cycle of constantly recurring errors results in loss of confidence in stock status reports, as well as in the inventory valuations with their distorting effect on reported profits.

The management of one company concerned with these problems has taken the following steps to improve the quality of reporting:

1. Issuing packets of prepunched cards on which the part number and part name are identified. The individual requisitioning material from stock need only fill in the quantity and the authorized signature. A more sophisticated approach would have been to use computer-produced pick lists, which are a great improvement over the prepunched cards.
2. Securing the entrance into the stockroom to eliminate theft by second- and third-shift personnel. This would require the requisitioner to summon the security guard (or watchman) to unlock the stockroom and check the requisition with the items being withdrawn.
3. Implementing cycle counting procedures throughout the year. The GH Corpora-

tion (name disguised), which had 18,250 different part numbers in stock, implemented cycle counting procedures using the following steps:

a. Identifying the inventory by four categories, showing:

- The number of items in each category.
- The percentage of each category to the total number of items.
- The percentage of the value of each category to the total inventory value.

	NUMBER OF ITEMS	% OF TOTAL ITEMS	% OF TOTAL VALUE
A items	1,350	7.4	48
B items	2,300	12.6	26
C items	3,200	17.5	16
D items	11,400	62.5	10
	18,250	100.0	100

b. Setting up a cycle count frequency using the 80/20 rule. Since the A and B items account for 74% of the total inventory value and require only 20% of the items to be counted, cycle counts for these two categories are scheduled more frequently. The D items, which represent over 60% of the total number of items and only 10% of the total value, can be scheduled for counting once a year. Since many of the D items were low-priced standard items such as screws, washers, grommets, and rivets, the decision was made to issue them in small packages rather than to count out the exact number required for a specific lot. The balance would remain at the work station, since the usage was continuous. This method of handling the small items reduced the number of requisitions and simplified the cycle counting procedure for the D items. The frequency cycle for taking the counts is based on the following table:

	COUNTS PER YEAR	TOTAL ITEMS COUNTED/YEAR	TOTAL ITEMS COUNTED/DAY
A items	6	8,100	33
B items	4	9,200	37
C items	2	6,400	26
D items	1	11,400	46
			142

The computer was programmed to select the items to be counted each day. These items are listed on a printout providing space for filling in the quantities counted. When each day's counts are turned in, a new printout is prepared in which the physical counts are compared with the on-hand balances to determine which part numbers are in error.

Cycle Counting in Perspective

Cycle counting is a full-time job. The personnel requirements for this task are dependent upon the number of items in inventory, the nature of the product, and the manufacturing processes, as well as the types of storage facilities that are required.

In a company with 18,000 to 20,000 parts in inventory, effective cycle counting procedures require 140 to 150 items to be counted each workday.

Cycle counting cannot be handled on a part-time basis by the stock handlers. This function should be the responsibility of the internal auditing department. In the typical manufacturing plant, inventories can make up between 30 to 40% of the capital investment. Since one of the functions of the financial executive is to act as caretaker of the company's assets, it makes sense for the cycle counter to report to the internal audit manager. This has the advantage of requiring the Internal Audit Department to come to grips with the day-to-day problems of controlling inventory, rather than merely observing the physical inventory taken once a year.

Companies that may hesitate to implement cycle counting procedures because of the need for an additional clerk or two should consider the following:

If a wrong part number has been credited with the quantities of a certain item that have been received, the MRP procedures will reduce the order quantity by a like amount, thus creating a potential shortage. Conversely, when a negative balance has been caused by "illegal" issues of material or improper recording of transactions, an excess order will be produced, thus inflating the inventory. Issuance of the incorrect quantity can also distort the balance.

OPEN ORDERS IN EXCESS OF NEEDS

Exhibit 7 illustrates a case in which there are 451 units of Part Number 20611 on hand (column 3) with an MRP requirement of 149 units (columns 5 and 6). The on-hand quantity of 451 units, less the MRP requirement of 149 units, leaves an on-hand balance of 302 units to cover any additional needs. The open orders for 500 additional units shown in column 9 are therefore far in excess of needs.

What happened to cause this situation? Somewhere along the line, there were sufficient requirements to justify this order quantity. However, the requirements (customer orders) were canceled, but the purchase and/or shop orders authorizing fabrication were not. The system recognized that it must always balance requirements with orders, but it could not automatically cancel these orders. Since the cancellation process is a highly labor-intensive task that frequently is delayed until other more pressing matters are attended to, the open orders remain on the books until they are either canceled or processed. In many cases, cancellation is delayed and the open orders are filled, resulting in increased stocks of parts that are no longer needed.

Exhibit 8 illustrates a similar situation. Although the quantities involved are somewhat less than those in the preceding example, the unit values are substantially greater.

EXHIBIT 7
COMMON ERRORS IN INVENTORY MANAGEMENT

1	2	3	4	5	6	7	8	9	10	11	12
Part Number	Part Name	on Hand	Reqmt. Over-due	Reqmt. 1st 3 Months	Reqmt. Next 9 Months	Open Orders Over-due	Open Orders 1st 3 Months	Open Orders Next 9 Months	Reqmt. Total	Avg. Usage per Month	Invty. Value
20611	BASE	451	0	1	148	0	0	500	149	5.2	182

Note: Columns 3 through 11 are expressed in units; column 12, in dollars.

EXHIBIT 8
COMMON ERRORS IN INVENTORY MANAGEMENT

1	2	3	4	5	6	7	8	9	10	11	12
Part Number	Part Name	On Hand	Reqmt. Over-due	Reqmt. 1st 3 Months	Reqmt. Next 9 Months	Open Orders Over-due	Open Orders 1st 3 Months	Open Orders Next 9 Months	Reqmt. Total	Avg. Usage per Month	Invty. Value
90120	SHAFT	9	0	0	1	0	0	2	1	.3	2,369
62334	BOLT	28	0	2	1	0	0	4	3	0	6,777

Note: Columns 3 through 11 are expressed in units; column 12, in dollars.

ERRONEOUS OPEN ORDERS RESULTING IN OBSOLETE INVENTORY

The case illustrated in Exhibit 9, though extreme, is real. Although Part Number 71655 had been obsolete for over a year, the files were found to contain an order for 274 units (see column 9 in Exhibit 9). This discovery raised several questions. Was the order valid but misidentified in the files? If so, was a duplicate order placed for the correct part number? If so, this would mean excess inventory amounting to about $17,000. If there was no misidentification of the part number, the $17,000 would represent obsolete rather than excess inventory.

Before any determination could be made, it was necessary to check other files in order to determine the following:

1. Whether the part number was incorrect. If so, what is the order status of the correct part number?
2. If, because of the misidentification, a duplicate order was placed, is it too late to cancel it?
3. If the part number was not misidentified, has the error been discovered and cancellations issued?

In this case, the part number was correct but no cancellation had been made. Further investigation revealed that part of the order was already in the receiving area and the balance was en route. Since the part was not standard, it could not be returned to the vendor for resale to another customer. This error meant that the inventory would soon contain $17,000 in obsolete stock.

Misidentification of the part number or misstatement of the quantities issued are not the only reasons for incorrect ordering. An erroneous forecast can have a similar

EXHIBIT 9
COMMON ERRORS IN INVENTORY MANAGEMENT

1	2	3	4	5	6	7	8	9	10	11	12
Part Number	Part Name	On Hand	Reqmt. Over-due	Reqmt. 1st 3 Months	Reqmt. Next 9 Months	Open Orders Over-due	Open Orders 1st 3 Months	Open Orders Next 9 Months	Reqmt. Total	Avg. Usage per Month	Invty. Value
71655	ROLL	0	0	0	0	0	0	274	0	0	0

Note: Columns 3 through 11 are expressed in units; column 12, in dollars.

effect. Even if the forecast is accurate but a change is made later—and not taken into account—this will cause the same problem that can result from an unprocessed customer order cancellation.

The type of error shown in Exhibit 9 would be fairly easy to catch if open orders for each part were compared with the "Requirement Total" shown in Column 10. Tests of this type should be made regularly after each batch of new orders is entered into the system and when any change is made in the forecast.

DISCREPANCIES BETWEEN MRP AND OPEN ORDERS

In an earlier example of open orders that were in excess of requirements, it was noted that the system recognized that it must always balance material requirements with orders but that it could not automatically cancel or reduce orders.

Exhibit 10 shows a situation in which a customer for Part #32761 canceled his order. The cancellation was due to delays in filling the order. This, in turn, was caused by delays on the part of the supplier of the material from which the cams were bought. It was too late to cancel the material shipment from the supplier because the material was already en route. This problem could also be caused by a change in forecast because orders did not come in as forecasted.

Apart from the foregoing, the status report illustrated in Exhibit 10 raises a question. Is the ordering based on MRP or on past usage? Actually, the 200 units on order are much closer to the average usage of 21.3 units per month than to the 49 units projected by the MRP procedures (usage of 21.3 units × 12 months = 256 units).

This raises the question of whether there is a lack of confidence in the quality of the MRP procedures being followed. Are realistic lead times being used? Is management making sure that policies for ordering are based on sound MRP procedures? Too often, there is a tendency to program the computer without introducing the judgmental factors necessary to make a system operate effectively.

Exhibit 11 is an example of a situation in which ordering has no relationship to either MRP or past usage. The open orders amount to 2.4 times the MRP requirements (397 ÷ 168 = 2.4 times). If the ordering had been based on average usage, the requirements and open orders would be 42 (3.5 per month × 12 months = 42). There are quite a few judgmental factors in MRP procedures. Some of these change with time and environment, requiring modifications to be made in order to reflect the altered situation. Most MRPs can handle a large number of special situations by the use of a code in the program to tell the system whether a part is to be automatically or manually reordered, for example. Unfortunately, the code is not always used when it should be.

EXHIBIT 10
COMMON ERRORS IN INVENTORY MANAGEMENT

1	2	3	4	5	6	7	8	9	10	11	12
Part Number	Part Name	On Hand	Reqmt. Over-due	Reqmt. 1st 3 Months	Reqmt. Next 9 Months	Open Orders Over-due	Open Orders 1st 3 Months	Open Orders Next 9 Months	Reqmt. Total	Avg. Usage per Month	Invty. Value
32761	CAM	−15	49	0	0	200	0	0	49	21.3	0

Note: Columns 3 through 11 are expressed in units; column 12, in dollars.

EXHIBIT 11
COMMON ERRORS IN INVENTORY MANAGEMENT

1	2	3	4	5	6	7	8	9	10	11	12
						Open Orders Over-due	Open Orders 1st 3 Months	Open Orders Next 9 Months		Avg. Usage per Month	
Part Number	Part Name	On Hand	Reqmt. Over-due	Reqmt. 1st 3 Months	Reqmt. Next 9 Months				Reqmt. Total		Invty. Value
42367	SUPPORT	−40	168	0	0	397	0	0	168	3.5	0

Note: Columns 3 through 11 are expressed in units; column 12, in dollars.

OBSOLETE INVENTORY

Part #60841, shown in Exhibit 12, is being carried in the system because there are 13 units on hand with no requirements for their use and no past usage. These parts will remain in inventory until a management decision is made on their disposition.

Part #71655–1 is a companion to part #71655 which is also obsolete, as discussed in connection with Exhibit 9.

One of the difficulties in minimizing the number of obsolete items is the overwhelming number of items to be checked; this requires a labor-intensive effort of major proportions. Even when the obsolete items are identified, managements have been found, in some cases, to be reluctant to write off such inventories because of the unfavorable impact on profits. The write off is delayed month after month in the hope that profits will increase—thus reducing the effect on profitability.

It has been estimated that obsolete and slow-moving items make up as much as 20% of the inventory value. Serious consideration should be given to the development of computerized audits that would, on an exception basis, print out imbalanced relationships between MRP requirements and historical usage. It is entirely possible that some imbalances, particularly in the history of usage, may change, as would other factors referred to earlier. These would affect the reliability of the status reports. Regular exception audits, which will be discussed next, would focus attention on the irregularities.

EVALUATING THE RESULTS OF EXCEPTION AUDITS

There is frequently a tendency to take an overly perfectionist approach in monitoring what is acceptable and what is not. In our fast-moving, complex, highly competitive economy, acceptability must be based on a reasonable range rather than a precise, mathematically derived measure.

EXHIBIT 12
COMMMON ERRORS IN INVENTORY MANAGEMENT

1	2	3	4	5	6	7	8	9	10	11	12
						Open Orders Over-due	Open Orders 1st 3 Months	Open Orders Next 9 Months		Avg. Usage per Month	
Part Number	Part Name	On Hand	Reqmt. Over-due	Reqmt. 1st 3 Months	Reqmt. Next 9 Months				Reqmt. Total		Invty. Value
60841	COLLAR	13	0	0	0	0	0	0	0	0	620
(3) 71655–1	ROLL	0	0	0	0	0	0	274	0	0	0

Note: Columns 3 through 11 are expressed in units; column 12, in dollars.
(3) Part #71655–1 is a companion roll to part #71655, discussed in Exhibit 5.

EXHIBIT 13
COMMON ERRORS IN INVENTORY MANAGEMENT

1	2	3	4	5	6	7	8	9	10	11	12
Part Number	Part Name	On Hand	Reqmt. Over-due	Reqmt. 1st 3 Months	Reqmt. Next 9 Months	Open Orders Over-due	Open Orders 1st 3 Months	Open Orders Next 9 Months	Reqmt. Total	Avg. Usage per Month	Invty. Value
49054	SHAFT	0	67	28	14	90	9	0	109	16.7	0
70300	ROLL	0	220	150	150	525	0	0	520	40.2	0
77140	GEAR	0	111	78	0	924	0	0	189	0	0

Note: Columns 3 through 11 are expressed in units; column 12, in dollars.

Exhibit 13 illustrates an acceptable approach which compares the requirements, open orders, and average usage, as well as detecting the existence of negative quantities. The exception report might be prepared with the following headings and figures taken from Exhibit 13:

PART #	REQMT. TOTAL	TOTAL OPEN ORDERS	12 MONTH USAGE	ON HAND
49054	109	99	200	–0–
70300	520	525	482	–0–
77140	189	924	0	–0–

Part #49054

The total requirements and total open orders are reasonably close. The total usage for 12 months, based on the average for the past 6 months, is about double the requirements and the open orders for the year. This situation should be examined. It is possible that usage of this part has dropped because of replacement by another part on some of the products—in which case the average usage figure should be adjusted for future measurements. No minus value was shown for the on-hand balance.

Part #70300

The total requirements, total open orders, and 12-month projected usage are within a close range, with no negative value indicated for the on-hand balance.

Part # 77140

This part number, like part #49054, would be listed on the exception report. In the case of part #77140, the question is automatically raised as to why open orders are about five times as great as the requirement total when the projected 12-month usage is shown as zero. The investigation revealed that this is a part for a new product with no past usage. The requirements are based on a forecast that did not anticipate the real demand. In view of the unanticipated demand, a large number of units were ordered. Subsequent requirements will be based on a revised forecast.

SUMMARY

On the stock exchanges, the impetus provided by the computer age made it possible to increase the number of shares handled each day by a multiple of 10. This same impetus permitted an even more striking improvement in inventory management techniques. These techniques involved the use of structured bills of materials in breaking down the forecasted production by the various parts (and raw materials) required to meet the production schedules—taking into account the purchasing and manufacturing lead times so necessary in meeting customer requirements on a timely basis. They also provided status reports showing new on-hand balances as parts were received into and withdrawn from stock. By-products of the system such as inventory valuation, computer-produced pick lists, and routings helped to extend the system beyond the point of mere stockkeeping.

While much has been accomplished in automating masses of detailed information, there has been a tendency in many companies to perform many of the functions by rote. The resulting product frequently consists of errors similar to those discussed in this chapter, with the result that the credibility of the system has been questioned. Implementation must include a second phase in which exception auditing is introduced to call attention to and expeditiously correct the weaknesses inherent in the system.

The strengths of computerized inventory management are quite obvious. The guidelines listed below will therefore deal with some of the weaknesses that must be corrected.

COMMON WEAKNESSES	CORRECTIVE MEASURES REQUIRED
On-hand balances show negative quantities.	Caused by misidentification or by premature issuance of material with no receipt recorded. Negative values should not be changed to zero dollars because this is tantamount to a writeup in inventory.
Open orders with suppliers exceed requirements indicated by the system.	Institute a procedure to promptly advise the Purchasing Department to cancel or reduce outstanding orders relating to products canceled by the customer. If this is not done on a timely basis, there will be an inventory buildup.
Large differences occur between material requirements and open orders.	Check material requirements with average usage. If both are not reasonably close, forecast could be incorrect.
Status report shows stock on hand with no requirements and no past usage.	In all likelihood, such stock is obsolete and should be written off.
When open orders have no relationship to requirements or to average usage, this could be due to a special situation.	Most MRPs provide a code to be used in special situations, but the codes are not always used when they should be.

8
Interface of Inventory Management and the Computerized Cost Accounting System

This chapter demonstrates how one company computerized its cost accounting system. It illustrates the treeing up of the manufacturing process sheets from which the material, direct labor, and production hours were obtained; the cost routing sheets (referred to by some as the "indented bill of material"); the various transaction reports; other by-product control reports; closing journal entries; ledger accounts; abbreviated income statement; and variance analyses.

Chapter 7 cited the difficulties in using card files as a means of managing inventory because of the great increase in the number of items carried in inventory.

This proliferation also affected cost accounting. Valuing items in inventory was practical only so long as the number of cards to be priced manually was not prohibitively high, for example, 18,500 items in the case of tire valves and related products in the company used in this cost accounting case example.

Companies that found it impractical to price thousands of individual cards, which were constantly in use by production personnel, were forced to find other means of costing production and inventories. Many cost accountants determined their manufacturing cost of sales by applying historical percentages of cost of sales to sales. Frequently, because the historical percentages proved to be incorrect for the current year, the year-end reconciliation of the physical to book inventory showed a large difference—indicating that profits during the earlier part of the year had been greatly overstated (sometimes understated). The general manager of one company stated the problem this way:

> We had 15,000 to 16,000 items in inventory, of which 2,600 were end products. Computers were still very expensive, so we could not track the costs through the various manufacturing operations in order to come up with the correct finished product cost with which to relieve the inventory when such products were sold. My accountant used the historical cost of sales to sales percentage (64%) that was fairly stable. One year when we compared our priced-up physical inventory with the value carried on the books, we came up with a shortage of almost a quarter of a million dollars. We took a second physical but the results were not much different. Applying our 20/20 hindsight, we then realized that the inflation rate for material and labor had jumped between 11 and 13%. Because of competition from overseas, we were limited in the amount that we could increase our selling prices. It was only natural for the inventory to be overstated if our cost of products sold was understated. It was no fun facing top management at one of the board meetings and explaining how this happened. The only good that came out of it was that the board authorized the purchase of computer equipment.

THE COMPUTER COMES TO THE RESCUE

The bill of material is the "blueprint" of how the product is made. It provides a list of the various items, processes, and processing times at the different stages of

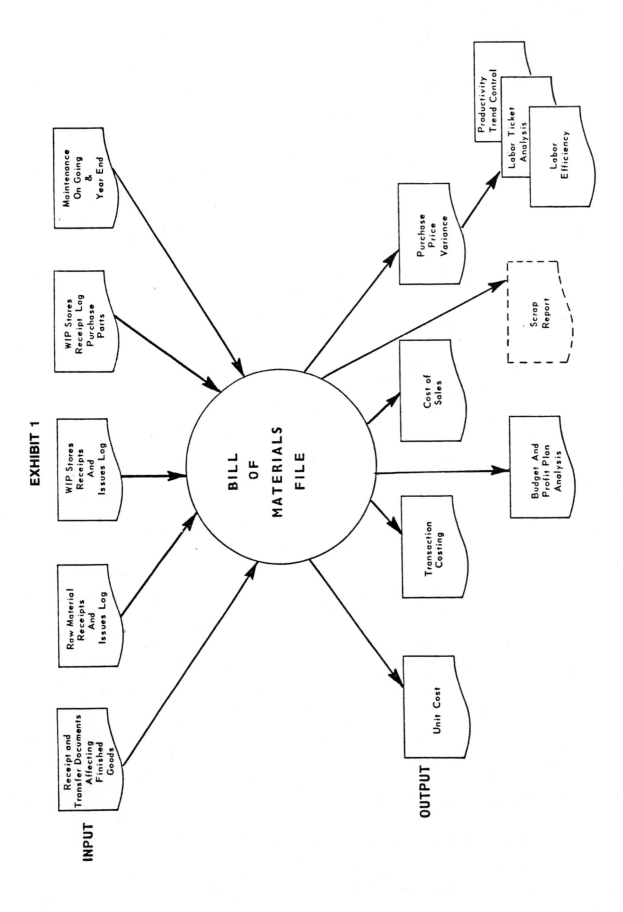

EXHIBIT 1

Note: Although the system will provide a scrap report, it will not be used to adjust inventory, because only good production accepted by the stockrooms will be reported.

production. Just as a bill of material is important to the physical production process in the manufacture of a product, so is the computerized cost routing sheet the central point in the computerized inventory and cost accounting control system. Exhibit 1 illustrates diagrammatically the relationship of the input and output documents to the manufacturing procedures. On the input side, it shows the various types of transaction documents that are also run against the bill of material information to produce such output documents as product costs, transaction costs, cost of sales, and variance analyses. An important part of the computerized procedures are the ongoing and year-end maintenance programs, the edit lists to assure more accurate input of information, and the "where-used" file.

The previous chapter, in citing the function of a systems analyst in setting up the MRP program, emphasized that a product-structuring capability must be built into the program to facilitate the breakdown of end products into their components. In cost accounting, the cost roll-up is used in reverse to accumulate costs upward as the various parts are fabricated and assembled into end products.

Another important feature is the capability of the where-used file, which can access parts that are common to two or more end products. Note in Exhibit 2 that component #06100746 is used in 684 end products, while component #06100100 is used in three. The cost standards as well as the stock status on-hand balances reside in an item master file.

This chapter will illustrate and explain the content of the cost routing sheet, where the information comes from, and how the product costs are developed. It will also illustrate transaction reports and describe the procedure for summarizing them and developing the closing journal entries.

An important step in the mechanics of automation for inventory management and cost accounting is the treeing up of the product structure. To illustrate this procedure, the tire valve stem (exclusive of the valve insert) will be used. (See the photograph of a tire valve in Exhibit 3.) This is the product line that showed a breakdown of 18,500 parts in raw materials, work-in-process, and finished goods. The process of

EXHIBIT 2
"WHERE USED" FILE

Component #06100746 used in 684 End Products:

02026910209	02026910307	02026910308	02026910309	02052950002
02054310003	02054310004	02054310020	02054310198	02054310209
02054310298	02054320003	02054320004	02054330001	02054330002
02054330129	02054340001	02054340002	02054340197	02054350002
02054350003	02054350020	02054350021	02054350197	02054350209
02054350210	02054360002	02054360003	02054360197	02054360198
02054360200	02054360209	02054360210	02054370003	02054370020
02054380003	02054380020	02055720002	02055720003	02055720019
02055720020	02055720021	02055720209	02055720210	02055730002
02055730003	02055730019	02055730020	02055730021	02055730209
90057620099	90057620090	90057620092	90057620096	90057620197
99009900099	99009900100	99052880336	99052890126	99052932401
99053880097	99052453212	99052567820	99061880132	99073201063
99132647761	99133677642	99213674541	99224675132	99567362111

Component #06100100 used in 3 End Products:

39031001001	39076160419	39078131335

EXHIBIT 3
PHOTOGRAPH OF A TIRE VALVE IN VARIOUS STAGES OF MANUFACTURE.

LINE DRAWING OF
BRASS STEM AFTER
HEADING AND
THREADING

LINE DRAWING
OF COMPLETED
TIRE VALVE STEM

BRASS COIL
PURCHASED IN
15,000 POUND
COILS

BRASS STEM
AFTER CUTOFF
AND HEADING

BRASS STEM
AFTER HEADING,
THREADING AND
DEGREASING

TUBULATED DISC

TUBULATED DISC
MOLDED TO BRASS STEM

treeing up an end product manually would require at least a day to a day and a half each. Herein lies the advantage of the computer, which can track the physical movement of the thousands of items from raw material to finished goods at lightning speed and issue transaction reports for movement into and out of the various processing and stockroom points.

Source of Manufacturing Data

The required data is provided by the Engineering, Industrial Relations, Purchasing and Cost Accounting Departments. The required data include the following:

1. Material specifications
2. Quantity of material required
3. Manufacturing operations to be performed
4. Cost centers in which operations are to be performed
5. Set-up hours
6. Production hours
7. Labor grades of employees
8. Material cost
9. Direct labor cost
10. Overhead cost

These data are based on the requirements per 1,000 units. A reasonable allowance for losses of material must be included. In a component such as the brass tire valve stem, the starting weight per 1,000 stems is 37.8 pounds. However, because of the drilling and reaming operations that hollow out the inside of the stem to provide space for the valve, the finished weight of the brass stem is 17 pounds. This means that 55% of the material becomes a production loss. This is shown in the manufacturing process sheet in Exhibit 4. This process sheet also shows the material specifications, as well as the operations related to this level. The drilling and reaming operations that provide the space for the insertion of the valve are shown at level 02, along with the other related data for operations performed, time allowances, routing, and cost centers through which the work flows.

Reasonable allowances must also be made in the production hours required for the various operations to provide for such factors as start-up time, rest periods, and fatigue allowances where applicable. The sources of the data listed above are shown below:

1.	Material specifications	Engineering (Design Engineering)
2.	Quantity of material	Engineering (Design Engineering)
3.	Manufacturing operations	Engineering (Mfg. Engineering)
4.	Cost centers	Engineering (Mfg. Engineering)
5.	Set-up hours	Engineering (Mfg. Engineering)
6.	Production hours	Engineering (Mfg. Engineering)
7.	Labor grades	Industrial Relations
8.	Material cost	Purchasing Department and Cost Accounting
9.	Direct labor cost	Cost Accounting
10.	Overhead rates	Cost Accounting

Although the standard material costs would also be considered to be fixed for a year, changes in the inflation rate could require changes to be made in mid-year to avoid unrealistic variances. Since labor rates are usually controlled by multiyear contracts in many companies, these would not fluctuate as greatly as material costs. Overhead rates are usually predetermined for the year, except in unusual circumstances. An example of an unusual circumstance would be the introduction of, say, highly automated equipment that would radically alter the labor and depreciation costs.

Treeing Up the Manufacturing Process

Exhibit 4, referred to earlier, illustrates the treeing up-process diagrammatically. The center of the exhibit shows this in an organization chart fashion for the five levels involved. The underlying manufacturing process sheets are also shown for each of the levels. These include:

Item identification and machine code
Material specifications
Quantity of material required
Routing through the cost centers
Number and description of each operation
Equipment required
Set-up hours (where applicable)
Labor grades for set-up
Production hours
Labor grades for production
Cost centers

EXHIBIT 4
PRODUCT STRUCTURE OF TIRE VALVE STEM

MANUFACTURING I

ISSUE DATE	ISSUE #	REVISED:	P.C. 01	BASIC 02608	SUFFIX 172-2
DRAWING #		LAST C.A.	PART NAME STEM WITH PLAST		
			MTL. CODE		KIND
			SHAPE		SPEC.
			UNIT	PER/M GROSS	
			ROUTING		
			PACKING & FINISHE		

OPN. #	OPERATION DESCRIPTION	EQUIPME
	01-02608-172-2-0537 STEM W/PLASTIC DISC	
010	MAKE CARTON 018751 & APPLY LABEL 011856	BENCH
020	PACK 1000 IN 018751 CARTON; WEIGH & SEAL	BENCH W/SCAL

MANUFACTURING PROCESS SHEET

P.C. 01	BASIC 02608	SUFFIX 172-2	MACH. CODE 0005	REFERENCE
PART NAME STEM W/PLASTIC DISC - OPERATION 20			KIND ASSEMBLY	SIZE	TEMPER	HARDNESS
MTL. CODE TUBE		SPEC.		PER/M NET
SHAPE		PER/M GROSS
UNIT	
ROUTING COATING, MOLDING, MACHINING		EQUIPMENT

LEVEL 03

OPN. #	OPERATION DESCRIPTION		DEPT.	SET-UP HRS.	LAB. GRD.	PROD. HRS./M	LAB. GRD.	NO. MACH.	NO. MEN	COST CENTER
	01-02608-1-0008 SEMI-FINISHED STEM	COATING TANKS	PLATE			.05	7			0568
	01-02608-173-2-0002 PLASTIC DISC	MOLDING PRESS #5	MOLD			1.16	7			0981
010	FINISH STEM PER SPEC. #29									
020	MOLD & CURE									

MANUFACTURING PROCESS SHEET

P.C 01	BASIC 02608	SUFFIX 173-2	MACH. CODE 0002	REFERENCE
PART NAME PLASTIC DISC			KIND PLASTIC #316	SIZE 1" x 3/8"	TEMPER	HARDNESS
MTL. CODE		SPEC.		PER/M NET
SHAPE		PER/M GROSS
UNIT	
ROUTING		EQUIPMENT

LEVEL 04

OPN. #	OPERATION DESCRIPTION		DEPT.	SET-UP HRS.	LAB. GRD.	PROD. HRS./M	LAB. GRD.	NO. MACH.	NO. MEN	COST CENTER
	.0099 LBS. 97-00019-0000 PLASTIC D785A	41" MARK	MOLD			.08	6		1	1294
		#25 REGAL & CUTOFF	MOLD			.08	6		1	1294
010	MILL, TUBULATE & CUT TO SIZE									

TREEING UP THE

| CARTON LABEL AND PACK |
| LEVEL 01 |

| DRILL AND RE COMBINED UNIT |
| LEVEL 02 |

| COMBINE STEM AND DISC |
| LEVEL 03 |

| FORM PLASTIC DISC |
| LEVEL 04 |

| WEIGH AND MIX PLASTIC |
| LEVEL 05 |

MANUFACTURING PF

P.C. 97	BASIC 00019	SUFFIX 0000
PART NAME		PLASTIC D 78
MTL. CODE		KIND
SHAPE		SPEC.
UNIT	PER/M GROSS
ROUTING	MOLDING

OPN. #	OPERATION DESCRIPTION	EQUIPMEN
010	WEIGH OUT AND MIX PLASTIC INGREDIENTS	BENCH W/SCALE,

MATERIAL CODE	DESCRIPTION	BREAKDOWN PER
05-9562	PLASTIC #276	350.75
05-F401	MAGNESIUM LT	
05-4213	HEXO CL	87.67
	TOTAL POUNDS OF INGREDIENTS	1,000.00

Process Sheet (top, partial)

CODE 036	REFERENCE				SHOP ORDER #	
C					DATE ISSUED	
	SIZE				QTY. TO MAKE	
TEMPER	HARDNESS				RAW MTL. REQMT.	
PER/M NET					REQD. COMPLETION DATE	
S				LEVEL 01		

DEPT.	SET-UP HRS.	LAB. GRD.	PROD. HRS./M	LAB. GRD.	NO. MACH.	NO. MEN	COST CENTER
PKG.			.02	2			1369
PKG.			.05	2			1369

MANUFACTURING PROCESS SHEET (Level 02)

ISSUE DATE | DRAWING # | ISSUE # | REVISED: | LAST C.A.

P.C. 01 | BASIC | PART NAME 02608 | SUFFIX 172-2 | MACH. CODE 0537 | REFERENCE
STEM W/PLASTIC DISC
MTL. CODE | SHAPE | KIND | UNIT | SPEC. | PER/M GROSS | SIZE | TEMPER | SHOP ORDER # | DATE ISSUED
PER/M NET | HARDNESS | QTY. TO MAKE | RAW MTL. REQMT. | REQD. COMPLETION DATE

ROUTING: MACHINING, MACHINING, INSPECTION, PACKING

EQUIPMENT

OPN. #	OPERATION DESCRIPTION		DEPT.	SET-UP HRS.	LAB. GRD.	PROD. HRS./M	LAB. GRD.	NO. MACH.	NO. MEN	COST CENTER
010	DRILL & BLOW	BENCH MACHINE								
020	REAM & BLOW	BENCH MACHINE								
	INSPECT		MACHG.			1.67	2			0267
	01-02608-172-2-0005		MACHG.			1.18	2			0267
			QC							

LEVEL 02

MANUFACTURING PROCESS SHEET (Level 04)

ISSUE DATE | DRAWING # | ISSUE # | REVISED: | LAST C.A.

P.C. 01 | BASIC 02608 | PART NAME STEM | SUFFIX 1 | MACH. CODE 0008 | REFERENCE
MTL. CODE | SHAPE 20-2800 | KIND | UNIT LBS. | COIL | SPEC. 26-4 | PER/M GROSS 37.8 | BRASS | SIZE | TEMPER | .280 DIAMETER | HARDNESS
PER/M NET 17.0
SHOP ORDER # | DATE ISSUED | QTY. TO MAKE | RAW MTL. REQMT. | REQD. COMPLETION DATE

ROUTING: MACHINING, COATING, INSPECTION, COMPONENTS STOCKROOM

EQUIPMENT

OPN. #	OPERATION DESCRIPTION		DEPT.	SET-UP HRS.	LAB. GRD.	PROD. HRS./M	LAB. GRD.	NO. MACH.	NO. MEN	COST CENTER
010	CUT-OFF & HEAD	HEADER	MACHG	3.0	10					
020	ROLL THREAD	ROLLING MACHINE	MACHG	2.0	10	.15	5	2	1	0447
030	HEADING	HEADER	MACHG	12.0	13	.50	5	2	1	0450
050	DEGREASE	DEGREASER	COATG			.81	12			0761
	INSPECT		QC			.07	4			0568

LEVEL 04

Process Sheet (bottom left, partial — Level 05)

SHEET				
E	REFERENCE			
	SIZE			
PER	PER/M NET			

LEVEL 05

PT.	SET-UP HRS.	LAB. GRD.	PROD. HRS./M	LAB. GRD.	NO. MACH.	NO. MEN	COST CENTER
LD			4.65	88		3	1291

CESS ENG'G. | STDS. ENG'G.

MAKE
BRASS
STEM
LEVEL 04

COST ROUTING SHEET

As is typical in many companies that are automating their systems, difficulties arose in this company in trying to use existing product ID numbers. There was no consistency in the numbering procedures which had been developed over the years. In some instances, a combination of numerals and alphabetical designations had been used. In others, additional digits were added to designate special finishes or colors. To avoid the problems of attempting to use them, a new four-digit "machine code" was added to the regular number. Thus, the old product ID, familiar to the operating people, would always print out with the machine code used in the computer for identification purposes. In the cost routing sheet illustrated by Exhibit 5, the first two digits, identified as PC for product code, precede the basic five-digit number—which is then followed by the four-digit machine code. Note in the manufacturing process sheets that a suffix is also used, thus requiring 15 digits to be shown on some documents. While this may seem unnecessary, practical considerations deemed it to be obligatory.

Following is an explanation of the 15 column headings in Exhibit 5.

Col. 1: Opr. No. The operation numbers identify the steps in the manufacturing process of the product. These numbers are shown as 010, 020, 030, 040, 050, and so on. 010 may identify a drilling operation in one cost center but a coating process in another.

Col. 2: B/M Level The B/M (bill of material) level designates the position of the part number in the product structure.

Col. 3: Quantity Specifies how many of the items are required per completed part at that level. This must be viewed in conjunction with the last column, headed "UM," which stands for unit of measure. In this instance, the code 2 under "UM" means per 1,000. The quantity of 1.00000 therefore means that 1,000 components, for example, are required per 1,000 units completed at that level. When two units are required per finished unit, the quantity will be shown as 2.00000. In the case of raw materials shown as the 97 series of items at the bottom portion of the cost routing sheet the quantity is shown as .00990. This means that .00990 pound of material is required per 1,000 units of product.

Col. 4: Start Opn. The operation number in this column identifies the point in the process at which processing starts on an incoming component. Note that the first operation in cost center 1369 (level 01) relates to raw material (packaging and labels). The first operation is 010, which consists of making up the carton and applying the label. The incoming component from level 02 is packaged in operation 020. Thus, the start operation for the latter is indicated as 020.

Col. 5: Cost Cntr. The first two digits identify the department, while the second two identify various work centers within the department.

Col. 6: Std. Hrs./M The number of hours per 1,000 units needed to perform an operation. The hours mean labor hours when a hand operation is performed or machine hours when the operation is machine paced. (Machine hours can be synonymous with labor hours when there is a full-time operator for the machine being used.)

Col. 7: Labor Rate Quantifies the labor cost per hour for performing the particular operation. This rate, multiplied by the hours per 1,000, provides the standard direct labor cost. If an operator tends more than one machine, the labor rate per hour will be divided by the number of machines.

EXHIBIT 5
COST ROUTING SHEET
FOR PRODUCT 01–02608–5036

Product ID	(1) Opr No.	(2) BM Levl	(3) Quantity	(4) Start Opn.	(5) Cost Cntr.	(6) Stnd Hrs/M	(7) Labor Rate	(8) Variable Ovhead	(9) Fixed Ovhead	(10) R/M Code	(11) R/M Gross	(12) R/M Net	(13) Scrap Recovy	(14) Standard R/M Cost	(15) UM
01–02608–5036	010	01	1.00000	010	1369	.02	2.497	1.749	3.407	018751				128.6900	2
01–02608–5036	010	01	1.00000	010	1369					011856				8.0500	2
01–02608–5036	020	01	1.00000	020	1369	.05	2.497	1.749	3.407						
. 01–02608–0537	010	02	1.00000	010	0267	1.67	2.473	2.093	3.678						
. 01–02608–0537	020	02	1.00000	010	0267	1.18	2.473	2.093	3.678						
.. 01–02608–0005	010	03	1.00000	010	0568	.05	2.752	6.022	4.282						
.. 01–02608–0005	020	03	1.00000	010	0981	1.16	2.790	1.942	3.237						
... 01–02608–0008	010	04	1.00000	010	0447	.15	1.335	4.182	7.121	202800	37.800	17.000	313.75000	638.1700	2
... 01–02608–0008	020	04	1.00000	010	0450	.50	1.335	4.182	7.122						
... 01–02608–0008	030	04	1.00000	010	0761	.81	3.396	3.326	4.933						
... 01–02608–0008	050	04	1.00000	010	0568	.07	2.752	6.022	4.282						
... 01–02608–0002	010	04	1.00000	010	1294	.08	2.773	2.978	4.413						
..... 97–00019–0000	010	05	.00990	010	1291	4.65	2.773	2.978	4.413	059562	350.75000	350.75000		250.0000	2
..... 97–00019–0000	010	05	.00990	010						055401	17.54000	17.54000		88.0000	2
..... 97–00019–0000	010	05	.00990	010						051202	3.86000	3.86000		530.0000	2
..... 97–00019–0000	010	05	.00990	010						058110	4.56000	4.56000		530.0000	2
..... 97–00019–0000	010	05	.00990	010						057326	7.02000	7.02000		34.5000	2
..... 97–00019–0000	010	05	.00990	010						054202	35.08000	35.08000		260.0000	2
..... 97–00019–0000	010	05	.00990	010						057320	87.69000	87.69000		114.2100	2
..... 97–00019–0000	010	05	.00990	010						055407	86.64000	86.64000		160.0000	2
..... 97–00019–0000	010	05	.00990	010						057315	3.51000	3.51000		225.0000	2
..... 97–00019–0000	010	05	.00990	010						059536	70.15000	70.15000		102.5000	2
..... 97–00019–0000	010	05	.00990	010						059537	224.48000	224.48000		60.0000	2
..... 97–00019–0000	010	05	.00990	010						051214	21.05000	21.05000		11.7500	2
..... 97–00019–0000	010	05	.00990	010						054213	87.67000	87.67000		72.5000	2

Col. 8: Variable Overhead The variable portion of indirect costs. It is based on a flexible budget which identifies separately those costs that are likely to fluctuate with changes in the volume of production. This would include such costs as supplies, material handling, and equipment servicing.

Col. 9: Fixed Ovhead Also determined by the flexible budget. This category includes such costs as occupancy, supervision, and depreciation. Segregation of the variable and fixed overhead facilities additional analysis beyond that required in the routine cost system procedures.

Col. 10: R/M Code Identifies the raw material to which no labor has yet been applied. Included in this coding in the cost routing sheet are:

- Cartons and labels used.
- Brass rod for making the stem.
- Ingredients required for making the plastic disc.

Col. 11: R/M Gross The starting quantity of material for making the component or assembly. When material is unavoidably lost in the processing of a component, the finished weight is shown in column 12 as *R/M Net*. An illustration of this is operation 10 in cost center 0447. The brass rod must be drilled out and threaded. The gross weight of the rod is shown in column 11 as R/M Gross, while the finished weight is indicated in column 12 as R/M Net.

Col. 13: Scrap Recovery Shows the standard cost per 1,000 pounds of metal recovered from the process.

Col. 14: Standard R/M Cost Shows the standard cost of the raw material used in the product.

Col. 15: UM Unit of measure. The numeral "2" indicates "per thousand."

In comparing Exhibit 4 with Exhibit 5, it should be noted that the cost routing sheet doesn't provide for set-up hours as a separate item. When production runs are long, as with most products that are built to stock, the cost of set-up per unit is so small that set-up is included as part of the overhead rate. The manufacturing process sheets, used in Exhibit 4 do, however, indicate the set-up cost allowances, where applicable, for purposes of monitoring the efficiency with which the set-ups are made.

The cost standards as well as the stock status on-hand balances reside in an item master file. Both are updated with single rather than multiple entries.

THE MECHANICS OF COSTING

The program format illustrated in the cost routing sheet not only provides for tracking production and inventory quantities for use in inventory management; it also provides for costing the production and inventory for cost accounting purposes. Illustrative examples for costing material and labor are shown in Exhibits 6 and 7.

Developing the Product Cost—Material

Earlier in this chapter, it was noted that the starting quantity for making the brass tire valve stem was 37.8 pounds per 1,000. It was further noted that because of the hollowing out of the stem in a drilling operation, 20.8 pounds of brass, or 55% of the starting quantity, was considered to be necessary scrap.

EXHIBIT 6
DEVELOPING THE PRODUCT COST—MATERIAL

COST ROUTING SHEET
PRODUCT 01-02608-5036

	1 OPR NO.	2 BM LEVL	3 QUANTITY	4 START OPN.	5 COST CNTR	6 STND HRS/M	7 LABOR RATE	8 VARBLE OVHEAD	9 FIXED OVHEAD	10 R/M CODE	11 R/M GROSS	12 R/M NET	13 SCRAP RECOVY	14 STANDARD R/M COST	15 U M
PRODUCT ID															
01—02608—5036	010	01	1.00000	010	1369	.02	2.497	1.749	3.407	018751				128.6900	2
01—02608—5036	010	01	1.00000	010						011856				8.0500	2
01—02608—5036	020	01	1.00000	020	1369	.05	2.497	1.749	3.407						
. 01—02608—0537	010	02	1.00000	010	0267	1.67	2.473	2.093	3.678						
. 01—02608—0537	020	02	1.00000	010	0267	1.18	2.473	2.093	3.678						
.. 01—02608—0005	010	03	1.00000	010	0568	.05	2.752	6.022	4.282						
.. 01—02608—0005	020	03	1.00000	010	0981	1.16	2.790	1.942	3.237						
... 01—02608—0008	010	04	1.00000	010	0447	.15	1.335	4.182	7.121	202800	37.80	17.0	313.75	638.17	2
... 01—02608—0008	020	04	1.00000	010	0450	.50	1.335	4.182	7.122						
... 01—02608—0008	030	04	1.00000	010	0761	.81	3.396	3.326	4.933						
... 01—02608—0008	050	04	1.00000	010	0568	.07	2.752	6.022	4.282						
... 01—02608—0002	010	04	1.00000	010	1294	.08	2.773	2.978	4.413						
.... 97—00019—0000	010	05	.00990	010	1291	4.65	2.773	2.978	4.413	059562	350.75000	350.75000		250.0000	2
.... 97—00019—0000	010	05	.00990	010						055491	17.54000	17.54000		88.0000	2
.... 97—00019—0000	010	05	.00990	010						051202	3.86000	3.86000		530.0000	2
.... 97—00019—0000	010	05	.00990	010						058110	4.56000	4.56000		530.0000	2
.... 97—00019—0000	010	05	.00990	010						057326	7.02000	7.02000		34.5000	2
.... 97—00019—0000	010	05	.00990	010						054202	35.08000	35.08000		260.0000	2
.... 97—00019—0000	010	05	.00990	010						057320	87.69000	87.69000		114.2100	2
.... 97—00019—0000	010	05	.00990	010						055407	86.64000	86.64000		160.0000	2
.... 97—00019—0000	010	05	.00990	010						057315	3.51000	3.51000		225.0000	2
.... 97—00019—0000	010	05	.00990	010						059536	70.15000	70.15000		102.5000	2
.... 97—00019—0000	010	05	.00990	010						059537	224.48000	224.48000		60.0000	2
.... 97—00019—0000	010	05	.00990	010						051214	21.05000	21.05000		11.7500	2
... 97—00019—0000	010	05	.00990	010						054213	87.67000	87.67000		72.5000	2

COSTING THE BRASS
(COSTS ARE PER/M)

1. MULTIPLY GROSS WEIGHT (COL. 11) X STANDARD COST (COL. 14)

   37.8 Lbs. X 638.17/M = $24.13/M

2. SUBTRACT NET WEIGHT (COL. 12) FROM GROSS WEIGHT (COL. 11)

   37.8 Lbs. MINUS 17.0 Lbs. = 20.8 Lbs.

3. MULTIPLY DIFFERENCE BY SCRAP RECOVERY COST (COL. 13)

   20.8 Lbs. X 313.75/M = $6.53/M

4. FROM LINE 1 SUBTRACT LINE 3

   $24.13 MINUS $6.53 = $17.60/M

2,255 UNITS @ $17.60 = $39.68

COST OF SALES

PRODUCT ID	OPR NO.	QUANTITY	BRASS	NON-BRASS MATERIAL	LABOR	VARIABLE OVERHEAD	CUMULATIVE OPERATING COST	FIXED OVERHEAD	TOTAL COST
01 00131 AP1	0004 000 R	315,000	4,191.36	17.71	310.16	731.31	5,250.54	837.66	6,088
01 00131 A1782	0013 000 R	57,500	773.78	240.59	481.82	524.23	2,020.42	756.87	2,777
01 00131 17829	0017 000 R	243,800	3,167.79	899.12	2,187.49	2,315.74	8,570.14	3,324.75	11,894
01 01651 UAH1	0086 000 R	277,500	3,605.67	15.45	287.09	676.08	4,584.29	760.57	5,344
01 02351 7913	5250 000 R	1,200	15.59	11.59	17.31	14.93	59.42	20.94	80
01 02870 7913	5179 000 R	757	12.58	5.29	31.35	20.25	69.47	27.18	96
01 02608	5036 000 R	2,255	39.68	3.77	33.28	33.49	110.22	54.50	164
01 03407 0178	5032 000 R	8,550	137.70	29.88	148.94	186.67	503.19	241.74	744
PRODUCT TOTALS	R	952,062	12,535.35	1,472.22	3,904.79	4,940.38	22,852.74	6,655.99	29,508
PERCENT OF TOTAL COST			42.49	4.99	13.23	16.75	77.46	22.54	100.00

LEGEND: R = Rod

EXHIBIT 7
DEVELOPING THE PRODUCT COST—LABOR

COST ROUTING SHEET
PRODUCT 01-02608-5036

	1	2	3	4	5	6	7	8	9	10	11	12	13	14	15
PRODUCT ID	OPR NO.	BM LEVL	QUANTITY	START OPN.	COST CNTR.	STND HRS/M	LABOR RATE	VARBLE OVHEAD	FIXED OVHEAD	R/M CODE	R/M GROSS	R/M NET	SCRAP RECOVY	STANDARD R/M COST	U M
01—02608—5036	010	01	1.00000	010	1369	.02	2.497	1.749	3.4o7	018751				128.6900	2
01—02608—5036	010	01	1.00000	010						011856				8.0500	2
01—02608—5036	020	01	1.00000	020	1369	.05	2.497	1.749	3.407						
. 01—02608—0537	010	02	1.00000	010	0267	1.67	2.473	2.093	3.678						
. 01—02608—0537	020	02	1.00000	010	0267	1.18	2.473	2.093	3.678						
.. 01—02608—0005	010	03	1.00000	010	0568	.05	2.752	6.022	4.282						
.. 01—02608—0005	020	03	1.00000	010	0981	1.16	2.790	1.942	3.237						
... 01—02608—0008	010	04	1.00000	010	0447	.15	1.335	4.182	7.121	202800	37.800	17.000	313.75000	638.1700	2
... 01—02608—0008	020	04	1.00000	010	0450	.50	1.335	4.182	7.122						
... 01—02608—0008	030	04	1.00000	010	0761	.81	3.396	3.326	4.933						
... 01—02608—0008	050	04	1.00000	010	0568	.07	2.752	6.022	4.282						
... 01—02608—0002	010	04	1.00000	010	1294	.08	2.773	2.978	4.413						
.... 97—00019—0000	010	05	.00990	010	1291	4.65	2.773	2.978	4.413	059562	350.75000	350.75000		250.0000	2
.... 97—00019—0000	010	05	.00990	010						055401	17.54000	17.54000		88.0000	2
.... 97—00019—0000	010	05	.00990	010						051202	3.86000	3.86000		530.0000	2
.... 97—00019—0000	010	05	.00990	010						058110	4.56000	4.56000		530.0000	2
.... 97—00019—0000	010	05	.00990	010						057326	7.02000	7.02000		34.5000	2
.... 97—00019—0000	010	05	.00990	010						054202	35.08000	35.08000		260.0000	2
.... 97—00019—0000	010	05	.00990	010						057320	87.69000	87.69000		114.2100	2
.... 97—00019—0000	010	05	.00990	010						055407	86.64000	86.64000		160.0000	2
.... 97—00019—0000	010	05	.00990	010						057215	3.51000	3.51000		225.0000	2
.... 97—00019—0000	010	05	.00990	010											
.... 97—00019—0000	010	05	.00990	010											
.... 97—00019—0000	010	05	.00990	010											
.... 97—00019—0000	010	05	.00990	010											

COSTING THE LABOR
(COSTS ARE PER/M)

COST CENTER	OPN.	STANDARD HOURS/M	LABOR RATE(1)	LABOR COST
1369	010	.02	$2.497	$.05
1369	020	.05	2.497	.12
0267	010	1.67	2.473	4.13
0267	020	1.18	2.473	2.92
0568	010	.05	2.752	.14
0981	020	1.16	2.790	3.24
0447	010	.15	1.335	.20
0450	020	.50	1.335	.67
0761	030	.81	3.396	2.75
0568	050	.07	2.752	.19
1294	010	.08	2.773	.22
1291	010	4.65(2)	2.773	.13
				$14.76

(1) Based on hourly rate divided by number of machines operated.

(2) Factored by .0099 to reflect standard cost per/M units.

2,255 Units @ $14.76 = $33.28

COST OF SALES

PRODUCT ID	OPR NO.		QUANTITY	BRASS	NON-BRASS MATERIAL	LABOR	VARIABLE OVERHEAD	CUMULATIVE OPERATING COST	FIXED OVERHEAD	TOTAL COST
01 00131 AP1	0004	000 R	315,000	4,191.36	17.71	310.16	731.31	5,250.54	837.66	6,088
01 00131 A1782	0013	000 R	57,500	773.78	240.59	481.82	524.23	2,020.42	756.87	2,777
01 00131 17829	0017	000 R	243,800	3,167.79	899.12	2,187.49	2,315.74	8,570.14	3,324.75	11,894
01 01651 UAH1	0086	000 R	277,500	3,605.67	15.45	287.09	676.08	4,584.29	760.57	5,344
01 02351 7913	5250	000 R	1,200	15.59	11.59	17.31	14.93	59.42	20.94	80
01 02870 7913	5179	000 R	757	12.58	5.29	31.35	20.25	69.47	27.18	96
01 02608	5036	000 R	2,255	39.68	3.77	33.28	33.49	110.22	54.50	164
01 03407 0178	5032	000 R	8,550	137.70	29.88	148.94	186.67	503.19	241.74	744
PRODUCT TOTALS	R		952,062	12,535.35	1,472.22	3,904.79	4,940.38	22,852.74	6,655.99	29,508
PERCENT OF TOTAL COST				42.49	4.99	13.23	16.75	77.46	22.54	100.00

LEGEND: R = Rod

Exhibit 6 identifies these figures in the cost routing sheet and illustrates the application of standard costs in the section labeled "Costing the Brass." The costing is illustrated in four steps:

1. The gross weight is multiplied by the standard cost per 1,000 pounds of brass, with a resulting cost of $24.13 per 1,000 stems.
2. The net finished weight is subtracted from the starting weight to arrive at the pounds of brass lost.
3. The 20.8 pounds of brass lost is multiplied by the standard cost of scrap recovery, showing a credit of $6.53 per 1,000 stems.
4. The product cost per 1,000 stems at level 04 is arrived at by subtracting the $6.53 from the $24.13. This indicates a brass cost of $17.60 per 1,000 stems.

The cost of sales transaction listing shown in the lower third of Exhibit 6 indicates that 2,255 units of the 01 02608 5036 stem were sold at a total standard cost of $164. Of this, the standard cost of the brass content is shown as $39.68 (2,255 × $17.60).

Developing the Product Cost—Labor

Exhibit 7 illustrates the procedure for arriving at the labor cost for product 01 02608 5036. The standard hours per 1,000 units are added up (see the section entitled "Costing the Labor") for all the operations in all cost centers through which this product passes. These hours are then multiplied by the labor grade rates to arrive at a total labor cost by cost center. The addition of the total labor cost by cost center results in a total labor cost of $14.76 per 1,000 units. Then, multiplying the $14.76 by the 2,255 units that were sold, $33.28 of the total cost of the sales of this product is accounted for. The balance of the cost is made up of the nonbrass material and the overhead. The nonbrass material is calculated in much the same manner as brass, while the overhead is based on the direct labor or machine hours, whichever is applicable to the particular operation performed. Calculating overhead costing rates is covered in Chapters 1 and 2.

COSTING THE TRANSACTIONS

The costing of brass and labor in the cost of sales transaction listing in Exhibits 6 and 7 belongs under the heading of this section. There are other transactions that precede the relief of inventory when products are sold. These include the movement of raw material and partially completed products throughout the manufacturing process.

Transactions relating to the fabricated components and subassemblies involve the following stockrooms:

1. Raw material
2. Fabricated and purchased components (parts)
3. Finished goods

The fabricating and assembly cost centers would include cost centers in the following departments:

1. Automatics
2. General machinery
3. Molding
4. Plating, cleaning, and coating
5. Hand assembly and packaging
6. Automatic assembly including packaging

Departments 1, 2, 3, and 4 are fabricating departments in the primary work-in-process area, while departments 5 and 6 are assembly departments in the secondary work-in-process area.

The transactions relating to raw material affect the primary work-in-process area. The fabricated parts are then listed as transactions through the various cost centers within primary work-in-process until they are ready for transfer into the fabricated and purchased components stockroom. Reissues of the fabricated and purchased components into the secondary work-in-process area are treated as transactions much like issues out of the raw material stockroom. Finally, the fully assembled products are transferred into finished goods stock. The final stage in the transactions is, of course, the transfer out of finished goods to cost of sales.

Raw Material Issues

Exhibit 8 illustrates the costing of issues of raw material. These are categorized by broad types of material. The example shown covers chemicals. The individual items are listed in the sequence of the part numbers, each showing the unit of measure "2," indicating the cost per 1,000. The column headed "Extended Cost" is the result of multiplying the quantity by the standard unit cost per 1,000. Note that item 96–5408 shows a negative quantity and therefore a negative cost. This indicates either a return to stock or quantity correction of a previous issue. The extended costs showing a single asterisk to the right indicate subtotals. The double asterisks are group totals. The final total, $346,340.81, is the total of all items issued during the month, including the other categories as well as chemicals. This total for all issues will be shown

EXHIBIT 8
RAW MATERIAL ISSUES

CHEMICALS	DESCRIPTION	U/M	QUANTITY	STANDARD UNIT COST	EXTENDED COST	
96-5408	Powder =6 H	2	30	4750.0000	− 142.50	
			30		− 142.50	*
96-5410	Tetrafluoroethylene Resin = 6	2	184	4750.0000	874.00	
96-5410	Tetrafluoroethylene Resin = 6	2	138	4750.0000	655.50	
	Resin = 6					
96-5410	Tetrafluoroethylene	2	140	4750.0000	665.00	
	Resin = 6		683		3,244.25	*
965411	Naphtha	2	30	45.0700	1.35	
965411	Naphtha	2	60	45.0700	2.70	
965411	Naphtha	2	30	45.0700	1.35	
			120		5.40	*
			2,062		3,313.98	**
					346,340.81	**

later in a journal entry that relieves the raw material inventory account and charges work-in-process.

Fabricated Parts Transferred into the Stockroom

Most companies that fabricate parts for use in assembly at a later date utilize a work-in-process stockroom as a storage and staging area for fabricated components and subassemblies. When completed, they are transferred to the fabricated and purchased components stockroom. Exhibit 9 shows a typical transaction listing of the items being moved into the stockroom. Since no production operations are performed in the stockroom, the operation number used is 999. Note that the columnar format for costing is similar to that used for cost of sales, referred to in the lower third of Exhibits 6 and 7. In fact, all transfers through the manufacturing process will show the same format, because the work-in-process and finished goods inventories show this breakdown. Note, also, that the costs transferred to the stockroom are summarized by "To Department Totals" and "From Department Totals." Since this transaction listing includes parts used on the valve inserts as well as other related products, the brass column is broken down to show the brass strip and brass wire separately from the rod.

Cost of Sales

Although cost of sales was discussed in connection with Exhibits 6 and 7, it is included here again as Exhibit 10. Since the costing was previously explained, the purpose here is to point out that the computer automatically calculates the percentage of each element of cost to the total cost. This is done not only for the total cost of sales but for the various categories of products making up the total. This type of percentage breakdown can be helpful for analytical purposes.

Since the issues of material into work-in-process, transfers of fabricated items into the fabricated and purchased parts stockroom, and the cost of sales are representative of the method of costing transactions, there is no need to discuss the others at this time.

BY-PRODUCT CONTROL REPORTS

The computer speeds up many of the routine tasks previously performed by hand. Many of the data that provide information needed for cost accounting and inventory management contain valuable information that could be used for more complete management control.

When the work was performed manually, time did not permit culling out such data and reassembling them into more comprehensive controls. The computer now makes such data more readily accessible and programmable into useful reports. Since material accounts for almost half of the total manufacturing cost in many companies, and in many instances far in excess of half, material will be used to provide illustrative examples.

Purchased Parts Price History

Price information on purchases is maintained manually in the purchasing departments of many companies. Since much of this information is posted by hand, any meaningful

EXHIBIT 9
FABRICATED PARTS TRANSFERRED TO FABRICATED AND PURCHASED PARTS STOCKROOM

Product ID	Opr No.	Quantity	Brass	Non-Brass Material	Labor	Variable Overhead	Cumulative Operating Cost	Fixed Overhead	Total Cost
31 05163	0009	999 R	360	3.16	4.54	34.96	43.52	86.18	70.52	156.70
33 00798 D15	0016	999	250		13.13	.00	.00	13.13	.00	13.13
39 01451 198	0019	999 R	1,900	2.36	.00	27.49	3.49	34.87	4.52	39.39
		W		1.53						
39 04414 6	0019	999 R	710	4.36	2.65	18.59	7.40	33.19	9.90	43.09
		S		.19						
39 09155 6	0048	999 R	830	1.75	8.78	51.24	12.54	74.37	21.36	95.73
		W		.06						
41 00931 5	0049	999	300		.17	1.84	1.62	3.63	2.74	6.37
51 01593 4	0029	999	1,000		25.55	9.68	11.15	46.38	13.38	59.76
53 07642 2	0019	999	1,000		2.61	.00	.00	2.61	.00	2.61
53 08385 A3	0109	999	41,620		19.98	155.02	129.55	304.55	223.07	527.62
67 03670 197	0079	999	10		5.85	.00	.00	5.85	.00	5.85
67 08600 16	0119	999	8		.15	.11	.06	.32	.12	.44
67 08600 22	0159	999	7		.24	.57	.63	1.44	1.00	2.44
67 08600 23	0169	999	7		.11	.67	.81	1.59	1.32	2.91
67 08600 45	0269	999	9		.57	.49	.68	1.74	.83	2.57
67 08601 12	0089	999	10		5.20	.00	.00	5.20	.00	5.20
"TO" DEPT. TOTALS	R	48,021	11.63	89.53	300.66	211.45	615.05	348.76	963.81
	S		.19						
	W		1.59						
"FROM" DEPT. TOTALS	R	48,021	11.63	89.53	300.66	211.45	615.05	348.76	963.81
	S		.19						
	W		1.59						

LEGEND: R = Rod; S = Strip; W = Wire

EXHIBIT 10
COST OF SALES

PRODUCT ID	OPR NO.		QUANTITY	BRASS	NON-BRASS MATERIAL	LABOR	VARIABLE OVERHEAD	CUMULATIVE OPERATING COST	FIXED OVERHEAD	TOTAL COST
01 00131 AP1	0004 000	R	315,000	4,191.36	17.71	310.16	731.31	5,250.54	837.66	6,088
01 00131 A1782	0013 000	R	57,500	773.78	240.59	481.82	524.23	2,020.42	756.87	2,777
01 00131 17829	0017 000	R	243,800	3,167.79	899.12	2,187.49	2,315.74	8,570.14	3,324.75	11,894
01 01651 UAH1	0086 000	R	277,500	3,605.67	15.45	287.09	676.08	4,584.29	760.57	5,344
01 02351 7913	5250 000	R	1,200	15.59	11.59	17.31	14.93	59.42	20.94	80
01 02870 7913	5179 000	R	757	12.58	5.29	31.35	20.25	69.47	27.18	96
01 02608	5036 000	R	2,255	33.68	3.77	33.28	33.49	110.22	54.50	164
01 03407 0178	5032 000	R	8,550	137.70	29.88	148.94	186.67	503.19	241.74	744
PRODUCT TOTALS		R	952,062	12,535.35	1,472.22	3,904.79	4,940.38	22,852.74	6,655.99	29,508
→ PERCENT OF TOTAL COST				42.49	4.99	13.23	16.75	77.46	22.54	100.00 ←

LEGEND: R = Rod

EXHIBIT 11
PURCHASED PARTS PRICE HISTORY

Part No.	Vendor	Invoice No.	P.O. #	Invoice Date	Quantity	U/M	Total Actual Cost	Actual Unit Cost
01–2868	Ajax Supply Company	42367	02873	2/2	100	ea.	53.80	.538
01–2868	Ajax Supply Company	42367	05091	3/5	400	ea.	215.20	.538
01–2868	Ajax Supply Company	42646	03047	3/6	100	ea.	53.80	.538
01–2868	Ajax Supply Company	43359	06068	5/7	100	ea.	53.80	.538
01–2868	Ajax Supply Company	43363	06949	6/7	900	ea.	522.90	.581
01–2868	Ajax Supply Company	43424	06729	6/8	300	ea.	176.40	.588
01–2868	Ajax Supply Company	43426	07657	7/12	600	ea.	352.80	.588
01–2868	Ajax Supply Company	43468	07657	8/18	600	ea.	352.80	.588
01–2868	Ajax Supply Company	43686	07729	9/12	300	ea.	176.40	.588
01–2868	Ajax Supply Company	45898	07892	10/13	500	ea.	345.00	.690
01–2868	Ajax Supply Company	46667	07884	10/16	502	ea.	376.50	.750
01–2868	Ajax Supply Company	48882	08861	11/23	501	ea.	375.75	.750
01–2868	Ajax Supply Company	52601	08960	12/14	500	ea.	375.00	.750
					5403		3,430.15	.635
43–9267	Berkshire Products	41031	02802	1/30	25	ea.	408.17	16.327
43–9267	Berkshire Products	42308	02815	2/5	125	ea.	2,040.85	16.327
43–9267	Berkshire Products	42309	05020	2/18	25	ea.	408.17	16.327
43–9267	Berkshire Products	42656	03023	3/6	50	ea.	816.34	16.327
43–9267	Berkshire Products	42333	05621	4/2	75	ea.	1,224.51	16.327
43–9267	Berkshire Products	43852	06842	5/9	25	ea.	408.17	16.327
43–9267	Berkshire Products	43962	06731	6/17	25	ea.	416.50	16.660
43–9267	Berkshire Products	43975	07662	7/12	35	ea.	583.10	16.660
43–9267	Berkshire Products	44502	07894	8/14	85	ea.	1,416.10	16.660
43–9267	Berkshire Products	45652	07992	9/16	65	ea.	1,082.90	16.660
43–9267	Berkshire Products	46867	08012	10/18	15	ea.	249.90	16.660
43–9267	Berkshire Products	49001	08862	11/21	56	ea.	932.96	16.660
43–9267	Berkshire Products	51621	09002	12/16	57	ea.	949.62	16.660
					663		10,937.29	16.496

analysis would require burdensome manual analysis which would be both time-consuming and costly. Introduction of the computer provides an excellent opportunity to develop a price history by individual items for various suppliers over a period of time.

Exhibit 11 illustrates two items for which such an analysis was made. The listing shows the vendor (or vendors when more than one source is used), invoice number, invoice date, quantity purchased, unit in which purchased, total actual cost, unit cost, and average unit cost in a desired period of time.

The unit cost history is useful in monitoring the historical price trends and the influence of quantity purchases on individual unit prices. The report can be rearranged so that price comparisons can be made of similar items supplied by more than one vendor. This type of report can also be very useful in setting material price standards for cost accounting purposes.

Purchase Price Variance Report

In companies using standard costs, the purchase price variances are usually calculated at the time the vendor invoices are being processed for payment. This facilitates the matching of the purchase price variance with the specific invoice to which it applies. Introduction of the computer facilitated the preparation of purchase price variance reports that listed every single purchase—showing the quantity purchased, the standard unit cost, total actual cost, total standard cost, and the variance of the total actual cost from the total standard cost. Such a report is illustrated in the upper half of Exhibit 12.

Many data processing departments, when initially programming such reports, list every item purchased, irrespective of the magnitude of the variance between actual and standard costs. The result has been complaints by operating personnel such as the following, which was made by the plant manager of a company using many different parts that were purchased from the outside:

I think the theory of standard costs and variances is great, but why must I receive a printout each month that requires me to pore through 50 to 75 pages of items purchased during the month? I have more important things to do. First of all, weekly reports would be more useful to me than monthly reports. Additionally, I would like only the major items reported on an exception basis. This would include:

1. Those items in which the variance exceeds 5% of the standard cost.
2. Those items in which the variance is in excess of $100, regardless of the percentage.

This plant manager, in describing the format that would be more useful to him, commented further that the previous month's total purchase price variance was favorable in the amount of $16,191.67. He expressed his reaction as follows:

I get very suspicious of the type of effort that went into setting standard prices when I see a 6.4% favorable price variance—particularly when the wholesale price index showed an 8% increase during the year. This tells me that the purchasing department was playing it safe. What also bothers me is that the cost department accepted these standards without a single question or challenge.

The lower portion of Exhibit 12 illustrates a purchase price variance report showing only the major items on an exception basis. Note that this excludes such minor

EXHIBIT 12
PURCHASE PRICE VARIANCE BY ITEM

P.O. NO.	ITEM CODE	QUANTITY	U/M CODE	U/M	STD. UNIT COST	ACTUAL COST	STANDARD COST	VAR-IANCE
49999	03 3472	3346	2	LBS	702.700	2,754.43	2,351.23	− 403.20
50344	20 2980	810	2	LBS	620.190	490.21	502.35	12.14
49760	21 3190	1851	2	LBS	625.000	1,110.97	1,156.88	45.91
50134	21 3476	4372	2	LBS	625.000	2,733.37	2,732.50	− .87
50333	21 3476	7378	2	LBS	625.000	4,428.28	4,611.25	182.97
50050	21 3650	344	2	LBS	724.490	206.47	249.22	42.75
50217	21 4450	555	2	LBS	580.000	306.75	321.90	15.15
49799	21 4450	1238	2	LBS	580.000	684.24	718.04	33.80
50591	22 0781	127	2	LBS	1,287.780	109.83	163.55	53.72
50218	22 1562	110	2	LBS	828.000	89.56	91.08	1.52
49215	22 1660	1000	2	LBS	828.000	814.20	828.00	13.80
49216	22 1660	6018	2	LBS	828.000	4,899.86	4,982.90	83.04
49216	22 1660	4383	2	LBS	828.000	3,130.34	3,629.12	498.78
49185	23 0245	6810	2	LBS	625.000	4,087.36	4,256.25	168.89
49186	23 0245	26689	2	LBS	625.000	16,152.18	16,680.63	528.45
49186	23 0245	17314	2	LB$	625.000	10,391.86	10,821.25	429.39
49186	23 0245	20517	2	LBS	625.000	12,416.89	12,823.13	406.24
48958	23 0332	6614	2	LBS	630.000	4,002.79	4,166.82	164.03
48958	23 0332	3726	2	LBS	630.000	2,329.50	2,347.38	17.88
49398	23 0437	7152	2	LBS	585.000	3,988.67	4,183.92	195.25
48971	23 0437	13939	2	LBS	585.000	7,773.78	8,154.32	380.54
49996	23 0438	534	2	LBS	585.000	297.81	312.39	14.58
49670	23 0467	2522	2	LBS	585.000	1,454.44	1,475.37	* 20.93
50345	23 0531	5066	2	LBS	576.000	2,777.18	2,918.02	140.84
49659	23 0625	1010	2	LBS	549.000	524.90	554.49	29.59
50222	23 0625	1520	2	LBS	549.000	789.94	834.48	44.54
						232,934.06	249,125.73	16,191.67

PURCHASE PRICE VARIANCE BY MAJOR ITEM*

P.O. No.	Item Code	Quan-tity	U/M Code	U/M	Std. Cost Unit	Actual Cost	Standard Cost	Variance**
49997	03 3472	3346	2	lbs.	702,700	2,754.43	2,351.23	403.20 U
50333	21 3476	7378	2	lbs.	625,000	4,428.28	4,611.25	182.97 F
50050	21 3650	344	2	lbs.	724,490	206.47	249.22	42.75 F
50591	22 0781	127	2	lbs.	1,287.780	109.83	163.55	53.72 F
49216	22 166$	4383	2	lbs.	828,000	3,130.34	3,629.12	498.78 F
49185	23 0245	6810	2	lbs.	625.000	4,037.36	4,256.25	168.89 F
49186	23 0245	26689	2	lbs.	625.000	16,152.18	16,680.63	528.45 F
49186	23 0245	17314	2	lbs.	625.000	10,396.86	10,521.25	429.39 F
49180	23 0245	7859	2	lbs.	625.000	4,716.97	4,911.85	194.91 F
49186	23 0245	20517	2	lbs.	625.000	12,416.89	12,823.13	406.24 F
48958	23 0332	6614	2	lbs.	630.000	3952.79	4,116.82	164.03 F
49398	23 0437	7152	2	lbs.	585.000	3,988.67	4,183.92	195.25 F
48971	23 0437	13939	2	lbs.	585.000	7,773.78	8,154.32	380.54 F
50345	23 0531	5066	2	lbs.	576.020	2,777.18	2,918.02	140.84 F

* MAJOR ITEMS ARE THOSE VARIANCES THAT ARE 5% OR MORE AND THOSE THAT EXCEED $100.
** U = UNFAVORABLE   F = FAVORABLE

items as $0.87 on a purchase of over $2,700 and the small items whose percentage variance is less than 5%. The comments by this plant manager showed that he was interested in controlling his costs and was able to do so without requiring voluminous reports. Other operating executives may prefer to establish different guidelines for exception reporting. Another company wanted no variances of under $100 reported even if they exceeded 5%. Such determinations vary from company to company, depending upon the nature of the materials used and the demand and supply situation in the marketplace.

Material Receipts Compared with the Plan

The controller of one company noted that a large number of invoices were being received from suppliers in advance of the delivery date specified on the purchase order. This meant that the material might also be delivered in advance of the date specified for delivery. In a sample of 100 such cases, it was found that material was being received 3.2 days early, on the average. This premature delivery meant that the company's inventory was excessive to the extent that orders were received early. It also meant that part of the discount allowed for payment within 10 days was being paid prematurely, thus depriving the company of the use of this cash. Additionally, this tended to dilute the calculation of return on investment because inventories were higher than planned.

EXHIBIT 13
MATERIAL RECEIPTS COMPARED WITH PLAN

Part No.	Purchase Order No.	Description	U/M	Quantity	Standard Unit Cost	Total Standard Cost
01-0126	46236	Casting	ea.	1	22.994	20.994
01-0327	46337	Casting	ea.	10	93.789	937.890
02-0462	40454	Casting	ea.	10	275.000	2,750.000
02-0561	46567	Casting	ea.	10	181.?70	1,810.300
03-0102	46567	Casting	ea.	1	148.870	148.870
04-9362	47668	.067" × 48" Coiled Steel	lb.	20,000	.105	2,100.000
04-98?7	47887	.051" × 36" Coiled Steel	lb.	20,000	.108	2,160.000
05-0002	48882	.020" × 10" Coiled Steel	lb.	5,000	.122	610.000
05-0763	46567	.018" × 9" Coiled Steel	lb.	5,000	.108	540.000
05-0972	46338	.016" × 12" 70/30 Brass	lb.	1,000	.100	600.000
05-27?7	43536	.010" × 16" 70/30 Brass	lb.	2,000	.580	1,160.000
06-9872	43678	Teflon Tetraflouride	lb.	184	4.750	874.000
06-9962	44587	Teflon Tetraflouride	lb.	138	4.750	655.500
07-3212	45867	#110 Switch Plates	ea.	35	.500	17.500
07-3556	43655	#220 Switch Plates	ea.	1,000	1.500	1,500.000
07-5456	42337	Nylon Grommets	ea.	25,000	.028	700.000
07-6768	4124?	Plastic Washers	ea.	100,000	.030	3,000.000
20-3246	46687	#10 Webbing	yd.	1,000	3.070	3,070.000
20-4678	46667	#26 Webbing	yd.	5,000	4.020	20,100.000
20-5762	45452	#32 Plastic Material	yd.	10,000	.500	5,000.000
20-6879	46601	#41 Plastic Material	yd.	5,000	1.100	5,500.000
22-1334	45827	2122 Ferrules	ea.	100	2.100	210.000
22?23?7	45990	3538 Ferrules	ea.	200	3.000	600.000
23-3679	42876	½ HP. Motor	ea.	100	10.000	1,000.000
23-4627	43378	1 HP. Motor	ea.	300	46.500	13,950.000
		Total w/e 10/7				95,968.000 *
		Planned Purchases				87,690.000

* ACTUAL RECEIPTS IN EXCESS OF PLAN BY 9.4%

NOTE: Although this report shows a single percentage for the week's purchases, some may prefer to calculate a percentage by line item.

Exhibit 13 illustrates the format of a report that was prepared weekly to monitor deliveries against planned (scheduled) dates. This report lists the part number, purchase order number, description of the material ordered, quantity, and standard cost. The total standard cost of the material received during each week was compared with the total standard cost of the material scheduled for delivery during that same week. The difference indicates the dollar value of material shipped prematurely. The difference between actual receipts and planned purchases in this case was in excess of 9%, compared with 2% which was the amount allowed. This report was forwarded to the Purchasing Department each week, as well as to the general manager. The Purchasing Department was instructed to notify the suppliers of the premature shipment and to advise them that discounts would be calculated from the date the delivery was scheduled to have arrived rather on the date of receipt. In the event that material was received late, the date from which the discount allowance was counted would be from the date of receipt. After this report was in use for 6 weeks, the difference between the actual and planned dates of receipt dropped from over 9% to 3%, based on the standard cost of the material involved.

The treasurer of another company was also quite conscious of early and late deliveries of material by suppliers. He expressed his views as follows:

Timeliness to me means delivery on schedule—not late and not too early. The objection to late delivery is obvious; to early delivery, not so obvious. It is to the advantage of the vendor to ship to the customer as soon as possible—even if ahead of schedule. The vendor thus reduces the amount of capital tied up in his inventory and improves his return on investment. While advantageous to the seller, this practice has the opposite effect on the buyer. If the buyer company receives the shipment ahead of schedule, its investment is needlessly increased and its return on investment reduced.

The report format used by this company is shown in Exhibit 14. The report is based on a comparison of the scheduled delivery date, contained in the purchase order, with the date of receipt of the material. The last column, "Vendor Performance," indicates the number of days that delivery was made before or after the authorized delivery date. Such a report is useful in determining which vendors come closest to approximating the authorized receipt date. Those who habitually make delivery late or ahead of time can be given a warning.

Exhibits 13 and 14, though different in format, are similar in principle and intent. Companies seeking to control the size of their inventories will find that monitoring vendor adherence to scheduled delivery dates (within reason) is one of the many methods of accomplishing this goal.

SUMMARIZING THE TRANSACTION REPORTS

In an earlier section entitled "Costing the Transactions," the mechanics of costing were demonstrated for the brass required in making the stem, as well as the direct labor cost for the various cost centers. The format of the transaction reports was also illustrated. The section "By-Product Control Reports," discussed the modifications that could be made to the information contained in the transaction reports to provide management with additional information. Although the illustrative examples were limited to material, the concept could be applied to the other elements of cost as well.

This section will deal with the consolidation of the various transaction reports with a view to determining the cost of production for the month and the changes

EXHIBIT 14
VENDOR DELIVERY PERFORMANCE
Week Ending _____ / _____ / _____

Vendor	Part No.	Description	Purch. Order Number	Qty.	U/M	Total Standard Cost	Scheduled Delivery Date	Received Date	Vendor Performance[1]
ABC Corp.	1440 202	Angle	C45100	1,440	In	514.00	5/17/x5	5/23/x5	6 L
ABC Corp.	1452 316	Channel	C45101	2,400	In	1,200.00	5/22/x5	5/19/x5	3 E
ABC Corp.	1535 360	Flat	C45205	2,400	In	1,320.00	5/22/x5	5/23/x5	1 L
						3,034.00*			
ABZ Corp.	1440 220	Angle	C45100	1,440	In	576.00	5/15/x5	5/22/x5	7 L
						576.00*			
B.Z. Co.	1535 274	Flat	C45206	240	In	144.00	5/09/x5	5/20/x5	11 L
B.Z. Co.	1622 334	Bar Round	C46170	240	In	120.50	5/15/x5	5/21/x5	6 L
B.Z. Co.	1622 342	Bar Round	C46275	240	In	132.00	5/16/x5	5/23/x5	7 L
						396.50*			
						4,006.50**			

[1] Indicates the number of days early or late

in inventory. The transaction reports, listed below, are shown in Exhibit 15 together with the closing journal entries. The transactions are numbered from 1 to 10, as are the journal entries.

1. Purchase price variance by item
2. Raw material issues
3. Fabricated parts transferred into fabricated and purchased parts inventory
4. Transfers from finished goods to fabricated and purchased parts inventory
5. Transfers from fabricated and purchased parts inventory to production
6. (Omitted because there were no transactions)
7. Components in finished goods stock returned to production
8. Completed production transferred to finished goods inventory
9. Change in work-in-process floor inventory
10. Cost of sales

A discussion of each of the above-listed transactions follows:

1. *Purchase price variance by item.* This report was discussed in the section "By-product Control Reports," in which it was suggested that the analysis of variances be presented to the purchasing department and to management on an exception basis in order to avoid numerous pages of detail. Note that the total purchase price variance is $16,352.54, made up of $16,191.67 relating to purchases into the raw material inventory and $160.87 relating to purchases into the fabricated and purchased parts inventory. Note also that the purchase price variance of $16,352.54 is favorable because the standard cost is greater than the actual cost. Since the company values its production and inventory at standard cost, the raw material inventory was increased in value by the amount of the variance to bring it up to the standard cost.

Before proceeding to the other transaction reports, it would be well to discuss the method of recording the variances and to give some explanation of the "uncosted items" shown in the various reports.

Recording variances: Since, in a standard cost system, actual costs must be compared with a standard, it is necessary to use a "clearing account" to measure the differences. This clearing account is referred to by different names. Some call it a "manufacturing cost control account," while others call it a "variance clearing account." The company used in this case example identifies the clearing account as:

• Material variance
• Labor variance
• Indirect labor and overhead variance

The more detailed breakdown of the above variance accounts is illustrated later in the chapter.

Uncosted items: One of the real-world problems in establishing standard costs at the beginning of each year is the determination of which of the thousands of items fabricated and assembled will be active in the coming year—after a period of inactivity. Another problem is the determination of what new parts and end products will be introduced in the coming year. Failure to predict uncertainties of this nature

EXHIBIT 15
SUMMARY OF TRANSACTION REPORTS

1 PURCHASE PRICE VARIANCE BY ITEM

P.O. NO.	ITEM CODE	QUANTITY	U/M CODE	UNIT COST	ACTUAL COST	STANDARD COST	VARIANCE
49999	03 3472	3346	2	702.700	2,754.43	2,351.23	− 403.20
50344	20 2980	810	2	620.190	490.21	502.35	12.14
49760	21 3190	1851	2	625.000	1,110.97	1,156.88	45.91
48958	23 0332	6614	2	630.000	4,002.79	4,166.82	164.03
48958	23 0332	3726	2	630.000	2,329.50	2,347.38	17.88
49398	23 0437	7152	2	585.000	3,988.67	4,183.92	195.25
48971	23 0437	13939	2	585.000	7,773.78	8,154.32	380.54
49996	23 0438	534	2	585.000	297.81	312.39	14.58
49670	23 0467	2522	2	585.000	1,454.44	1,475.37	20.93
50345	23 0531	5066	2	576.000	2,777.18	2,918.02	140.84
49659	23 0625	1010	2	549.000	524.90	554.49	29.59
50022	23 0625	1520	2	549.000	789.94	834.48	44.54
					232,934.06	249,125.73	16,191.67

STANDARD COST EQUALS QUANTITY X UNIT COST

2 RAW MATERIAL ISSUES

CHEMICALS	DESCRIPTION	U/M	QUANTITY	STANDARD UNIT COST	EXTENDED COST
96-5408	Powder =6 H	2	30	4750.0000	− 142.50 *
		2	30		− 142.50 *
96-5410	Tetrafluoroethylene Resin = 6	2	184	4750.0000	874.00
96-5410	Tetrafluoroethylene Resin = 6	2	138	4750.0000	655.50
96-5410	Resin = 6	2	140	4750.0000	665.00 *
	Tetrafluoroethylene Resin = 6		683		3,244.25 *
965411	Naphtha	2	30	45.0700	1.35
965411	Naphtha	2	60	45.0700	2.70
965411	Naphtha	2	30	45.0700	1.35
			120		5.40 **
			2,062		3,313.98 **
					346,340.81

3 FABRICATED PARTS TRANSFERRED INTO FABRICATED AND PURCHASED PARTS INVENTORY

From:	Brass	Non-Brass	Direct Labor	Variable Overhead	Fixed Overhead	Total
01	$ 13.41	89.53	300.66	211.45	348.76	963.81
02	1.50	38.12	4.08	3.20	4.75	51.65
03	2,085.47	81.80	302.92	678.81	1,029.06	4,178.08
04	4,098.41	11,926.58	2,080.78	2,055.62	2,889.39	23,050.78
05	229,804.96	16,932.22	39,916.46	69,870.01	93,891.07	450,414.72
06	2,913.91	591.33	1,796.39	2,041.96	2,879.65	10,223.24
07	1,408.39	63.53	388.42	433.52	654.23	2,948.09
08	15,413.32	2,473.79	10,881.12	14,917.32	22,872.35	66,557.90
09	541.54	1,204.47	3,340.78	3,096.48	4,880.48	13,063.75
10	97.36	246.72	26.32	28.35	39.43	438.18
11	1,390.27	1,611.96	539.96	628.49	950.28	5,120.96
12						36.72
Total Costed	257,768.54	35,296.77	59,577.89	93,965.23	130,439.45	577,047.88
Uncosted items	6,666.95	2,003.78	1,495.59	2,368.74	3,444.58	15,979.64
	$ 264,435.49	37,300.55	61,073.48	96,333.97	133,884.03	593,027.52

301,736.04
230,218.00

7 COMPONENTS IN FINISHED GOODS STOCK RETURNED TO PRODUCTION

To:	Brass	Non-Brass	Direct Labor	Variable Overhead	Fixed Overhead	Total
01	$ 347.41	119.19	243.64	277.24	413.38	1,400.86
02	16.48	96.01	17.43	15.64	25.46	171.02
04	13.08	1.58	28.39	29.87	46.15	119.07
06		61.99	.50	.35	.68	63.52
07	37.87	.12	1.57	3.41	5.69	48.66
08		.05	.21	.37	.57	1.70
11	315.01	850.44	213.87	215.11	333.43	1,927.86
12	1,637.18	1,887.21	1,504.84	1,419.30	2,173.41	8,621.94
32	21.28	77.66	21.30	20.58	31.88	172.70
41	1.42	1.92	2.27	2.20	3.26	11.07
42	.58	.49	.51	.66	.81	3.05
43	1.12	1.06	.62	.60	.93	4.33
47	269.84	63.51	172.31	186.96	289.44	982.06
Total Costed	2,661.32	2,161.39	2,207.75	2,172.29	3,325.09	13,527.84
Uncosted items	547.84	85.95	40.25	47.92	19.42	741.38
	$ 3,209.16	3,247.34	2,248.00	2,220.21	3,344.51	14,269.22

CLOSING JOURNAL ENTRIES

(1)

Material Variance		16,191.67
Raw Material Inventory	16,352.54	
Fabricated and Purchased Stores (WIP)	160.87	

To record purchase price variance.

(2)

Material Variance		346,340.81
Raw Material Inventory	346,340.81	

To record issues of raw material to production floor.

(3)

Fabricated and Purchased Parts Inventory		593,027.52
Material Variance	301,736.04	
Labor Variance	61,073.48	
Indirect Labor and Overhead Variance	230,218.00	

To record production of fabricated parts transferred into fabricated and purchased parts stores

(4)

Fabricated and Purchased Parts Inventory		1,956.56
Finished Goods Inventory	1,956.56	

To record transfers of items in finished goods to fabricated and purchased parts stores.

COMPLETED PRODUCTION TRANSFERRED TO FINISHED GOODS INVENTORY

	Brass	Non-Brass	Direct Labor	Variable Overhead	Fixed Overhead	Total
Costed	$214,710.48	123,008.74	108,217.04	121,741.51	181,154.82	748,832.59
Uncosted	7,264.81	5,825.78	5,386.64	5,965.95	8,725.37	33,168.55
	$221,975.29	128,834.52	113,603.68	127,707.46	189,880.19	782,001.14

CHANGE IN WORK-IN-PROCESS FLOOR INVENTORY

	Brass	Non-Brass	Direct Labor	Variable Overhead	Fixed Overhead	Total
Finished Goods Produced:	$221,975.29	128,834.52	113,603.68	127,707.46	189,880.19	782,001.14
From Finished Goods to Production Floor:						
From Fabricated Stores to Production Floor:	3,209.16	3,247.34	2,248.00	2,220.21	3,343.51	14,268.22
	270,320.97	126,752.99	63,767.95	100,094.54	137,448.65	698,385.10
	(51,554.84)	(1,165.81)	47,587.73	25,392.71	49,088.03	69,347.82

---

(5)

Work-in-Process Floor Inventory 698,385.10
  Fabricated and Purchased Parts Inventory 698,385.10
  To record issues of fabricated and
  purchased parts to production floor.

(6)

No entry this month.

(7)

Work-in-Process Floor Inventory 14,269.22
  Finished Goods Inventory 14,269.22
  To record items in finished goods
  transferred to the production floor.

(8)

Finished Goods Inventory 782,001.14
  Work-in-Process Floor Inventory 782,001.14
  To record production transferred
  to finished goods.

(9)

Work-in-Process Floor Inventory 69,347.82
  Material Usage Variance (brass & non-brass) .... 52,720.65 .... 47,587.73
  Labor Variance
  Indirect Labor and Overhead Variance 74,480.74
  To record standard cost of production.

(10)

Cost of Sales 753,596.69
  Finished Goods Inventory 753,596.69
  To record shipments during month.

- · - · - · - · - · - · - · - · - · -

Cost of Sales 62,364.67
Indirect Labor and Overhead Variance .... 40,740.02 .... 81,133.75
  Material Variance
  Labor Variance 21,970.94
  To close out Variance Accounts.

TRANSFERS FROM FINISHED GOODS TO FABRICATED AND PURCHASED PARTS INVENTORY

	Brass	Non-Brass	Direct Labor	Variable Overhead	Fixed Overhead	Total
Total Costed	$ 47.72	537.22	217.03	188.69	273.50	1,264.16
Uncosted items	31.60	471.41	69.30	47.90	72.19	692.40
	$ 79.32	1,008.63	286.33	236.59	345.69	1,956.56

TRANSFERS FROM FABRICATED AND PURCHASED PARTS INVENTORY TO PRODUCTION

To:	Brass	Non-Brass	Direct Labor	Variable Overhead	Fixed Overhead	Total
01	$ 48,524.50	21,270.43	18,750.18	23,636.47	32,404.98	144,586.56
02	14,120.43	5,520.33	9,464.68	13,374.62	20,628.73	63,108.79
04	2,454.31	15,257.61	1,861.74	2,285.78	3,029.04	24,888.48
05	152,774.51	6,920.74	14,377.23	24,868.29	34,414.69	233,335.46
06	5,803.94	15,186.86	1,737.66	2,538.59	3,463.66	28,730.71
07	25,787.14	495.34	9,930.40	21,765.50	28,195.78	86,174.16
08	189.76	565.40	41.22	50.95	70.46	917.79
11	1,769.73	373.78	1,077.12	1,791.47	1,738.56	6,750.66
12	14,507.04	59,294.59	5,319.20	7,813.14	10,714.46	97,648.43
13	.34		.07	.11	.17	.69
Total Costed	265,931.70	124,885.08	62,559.50	98,124.92	134,660.53	686,161.73
Uncosted items	4,389.27	1,867.91	1,208.45	1,969.62	2,788.12	12,223.37
	$ 270,320.97	126,752.99	63,767.95	100,094.54	137,448.65	698,385.10

COST OF SALES

PRODUCT ID	OPR NO.	QUANTITY	BRASS	NON-BRASS MATERIAL	LABOR	VARIABLE OVERHEAD	CUMULATIVE OPERATING COST	FIXED OVERHEAD	TOTAL COST
01 00131 AP1	0004 000 R	315,000	4,191.36	17.71	310.16	731.31	5,250.54	837.66	6,088
01 00131 A1782	0013 000 R	57,500	773.78	240.59	481.82	524.23	2,020.42	756.87	2,777
01 00131 17829	0017 000 R	243,800	3,167.79	899.12	2,187.49	2,315.74	8,570.14	3,324.75	11,894
01 01651 UAH1	0086 000 R	277,500	3,605.67	15.45	287.09	676.08	4,584.29	760.57	5,344
01 02351 7913	5250 000 R	1,200	15.59	11.59	17.31	14.93	59.42	20.94	80
01 02870 7913	5179 000 R	757	12.58	5.29	31.35	20.25	69.47	27.18	96
01 02608	5036 000 R	2,255	39.68	3.77	33.28	33.49	110.22	54.50	164
01 03407 0178	5032 000 R	8,550	137.70	29.88	148.94	186.67	503.19	241.74	744
PRODUCT TOTALS		952,062	12,535.35	1,472.22	3,904.79	4,940.38	22,852.74	6,655.59	29,508
PERCENT OF TOTAL COST			42.49	4.99	13.23	16.75	77.46	22.54	100.00

LEGEND: R = Rod

TOTAL ALL SALES CATEGORIES $ 753,597

accurately results in transactions that cannot be costed by the normal computerized costing process. As a result, when such uncosted items are discovered, temporary standards are introduced manually until the more permanent standards can be added to the files. Although the "uncosted" category is difficult to avoid, the dollar value should be only a small percentage of the value of the transactions that are costed.

2. *Raw material issues.* This transaction report was explained earlier to provide the groundwork for the discussion of by-product reports that would be helpful for better management control. The total standard cost of issues ($346,340.81) is charged to the material variance clearing account and credited to the raw material inventory to reflect the issues.

3. *Fabricated parts transferred into fabricated and purchased parts inventory.* This transaction report lists and costs the fabricated parts that have been *accepted* into the fabricated and purchased parts stockroom. Although the computer accumulates the input costs as they are incurred, the standard cost of the part at the point when it is accepted into stock is the value added to inventory. This avoids dependence on the accuracy of spoilage reports, which in many cases are incomplete. This will be explained in greater detail when transaction report 9 is discussed.

It should be noted that although many fabricated items physically bypass the stockroom and move on to the assembly operations, they are nonetheless recorded as if they had been received into stock and issued. The "From" and "To" entries are made simultaneously. The total of $593,027.52 transferred into this stockroom is shown in journal entry 3 (which corresponds to the number shown for this transaction report in Exhibit 15) as a debit (charge) to the fabricated and purchased parts inventory. The breakdowns of this total by material, direct labor, and overhead are shown as credits to the respective variance clearing accounts.

4. *Transfers from finished goods to fabricated and purchased parts inventory.* Fabricated parts are found in the finished goods stockroom for several reasons:

- They are sold as replacement parts.
- They may be sold to companies that purchase the parts and make the end products.
- When goods are returned from customers because of a defect, they may be disassembled and the salvaged parts returned to the fabricated and purchased parts stockroom.

The $1,956.56 total value of some or all of the above in this month has been transferred back to the parts stockroom. The journal entry bearing the same number as this transaction report (#4) shows the charge to the parts stockroom and the credit to finished goods inventory.

5. *Transfers from fabricated and purchased parts inventory to production.* These transfers could be made up of some of the parts that move directly from the fabrication area to assembly without physically being received into the stockroom. This was mentioned in the discussion of transaction report 3 when reference was made to the "From" and "To" entries that are made simultaneously. The bulk of the items have been transferred to such departments as 01 (Automatic Machinery), 04 (General Machinery) and 05 (Plating, Coating, and Clean-

ing). Although some of these may be returned to the parts stockroom, most are moved to the assembly departments. Note the reference "To Production" in the caption of this transaction report. Journal entry 5 shows a charge of the total standard cost of transfers in the amount of $698,385.10 to the work-in-process floor inventory and a credit of the same amount to the fabricated and purchased parts inventory. Both are work-in-process inventories, but a separation is made between the work-in-process in stock that is maintained on a perpetual basis and the work-in-process that remains on the factory floor at the various work stations. This will be discussed further when we cover transaction report 9.

6. *Customer returns.* Customer returns for which credits have been issued are covered by this transaction report and the journal entry bearing this same number. Because there were no credits issued in this period, no transaction report is shown and no charges or credits are shown in the related journal entry.

7. *Components in finished goods stock returned to production.* These transactions are similar to those covered earlier in (4), except that the transfer is being made to the work-in-process floor inventory rather than to the fabricated and purchased parts inventory. The journal entry charges the work-in-process floor inventory and credits the finished goods inventory in the amount of $14,269.22.

8. *Completed production transferred to finished goods inventory.* This transaction report shows the cost of finished products that have been transferred to the finished goods inventory. Accordingly, journal entry 8 charges the finished goods inventory and credits the floor work-in-process inventory for the total amount of $782,001.14.

9. *Change in work-in-process floor inventory.* One of the difficult problems in accurate reporting of production is correct accountability for spoilage. When spoiled production is understated, inventory values will be overstated, with the result that a phantom inventory will build up on the books. This results in overstatement of profits during the year, followed by a writedown of these profits at year-end when the value of the physical inventory is compared with the book value. With the advent of automatic equipment that spews out parts by the million, many parts fall through open areas around the machines. These are difficult to retrieve economically. At best, such parts can be swept up and placed in scrap barrels for recovery of the scrap value.

In operations in which the material can be remelted—plastics molding and die casting material, for example—production counts are often determined by multiplying the number of cavities in the mold by the number of cycles registered on the counting mechanism. Frequently, because of variations and unevenness in mold temperatures, as well as defects in some of the cavities, many parts counted as good production are thrown back for remelting. These are counted as production again the second time when reused.

The solution to this problem is to recognize production only when the component (part) is accepted into the work-in-process stockroom (fabricated and purchased parts stockroom) or into finished goods stock. This leaves only the floor work-in-process to be accounted for, which is a two-step process:

a. Net out the production transferred into finished goods with the issues of components transferred out of the stockrooms to the production floor.

b. Account for the inventory in the "pipeline" on the factory floor by a constant figure. If the pipeline inventory fluctuates widely, a monthly physical inven-

EXHIBIT 16

CALCULATING THE WORK-IN-PROCESS FLOOR INVENTORY*

7 — COMPONENTS IN FINISHED GOODS STOCK RETURNED TO PRODUCTION

To:	Brass	Non-Brass	Direct Labor	Variable Overhead	Fixed Overhead	Total
01	$ 347.41	119.19	243.64	277.24	413.38	1,400.86
02	16.48	96.01	17.43	15.64	25.46	171.02
04	13.08	1.58	28.39	29.87	46.15	119.07
06		61.99	.50	.35	.68	63.52
07	37.87	.12	1.57	3.41	5.69	48.66
08	.05	.21	.50	.37	.57	1.70
11	315.01	850.44	213.87	215.11	333.43	1,927.86
12	1,637.18	1,887.21	1,504.84	1,419.30	2,173.41	8,621.94
32	21.28	77.66	21.30	20.58	31.88	172.70
41	1.42	1.92	2.27	2.20	3.26	11.07
42	.58	.49	.51	.66	.81	3.05
43	1.12	1.06	.62	.60	.93	4.33
47	269.84	63.51	172.31	186.96	289.44	982.06
Total Costed	2,661.32	2,161.39	2,207.75	2,172.29	3,325.09	13,527.84
Uncosted items	547.84	85.95	40.25	47.92	19.42	741.38
	$ 3,209.16	3,247.34	2,248.00	2,220.21	3,344.51	14,268.22

8 — COMPLETED PRODUCTION TRANSFERRED TO FINISHED GOODS INVENTORY

	Brass	Non-Brass	Direct Labor	Variable Overhead	Fixed Overhead	Total
Total Costed	$214,710.48	123,008.74	108,217.04	121,741.51	181,154.82	748,832.59
Uncosted	7,264.81	5,825.78	5,386.64	5,965.95	8,725.37	33,163.55
	$221,975.29	128,834.52	113,600.68	127,707.46	189,880.19	782,001.14

5 — TRANSFERS FROM FABRICATED AND PURCHASED PARTS INVENTORY TO PRODUCTION

To:	Brass	Non-Brass	Direct Labor	Variable Overhead	Fixed Overhead	Total
01	$ 48,524.50	21,270.43	18,750.18	23,636.47	32,404.98	144,586.56
02	14,120.43	5,520.33	9,464.68	13,374.62	20,628.73	63,108.79
04	2,454.31	15,257.61	1,861.74	2,285.78	3,029.04	24,888.48
05	152,774.51	6,920.74	14,377.23	24,868.29	34,414.69	233,355.46
06	5,803.94	15,186.86	1,737.66	2,538.59	3,463.66	28,730.71
07	25,787.14	495.34	9,930.40	21,765.50	28,195.78	86,174.18
08	189.76	565.40	41.22	50.95	70.46	917.79
11	1,769.73	373.78	1,077.12	1,791.47	1,738.56	6,750.66
12	14,507.04	59,294.59	5,319.20	7,813.14	10,714.46	97,648.43
13	.34		.07	.11	.17	.69
Total Costed	265,931.70	124,885.08	62,559.50	98,124.91	134,660.53	686,161.73
Uncosted items	4,389.27	1,867.91	1,208.45	1,969.62	2,788.12	· 12,223.37
	$ 270,320.97	126,752.99	63,767.95	100,094.54	137,448.65	698,385.10

9 — CHANGE IN WORK-IN-PROCESS FLOOR INVENTORY

	Brass	Non-Brass	Direct Labor	Variable Overhead	Fixed Overhead	Total
Finished Goods Produced:	$221,975.29	128,834.52	113,603.68	127,707.46	189,880.19	782,001.14
From Finished Goods to Production:	3,209.16	3,247.34	2,248.00	2,220.21	3,343.51	14,268.22
From Fabricated Stores to Production:	270,320.97	126,752.99	63,767.95	100,094.54	137,448.65	698,385.10
	(51,554.84)	(1,165.81)	47,587.73	25,392.71	49,088.03	69,347.82

* This exhibit is an excerpt from Exhibit 15

tory of major items must be taken and the work-in-process inventory adjusted. If the adjustment is not made, the difference will be reflected as a variance. The transactions in transaction report 9 assume a constant pipeline inventory.

The transaction reports from which the figures in transaction 9 were taken are shown in Exhibit 16, which shows the interaction of transaction reports 7, 8, and 5 with 9.

10. *Cost of sales.* The cost of sales format was referred to several times earlier in this chapter. Like the others the columnar format showing the elements of cost is the same. The balance of the three variance clearing accounts is closed out into the cost of sales account. Although this is shown in journal entry 11, there is no transaction listing because this entry is the result of posting balances from previously made journal entries.

MANUFACTURING COST SUMMARY

The Manufacturing Cost Summary, shown in Exhibit 17, lists the following data:

- Closing journal entries which were used in Exhibit 15 to reconcile the entries with the transaction reports from which these entries were taken.
- Factory ledger accounts to which the journal entries were posted.
- Abbreviated Income statement.
- Breakdown of variances.

As can be seen from Exhibit 15, the journal entries summarize the 10 transaction reports. The function of the ledger accounts is to recast the journal entries into the various accounts in order to determine the impact of the transactions on these accounts. This facilitates the determination of the month's income statement. Note that the standard cost of sales is subtracted from the sales (not included in this exhibit) and the standard gross profit is determined. When the total variances which had been closed into the cost of sales account are deducted from the standard gross profit, the actual gross profit is reflected. This is shown at the bottom of the left side of the exhibit.

Variance Summary

The variances are usually shown on the income statement in total to facilitate faster closing and earlier determination of the results for the month. However, the variances are broken down further beyond the detail contained in the journal entries. The upper part of the exhibit, on the right side, starts with a broad breakdown which, within material, shows the purchase price and material usage variances separately. Direct labor was broken down to reflect the rate variance and efficiency variance separately. The spending variance for overhead was calculated first and then subtracted from total overhead to arrive at the volume variance.

Breakdown of Variances

The further breakdown was required to pinpoint the figures by responsibility. The purchase price variance, for example, is shown for brass and nonbrass material so

EXHIBIT 17
MANUFACTURING COST SUMMARY

CLOSING JOURNAL ENTRIES

(1)

Material Variance		
Raw Material Inventory	16,352.54	
Fabricated and Purchased Stores (WIP)		16,191.67
		160.87
To record purchase price variance.		

(2)

Material Variance	346,340.81	
Raw Material Inventory		346,340.81
To record issues of raw material to production floor.		

(3)

Fabricated and Purchased Parts Inventory	593,027.52	
Material Variance		301,736.04
Labor Variance		61,073.48
Indirect Labor and Overhead Variance		230,218.00
To record production of fabricated parts transferred into fabricated and purchased parts stores		

(4)

Fabricated and Purchased Parts Inventory	1,956.56	
Finished Goods Inventory		1,956.56
To record transfers of items in finished goods to fabricated and purchased parts stores.		

(5)

Work-in-Process Floor Inventory	698,385.10	
Fabricated and Purchased Parts Inventory		698,385.10
To record issues of fabricated and purchased parts to production floor.		

(6)

No entry this month.

(7)

Work-in-Process Floor Inventory	14,269.22	
Finished Goods Inventory		14,269.22
To record items in finished goods transferred to the production floor.		

(8)

Finished Goods Inventory	782,001.14	
Work-in-Process Floor Inventory		782,001.14
To record production transferred to finished goods.		

(9)

Work-in-Process Floor Inventory	69,347.82	
Material Usage Variance (brass & non-brass)	52,720.65	
Labor Variance		47,587.73
Indirect Labor and Overhead Variance		74,480.74
To record standard cost of production between the fabricated parts level and finished goods level.		

(10)

Cost of Sales	753,596.69	
Finished Goods Inventory		753,596.69
To record shipments during month.		

VARIANCE SUMMARY

MATERIAL VARIANCES

Purchase Price Variance	$(16,192)	
Material Usage Variance	97,326	81,134

DIRECT LABOR

Rate Variance	6,534	
Efficiency Variance	15,437	21,971

OVERHEAD

Spending Variance	12,887	
Volume Variance	(53,627)	(40,740)
		$ 62,365

BREAKDOWN OF VARIANCES

MATERIAL RELATED

Purchase Price		
Brass	$(16,598)	
Non-Brass	406	$(16,192)
Material Usage		
Brass	$ 73,499	
Non-Brass	23,827	
		$ 97,326

DIRECT LABOR RELATED

Rate		6,534
Efficiency		
Automatics	$ 5,162	
General Machinery	(872)	
Plating & Coating	1,242	
Hand Assembly	6,842	
Automatic Assembly	3,063	
		$ 15,437

OVERHEAD RELATED

Volume Variance $(53,627)

Spending

Automatics	
Indirect Labor	$ 1,842
Fringe Benefits	98
O/T Premium	165
Supplies	50
Small Tools	86
	$ 2,241

General Machinery	
Indirect Labor	$ 672
Fringe Benefits	121
O/T Premium	(22)
Supplies	65
Small Tools	41
	$ 877

Plating & Coating	
Indirect Labor	$ (25)
Fringe Benefits	(5)
O/T Premium	–
Supplies	155
Small Tools	5
	$ 130

Hand Assembly	
Indirect Labor	$ 3,065
Fringe Benefits	260
O/T Premium	128
Supplies	87
Small Tools	62
	$ 3,602

Automatic Assembly	
Indirect Labor	214
Fringe Benefits	35
O/T Premium	10
Supplies	12
Small Tools	22
	$ 293

Overall Plant	
Electricity	$ 795
Real Estate Taxes	360
Maintenance Department	4,414
Dues & Subscriptions	175

TOTAL OVERHEAD SPENDING $ 12,887

---

	(11)
Cost of Sales	62,364.67
Indirect Labor and Overhead Variance	40,740.02
Material Variance	81,133.75
Labor Variance	21,970.94
To close out Variance Accounts.	

LEDGER ACCOUNTS

Raw Material Inventory

(1) 16,352.54	(2) 346,340.81

Fabricated and Purchased Parts Inventory

(3) 593,027.52	(1) 160.87
(4) 1,956.56	(5) 698,385.10

Work-in-Process Floor Inventory

(5) 698,385.10	(8) 782,001.14
(7) 14,269.22	
(9) 69,347.82	

Finished Goods Inventory

(8) 782,001.14	(4) 1,956.56
	(7) 14,269.22
	(10) 753,596.69

Material Variance

(2) 346,340.81	(1) 16,191.67
(9) 52,720.65	(3) 301,736.04
	(11) 81,133.75

Labor Variance

Actual Labor 130,632.15	(3) 61,073.48
	(9) 47,587.73
	(11) 21,970.94

Indirect Labor and Overhead Variance

Actual Overhead 263,958.72	(3) 230,218.00
(11) 40,740.02	(9) 74,480.74

Cost of Sales

(10) 753,596.69	
(11) 62,364.67	

ABBREVIATED INCOME STATEMENT

Sales	$1,260,350
Standard Cost of Sales	753,597
Standard Gross Profit	506,753
Variances	62,365
Actual Gross Profit	$ 444,388

that the appropriate buyers would be shown the amount of variance for which they were responsible. In the case of the favorable variance for brass, it was mentioned earlier that this was not necessarily an indication of better buying but rather of establishing excessively high standards.

The material usage variance was also broken down by brass and nonbrass material in order to pinpoint the cause more precisely. Although not shown here, the breakdown of brass by rod, wire, and strip permitted a better determination of the foreman whose cost center caused the excess usage. The same applies to nonbrass material.

Further pinpointing of the direct labor rate variance was considered to be the responsibility of the Industrial Relations Department. An unfavorable rate variance is usually caused by assignment of a higher-rated employee to a lower-rated job.

Labor efficiency variances are identified by the departments in which they were incurred.

Overhead-related variances were broken down as follows:

- Management was considered to be responsible for any volume variances because sales affected the volume of production. In this period, the variance was favorable because the plant operated above normal capacity. It is possible, however, that a fully loaded plant could have an unfavorable variance if a high percentage of production is defective or if the scheduling of production is not properly made. This cannot be determined without further analysis.
- The spending variance for most expenses has been broken down by the cost centers for the expenses considered to be controllable by the foremen. The indirect category includes only the factory foremen and some part-time clerical help. The administrative type of indirect labor such as that of the plant manager, cost accounting, industrial engineering, production control, purchasing, and quality control personnel are included in fixed overhead and are therefore reflected in the volume variance.
- Examples of certain expenses which might be considered to be applicable to the individual cost centers are shown in the overall plant category because they are monitored by the following individuals:

> Chief electrician (electricity)
> Management (real estate taxes)
> Plant engineer (maintenance costs)
> Industrial Relations Department (dues and subscriptions)

The cost of computerizing the cost system is not small, even with the great reductions that have taken place in computer costs and the availability of software. When a company embarks on a program for computerizing the cost accounting system, it should computerize its materials management procedures as well. The reverse is also true. The physical units that are reported in the transaction listings and provide the basis for inventory management should be the same as those that are valued by the cost department in arriving at general ledger inventory values.

As competitive pressures continue to intensify, computerized inventory management and cost accounting will contribute increasingly to the economic survival of American industry. The procedures outlined in this and the preceding chapter provide a framework which should buttress management's needs for more effective controls.

GUIDELINES FOR GETTING THE MOST
FROM YOUR COMPUTERIZED COST SYSTEM

1. When computerizing the cost system, make certain that all three elements of manufacturing cost (material, direct labor, and overhead) are identified individually at each bill of material level. (See column headings in Exhibit 10).
2. If one of the materials represents a predominant portion of material cost, as in the case of brass, show this separately from nonbrass material. Break down the overhead cost between the variable and fixed segments.
3. Segmentation of the elements referred to in guideline 2 facilitates the analysis of cost reduction possibilities in the various products.
4. Make the most of the computerized cost system for such byproduct reports as:
   a. Purchase parts price history (Exhibit 11)
   b. Purchase price variance analysis (Exhibit 12)
   c. Material receipts versus planned receipts (Exhibit 13)
   d. Vendor delivery performance (Exhibit 14)
5. Don't rely on scrap reports to adjust production of parts and subassemblies previously recorded as production at individual work stations (operations). Recognize as input into inventory only the good production accepted into controlled storage areas. (See transaction reports in Exhibit 15.)

See also the following chapter.

9
Integrating Inventory Management with Cost Accounting and Fulfilling Dual Costing Needs

The purpose of this chapter is to call attention to the need for a data base that will satisfy two cost accounting needs. These call for:

1. *Maintaining complete purity of the three elements throughout the manufacturing process.*
2. *Combining the three elements of cost and progressively accumulating them through the entire manufacturing process as material.*

Why these two methods of costing are needed and how they are used is the subject of this chapter.

The two preceding chapters deal with inventory. The first of these is concerned with the flow and control of the physical units; the second pertains to the procedures for valuing the physical units flowing through the various operations.

THE COMPUTER FACILITATES THE "UNO NUMERO" CONCEPT*

Prior to the availability of the computer, it was impractical in many companies to cost the physical units within the manufacturing process. It was therefore necessary to charge all costs to a single inventory pool and relieve this pool by the quantities shipped and by any reported production rejects. Chapter 8 illustrates how the inventory costing can be based on the actual movement of the physical units through the various operations. The computer facilitates the application of the uno numero concept, in which the same physical units tracked by the materials management group are used by the Cost Department for valuation purposes.

VARIATIONS IN THE COSTING PROCESS

Some, possibly most, companies, in developing the data base for costing, accumulate the material, direct labor, and overhead costs incurred in each department and transfer the total as a material cost to the next department. That department, in turn, accumulates all its costs, including the receipts from the prior department, and transfers the total as a material cost to the succeeding department, and so on.

This process is demonstrated in Exhibit 1. Before discussing this exhibit, it might be well to describe the process for making a cathode ray tube (CRT) which is the illustrative example used.

---

* "Uno numero" (one number) refers to the concept of using the same source document rather than obtaining figures from different sources that may not agree.

EXHIBIT 1
MANUFACTURING COST OF CATHODE RAY TUBES TRANSFERRING THE THREE ELEMENTS TO THE NEXT DEPARTMENT AS MATERIAL

	Wash and Coat Bulbs			Assemble, Exhaust, Seal and Base			Test and Pack			Finish and Repack		
	Theo. Cost/M	% Eff.	Std. Cost/M	Theo. Cost/M	% Eff.	Std. Cost/M	Theo. Cost/M	% Eff.	Std. Cost/M	Theo. Cost/M	% Eff.	Std. Cost/M
Material												
Bulbs	$6,500.00	96	6,770.83									
Phospor #43	137.75	60	229.58									
Phospor #75	99.13	60	165.22									
Kasil	12.48	60	20.80									
Acetic Acid	3.28	60	5.47									
Graphite Coating	3.50	90	3.89									
TOTAL	$6,756.14		7,195.79									
Washed and Coated Bulbs				8,106.04	94	8,623.45						
Electron Guns				1,022.56	92	1,111.48						
Basing Material				27.54	90	30.60						
TOTAL				9,156.14		9,765.53						
Based CRTs							11,347.72	74.5	15,231.84			
Salvage Credits									(1,711.35)			
Packing Material							247.25	95.0	260.26			
Miscellaneous Material							53.57	85.6	62.58			
TOTAL							11,648.54		13,843.33			
Finished and Repacked CRTs										15,873.40	100	15,873.40
DIRECT LABOR												
Wash and Coat Bulbs	109.90	46	238.91									
Assemble and Seal In				44.69	60	74.49						
Exhaust				75.72	60	126.20						
Base				56.50	70	80.71						
TOTAL				176.91		281.40						
Test and Pack							57.37	57.2	100.30			
Finish and Repack										11.91	79.6	14.96
OVERHEAD												
Wash and Coat Bulbs			671.34									
Assemble and Seal In						213.79						
Exhaust						957.86						
Base						129.14						
TOTAL						1,300.79						
Test and Pack									1,929.77			
Finish and Repack												53.11
TOTAL STD. MANUFACTURING COST			$8,106.04			11,347.72			15,873.40			15,941.47

The Manufacturing Process

The manufacture of CRTs in this company is done in four steps, which are described below:

1. *Wash and coat bulbs.* Manufacture of a CRT begins with the glass bulb, or "envelope," as it is sometimes called. In this department, the inverted bulbs, fixed to a moving conveyor after the washing operations, are filled with a liquid containing phosphors in suspension. After the phosphors settle on the inside face of the bulb, the fluid is poured out by a tilting action of the conveyor. The bulb is then rinsed carefully in order not to disturb the screen. It is then passed through a baking oven. The next operation in this department consists of coating the inside of the neck and a portion of the flare with a black substance made up of graphite. (Some companies use an aluminizing process rather than a graphite coating.) This acts as a conductor to direct the electrons toward the screen.

   The materials used to make the coated (screened) bulb are the first six items in Exhibit 1 listed under "Material." Note that the first column of material cost figures in the "Theo. Cost/M" column are adjusted by the percent efficiency to provide an allowance for unavoidable losses of material. These percentages are applied to the theoretical cost/M to arrive at the standard cost/M. The total standard cost/M for the material used in the Wash and Coat Bulbs Department is $7,195.79.

   The same principle is applied to the direct labor—for which the efficiency percentage is 46%. Since overhead rates have been based on standard direct labor, the overhead figures show no theoretical cost or percent efficiency in any of the departments. The total standard cost for material, direct labor, and overhead is $8,106.04. This total becomes the material cost in the next department under the material caption "Washed and Coated Bulbs."

2. *Assemble, exhaust, seal in, and base.* The first step in this department is to insert an electron gun (mount) into the neck of the bulb. The glass wafer at the end of the gun is fused to the neck of the bulb by a sealing-in process which consists of playing a gas flame on the neck of the bulb as it rotates. An exhaust operation then removes the air from the inside of the bulb. The exhausting is done through a glass tube that protrudes through the glass wafer beyond the edge of the bulb. Upon completion of this operation, the glass tube is heated and sealed off by fusing. The final step is threading the wires from inside the gun into the pins of the plastic base. The base is then cemented to the end of the neck, and the ends of the pins are soldered to hold the wires and to assure electrical contact.

   The total standard cost of the based CRTs, amounting to $11,347.72 per 1,000, becomes the theoretical cost for the test and pack operation in the Test and Pack Department.

3. *Test and pack.* The based CRTs are tested in this department and packed. The cost of $11,347.72 per 1,000 is adjusted by an efficiency percentage of 74.5 to arrive at a standard cost of $15,231.84 per 1,000. In addition to adding the cost of packing material and other miscellaneous material, a credit of $1,711.35 is deducted. This represents credit received for recovery of bulbs from based tubes which were found to be defective. The total standard cost per 1,000

EXHIBIT 2

MANUFACTURING COST OF CATHODE RAY TUBES MAINTAINING PURITY OF THE THREE COST ELEMENTS IN ALL FOUR DEPARTMENTS

	Wash and Coat Bulbs			Assemble, Exhaust, Seal and Base			Test and Pack			Finish and Repack		
	Theo. Cost/M	% Eff.	Std. Cost/M	Theo. Cost/M	% Eff.	Std. Cost/M	Theo. Cost/M	% Eff.	Std. Cost/M	Theo. Cost/M	% Eff.	Std. Cost/M
MATERIAL												
Bulbs	$6,500.00	96	6,770.83	6,770.83	94	7,203.01	7,203.01	74.5	9,668.47	9,668.47	100	9,668.47
Phosphor #43	137.75	60	229.58	229.58	94	244.23	244.23	74.5	327.83	327.83	100	327.83
Phosphor #75	99.13	60	165.22	165.22	94	175.77	175.77	74.5	235.93	235.93	100	235.93
Kasil	12.48	60	20.80	20.80	94	22.13	22.13	74.5	29.70	29.70	100	29.70
Acetic Acid	3.28	60	5.47	5.47	94	5.82	5.82	74.5	7.81	7.81	100	7.81
Graphite Coating	3.50	90	3.89	3.89	94	4.14	4.14	74.5	5.56	5.56	100	5.56
Electron Guns				1,022.56	92	1,111.48	1,111.48	74.5	1,491.92	1,491.92	100	1,491.92
Basing Material				27.54	90	30.60	30.60	74.5	41.07	41.07	100	41.07
Salvage Credits									(1,711.35)	(1,711.35)	100	(1,711.35)
Packing Material							247.25	95.0	260.26	260.26	100	260.26
Miscellaneous Material							53.57	85.6	62.59	62.59	100	62.59
TOTAL MATERIAL	$6,756.14		7,195.79	8,245.89		8,797.18	9,098.00		10,419.79	10,419.79		10,419.79
DIRECT LABOR												
Wash and Coat Bulbs	$ 109.90	46	238.91	238.91	94	254.16	254.16	74.5	341.15	341.15	100	341.15
Assemble and Seal In				44.69	60	74.49	74.49	74.5	99.99	99.99	100	99.99
Exhaust				75.72	60	126.20	126.20	74.5	169.40	169.40	100	169.40
Base				56.50	70	80.71	80.71	74.5	108.33	108.33	100	108.33
Test and Pack							57.37	57.2	100.30	100.30	100	100.30
Finish and Repack										11.91	79.6	14.96
TOTAL DIRECT LABOR	$ 109.90		238.91	415.82		535.56	592.93		819.17	831.08		834.13
OVERHEAD												
Wash and Coat Bulbs			671.34	671.34	94	714.19	714.19	74.5	958.64	958.64	100	958.64
Assemble and Seal in						213.79	213.79	74.5	286.97	286.97	100	286.97
Exhaust						957.86	957.86	74.5	1,285.72	1,285.72	100	1,285.72
Base						129.14	129.14	74.5	173.34	173.34	100	173.34
Test and Pack									1,929.77	1,929.77	100	1,929.77
Finish and Repack												53.11
TOTAL OVERHEAD			671.34	671.34		2,014.98	2,014.98		4,634.44	4,634.44		4,687.55
TOTAL STD. MANUFACTURING COST			8,106.04			11,347.72			15,873.40			15,941.47

153

tested and packed CRTs amounts to $15,873.40. As in the previous departments, this becomes the theoretical cost per 1,000 in the next department.

4. *Finish and repack.* After the testing and packing operation in the previous department, the CRTs are placed in inventory for a short period of time to assure that they do not develop a leak or other defect. As soon as this "hold" period has expired, the tubes are sprayed on the outside, baked to dry the finish, branded, and repacked.

Note that no losses are allowed in the finished and repacked CRTs. The percent efficiency factor, therefore, is 100%. The labor operation, however, is factored at 79.6% efficiency. This results in a total standard cost of $15,941.47 per 1,000 CRTs.

PROGRESSIVE ACCUMULATION OF COSTS FOR PRODUCT COSTING

Exhibit 1, referred to earlier, illustrates the total costing process through the four steps in the manufacture of CRTs. This exhibit shows the principle of transferring the total of the three cost elements in each department to the succeeding department as a material cost. The progressive accumulation of costs in this manner until a final cost has been determined for the completed product simulates the movement of the physical units.

As an example, the physical unit being transferred to the Assemble, Exhaust, Seal-In, and Base Department is a glass bulb with the screen on the inside face plate and a graphite coating on the inside of the neck. The cost passed on to the next department includes not only the glass bulb but also the coating materials, direct labor, and overhead. If there is breakage in the receiving department, a coated bulb has been lost. The value of the coated bulb is accounted for as a single total cost, not as eight line items made up of six materials, direct labor, and overhead.

In Exhibit 2, the costs are tracked through the same four departments by individual line items. While the total cost incurred in each department is exactly the same in both exhibits, the procedure followed in Exhibit 1 simplifies cost control because it monitors the product received from the preceding department as a whole, rather than by its parts.

MAINTAINING THE PURITY OF THE THREE COST ELEMENTS

Cumulative costing, as illustrated in Exhibit 1, simplifies the valuation of inventories and facilitates the calculation of individual product costs. However, there are other cost accounting applications in which the purity of the three elements of cost must be maintained, as shown in Exhibit 2. Some of these applications are:

1. Cost reduction studies for individual products.
2. Make or buy studies.
3. Marginal costing and pricing.
4. Breakeven analyses.

Note, in the following comparison of the three elements of cost, shown in the two exhibits, how direct labor and overhead for the finished product in Exhibit 1 amount to less than 1%, while material is more than 99%.

Table 1
Cumulative Costing Versus Maintenance of Purity
of the Three Elements

	FROM EXHIBIT 1		FROM EXHIBIT 2	
Material	$15,873.40	99.6%	10,419.79	65.4%
Direct labor	14.96	.1	834.13	5.2
Overhead	53.11	.3	4,687.55	29.4
Total	$15,941.47	100.0%	15,941.47	100.0

Exhibit 2, on the other hand, shows that the "pure" material cost is 65.4% of the total manufacturing cost, while overhead is 29.4% and labor 5.2%. Programming the computer for cost accounting requirements is not an either/or choice. Both methods are required to fulfill the different cost accounting needs.

Cost Reduction Studies for Individual Products

Analysis of cost reduction possibilities requires information regarding the material, direct labor, and overhead content of the products on a noncumulative basis, as illustrated in Exhibit 3. Note that the material content of products 6100, F011, and 7007 is 50% of the selling price or higher. This is in comparison with an average of 43% for all products in the family.

Information such as this could focus on the desirability of simplifying the design of the product or finding substitute material to reduce the cost.

The same applies to direct labor. Note in products 8100 and D166 that the labor as a percentage of the selling price is double the average for all eight products. This suggests the possibility of automating or simplifying the manufacturing process, if feasible.

Make or Buy Studies

In make or buy studies, it is particularly important to determine the estimated amount of overhead absorption that will be lost when the product or component is purchased on the outside. Here again, the breakdown of the three elements of cost must be pure.

Marginal Costing and Pricing

Marginal costing requires the breakdown of overhead by its variable and fixed portions so that the variable overhead can be included in the variable category along with material, direct labor, and any other nonmanufacturing variable costs such as sales commissions.

The total variable costs of the six products shown in Exhibit 4 are subtracted from the sales price of each to determine the balance left to cover the fixed costs and profit. These figures, shown in the upper half of the exhibit, are then divided by the total sales prices to show the percentages. To determine the relative profitability, one need only scan the last line on the exhibit to see that product E is the most profitable because the balance left for fixed costs and profits is the highest (57.5%).

EXHIBIT 3
BREAKDOWN OF PRODUCT PROFITABILITY FOR COST REDUCTION STUDY
(figures in $000)

PERIOD _____

Product Number	Sales $	%	Standard Material $	%	Standard Direct Labor $	%	Standard Variable Mfg. Ovhd. $	%	Total Std. Variable Costs $	%	Marginal Contribution $	%	Standard Fixed Mfg. Overhead $	%	Total Std. Mfg. Cost $	%	Standard Gross Profit $	%
P660	296	100	127	43	21	7	6	2	154	52	142	48	24	8	178	60	118	40
J200	1,380	100	456	33	138	10	55	4	649	47	731	53	207	15	856	62	524	38
2020	1,847	100	813	44	129	7	37	2	979	53	868	47	185	10	1164	63	683	37
6100	499	100	254	51	25	5	10	2	289	58	210	42	40	8	329	66	170	34
F011	1,649	100	824	50	99	6	33	2	956	58	693	42	149	9	1105	67	544	33
7007	867	100	460	53	69	8	26	3	555	64	312	36	104	12	659	76	208	24
8100	1,132	100	408	36	192	17	68	6	668	59	464	41	260	23	928	82	204	18
D166	130	100	42	32	23	18	9	7	74	57	56	43	38	29	112	86	18	14
TOTAL	7,800	100	3384	43	696	9	244	3	4324	55	3476	45	1007	13	5331	68	2469	32

EXHIBIT 4
CONTRIBUTION TO FIXED COST AND PROFIT AFTER VARIABLE COSTS

	Product A	Product B	Product C	Product D	Product E	Product F
Sales Price	$250.00	$300.00	$200.00	$350.00	$400.00	$360.00
Total Variable Cost						
Material	$102.25	$ 89.70	$ 71.00	$129.85	$103.20	$101.88
Direct Labor	3.75	20.70	20.80	37.80	31.60	29.52
Overhead	1.25	6.90	7.00	12.60	10.40	9.72
Other Variable	15.50	18.60	12.40	21.70	24.80	22.32
Total Variable	$122.75	$135.90	$111.20	$201.95	$170.00	$163.44
Balance left for Fixed Costs and Profit	$127.25	$164.10	$ 88.80	$148.05	$230.00	$196.56

VARIABLE MANUFACTURING COSTS AS A PERCENT OF THE SALES PRICE

	Product A	Product B	Product C	Product D	Product E	Product F
Sales price	100.0%	100.0%	100.0%	100.0%	100.0%	100.0%
Total Variable Cost						
Material	40.9%	29.9%	35.5%	37.1%	25.8%	28.3%
Direct Labor	1.5	6.9	10.4	10.8	7.9	8.2
Overhead	.5	2.3	3.5	3.6	2.6	2.7
Other Variable	6.2	6.2	6.2	6.2	6.2	6.2
Total Variable	49.1%	45.3%	55.6%	57.7%	42.5%	45.4%
Balance left for Fixed Costs and profit	50.9%	54.7%	44.4%	42.3%	57.5%	54.6%

Product D is the least profitable because the contribution to fixed costs and profits is the lowest (42.3%).

To make such an analysis, it is necessary to use pure rather than cumulative figures. If the latter had been used, the overhead costs would be intermingled with material and direct labor, rendering it impossible to make any meaningful analysis of the type shown in Exhibit 4.

Breakeven Analysis

The costs used in developing a breakeven analysis, as in marginal costing and pricing, must break out overhead into its variable and fixed components. Here, again, the costs must be pure rather than cumulative.

SHOWING THE COST BOTH WAYS

Some companies like to know their product costs both ways—cumulative and pure. This is illustrated for the manufacture of plastic cosmetic cases in Exhibit 5.

Calculating the Cost Elements on a Cumulative Basis

The total cost column shows the aggregate of material, labor, and overhead (burden) costs. The total cost of the molded tops, $7.60 per 1,000, is adjusted by a 4% waste factor when used in the Assembly Department. This brings the cost up to $7.90

EXHIBIT 5
PRODUCT: PLASTIC COSMETIC CASES

STANDARD PRODUCT COST SHEET

EFFECTIVE JAN. 1, XX

Quantity - 1000
(500 per case)

Materials or Operation Description	Code Number	Quantity Specified	% Waste	Standard	Unit of Measure	Material Rate	Material Cost	Labor Rate	Labor Cost	Burden Rate	Burden Cost	Total Cost
TOP												
Plastic	771	20.0	5	21.0000	lb.	.134	2.81					2.81
Molding	38			.3768	hr.					12.70	4.79	4.79
							2.81				4.79	7.60
BOTTOM												
Plastic	771	21.0	5	22.0500	lb.	.134	2.95					2.95
Molding	38			.4072	hr.					12.70	5.17	5.17
							2.95				5.17	8.12
ISSUE TO ASSEMBLY FLOOR												
Molded Plastic Top	151	1,000	4	1,040	M	7.600	7.90*					7.90 *
Molded Plastic Bottom	152	1,000	4	1,040	M	8.120	8.44#					8.44 #
Carton (holds 500)	6	2	5	2.1000	Ea.	.268	.56					.56
Bag	18	50	5	52.5000	Ea.	.031	1.63					1.63
Crate	6	2	5	2.1000	Ea.	.162	.34					.34
Assemble & Pack	64			1.0000	Hr.			2.58	2.58	6.32	6.32	8.90
							18.87		2.58		6.32	27.77
TRANSFER VALUE TO FINISHED GOODS	2131	1,000	1	1,010	M	27.77	28.06					28.06
							28.06					28.06
TOTAL COST BY ELEMENT							8.61		2.61		16.84	28.06

	$ PER CASE	%
SALES PRICE	17.35	100.0
STANDARD COST	14.03	80.8
GROSS PROFIT	3.32	19.2

* Molded top $7.60 + 4% waste = $7.90
# Molded bottom $8.12 + 4% waste = $8.44

per 1,000. Likewise, the $8.12 cost per 1,000 for the plastic bottoms is adjusted by the 4% waste factor in assembly, bringing the cost up to $8.44 per 1,000.

The adjusted costs of the tops and bottoms, plus the costs incurred in the Assembly Department, amount to $27.77 per 1,000. This cost is then adjusted for a 1% waste allowance in finished goods, which brings the total product cost to $28.06 per 1,000.

Calculating the Cost Elements on a Pure Basis

The pure costs of the three elements are shown on the last line of the Standard Product Cost Sheet. Note that the three elements, material at $8.61 plus labor at $2.61 and overhead at $16.84, add up to $28.06. For illustrative purposes, the material costs on a pure basis are listed below to show how the cost of $8.61 per 1,000 was arrived at.

Material	Cost per 1,000
Plastic for tops	$2.81
Plastic for bottoms	2.95
	5.76
4% waste allowance in assembly	.23
Total plastic	5.99
Cartons, bags, and crates	2.53
	8.52
1% waste in finished goods inventory	.09
Total immaterial cost	$8.61

The same procedure would be followed for direct labor and overhead to arrive at the pure costs of these other two elements. Note that there is no labor cost shown in the molding operation. The reason is that machine hour rates are used for the molding presses. The labor is included in the machine hour rate, which is the figure shown in the overhead (burden) column.

FULFILLING USER NEEDS

As computer technology has advanced, data processing managers have become more conscious of the need to place a high priority on user needs. They have become aware, for example, that when inventory management procedures are computerized, a data base must be provided to cost the physical units as they move through the plant.

The cost manager, when providing the cost data, will usually fully approve the cumulative concept of costing as illustrated earlier in Exhibit 1—and rightly so.† However, many cost accountants fail to realize that the data base must also be programmed to provide costs that maintain the purity of the three elements of cost. This is mandatory when cost reduction and make or buy studies are required for products and components. Purity of the cost elements is also required for marginal costing and breakeven analysis.

---

† Note in the case example in the preceding chapter, that the company chose to carry the three elements of cost through the various processes on a pure, rather than a cumulative basis.

GUIDELINES TO ASSURE THAT USER NEEDS ARE FULFILLED

Systems analysts are frequently blamed for computerized systems that do not satisfy user needs. In many such cases, the user is just as much to blame. The following guidelines should be helpful in assuring that the system will fulfill expectations:

1. The cost manager must adequately assess his costing needs. Systems analysts are not skilled cost accountants; they cannot satisfy costing needs without a cooperative and fully organized effort on the part of the user.
2. The cost accountant must explain all procedures, reports, and analyses so that the systems analyst obtains an understandable picture of what is required.
3. When the programming has been completed, the manual and computerized systems must be run concurrently for a test period of a month or two.

These guidelines are not limited to cost accounting alone. They apply to other disciplines with equal force.

10
Inventory Valuation In An Inflationary Economy

The increase in the rate of inflation varies according to the state of the economy. The consensus of the business community is that our nation's massive budget deficit portends a long-term upward trend in inflation—a circumstance that mandates the use of LIFO for many companies to prevent an overstatement of profits.

This chapter discusses the advantages and disadvantages of LIFO, points to consider before adopting it, and various costing methods. Although simplified examples are used to illustrate the calculations, actual figures of several companies on LIFO are also included.

Inflation is a condition of generally rising prices in which the increases are more extensive than the decreases. Deflation, a period of falling prices, was quite prevalent during the 1920s and 1930s. Most of the 1950s and 1960s were fairly stable. However, the rate of inflation began to rise in the mid-1960s and continued to do so until the early 1980s when another period of stability was reached. If our past economic history is any guide, inflation will once again resume its long-term upward trend.

Although selling prices took inflation into account, many companies using first-in, first-out (FIFO) and weighted average methods of valuing inventories did not reflect the impact of inflation on the values assigned to the cost of sales. The result was overstated profits. As inflation rose higher and higher, the realization that financial statements were becoming more and more distorted prompted more serious consideration of other methods of inventory valuation. The logical candidate was the last-in, first-out (LIFO) method.

WHAT IS LIFO?

LIFO is a method of inventory valuation which assumes that the cost most recently incurred in the purchase or production of goods is the cost of items sold during the period. By charging current costs to operations, LIFO assumes that inventory on hand at the end of the period is made up of the oldest costs incurred to build inventory to its current level. This cost flow assumption contrasts to the assumption of the other frequently used valuation methods—FIFO and the weighted average (a modification of FIFO). The FIFO method assumes that the cost of items sold in a period is made up of the oldest costs in inventory just prior to sale. By charging the oldest costs in inventory to operations, FIFO assumes that inventory at the end of the period consists of the most recent costs incurred.

As a practical matter, FIFO more closely depicts the physical movement of goods than LIFO. Companies generally use the oldest items in inventory first so that they can continually roll the stock and prevent deterioration or obsolescence. In times of stable prices, FIFO has been widely used without the distortions created by inflation. However, in periods of continuous inflation, FIFO tends to result in "inventory profits" that result merely from holding inventory. The financial executive of one such comapny whose employees were on strike during a period when inflation rose to 13%, commented at a management meeting: "Our plant has been down for two months now and we made a $25,000 profit on our inventory."

Better Matching of Costs and Revenues

To illustrate the differences between LIFO and FIFO methods, assume that a company starts a business in which it buys and sells a single product (product A). The company begins operations with $13,000 in cash. At the beginning of the initial year of operations, the company purchases three units of product A at $4,000 per unit and establishes a sales price of $6,000 for each unit. During the year, the company sells the three units for a total of $18,000. As the company sells product A, it must replenish that inventory to remain in business. Because of high rates of inflation, the cost has increased to $4,400, or $13,200 for the three units purchased.

Now the company must decide whether to use the FIFO or LIFO method to price its ending inventory. From the standpoint of its inventory position, the company began operations with three units of product A and still has three units. In the absence of additional capital or borrowing, the company must provide sufficient cash from selling the product to replenish its inventory, meet other operating expenses, and generate an adequate return for its investors. Because the cost of product A continues to increase dramatically, the selection of an inventory valuation method becomes very important. What is reported in the financial statements depends largely on the inventory values.

If the company elects to use the FIFO method, the cost of each unit of product A that was sold will be assumed to be $4,000 (oldest cost). On the other hand, if LIFO is adopted, the cost would be $4,400 per unit. The effect of each on the income statement is shown below:

	FIFO	LIFO
Sales	$18,000	$18,000
Cost of sales	12,000	13,200
Gross profit	6,000	4,800
Operating expenses	3,000	3,000
Income before taxes	3,000	1,800
Taxes at assumed rate of 50%	1,500	900
Net income	$ 1,500	$ 900

The gross profit difference of $1,200 (increased cost of new units, $400 × three units) constitutes the inventory profits which result when FIFO is used to value ending inventory. Because the company must replenish its inventory at a higher cost, the $1,200 of inventory profits under FIFO is not available for distribution to shareholders. Under LIFO, current costs are matched against sales, and therefore inventory profits are not reported.

The cash flow effect (income tax savings) of using LIFO as opposed to FIFO is:

	FIFO	LIFO
Cash from sales of Product A	$18,000	$18,000
Cost of replenishing inventory	(13,200)	(13,200)
Operating Expenses	(3,000)	(3,000)
Income Taxes	(1,500)	(900)
	$ 300	$ 900

LIFO results in greater cash flow because of reduced income taxes. Lower taxes free up cash for operations and reduce the need to borrow and to incur financing charges.

Effect on the Balance Sheet

Companies need certain levels of inventory to remain in business. Under the LIFO concept, those levels are carried on the balance sheet at their original LIFO cost until they are decreased. Any increases are added at the current cost in the year of acquisition. In our example, the ending inventory would be priced at $12,000 (three units at $4,000 each) even though the current cost of the units is $13,200 ($4,400 each). In future years, as long as the inventory level remains above three units, the first three units of product A in the closing inventory would continue to be carried at $4,000 each. Increases in the level of the closing inventory above the three units (called a "layer," or increment) would be priced using current costs in the year the inventory level increases. If, in the second year, the company in the above example increased its inventory to four units, it would carry the first three at $4,000 each and the fourth unit (the current year's increment) at the current cost of, say, $5,000. The first four units in future years' inventories would continue to be carried at $17,000 until the closing inventory of any year falls below four units.

After LIFO has been used for a few years, the inventory amount on the balance sheet will undoubtedly become unrealistically low compared to the current cost of inventory. However, companies registered with the Securities and Exchange Commission (SEC) are required—and generally all others follow suit—to disclose the current cost of their inventories and the LIFO adjustment. Other disclosures also are permitted to report the impact of LIFO accounting. The ability to make such disclosures should reduce some companies' concerns about adopting LIFO.

Advantages of LIFO

Reginald H. Jones, former chairman of the General Electric Company, and William J. Brons, a Harvard Business School professor, were both strong proponents of LIFO. The advantages cited by them and by others are as follows:

1. It eliminates inventory profits through better matching of costs and revenues.
2. It reduces taxes and increases cash flow. A method of estimating the amount of tax reduction and the increase in cash flow is as follows: multiply the cost of the beginning inventory by the inflation rate and then by the marginal tax rate. The product of these is the estimated tax savings and increased cash flow. Applying figures to the above, the assumed inventory of $10,000,000 multiplied by the assumed inflation rate of 10% is $1,000,000. Then multiplying the $1,000,000 by the 46% tax rate will show a total tax saving of $460,000.
3. The lower values assigned to inventories in the balance sheet may result in lower personal property taxes if local authorities permit the use of LIFO for this purpose.
4. Lower net income may also reduce expenses based on reported income, such as profit sharing and bonus plans.
5. Companies subject to FASB Statement 33 and using LIFO to determine the cost of sales generally do not need to calculate supplemental cost of sales amounts, as the LIFO amounts approximate inflation-adjusted results.

Disadvantages of LIFO

While the advantages of LIFO can be significant, companies should consider the following potential disadvantages before adopting it:

1. After LIFO has been used for several years, inventory amounts in the balance sheet may be much lower than current inventory costs. Although companies usually disclose the current cost of inventories in their balance sheets, the low value reported could affect compliance with debt covenants.
2. Matching current costs with current revenues is an advantage in financial reporting only when inventory levels are increasing. If inventory levels are reduced (e.g., due to a strike or material shortages), older LIFO costs are matched with current revenues and reported income becomes inflated. Assume, for example, that the company in the earlier example is in its fourth year of operation and that product A currently costs $6,000 and is selling for $10,000. Because of a lack of available supply, the inventory of product A is reduced to two units at the end of the year. For this reason, one of the older units carried in inventory at a cost of $4,000 is charged to the cost of sales. This results in an unrealistic gross profit of $6,000 on the sale for both tax and financial reporting purposes.
3. LIFO is advantageous only if costs are increasing. If current costs have declined, LIFO costs might exceed the market value.
4. Under Internal Revenue Service (IRS) regulations, the opening inventory in the year LIFO is adopted must be stated at actual cost (e.g., FIFO cost) rather than the lower of cost or market. Thus, any market writedowns that had been deducted previously must be restored and therefore included in taxable income. If a company has market valuation reserves at the beginning of the taxable year in which it adopts LIFO, it must include such reserves in taxable income over a three-year period, beginning with the year of adoption of LIFO.
5. To prepare interim financial statements, companies must estimate the amount of year-end inventories.
6. LIFO is more complex than other inventory valuation methods and has been governed largely by IRS rules and regulations. As a result, LIFO may result in higher recordkeeping costs and require more management attention and planning.

Points to consider before adopting LIFO

Because of the complexity of the issues involved and the importance of adopting LIFO in the most beneficial manner, companies should thoroughly analyze their situation before adopting LIFO. Among the factors that should be considered are the following:

1. Is the existing cost accounting system capable of developing the needed LIFO data, or will modifications be required?
2. What is the most feasible method of adopting LIFO? How many pools should be used? Should the specific goods or the dollar-value method be used? What technique should be used to compute the dollar value?
3. Are existing personnel capable of performing the necessary procedures? If not, should they receive formal training?
4. Should the company adopt LIFO for its entire inventory or only a portion (e.g., should it be adopted for the material content of inventory, but not for

labor and overhead)? Should only a part of the material content be included?

5. Should a different LIFO method be used for financial reporting purposes than for tax purposes?
6. Should the company consider restructuring its operations (i.e., should it form new subsidiaries) and have its subsidiaries adopt LIFO for tax purposes but use FIFO in consolidation, thus taking advantage of the *Insilco decision?

APPLICATION TO USE THE LIFO INVENTORY METHOD

To adopt LIFO, a company must file IRS Form 970 with its tax return for the year of change. Upon adopting LIFO, it must restore to taxable income the market valuation reserves deducted in prior years. The Economic Recovery Tax Act of 1981 lessened the impact of restoring valuation reserves. Beginning with calendar 1982 tax returns, restoration is made ratably over a three-year period, starting with the year LIFO is adopted.

For financial reporting purposes, the adoption of LIFO is usually a change in accounting principles. Accounting Principles Board Opinion 20 requires disclosure, in the year of change, of the justification for the change and its effect on reported results. For publicly held companies, the SEC requires a preferability letter from the company's independent auditors.

Unlike most changes in income tax accounting methods, LIFO may be adopted without obtaining prior approval from the IRS. An election can be made at any time up to the due date (including extensions) of a company's federal income tax return simply by attaching a completed Form 970 (see below) to the return for the year of change. From a practical standpoint, however, the decision to change should be made at an earlier date.

Although the IRS cannot deny a taxpayer the right to use LIFO, it does approve the manner in which LIFO is applied and the extent to which it is used. It does this when it examines the company's return. Further, once a company has adopted LIFO, it usually cannot change its method of determining LIFO or switch to another inventory method without the prior approval of the IRS. Thus, it is very important for a company to take care not only in making the decision to adopt LIFO but also in deciding how to first apply it.

Form 970, "Application to Use LIFO Inventory Method," requires the inclusion of the following information:

1. The specific inventory to which the LIFO method is to be applied. A company may limit its LIFO election to any group of items. This phase of the LIFO election is extremely important. LIFO inventories should be described in a manner that provides for flexibility in the event of unpredictable future changes in product mix or processing components. The company should identify specific products only if it wants to limit its election to those products.
2. An agreement to make such adjustments as required by the District Director of Internal Revenue upon examination of the return.
3. Nature of the company's business.
4. The previous method of inventory valuation and a statement that actual costs will be used in the future regardless of market valuation.

---

* The Tax Court held, contrary to a 1970 IRS published ruling, that it was not a violation of the conformity requirements for a parent to issue non-LIFO consolidated financial statements reflecting the operating results of subsidiaries, even though LIFO was used for tax purposes.

Form **970** (Rev. November 1981) Department of the Treasury Internal Revenue Service	## Application to Use LIFO Inventory Method ▶ Attach to your tax return. ▶ For Paperwork Reduction Act Notice, see instructions on back.	OMB No. 1545–0042 Expires 11–30–84

Name ABC COMPANY	Identifying number *(See instructions)* E.I.N. 12-3456780
Address *(Number, street, city, State and ZIP code)* 163 MILL ROAD CLEVELAND, OHIO 44115	CHECK ONE: [X] Initial Election [ ] Subsequent Election

Statement of Election and Other Information:

A. I apply to adopt and use the LIFO inventory method provided by section 472. I will use this method for the first time (or modify this method) as of (date tax year ends) DEC. 31, 19X3...., for the following goods (give details as explained in instructions; use more sheets if necessary): THE TOTAL INVESTMENT IN INVENTORIES INCLUDING ALL MATERIALS, DIRECT LABOR AND MANUFACTURING OVERHEAD.

B. I agree to make any adjustments that the District Director of Internal Revenue may require, on examination of my return, to reflect income clearly for the years involved in changing to or from the LIFO method or in using it.

1. Nature of business A. MANUFACTURE OF STEEL. B. SALE OF STOCK STEEL BUILDING SUPPLIES. C. FABRICATION OF COPPER PER CUSTOMER DESIGN.

2. (a) Inventory method used until now LOWER OF COST OR MARKET (FIRST-IN, FIRST-OUT)

(b) Will inventory be taken at actual cost regardless of market value? If "No," attach explanation. . . . . [X] Yes [ ] No

3. (a) Was the closing inventory of the specified goods valued at cost as of the end of the immediately preceding tax year, as required by section 472(d)? If "No," attach explanation . . . . [ ] Yes [X] No

(b) Did you file an amended return to include in the prior year's income any adjustments that resulted from changing to LIFO? [ ] Yes [X] No See Rev. Proc. 76–6, 1976–1, C.B. 545. If "No," attach explanation.

4. (a) List goods subject to inventory that are not to be inventoried under the LIFO method

SUPPLIES

(b) Were the goods of the specified type included in opening inventory counted as acquired at the same time and at a unit cost equal to the actual cost of the total divided by the number of units on hand? If "No," attach explanation . . . . . [X] Yes [ ] No

5. (a) Did you issue credit statements, or reports to shareholders, partners, other proprietors, or beneficiaries, covering the first tax year to which this application refers? . . . . [X] Yes [ ] No

(b) If "Yes," state to whom, and on what dates TO THE SHAREHOLDERS, MARCH 12, 19X4

(c) Show the inventory method used in determining income, profit, or loss in those statements THE DOLLAR-VALUE LIFO METHOD.

6. Method used to determine the cost of the goods in the closing inventory over those in the opening inventory. *(See Regulations section 1.472–2.)* [ ] Most recent purchases [X] Earliest acquisitions during the year [ ] Average cost of purchases during the year [ ] Other—Attach explanation

7. Method used in valuing LIFO inventories [ ] Unit method [X] Dollar-value method

8. (a) If you use pools, list and describe contents of each pool THREE SEPARATE POOLS ARE USED FOR THE THREE DISTINCTLY DIFFERENT TYPES OF BUSINESS ACTIVITIES (NATURAL BUSINESS UNITS) OF THE COMPANY. SEE THE ATTACHED SCHEDULE FOR FURTHER DESCRIPTION.

(b) Describe briefly the cost system used SEE ATTACHED STATEMENT.

(c) Method used in computing LIFO value of dollar-value pools [ ] Double extension method [X] Other method *(If other, describe and justify—see instructions.)*

9. Did you change your method of valuing inventories for this tax year with the Commissioner's permission? If "Yes," attach a copy of the National Office's "grant letter" to this Form 970 . . . . [ ] Yes [X] No

10. Were you ever on LIFO before? If "Yes," attach a statement to list the tax years you used LIFO and to explain why you discontinued it . . . . [ ] Yes [X] No

Under penalties of perjury, I declare that I have examined this application, including any accompanying schedules and statements, and to the best of my knowledge and belief it is true, correct, and complete.

------------- Date	------------------------------ Signature of taxpayer	
------------- Date	------------------------------ Signature of officer	------------------------ Title

Example—Form 970

Instructions

(References are to the Internal Revenue Code.)

GENERAL INSTRUCTIONS

Paperwork Reduction Act Notice.—The Paperwork Reduction Act of 1980 says we must tell you why we are collecting this information, how we will use it, and whether you have to give it to us. We ask for the information to carry out the Internal Revenue laws of the United States. We need it to ensure that you are complying with these laws and to allow us to figure and collect the right amount of tax. You are required to give us this information.

Purpose.—Form 970 is an optional form that you can file with your income tax return to adopt or expand the LIFO inventory method described in section 472. If you prefer, you can file a statement that gives the information asked for on Form 970. (See Regulations section 1.472–3(a).) File the application with your return for the first tax year for which you intend to use or expand the LIFO method.

Change from LIFO method.—Once you adopt the LIFO method, it is irrevocable. You must use it in all later years unless the Commissioner allows you to change to another method.

Note: Effective for tax years beginning after December 31, 1981, the Economic Recovery Tax Act of 1981 (Act) added the following new tax law:

1. **Section 472(d)**—Three-year averaging permitted for increase in inventory value.

2. **Section 474**—Election by certain small businesses to use one inventory pool.

The Act also added section 472(f) that authorizes IRS to issue regulations permitting the simplification of LIFO by use of Government Indexes. The regulations will specify the effective date for using the indexes.

SPECIFIC INSTRUCTIONS

Identifying number.—An individual's identifying number is the social security number. For all others it is the employer identification number.

Initial Election or Subsequent Election.—If this is your first election to use the LIFO inventory method, check the box for Initial Election. If you are expanding a prior LIFO election, check the box for Subsequent Election.

Statement of Election and Other Information.—If this is an initial election, enter the tax year you will first use the LIFO method and specify the goods to which you will apply it. If this is a subsequent election, enter the tax year you will expand the LIFO method and specify the goods to which the LIFO method is being expanded.

Attach a detailed analysis of all your inventories as of the beginning and end of the first tax year for which you will use the LIFO method (tax year for which the LIFO method is being expanded if this is a subsequent election) and as of the beginning of the preceding tax year. Also, include the ending inventory reported on your return for the preceding tax year. Regulations sections 1.472–2 and 1.472–3 give more information about preparing this analysis.

Item 8.—Dollar-value method.—You may use the "dollar-value" LIFO method to determine the cost of your LIFO inventories, as long as you use it consistently and it clearly reflects income. Regulations section 1.472–8 gives details about this method.

If you are a manufacturer or processor who establishes dollar-value LIFO pools, you may use natural business unit pools, multiple pools, or raw materials content pools. See Regulations section 1.472–8(b).

If you are a wholesaler, retailer, jobber, or distributor, see Regulations section 1.472–8(c) for guidelines on establishing dollar-value LIFO pools.

To figure the LIFO value of a dollar-value pool, use a method described in Regulations section 1.472–8(e). If you do not use the "double-extension" or "index" method, attach a detailed statement to explain the method you do use and how it is justified under Regulations section 1.472–8(e)(1). For example, if you use a "link-chain" method, your statement should explain why the nature of the pool makes the other two methods impractical or unsuitable.

Signature.—Form 970 must be signed. If you are filing for a corporation, the form must be signed by the president, vice president, treasurer, assistant treasurer, chief accounting officer, or other corporate officer (such as tax officer) authorized to sign.

Example—Form 970

ABC Company
E.I.N. 12-3456780

Supplementary Schedule
Form 970—Application to Use LIFO Inventory Method

Question 3(a) and (b). Adjustments from Changing to LIFO

Because this election to adopt LIFO is made for a taxable year beginning after January 1, 1982 an amended return is not required to be filed. Pursuant to the new section 472(d) added by the Economic Recovery Tax Act of 1981, the market restoration adjustment will be taken into taxable income over a three-year period beginning with the taxable year ending December 31, 19X3.

Question 8(a). List and Description of Contents of Each Pool

Pool number—1

A natural business unit pool including the total inventory investment consisting of material, direct labor and manufacturing overhead associated with manufacturing steel reinforcing bars. An analysis of this pool follows:

	Years Ended December 31		
	19X1	*19X2*	*19X3*
Raw materials	$1,790,730	$1,601,666	$2,032,933
Finished goods	3,991,165	4,518,163	4,031,004
Work-in-process	979,097	824,062	860,453
Finished goods accessories	213,582	348,265	402,972
	$6,974,574	$7,292,156	7,327,362
Less adjustment to last-in, first-out method of cost determination			1,484,439
			$5,842,923

Pool number—2

A natural business unit that contains various stock steel items.

	Years Ended December 31		
	19X1	*19X2*	*19X3*
Stock steel	$3,964,915	$2,970,154	$7,817,614
Less adjustment to last-in, first-out method of cost determination			413,995
			$7,403,619

Example—Form 970

ABC Company
E.I.N. 12-3456780

Question 8(a). List and Description of Contents of Each Pool (continued)

Pool number—3

This pool consists of purchased copper which is fabricated according to customers'
design. An analysis of this pool follows:

	Years Ended December 31		
	19X1	*19X2*	*19X3*
Material	$2,009,239	$1,359,687	$1,689,621
Direct Labor	115,284	84,325	93,393
Production overhead	187,145	139,896	141,626
Drafting labor	78,083	81,255	113,858
Drafting overhead	59,119	69,066	92,031
Other materials	35,951	63,211	83,042
	$2,484,821	$1,797,440	2,213,571
Less adjustment to last-in, first-out method of cost determination			60,231
			$2,153,340

Question 8(b). Manner in Which Costs Are Computed

Pool number—1

Raw materials:

　　Purchased materials are priced on the basis of a three-month moving average of
　　invoiced costs, including freight cost.

Work-in-Process and Finished Goods:

　　A process cost system is used for manufactured materials. All elements of cost,
　　including material, labor and manufacturing overhead, are included in inventory
　　valuation. The Company's cost system is a full-absorption cost system.

Both labor and manufacturing overhead are charged on a rate per ton of processed
steel.

Pool number—2

Stock steel is priced on earliest acquisitions during the year based upon invoiced
costs, including freight.

Example—Form 970

ABC Company
E.I.N. 12-3456780

Question 8(b). Manner in Which Costs Are Computed (continued)

Pool number—3

Purchased copper is priced on the basis of invoiced costs, including freight, for earliest acquisitions during the year. A job order cost system is used. Materials are charged to the job order at invoice cost plus freight. Direct labor is charged to the job order (actual time on the job by each employee). Manufacturing overhead (including production overhead, drafting labor, drafting overhead and other materials) is charged to the job order as a percentage of direct labor costs.

Question 8(c). Method Used in Computing LIFO Value of Dollar-Value Pools

Pool number—1

The link-chain method has been used by the Company in computing the LIFO value of this dollar-value pool. The Company double-extended each element of cost (i.e., materials, direct labor, and manufacturing overhead) by current-year unit costs and by unit costs used in pricing the closing inventory of such items in the preceding year. The respective extensions of the two costs were then totaled, and the totals were used to compute a yearly index for the current year. After the first year, the Company will multiply the yearly index by the cumulative index at the beginning of such year to determine the percentage of current-year cost to base-year cost.

The Company believes that the LIFO values of its inventory determined in this manner will be more accurate than it would be computed under alternative methods. The trend of production method and technological changes in this particular industry is such that the Company believes it will become increasingly difficult in future years to determine base-year costs of new or changed processing methods. The consistent use of the link-chain method adopted by the Company will obviate estimates and other imprecise procedures inherent in other methods of establishing base-year costs as new processes evolve.

Pool number—2

A link-chain method has been used by the Company in computing the LIFO values of this dollar-value pool. A statistical sampling method was used to select a representative portion of the items in the inventory. This selected sample of items was then used to determine the cost index and volume increase by use of the combined ratio method of statistical evaluation. The precision limits used to determine the sample size were based on the guidelines specified in Revenue Procedure 64-4 concerning the use of the installment method by retailers for revolving credit sales. (These precision limits were achieved in the Company's sample.)

Example—Form 970

ABC Company
E.I.N. 12-3456780

Question 8(c). Method Used in Computing LIFO Value of Dollar-Value Pools (continued)

Because of the large number of items in this business unit's pool and since new items of inventory are regularly entering this pool, the Company believes a link-chain index approach is the only appropriate and practical method to use. As tax years become further removed from the base year, much of the accruacy in developing current to base-year indexes that is available in the link-chain method would be lost in the use of any other method. One reason for this is that established price levels of new inventory items can be achieved with greater objectivity by establishing price levels one year back than by attempting to establish by reconstruction what price levels for a particular new item would have been in some remote base year.

Pool number—3

The link-chain method has been used by the Company in computing the LIFO value of this dollar value pool. The company double extended the direct labor, manufacturing overhead and a representative portion of the materials inventory in the pool by current-year unit costs and by unit costs used in pricing the closing inventory of such items in the preceding year. The respective extensions of the two costs were then totaled, and the totals were used to compute a yearly index for the current year. For subsequent years, the Company will multiply the yearly index by the cumulative index at the beginning of such year to determine the percentage of current-year cost to base-year cost.

The Company believes the link-chain index method of determining the LIFO value of this pool will be more accurate than any alternative method. Materials constitute approximately 70% of the cost content of this pool; and, since the activities of this business unit consist of custom-fabricating copper into various products per customer specifications, its inventory from year to year is susceptible to change, particularly in material specifications, including grades, mix and architectural design. As time goes by, it would become increasingly difficult to establish base-year costs of different materials in this business unit's inventory. Under these conditions, it is believed either the double-extension or other index methods would be impractical and would lose much of the accuracy available in the link-chain index method.

5. Whether the specified inventory on hand at the end of the immediately preceding taxable year was valued at cost as required, and whether an amended return will be filed. (For taxable years beginning in 1982, the taxpayer is required to take this adjustment to taxable income ratably over a three-year period beginning with the year of change.) Also, the company must state whether the opening inventory of the year of adoption was valued at average cost.
6. Any inventory that will not be valued by the LIFO method.
7. Whether financial reports covering the year of adoption were issued. If so, indicate to whom and on what dates, and the inventory method used.
8. The method used to determine the LIFO cost of the current year's increase in inventory (i.e., earliest, latest, average acquisition cost, or another appropriate method).
9. The method of valuing LIFO inventories (i.e., specific goods method or dollar-value method).
10. The pools (the term used to describe the method of accumulating or grouping similar inventory items) used, including a description of each pool (see the example on Form 970)
11. A description of the cost system used (see the example on Form 970).
12. If the dollar-value LIFO method is used, the technique of computing the LIFO value of the dollar-value pools (i.e., double-extension, index, or link chain). If an index or link-chain technique is used, the instructions call for a statement accompanying Form 970 describing the technique selected and justifying its use. Also, the IRS regulations require the taxpayer to file a copy of this statement with the Commissioner of Internal Revenue in Washington, D.C.
13. Whether the company made another change in its method of valuing inventories for this tax year with IRS permission.
14. Whether the company has used LIFO before.
15. An analysis of the inventories at the beginning and end of the year in which LIFO is elected and at the beginning of the preceding year. This analysis should be attached to Form 970.

Because the elections made upon adopting LIFO will affect the company for years to come, and because it may be difficult and costly to obtain future IRS approval for a change in method, the elections should be given careful consideration. The best advice is to obtain expert assistance in completing Form 970.

LIFO COSTING METHODS

Specific Goods Method

The specific goods method is generally considered the easiest LIFO costing method to understand. Under this method, each item or group of very similar items is, in effect, treated as a separate inventory pool. Inventory quantities are measured in terms of physical units such as:

- Tons of steel
- Pounds of cotton
- Barrels of oil
- Tons of coal

All units in the opening inventory are considered to have been purchased at the average price. After restoring writedowns, a company obtains the opening inventory cost of each item by dividing the total inventory cost by the number of units. To the extent that the number of units has increased during the year, there is a current year's increment. This is priced using the approach the company designated on Form 970.

Applying the Specific Goods Method

Exhibit 1 illustrates the calculation of LIFO using the specific goods method and compares the results to those obtained using FIFO. The ABC Company has adopted LIFO as of the beginning of the current year. The company purchases, processes, and sells cotton and has elected to use the specific goods method of LIFO for the raw material content (cotton) of its inventory. The following is a comparison of the results using the LIFO and FIFO methods:

EXHIBIT 1
APPLYING THE SPECIFIC GOODS METHOD

	LIFO	FIFO
Year 1		
Beginning inventory	$ 700,000	700,000
1,000,000 pounds @ $0.70		
Purchases		
3,000,000 pounds @ $0.80	2,400,000	2,400,000
Inventory available: 4,000,000 pounds	$3,100,000	3,100,000
Sales		
2,500,000 pounds @ $1.20	$3,000,000	3,000,000
Cost of goods sold		
LIFO (2,500,000 pounds @ $0.80)	2,000,000	
FIFO (1,000,000 pounds @ $0.70 + 1,500,000 pounds @ $0.80)		1,900,000
Gross profit	$1,000,000	1,100,000
Ending inventory		
LIFO (1,000,000 pounds @ $0.70 + 500,000 pounds @ $0.80)	$1,100,000	
FIFO (1,500,000 pounds @ $0.80)		$1,200,000
Year 2		
Beginning inventory		
LIFO (1,000,000 pounds @ $0.70 + 500,000 pounds @ $0.80)	$1,100,000	
FIFO (1,500,000 pounds @ $0.80)		1,200,000
Purchases		
5,000,000 pounds @ $0.95	4,750,000	4,750,000
Inventory available (6,500,000 lbs.)	$5,850,000	5,950,000
Sales		
4,500,000 pounds @ $1.40	$6,300,000	6,300,000
Cost of goods sold		
LIFO (4,500,000 pounds @ $0.95)	4,275,000	
FIFO (1,500,000 pounds @ $0.80 + 3,000,000 pounds @ $0.95)		4,050,000
Gross profit	$2,025,000	$2,250,000
Ending inventory		
LIFO		
1,000,000 pounds @ $0.70	$ 700,000	
500,000 pounds @ 0.80	400,000	
500,000 pounds @ 0.95	475,000	
FIFO (2,000,000 pounds @ $0.95)		1,900,000
	$1,575,000	$1,900,000

In the above example, the gross profit under LIFO is $100,000 less than the gross profit using FIFO because the LIFO cost of sales is computed using the most recent costs incurred ($0.80 per pound). The unit cost in the beginning LIFO inventory is retained to the extent that the quantity in the ending inventory equals or exceeds that in the beginning inventory. Any current-year increase in quantity (500,000 pounds in the example) is priced using current-year costs ($0.80 per pound). If the company had another item in its inventory not closely related to cotton (e.g., nylon), that other item would require a separate LIFO computation.

To carry the example further, and to illustrate the cumulative benefits that may result when LIFO is used, assume the following facts for the next year:

Carrying the example into the second year illustrates that in a period of rising inventory costs, the difference in the balance sheet amounts under LIFO and FIFO quickly widens. The $100,000 difference at the end of the first year has increased to $325,000 ($1,900,000 − $1,575,000) at the end of the second year. Assuming a 46% tax rate, the tax savings amount to $149,500.

Pooling

Inventory items may be included in the same pool under the specific goods method only if they are of the same kind. Cotton and rayon, for example, cannot be pooled. Therefore, companies with a variety of items in their inventory generally have more than one pool. IRS regulations state that each type of raw material in the opening inventory must be compared with a similar type in the closing inventory. Separate pools must be established for raw materials that are not similar. Separate pools should also be created for different quality items. As an example, sound accounting would indicate separate pools for different grades of a product if the difference in price range could lead to a distortion of the LIFO cost.

The IRS regulations give an example of a company that pools its specific goods inventory by raw material content. This company has a specific raw material not only in raw materials but also in work-in-process and finished goods. To calculate the total raw material quantity, the company would add amounts included in work-in-process and finished goods to the amount in raw materials. This would yield the total quantity on hand. As an example, a company that processes cotton into fabric could pool unprocessed raw cotton with the raw material content of the cotton that has been processed into finished fabric.

Advantages and Disadvantages of the Specific Goods Method

The advantage of the specific goods method is that it is easy to visualize because LIFO costs are associated with specific items in inventory. This method has been used most frequently by companies that have basic inventory items, such as steel, cotton, sugar, oil, or other commodities.

However, the specific goods method has certain disadvantages, especially if a company has a wide variety of inventory items or changes frequently (e.g., for technological reasons). The specific goods method may be costly to administer and may, in the long run, produce unwanted LIFO liquidations.

Because each item represents essentially a separate pool, if a company's mix of goods is expected to change because of style changes or technology, and if the quantities of some goods will increase and others decrease, liquidations are inevitable. When such liquidations occur, the LIFO objective of matching current costs and revenues is not achieved. In this situation, the specific goods method will result in higher reported income, even though the investment in total inventory may not have changed substantially.

The introduction of new products can also be a disadvantage under the specific goods method, again because each new dissimilar item results in a new pool and a separate LIFO computation. Assume, for example, that the company in our illustrative example decides to replace cotton with various synthetic fabrics in its product line. Because the synthetic fabrics are not considered to be similar to cotton for purposes of specific goods pooling, they cannot be substituted; nor can they preserve the LIFO base and the lower cost increments associated with the cotton inventory. As a result, the company would effectively go off LIFO in that year for its cotton inventory; current costs would be used to value the new synthetic inventories, and the older costs associated with the cotton inventory would be charged to the cost of goods sold as cotton is used or disposed of. If the company used the dollar-value method with a natural business unit pool, it might be able to retain the older layers.

Pricing Increments (Layers)

Regardless of the method used to compute LIFO values (i.e., specific goods or dollar value), an approach must be selected for pricing the current year's increases in inventory levels (the current year's layer or increment) (see Exhibit 2). The IRS regulations provide four optional methods for determining the cost of the current year's increment:

1. Latest acquisition cost.
2. Earliest acquisition cost.
3. Average acquisition cost.
4. Any other appropriate method which, in the opinion of the IRS, clearly reflects income.

Once one of these approaches has been designated on Form 970, it must be applied consistently in all subsequent years unless the IRS grants permission to change. As long as they are properly designated on Form 970, it appears that a company can use different approaches for different pools. The first three alternatives are illustrated below, using the following facts:

1. Assume that a company adopts the specific goods method of LIFO in 19X5 and that the inventory in one pool at the beginning of the year consists of 4,000 items at $5,75 per item. Purchases for the year are shown in #1 in Exhibit 2.
2. The closing inventory consists of 8,000 items. If the company were using FIFO, the cost would be $50,700, calculated as shown in #2 in Exhibit 2.
3. Calculations of the LIFO cost using the various approaches for pricing the current year's increment of 4,000 units (8,000 units at year end less 4,000 units at the beginning of the year) are shown in #3 in Exhibit 2.

It is evident from the example shown in #3 that the earliest acquisition approach results in the lowest LIFO inventory cost during periods of steadily rising prices and conforms more closely to the LIFO theory than the other methods. However, each of the three approaches has advantages and disadvantages:

- *Latest acquisition cost.* This approach is attractive because it is frequently the easiest to apply. Many companies using LIFO maintain their inventory records on FIFO. If the latest acquisition approach is used, current-year unit costs are available from the FIFO inventory valuation. One disadvantage of this approach

**EXHIBIT 2
PRICING THE INCREMENTS
BY THREE METHODS**

1

Purchases for Year	Units	Unit Cost	Amount
January	3,000	$5.80	$ 17,400
February	3,000	6.00	18,000
March	20,000	6.10	122,000
November	2,000	6.30	12,600
December	5,000	6.40	32,000
	33,000	$6.12	$202,000

2

Purchases	Units	Unit Cost	Amount
December	5,000	$6.40	$32,000
November	2,000	6.30	12,600
March	1,000	6.10	6,100
	8,000		$50,700

3

	Earliest Acquisition	Average Acquisition	Latest Acquisition
1. Opening inventory — 4,000 units at $5.75	$23,000	23,000	23,000
2. Pricing of current-year increment:			
Latest acquisition			
4,000 @ $6.40			25,600
Earliest acquisition			
January — 3,000 @ 5.80	17,400		
February — 1,000 @ $6.00	6,000		
Average acquisition			
4,000 @ $6.12		24,480	
3. LIFO cost of ending inventory	$46,400	$47,480	$48,600

is that it results in the highest value for an increment (and therefore the highest taxable income) if costs have been consistently rising throughout the year. Another disadvantage is that the company has to wait until after the end of the year to compute the current year's cost.

• *Earliest acquisition cost.* In periods of steadily increasing prices, this approach prices increments at lower costs than the other approaches. This results in the lowest tax and maximizes the removal of inventory profits for financial reporting purposes. Another advantage is that current-year unit costs may be computed in the early part of the year. The major disadvantage of this approach is that it may require additional clerical effort, since it usually requires a separate calculation.

• *Average acquisition cost.* This approach represents a middle ground between the other two. Its advantage over the latest acquisition cost is that it results in a lower LIFO value during periods of rising prices. Also, the average acquisition cost method may be advantageous if a purchase contract provides adjustments or rebates, for example, based on annual purchases or in other situations where there are significant seasonal fluctuations in cost. However, it also has two major disadvantages: (1) it requires even more clerical effort than the earliest acquisition method and (2) it usually must be calculated after year end.

In addition to the approaches described above, companies may use any other method which, in the opinion of the IRS, clearly reflects income. As an example, a manufacturer that annually revises standard costs in the third quarter may wish to use such standard costs in pricing LIFO increments. This does not fit within any of the approaches described above, but it might be acceptable if it clearly reflects income.

Apparently because of a desire for simplification in computational techniques, other methods are used in practice, even though they may apply slightly higher costs to increases in inventory quantities than those that would result from using the earliest acquisition approach. In some cases, if the savings are minimal, the additional effort needed to use the earliest acquisition approach may not be cost justified. Companies adopting LIFO should consider such factors in choosing the approach with the most favorable cost-benefit relationship.

Dollar-Value Method

Many of the disadvantages associated with the specific goods method are overcome by the use of the dollar-value method. Under this approach, inventory quantities are measured in terms of fixed dollar equivalents (base-year costs) rather than in terms of the quantities and prices of specific goods. Similar items of inventory are accumulated to form inventory pools, and increases or decreases in each pool are identified and measured in terms of the total base-year cost of the inventory in the pool rather than the physical base-year quantities of individual items.

To determine whether the inventory has changed, a company states dollars in terms of a common base year (the year LIFO is adopted). Changes in quantities and product mix within a pool may occur without affecting the total dollar value of the pool. The factors relating to selection of dollar-value LIFO pools will be discussed later in this section.

Throughout this section, we refer to the calculation of internal inflation indexes using one of the various dollar-value techniques. In March 1982 the IRS issued final regulations allowing companies to elect to use certain government-generated indexes when making dollar-value LIFO computations.

There are two basic ways to apply the dollar-value method—the double-extension and link-chain methods. Both techniques have a common objective—to determine the base-year cost of current-year inventory quantities. The double-extension technique achieves this objective directly by converting current-year quantities directly to base-year costs. The link-chain method, on the other hand, achieves this objective indirectly by developing an index based on current-year cost increases and multiplying that index by the prior-year cumulative index. Base-year costs are then calculated under the link-chain technique by dividing total current-year costs by the current-year cumulative index. There is also an index method that can be used when it is inpractical to perform a complete double extension of the inventory.

Double-Extension Technique (Using Base-Year Costs)
The double-extension technique extends ending inventory quantities twice—once at current-year costs and once at base-year costs. This double-extension procedure provides the current-year index (total current-year cost divided by total base-year cost).

To determine the net inventory change for the year, a company compares the ending inventory expressed in terms of base-year costs to the beginning of the year inventory expressed in terms of base-year costs. If the inventory has increased, the company converts the net increase or increment in base-year dollars to a LIFO cost by applying the current-year index. If the inventory has decreased, however, the net decrement in base-year costs is assumed to come from the most recent prior-year LIFO layers included in the beginning inventory.

When an item enters the inventory for the first time, a company must either use its current cost or determine its base-year cost. Under IRS regulations, current cost must be used unless the company is able to reconstruct a base-year cost. Failure to reconstruct a base-year cost may result in improper matching of current costs and revenues for financial reporting purposes.

A company that uses the double-extension technique must retain indefinitely a record of base-year unit costs of all items in inventory at the beginning of the year in which LIFO was adopted, as well as any base-year unit costs developed for new items added in subsequent years.

Illustrative Example of the Double-Extension Technique. Exhibits 3 and 4 illustrate the application of the double-extension technique of dollar-value LIFO for one pool using the latest acquisition method. Assume that the company's opening inventory on January 1, 19X1 (the date LIFO is adopted), totaled $150,000. Ending inventory for the next three years follows:

EXHIBIT 3
APPLICATION OF THE DOUBLE-EXTENSION
TECHNIQUE OF DOLLAR-VALUE LIFO

Item	Quantities in Ending Inventory	Base-Year Cost Unit Cost	Base-Year Cost Amount	Current-Year Cost(1) Unit Cost	Current-Year Cost(1) Amount	Index (2)
Year Ended December 31, 19X1						
A	8,000	$ 1.00	$ 8,000	$ 1.15	$ 9,200	
B	7,000	4.00	28,000	4.30	30,100	
C	10,000	7.00	70,000	7.60	76,000	
D	12,000	6.00	72,000	6.35	76,200	
			178,000		191,500	107.58
Year Ended December 31, 19X2						
A	12,000	1.00	12,000	1.30	15,600	
B	6,000	4.00	24,000	4.75	28,500	
C	7,000	7.00	49,000	8.15	57,050	
D	15,000	6.00	90,000	6.80	102,000	
E	7,000	9.00(3)	63,000	10.30	72,100	
			238,000		275,250	115.65
Year Ended December 31, 19X3						
A	18,000	1.00	18,000	1.50	27,000	
D	17,000	6.00	102,000	7.50	127,500	
E	10,000	9.00	90,000	11.20	112,000	
F	5,000	8.00(3)	40,000	9.75	48,750	
G	3,000	10.00(3)	30,000	12.35	37,050	
			$280,000		$352,300	125.82

EXHIBIT 3 (*Continued*)

Computation of LIFO Cost

December 31, 19X1			
January 1, 19X1 base	$150,000	100.00	$150,000
December 31, 19X1 increment	28,000	107.58	30,122
	$178,000		$180,122
December 31, 19X2			
January 1, 19X1 base	$150,000	100.00	$150,000
December 31, 19X1 increment	28,000	107,58	30,122
December 31, 19X2 increment	60,000	115.65	60,390
	$238,000		$249,512
December 31, 19X3			
January 1, 19X1 base	$150,000	100.00	$150,000
December 31, 19X1 increment	28,000	107.58	30,122
December 31, 19X2 increment	60,000	115.65	69,390
December 31, 19X3 increment	42,000	125.82	52,844
	$280,000		$302,356

(1) The latest acquisition method is used to determine current-year cost. The current-year cost of the 8,000 units of item A on December 31, 19X1, for example, is $1.15 per unit, or a total of $9,200. This represents the actual purchase cost of the last 8,000 units of item A purchased during 19X1. It also would be acceptable to use the earliest or average acquisition costs to price the current year's increment. In electing LIFO, a company must specify on Form 970 the method it will use. This method must be followed consistently when computing the LIFO inventory.

(2) The index is determined by dividing the total amount of the current-year cost by the total amount of the base-year cost (e.g., 19X1—$191,500 divided by $178,000 = 107.58).

(3) Reconstructed base-year costs using vendor price lists in existence on January 1, 19X1.

The advantages of using the dollar-value method rather than the specific goods method are apparent from this example. The composition of the inventory pool changed from year to year but because the total base-year cost in the entire pool continued to increase, no liquidation of any LIFO layer occurred. If the specific goods method had been used, each item probably would, in effect, have been a separate pool (assuming the items were not similar enough to be pooled). When items B and C were removed from inventory (19X3), those pools would have been liquidated. Because a liquidation has the effect of charging lower prior-year amounts to the cost of sales, the LIFO objective of matching current costs and revenues is not achieved. Further, a new current-year cost (rather than a reconstructed base-year cost) would have been used for new items added to the inventory (E in 19X2 and F and G in 19X3) had the specific goods method been used. (See Exhibit 2 for an illustrative example of the reduction of an increment.)

The double-extension technique under the dollar-value method has several significant disadvantages, however, when compared to other dollar-value techniques:

1. It is generally more time-consuming to compute because it usually must be done for all items in the inventory.
2. If large numbers of new items enter the inventory each year or if technological change is significant, it is difficult to reconstruct base-year costs for new items entering a pool. If base-year costs are not reconstructed, a proper matching of costs and revenues may not be made.

EXHIBIT 4

DOUBLE EXTENSION LIFO ILLUSTRATING
THE CONVERSION OF AN INCREMENT TO CURRENT COST
AND REDUCTION OF AN INCREMENT

CONVERTING A LAYER (INCREMENT) TO CURRENT COST

YEAR ENDED 12/31/84
1/1/84 INVENTORY = BASE YEAR COST

Components	Number In Stock	Unit Cost	Total Cost
16794	1,000	$2.00	$2,000
19142	4,000	4.00	16,000
13181	2,000	5.00	10,000
			$28,000

YEAR ENDED 12/31/84 INVENTORY
VALUED AT 1/1/84 BASE YEAR COST

	Number In Stock	Unit Cost	Total Cost
	1,000	$2.00	$2,000
	2,000	4.00	8,000
	6,000	5.00	30,000
			$40,000

	INDEX
	100%
	125

12/31/84 INVENTORY
AT BASE-YEAR COST

$ 28,000
  12,000
$ 40,000

Base Year Inventory Value
12/31/84 Layer

YEAR ENDED 12/31/84 INVENTORY
VALUED AT CURRENT COST

	Number In Stock	Unit Cost	Total Cost
	1,000	$4.00	$4,000
	2,000	5.00	10,000
	6,000	6.00	36,000
			$50,000

12/31/84 INVENTORY
AT LIFO VALUE

$28,000
 15,000
$43,000

REDUCTION OF A LAYER

YEAR ENDED 12/31/85 INVENTORY
VALUED AT 1/1/84 BASE YEAR COST

Components	Number In Stock	Unit Cost	Total Cost
16794	1,000	$2.00	$2,000
19142	3,000	4.00	12,000
13181	4,000	5.00	20,000
			$34,000

12/31/85 INVENTORY
AT BASE-YEAR COST

$ 28,000
   6,000
$ 34,000

Base Year Inventory Value
Balance of 12/31/84 Layer

YEAR ENDED 12/31/85 INVENTORY
VALUED AT CURRENT COST

	Number In Stock	Unit Cost	Total Cost
	1,000	$4.25	$4,250
	3,100	3.50	10,850
	5,000	6.50	32,500
			$47,600

	INDEX
	100%
	125

12/31/84 INVENTORY
AT LIFO VALUE

$ 28,000
   7,500
$ 35,500

Indexing

Some companies that have elected the double-extension technique currently use an index method even though they did not elect the index technique when they originally adopted LIFO. As an example, a company may not be able easily to reconstruct the base-year cost of 5% of its inventory. As was mentioned earlier, the company has the option of using current-year costs instead of base-year costs. Rather than do this, some companies use an index technique. Such a company, for example, might double-extend only 95% of its inventory to develop an index of current-year to base-year costs. It might then apply this index to 100% of the inventory to arrive at total base-year costs.

IRS regulations do not specifically allow companies electing the double-extension method to use an index technique. Nevertheless, it is frequently done in practice, and the IRS does not appear to be taking exception to it. Furthermore, using current-year costs in lieu of reconstructed base-year costs can result in recording LIFO costs in excess of current-year costs. The use of an index technique usually avoids this problem.

Link-Chain Technique

The double-extension technique can cause significant problems, particularly when the base year extends back a number of years. Changes in specifications and manufacturing methods are common in many industrial companies. The link-chain method eliminates the burden of reconstructing base-year costs and is therefore a more efficient means of computing LIFO.

Under the link-chain method, the ending inventory is double-extended at both current-year and prior-year unit costs. The technique may be applied by double-extending either all items in the inventory or a representative sample of them. The respective extensions are then totaled, and the totals are used to compute a current-year index. This current-year index is multiplied by the prior-year cumularive LIFO index to develop a current-year cumulative index. Total current-year costs are then divided by the current-year cumulative index to determine base-year costs. If base-year costs have decreased, however, the net decrement is assumed to come from the most recent prior-year LIFO layers included in the beginning inventory.

IRS regulations allow a company to use the link-chain method when it can demonstrate that changes in inventory items are frequent and thus neither the double-extension nor the index technique is practical. The IRS has never issued specific tests that must be met to use the link-chain method. Although it prefers the double-extension and index techniques, many companies have discovered that link-chain is the only practical means of determining the LIFO cost of their inventories. Companies initially adopting LIFO should consider electing link-chain. If they do not, they may find that IRS approval of a later change to this method is difficult to obtain.

Except for the first year, percentages of current-year to base-year costs computed according to the double-extension and link-chain techniques may vary to some degree, even though they are computed for the same inventories. These variances are due to the differences in inventory mix entering into the computations. Under the double-extension technique, the percentage of current-year to base-year costs in any year depends on the mix of items in the closing inventory of the current year. Each year's index is computed independently of that of other years. In the link-chain technique, the percentage of current-year to base-year costs depends not only on the mix of items in the closing inventory in the current year but also on the mix in the closing inventories of all years used in computing the cumulative index. The example below illustrates the differences between these two techniques.

Illustrative Example of the Link-Chain Method.   Exhibit 5, which uses the same inventory items and unit costs as Exhibit 3, illustrates the link-chain technique and compares the results with those achieved using the double-extension technique. Because this example involves only a few items, the entire inventory has been double-extended. As discussed above, a representative sample may also be used with the link-chain method. As in the double-extension example, assume that the yearly increments are priced using the latest acquisition method and that the company's opening inventory on January 1, 19X1 (the date of adoption of LIFO), totals $150,000.

   The double-extension and link-chain techniques produce fairly similar results in this simplified example. Changes in inventory mix and different ways of handling new inventory items usually create differences between the results obtained. If new items are included in the calculation of an index under link-chain, a unit cost would be reconstructed using prior-year rather than base-year costs.

Advantages and Disadvantages of the Link-Chain Technique.   The link-chain technique reduces the burden of LIFO computations by not requiring base-year unit costs. Companies adopting LIFO should consider this advantage when electing a method for making the LIFO computation.

EXHIBIT 5
LINK-CHAIN TECHNIQUE COMPARED WITH DOUBLE EXTENSION

Item	Quantities in Ending Inventory	Prior-Year Cost		Current-Year Cost (1)		Index	
		Unit Cost	Amount	Unit Cost	Amount	Current Year (2)	Cumulative (3)
Year Ended December 31, 19X1							
A	8,000	$ 1.00	$ 8,000	$ 1.15	$ 9,200		
B	7,000	4.00	28,000	4.30	30,100		
C	10,000	7.00	70,000	7.60	76,000		
D	12,000	6.00	72,000	6.35	76,200		
			$178,000		$191,500	107.58	107.58
					÷107.58		
				Base-Year Cost	$178,000(4)		
Year Ended December 31, 19X2							
A	12,000	$ 1.15	$ 13,800	$ 1.30	$ 15,600		
B	6,000	4.30	25,800	4.75	28,500		
C	7,000	7.60	53,200	8.15	57,050		
D	15,000	6.35	95,250	6.80	102,000		
E	7,000	9.60(5)	67,200	10.30	72,100		
			$255,250		$275,250	107.84	116.01
					÷116.01		
				Base-Year Cost	$237,264		
Year ended December 31, 19X3							
A	18,000	$ 1.30	$ 23,400	$ 1.50	$ 27,000		
D	17,000	6.80	115,600	7.50	127,500		
E	10,000	10.30	103,000	11.20	112,000		
F	5,000	9.15(5)	45,750	9.75	48,750		
G	3,000	11.60(5)	34,800	12.35	37,050		
			$322,550		$352,300	109.22	126.71
					÷126.71		
				Base-Year Cost	$278,036		

EXHIBIT 5 (*Continued*)

COMPUTATION OF LIFO COST

	Base-Year Cost	Index	LIFO Cost Using Link-Chain	(6) LIFO Cost Using Double-Extension
December 31, 19X1				
January 1, 19X1 Base	$150,000	100.00	$150,000	$150,000
December 31, 19X1 increment	28,000	107.58	30,122	30,122
	$178,000		$180,122	$180,122
December 31, 19X2				
January 1, 19X1 Base	$150,000	100.00	$150,000	$150,000
December 31, 19X1 increment	28,000	107.58	30,122	30,122
December 31, 19X2 increment	59,264	116.01	68,752	69,390
	$237,264		$248,874	$249,512
December 31, 19X3				
January 1, 19X1 Base	$150,000	100.00	$150,000	$150,000
December 31, 19X1 increment	28,000	107.58	30,122	30,122
December 31, 19X2 increment	59,264	116.01	68,752	69,390
December 31, 19X3 increment	40,772	126.71	51,662	52,844
	$278,036		$300,536	$302,356

(1) The latest acquisition method is used to determine the current-year cost. The current-year cost of the 8,000 units of item A on December 31, 19X1, for example, is $1.15 per unit, or a total of $9,200. This represents the actual purchase cost of the last 8,000 units of item A purchased during 19X1. It would also be acceptable to use the earliest or average acquisition costs to price the current year's increment. In electing LIFO, a company must specify on Form 970 the method it will use. This method must be followed consistently when computing LIFO inventory.

(2) The current-year index is determined by dividing the cost of the inventory at the current-year cost by the prior-year costs. For the year ending December 31, 19X1, the index is calculated as follows: $191,500 ÷ $178,000 = 107.58.

(3) The cumulative index is determined by multiplying the prior year's cumulative index by the current-year index. For the year ending December 31, 19X2, the cumulative index is calculated as follows: 107.58 × 107.84 = 116.01.

(4) The base-year cost for determining whether there is an increment or decrement for the year is calculated by dividing the inventory cost at current-year prices by the cumulative index. For the year ending December 31, 19X1, there is an increment of $28,000 ($178,000 − $150,000).

(5) Costs per vendor price lists at the end of the year for new items in the ending inventory.

(6) These amounts are taken from Exhibit 3.

However, there are some potential problems that companies should be aware of:

1. As previously discussed, the use of the link-chain rather than the double-extension technique must be justified for tax purposes. The IRS may challenge the use of link-chain.

2. The link-chain method calculates base-year costs on the basis of a cumulative index which may be more or less than the inflation rate of the inventory on hand. For example, the cumulative index of a company that adopted LIFO 30 years ago would include the effect of price changes in each of the preceding 30 years, including that of items no longer stocked. In contrast, under the double-extension method, the actual base-year cost is calculated only for inventory currently on hand, so that the inflation index relates directly to those goods.

Index Method of Computing Double-Extension or Link-Chain Methods

For some companies, it may be impractical to compute the LIFO index by performing a complete double-extension of ending inventory quantities. This situation might arise when:

1. The company has a manual cost system, making the time required to list all prior- (or base-) year costs and perform the double-extension calculation prohibitive.
2. The company has a computerized cost system in which current costs are available but prior- (or base-) year costs are not.
3. The company wishes to use current-year costs based on the earliest purchases, but its records are not maintained on that basis.

In situations such as these, it might be appropriate to use an index technique to compute all or part of the LIFO cost of a pool. The IRS regulations state, in part:

> An index may be computed by double-extending a representative portion of the inventory in a pool or by use of other sound and consistent statistical methods. The index used must be appropriate to the inventory pool to which it is to be applied. The appropriateness of the method of computing the index and the accuracy, reliability, and suitability of the use of such index must be demonstrated to the satisfaction of the district director in connection with the examination of the taxpayer's income tax returns.

The IRS has not provided definitions of the terms "representative portion" and "sound and consistent statistical methods." However, two basic approaches have been applied in practice—one involving double-extending items that comprise at least 70% of the total value of the LIFO pool in question, and the other involving statistical sampling.

Although 70% is an arbitrary figure, it is believed to be acceptable by the IRS. If the 70% method is used, care should be taken to ensure that the items that are double-extended are representative of the entire population (e.g., no individually significant items should be left out merely because their prices have decreased).

LIFO REPORTING IN INDUSTRY

The illustrative examples in the step-by-step explanation of the techniques used in developing LIFO cost utilized hypothetical figures for ease of demonstrating the principles. The cost accountant who is new to LIFO costing must, at some point, develop from these examples a suitable format for recording the figures on a continuing basis. This section explains several formats actually in use by three companies. The figures are actual; therefore, the years have been altered to provide greater anonymity to the company.

Specific Goods

Exhibit 6, illustrates the reporting format for calculating the LIFO and the LIFO reserve for cotton. The figures on the left side of the report list the pounds of cotton added to inventory for the years 1974 through 1985. The pounds added in each year have been costed at each year's LIFO value. The total of all layers added through 1985 divided by the total LIFO value of these layers shows a LIFO value of $0.153 per pound ($6,883,892 divided by 45,000,000 pounds). These three figures have been transferred to the right side of the report for calculation of the 1985 LIFO reserve. Note that the 45,000,000 pounds of cotton have been broken down by location and then multiplied by the current value per pound of $0.527 to arrive at a total current value of $23,715,000. The 45,000,000 pounds, previously determined to have a LIFO

EXHIBIT 6

LIFO USING SPECIFIC GOODS METHOD

CALCULATION OF
LIFO AND LIFO RESERVE
FOR COTTON

	INVENTORY LAYERS IN POUNDS	COST PER POUND	TOTAL LIFO VALUE
1974 (Base Year)	19,530,000	$ .098	$ 1,904,869
1975	4,316,000	.107	460,951
1976	1,984,000	.113	224,630
1977	101,000	.118	11,921
1978	3,343,000	.117	390,200
1979	3,930,000	.113	445,944
1980	440,000	.398	174,978
1981	219,000	.293	64,020
1982	4,812,000	.262	1,258,461
1983	3,496,000	.297	1,039,114
1984	1,067,000	.298	318,113
1985	1,762,000	.336	590,691
Cumulative	45,000,000	$ .153	$ 6,883,892

INVENTORY BY LOCATION	CALCULATION OF 1985 LIFO RESERVE
Plant 1	687,000
Plant 2	3,065,000
Plant 3	3,134,000
Plant 4	248,000
Plant 5	2,656,000
Total all plants	9,790,000
Warehouse inventories	35,210,000
Total all locations	45,000,000
Current Value Per Pound	$ .527
Total Current Value	$ 23,715,000
LIFO Value Per Pound	$ .153
Total Lifo Value	$ 6,884,000
LIFO Reserve	$ 16,831,000

EXHIBIT 7

LIFO USING CHAIN LINK METHOD

CALCULATION OF
LIFO AND LIFO RESERVE
FOR NON-COTTON MATERIAL

Year	CURRENT VALUE	BASE YEAR VALUE	LINK CHAIN METHOD CURRENT YEAR	CUMULATIVE	LAYERS IN BASE YEAR $	LIFO VALUE	LIFO RESERVE
1972*	5,129,855	5,129,855	1.000	1.000	5,129,855	5,129,855	-0-
1973	7,077,132	6,404,644	1.105	1.105	1,274,789	1,408,642	538,635
1974	9,782,838	7,513,700	1.178	1.302	1,109,056	1,443,991	1,800,350
1975	11,068,572		1.039		} 7,513,700	} 7,982,488	
1976	12,312,184		1.028				
1977	11,011,931		.993				
1978	13,076,562	$7,513,700	1.012				
1979	12,230,562		1.008	1.302	-	-	2,637,856
1980	13,020,314	9,306,872	.993	1.399	626,558	876,555	2,551,053
1981	14,158,623	10,304,675	.982	1.374	997,803	1,370,981	2,318,381
1982	14,261,406	10,455,576	.993	1.364	150,901	205,829	2,215,335
1983	16,330,341	12,132,497	.987	1.346	1,676,921	2,257,136	2,027,134
1984	24,736,963	19,028,433	.966	1.300	6,895,936	8,964,717	1,469,039
1985	35,732,618	27,152,618	1.012	1.316	8,124,012	10,691,200	1,773,494

* 1972 – Base Year

Formula boxes (shown within the table):

Base Year Value column:
Base Year Value = Current Value ÷ Cumulative Index.
$$\frac{\$9,782,838}{1.302} = \$7,513,700$$

Cumulative column:
Cumulative Index = Previous Year's Cum. Index x Current Year Index.
$$1.105 \times 1.178 = 1.302$$

Layers in Base Year $ column:
1974 Layer = Current Year's Base Value Less Previous Year's Base Value.
$$\$7,513,700 - 6,404,644 = \$1,109,056$$

LIFO Value column:
1974 LIFO Layer Value = 1974 Layer at Base Value x Cumulative Index
$$\$1,109,056 \times 1.302 = \$1,443,991$$

LIFO Reserve column:
LIFO Reserve = Current Year's Value – Cumulative LIFO Value
$$\$9,782,838 - 7,982,488 = \$1,800,350$$

value of $6,883,892 (rounded to $6,884,000), are subtracted from the current value of $23,715,000 to arrive at the LIFO reserve of $16,831,000.

LIFO using the Link-Chain Method

Exhibit 7 shows, for each of the 14 years, the current value of the inventory, along with the base value for each year. The link chain index is also shown for each year. The base-year value of each year's layers, as well as the LIFO value and LIFO reserve, are listed for each year. The calculations for each column are explained on the exhibit.

LIFO for a Distributor

Exhibit 8 illustrates a five-year calculation of LIFO and LIFO reserve for a distributor of plumbing supplies who sells at wholesale prices to mechanical contractors and plumbing supply stores.

Of the 52 figures shown for the five-year period, 16, or 30% of the total, are carryovers from the prior year. These are:

- The beginning LIFO inventory on line A for each new year is carried over from ending LIFO inventory of the preceding year. In the years in which increases occur, the carryover is made from line J; when decreases occur, the carryover is made from line N.
- Likewise, the prior year's ending inventory at base cost (line F) is carried over as the beginning inventory at the prior year's base value (line G).

Valuing the Current Year's Ending Inventory at Current and Base-Year Costs

This double valuation is achieved by the use of the double-extension technique. The number of units of each product is extended by the current year's cost and also by the cost at the beginning of the year. The former is posted to line B and the latter to line C.

Developing the Current Index and the Cumulative Index

The current year's index, shown on line D, is obtained by dividing the ending inventory by the base-year cost (line C).

The cumulative index, shown on line E, is calculated by multiplying the current year's index on line D by the prior year's cumulative index on line E. The result of this multiplication is posted to line E of the current year.

Year-End Inventory at Base Year Cost

This value is obtained by dividing the ending inventory at the current cost (line B) by the cumulative index shown on line E.

Calculating the Inventory Increase

The amount of inventory increase is obtained by subtracting the beginning inventory at the prior year's base value (line G) from the current year's ending inventory at the base-year value (line F). This difference is the inventory increase in base dollars shown on line H. Line I identifies the current cost of the inventory increase, which is calculated by multiplying the figure on line H by the cumulative index on line E less 1.00.

EXHIBIT 8

CALCULATION OF LIFO AND LIFO RESERVE FOR PLUMBING SUPPLIES

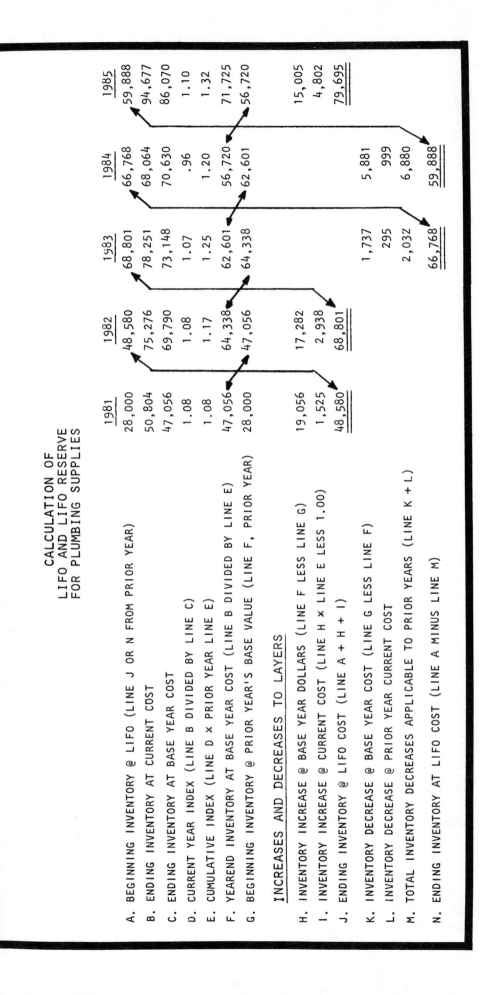

	1981	1982	1983	1984	1985
A. BEGINNING INVENTORY @ LIFO (LINE J OR N FROM PRIOR YEAR)	28,000	48,580	68,801	66,768	59,888
B. ENDING INVENTORY AT CURRENT COST	50,804	75,276	78,251	68,064	94,677
C. ENDING INVENTORY AT BASE YEAR COST	47,056	69,790	73,148	70,630	86,070
D. CURRENT YEAR INDEX (LINE B DIVIDED BY LINE C)	1.08	1.08	1.07	.96	1.10
E. CUMULATIVE INDEX (LINE D × PRIOR YEAR LINE E)	1.08	1.17	1.25	1.20	1.32
F. YEAREND INVENTORY AT BASE YEAR COST (LINE B DIVIDED BY LINE E)	47,056	64,338	62,601	56,720	71,725
G. BEGINNING INVENTORY @ PRIOR YEAR'S BASE VALUE (LINE F, PRIOR YEAR)	28,000	47,056	64,338	62,601	56,720
INCREASES AND DECREASES TO LAYERS					
H. INVENTORY INCREASE @ BASE YEAR DOLLARS (LINE F LESS LINE G)	19,056	17,282			15,005
I. INVENTORY INCREASE @ CURRENT COST (LINE H × LINE E LESS 1.00)	1,525	2,938			4,802
J. ENDING INVENTORY @ LIFO COST (LINE A + H + I)	48,580	68,801			79,695
K. INVENTORY DECREASE @ BASE YEAR COST (LINE G LESS LINE F)			1,737	5,881	
L. INVENTORY DECREASE @ PRIOR YEAR CURRENT COST			295	999	
M. TOTAL INVENTORY DECREASES APPLICABLE TO PRIOR YEARS (LINE K + L)			2,032	6,880	
N. ENDING INVENTORY AT LIFO COST (LINE A MINUS LINE M)			66,768	59,888	

Calculating the Inventory Decrease

The calculation of the inventory decrease at the base-year cost is the reverse of the calculation of the inventory increase. Instead of subtracting line G from line F, line F is subtracted from line G inasmuch as the latter figure is the larger of the two. The decrease at the base-year cost is shown on line K.

Line L shows the decrease in inventory at the prior year's current cost. This is obtained by multiplying line K by the prior year's cumulative index less 1.00. In subsequent years in which there is an inventory decrease, the same procedure is followed until the prior year's increase has been used up. If the preceding year's increase is used up, the remaining amount is applied to the next previous year's layer.

Ending Inventory at LIFO Cost

For the years in which there has been an inventory increase, this figure is obtained by adding the beginning inventory at the LIFO value (line A) plus the increases at the base-year value and at the current cost (lines H and I).

For the years in which inventory decreases have occurred, the beginning inventory at the LIFO value (line A) is reduced by the total decrease shown on line M.

LIFO IN COMPANIES USING STANDARD COST SYSTEMS

If interim period inventories are valued at a standard cost, estimates of interim LIFO adjustments usually can be made by charging or crediting variances as incurred to the cost of goods sold. Changes in the dollar value of inventory priced at standard cost represent changes in the inventory levels (i.e., an increment or decrement). The following example illustrates this approach:

ABC Company's beginning inventory consists of 5,000 units of product A with a FIFO cost of $5 per unit (total, $25,000) and a LIFO reserve of $5,000 (LIFO cost is 5,000 units at $4 each). The company has a standard cost system and uses the dollar-value method and the earliest-acquisition approach for valuing current layers. At the beginning of the year, the company adjusts its standard cost to $5.50 per unit, the estimated cost of the earliest purchases, and adjusts the beginning inventory for the revised standard cost by making the following entry:

Inventory (5,000 units × $5.50) − (25,000) $2,500
  LIFO reserve $2,500

If this entry was not made, the company would credit the inventory account at the current-year standard cost of $5.50 even though the inventory was recorded at only $5 per unit; a negative balance in inventory could possibly occur.

During the year, all production is recorded at $5.50, with variances charged to the cost of sales and all sales costed out at the standard cost of $5.50 per unit. Assume the production during the year as shown in Exhibit 9.

Exhibit 9 assumes that the company's standard cost established at the beginning of the year approximates the earliest acquisition costs. Any necessary revisions would be treated as changes in estimates for purposes of interim financial reporting. Also, because the above example is for a company with only one product, it does not include the effect of inventory mix changes. If a significant change in mix occurred

EXHIBIT 9
MAKING LIFO ADJUSTMENTS TO STANDARD COSTS

	Number of Units	Actual Unit Cost	Total Cost
	8,000	$ 5.50	$ 44,000
	6,000	5.60	33,600
	5,000	5.65	28,250
	8,000	5.70	45,600
	6,000	5.72	34,320
	33,000	$ 5.63	185,770
Less amount of cost recorded as inventory (33,000 × $5.50)			181,500
Total variances charged to cost of sales			4,270
Standard cost of units sold (32,000 × $5.50)			$176,000
Total cost of goods sold			$180,270

Year-end LIFO Calculation

Current-year cost (6,000 × $5.50)		$ 33,000
Base-year cost (6,000 × $4.00)		24,000
Current year's index (33,000 divided by $24,000)		137.50

	Base-Year Cost	Index	LIFO Cost
Base	$20,000	100.00	$ 20,000
Current layer	4,000	137.50	5,500
	$24,000		$ 25,500

	LIFO Cost
Inventory at current-year cost	$ 33,000
Inventory at LIFO cost	25,500
LIFO reserve required	$ 7,500
LIFO reserve per books:	$ 5,000
Entry made at beginning of year	2,500
	$ 7,500

Transaction Summary in Units

Beginning inventory	5,000
Units produced	33,000
Total available	38,000
Fewer units sold	32,000
Ending inventory	6,000

that was not anticipated, the effect on the LIFO computation would be treated as a change in the estimate.

The company in this example would not be required to compute interim LIFO indexes. The amount of variances charged to the cost of sales would increase throughout the year and would represent the current cost (standard cost plus or minus the variance). Any decrease in the total standard cost of each pool would represent a liquidation. If a liquidation occurs at an interim date, the company must decide whether it will be restored by the end of the year.

This method can also be used under the latest-acquisition approach. It would be more difficult, however, because the company would be required to set its standards at the beginning of the year based on its estimated year-end costs. In this situation, the company would need to monitor the variances closely and evaluate regularly the reasonableness of the estimated standards.

SELECTING THE DOLLAR—VALUE POOLS

One of the most important aspects of dollar-value LIFO is selection of the pools to be used in the computations. A company can avoid many of the disadvantages of the specific-goods method by carefully assigning inventory items to pools in a dollar-value LIFO application.

As previously discussed, LIFO's basic objective is to match current costs with current revenues. Generally, the fewer the pools, the less chance there is of liquidating the oldest and lowest-cost layers. This is true because the more items there are in a pool, the more likely it becomes that decreases in some items will be offset by increases in others, thus avoiding liquidations of layers. Fewer pools also minimize the administrative burden associated with accounting for LIFO inventories.

The LIFO election and its pooling concepts apply to individual corporations, not to consolidated groups. For tax purposes, each subsidiary must establish its own separate pools. If an affiliated group filing a consolidated tax return has three subsidiaries in the same line of business, a single LIFO pool encompassing the operations of all three cannot be adopted, even if one performs central purchasing for all of them.

Once a company has established its method of pooling in the year LIFO is adopted, that method must be followed for all subsequent years unless permission to change is granted by the IRS or unless a change is required by the IRS upon examination. A method of pooling is considered an accounting method.

The Natural Business Unit Pool

The broadest definition of a pool permitted by the IRS is the natural business unit pool. Under the regulations, if the natural business unit method is used, a pool "shall consist of all items entering into the entire inventory investment for a natural business unit of a business enterprise." The use of this method generally is limited to manufacturers and processors. However, if the IRS's permission is obtained, a wholesaler or retailer may also be able to use it. Such approval for wholesalers, retailers, jobbers, or distributors will be granted only where a company can clearly demonstrate that this method of pooling is appropriate and clearly reflects income. Such permission appears to be rarely granted. A retailer or wholesaler with only one class of goods would not need IRS permission to have only one pool—which would not, however, be a natural business unit.

If a manufacturer or processor has only one natural business unit, one pool should be used for all of its inventories, including raw materials, work-in-process, and finished goods. However, if a company's operations include more than one natural business unit, more than one pool must be established. A manufacturer may use natural business unit pooling for each natural business unit within the company and multiple pooling for other units.

A manufacturer or processor electing to pool by natural business units may not exclude labor and overhead from the LIFO pool. Also, a manufacturer using a multiple-pool dollar-value method for raw materials only may not change to a single natural business unit pool without including labor and overhead and, of course, obtaining IRS permission.

In determining the number and identity of natural business units for pooling, the regulations conclude that whether a company has more than one natural business unit is a question of fact to be determined under the specific circumstances. Important considerations include the following:

1. Are natural business divisions used for internal management purposes, such as separate profit-and-loss records for individual operations?
2. Are there separate and distinct production facilities and processes?

For a manufacturer or processor, a natural business unit normally consists of the entire productive capacity of an operation making one product line (or more than one if they are related) and includes, if applicable, purchasing and processing of the materials and selling of the produced goods. Thus, in the case of a manufacturer or processor, the maintenance and operation of a raw materials warehouse generally does not constitute, in itself, a natural business unit because it does not engage in production or sales.

If a manufacturer or processor is also engaged in wholesaling or retailing goods acquired from others, these goods are not considered part of any manufacturing or processing natural business unit.

Some companies using natural business unit pooling have been challenged by the IRS regarding purchased versus produced goods. This could occur when a company, because of lack of capacity or for some other reason, purchases goods that it normally produces and includes them in its inventory to meet sales needs. The IRS has taken the position that the company is a wholesaler of these goods, and therefore is not part of the natural business unit for pooling purposes. This may also apply when companies supplement produced inventory items with purchased items.

As an example, suppose a shoe manufacturer cannot produce enough shoes in its own plant to keep up with increased demand. The company could subcontract with another shoe manufacturer to produce shoes identical to its own. Even though the shoes are identical, the IRS could claim that those manufactured by the outsider do not belong in the same natural business pool with those manufactured by the company. As a result, part of the natural business unit pool may be liquidated, and a new pool created for subcontracted shoes with a current-year layer. For financial reporting purposes, a company probably would not report the reduced cost of sales resulting from a liquidation solely because the shoes were manufactured by a subcontractor.

The regulations contain the following three examples for defining natural business unit pools:

1. A corporation has two divisions. In one, it manufactures automatic clothes washers and dryers, electric ranges, and dishwashers. In the other, it manufactures radios and television sets. The manufacturing facilities used in each division are distinct from those used in the other. Under these circumstances, there are considered to be two natural business units. Therefore, two pools should be used—one for each division.
2. A company produces plastics in one of its plants. It sells substantial quantities of plastics and ships the remainder to a second plant of the company, which turns the plastic into toys. The plants are operated as separate divisions. Because

of the separate divisions and different product lines, the company is considered to have two natural business units.

3. A company manufactures paper. At one stage of processing, uncoated paper is produced and a substantial amount is sold. The remainder is transferred to the company's finishing mill, where a coated paper is produced and sold. The company has only one natural business unit, because coated and uncoated papers are considered to be within the same product line.

Multiple Pools

In electing dollar-value LIFO, a company could use the multiple-pool method. Separate pools could be established for similar raw materials and for each class or type of work-in-process and finished goods. Although natural business units usually provide the broadest definition of a pool (and therefore the greatest protection against liquidation of low-cost LIFO layers), the following are typical situations when a company might elect the multiple-pool method:

1. The company does not qualify for a natural business unit pooling because it is not a manufacturer or processor.
2. A manufacturer or processor wants to elect LIFO for only a portion of its inventory. For example, anticipated changes in prices, production techniques, or other technological changes might lead to a decision to adopt LIFO only for the raw material content of inventory (including that of work-in-process and finished goods). Other cost elements of the inventory (labor and overhead) would be accounted for using FIFO or another acceptable method, rather than LIFO.

According to the regulations, each of the multiple pools should consist of "substantially similar" inventory items. In determining their similarity, all the facts and circumstances should be considered. Detailed rules applicable to all companies are not feasible. However, according to the IRS, some important considerations include:

1. Similarity in the types of raw materials used or in the processing operations applied.
2. Interchangeability of the raw materials.
3. Similarity in the use of products.
4. The consistency with which the groupings are followed for internal accounting and management purposes.
5. The groupings customary in the company's industry.
6. The nature of the inventory items subject to the dollar-value method and their significance to the company's business operations. Where similar types of goods are inventoried in natural business units and multiple pools, the IRS may allocate these goods among the natural business units and multiple pools if the IRS determines it necessary to clearly reflect income.

Some of the multiple pooling principles described in the IRS regulations are as follows:

1. Raw materials which are substantially similar should be pooled together. Raw materials of unlike nature, however, should not be included in one pool even though they become part of identical finished products.

2. Finished goods and work-in-process should be placed in pools classified by major classes or types of goods. The same class or type of finished goods and work-in-process should ordinarily be included in the same pool.
3. A miscellaneous pool may be used, but it should consist only of items which are not includable in other pools and are relatively insignificant in dollar value compared with other inventory items.

Companies should consider several factors in the selection of dollar-value LIFO pools, with the objective of minimizing the likelihood that any LIFO layers will be liquidated. For example, if a company has three items and the total number of units is expected to remain fairly constant, but the mixture of the items is expected to vary significantly from year to year, it would be advantageous to place all three items in the same pool if possible.

Wholesalers, Retailers, and Others

For businesses dealing in the purchase and resale of merchandise, the regulations provide little specific guidance except to state that these inventories should be placed into pools "by major lines, types or classes of goods. In determining such groupings, customary business classifications of a particular trade in which the taxpayer is engaged is an important consideration." An example cited is pooling by department in a department store. This practice is fairly uniform throughout the retailing trade.

SUMMARY

The unprecedented inflation that reached successively higher peaks in 1970, 1975, and 1980 have resulted in greater and greater illusory inventory profits for most manufacturing companies not using LIFO costing procedures. With the government engaged in the largest spending programs in the history of our nation—resulting in massive budget deficits—the future can only portend even higher rates of inflation.

The financial executive, in serving his management as financial advisor, must, like the sentry at a military outpost, warn of impending danger. Unlike the sentry, who merely sounds an alarm, the financial executive must be armed with convincing facts and figures that will prove to his management the illusory nature of inventory profits, the resulting higher taxes, and the reduced cash flow. The mechanics for proving his case are contained in this chapter and await application when inflationary forces resume their upward trend.

SECTION 3
PRODUCTIVITY AND PROFITS

Effective utilization of the investment in a business is the most important single factor affecting profitability. The greater the investment, the greater the impact of utilization on productivity and profitability. Modern commuter railroads are illustrative of a high-investment business that suffers from underutilization. Locomotives of one commuter line in the East are used less than one-third of the time, while passenger cars roll less than 20% of the time. Even train crews are used less than half the number of hours for which they are paid. This explains why commuter lines are so heavily subsidized by the government.

Fortunately, most businesses have greater flexibility in terms of the options available to them in controlling investment and its utilization. One option is to expand by degrees, first through overtime and then by adding an additional shift for bottleneck operations. When productivity of the existing investment has been maximized, the company can then increase its investment in additional equipment (and facilities) without a large reduction in its utilization of the increased investment. Chapter 11 illustrates how profits can be adversely affected when capacity is increased without a corresponding increase in utilization. It also explains the importance of monitoring the utilization of equipment, computing the machine hours available for production, and the interplay of utilization and efficiency.

The control and justification of expenditures for fixed assets often concentrate heavily on after-the-fact paperwork controls—to the exclusion of a greater in-depth evaluation of the true productivity of the fixed assets to be purchased or rebuilt. Often when an acceptable payback period of, say, two years has been calculated and the purchase made, utilization falls far short of expectations. This is usually caused by problems that had not been taken into account in calculating the payback period. Chapter 12 provides specific examples and addresses the question "Could these problems have been anticipated?"

Chapter 13 discusses productivity measurement, not only by segments of the company but also at the division and company levels. At the levels in which income statements are prepared, the profit (or loss) can be broken down to isolate the portion of the profit (or loss) due to productivity and the amount due to changes in the cost/selling price relationships. The chapter describes how this can be done in two simple steps.

11
Production Capacity and Utilization of Investment

This chapter illustrates how a 9.7% profit at 85% capacity before expansion can drop to 7.8% at 90% capacity after expansion if the sales volume does not increase proportionately. This suggests that expansion in capacity not be made in one giant leap. Such interim capacity increases as overtime, an additional shift for bottleneck operations and improvements in the utilization of equipment should be used to "test the waters" before a full commitment for additional facilities is made.

Management in our modern society is frequently faced with the problem of deciding whether it should expand production capacity. Once the decision to expand is made, the question arises as to whether this should take the form of overtime, purchase of additional equipment, or physical expansion of facilities by adding to the present building or by relocating.

The final decision must be tempered by considering the effect on profits of the various alternatives. With that in view, the following points will be discussed:

- Effect of increased capacity on profits
- Overtime in lieu of expansion
- Fallacy of excess equipment
- Impact of expansion on utilization

OPTIMUM UTILIZATION OF FACILITIES: THE KEY TO PROFITABILITY

Optimum utilization of production facilities is a key factor in profitable operations. This was evident in the mid-1960s, a period of large corporate earnings, when utilization of facilities averaged better than 90% of capacity. In the early 1960s utilization was closer to 80%, compared with recessionary periods, when it dropped to 70%.

As the demand for products continues to increase, management must decide whether an increase in facilities is warranted. If the facilities are expanded and the anticipated sales volume does not materialize, the cost of the added facilities becomes a deterrent to improved earnings. The decision to expand, then, is a calculated risk at best.

It is possible, however, to make certain evaluations on the impact of volume (or lack of volume) on profits. The determination of profit/volume relationships under various alternative conditions can be a helpful aid in reducing the risk factor in making such decisions.

Each dollar that the customer pays for goods and services includes an allowance for reimbursing the seller for his fixed expenses. The seller's profit is largely dependent upon the relationship of the allowance for fixed costs provided for in the selling price to the fixed costs actually incurred.

When the marginal income (total sales dollars less variable costs) is equal to the fixed costs, we have a breakeven situation. This is illustrated in Exhibit 1 at the 70% capacity level.

EXHIBIT 1
PROFITS AT VARIOUS LEVELS OF CAPACITY

	70% Capacity	80% Capacity	85% Capacity	90% Capacity
Sales Volume	$700,000	$800,000	$850,000	$900,000
Variable Costs	315,000	360,000	382,500	405,000
Marginal Income	$385,000	$440,000	$467,500	$495,000
Fixed Costs	385,000	385,000	385,000	385,000
Profit	–0–	$ 55,000	$ 82,500	$110,000
% Profit	–0–	6.9%	9.7%	12.2%

At the 80% capacity level, the amount by which the marginal income exceeds the actual fixed costs ($440,000 − $385,000) equals profit ($55,000 or 6.9% of sales). At the 85% and 90% capacity levels, the amounts for the same items are $82,500 and $110,000, respectively, or 9.7% and 12.2% of sales. This example illustrates the effect of increased utilization of facilities on profits—assuming that other things remain equal.

Effect of Increased Capacity on Profits

Frequently, when management finds that the company is operating at levels exceeding 90% of capacity, it decides to expand. Once new facilities are added, what previously represented 90% capacity may be, say, 75% of the expanded facilities. Obviously, an expansion of capacity without an increase in sales volume reduces profits, as borne out by the figures in Exhibit 2.

Note that the profits have decreased by the additional amount of fixed costs which were required to expand productive capacity. A comparison of the profits before and after expansion, as shown in Exhibits 1 and 2, is as follows:

SALES VOLUME	PROFITS BEFORE EXPANSION	PROFITS AFTER EXPANSION
$700,000	–0–	($40,000)
800,000	$ 55,000	15,000
850,000	82,500	42,500
900,000	110,000	70,000

Computations such as these can never answer the question of whether to expand or by how much. But they can give a good indication of the effect on profits if the

EXHIBIT 2
EFFECT OF EXPANDED CAPACITY ON PROFITS

	70% Capacity	80% Capacity	85% Capacity	90% Capacity
Sales Volume	$700,000	$800,000	$850,000	$900,000
Variable Costs	315,000	360,000	382,500	405,000
Marginal Income	$385,000	$440,000	$467,500	$495,000
Fixed Costs	425,000	425,000	425,000	425,000
Profit	($ 40,000)	$ 15,000	$ 42,500	$ 70,000
% Profit		1.9%	5.0%	7.8%

expansion program goes through and the additional sales volume does not fulfill expectations.

Overtime in Lieu of Expansion

When there are indications that planned expansion of facilities may not be followed by sufficient increases in volume, many companies resort to the use of overtime. A 10-hour day, for example, will result in 25% more working hours.

Often, however, the economics of working overtime is questionable because of the premium pay when employees are paid time-and-a-half. To determine whether overtime is feasible, it is necessary to compare the added premium cost of labor with the amount of fixed costs which will be absorbed in the added production. While the example which follows considers only the premium cost of overtime, there are other costs, such as fringe benefits or shift differential pay. It has been assumed, however, that fixed costs will remain unchanged.

Overtime Pay Computation

Department A has 200 employees working a 40-hour week. At an hourly rate of $7.50, the total straight-time payroll for a 21-day month amounts to $252,000. To obtain an additional 10% production, the increase in the straight-time payroll would be $25,200. At time-and-a-half, the premium pay, therefore, would be $12,600.

Fixed Cost Absorption Computation

If production were increased in department A by 10% with no expenditure for additional equipment, existing fixed costs would be absorbed by increased production. If existing fixed costs were $168,000 per month, the amount absorbed by increased production would be 10% of $168,000 or $16,800. Since the overtime over and above straight time amounts to $12,600 while the fixed costs absorbed into the additional production are $16,800, $4,200 is gained by working overtime.

Fallacy of excess equipment

Over a period of years, companies accumulate machines which have long since been replaced by newer ones. The rationale for retaining such equipment is that the extra capacity "comes in handy" during peak periods when customers are demanding shipment of their orders. This argument is often reinforced by computations which show that the hourly cost of operating such equipment is miniscule.

One company divided the depreciation on excess machinery by the number of available machine hours in the year. There were 12 machines whose annual depreciation was $72,000. This was divided by 2,000 hours per machine, or a total of 24,000 machine hours per year, to arrive at an hourly cost of $3. At such a low cost, who could argue with the justification of holding on to the equipment?

The truth was that the 12 machines occupied some 5,000 square feet, which forced the company to rent outside space for storage of raw materials. The rental of this outside space plus the security service, extra insurance, cleaning service, and utilities added approximately $36,000 per year to the overhead cost. In addition, an extra maintenance man was tied up servicing the 12 machines. His wages with fringe benefits amounted to $24,000 per year. Thus, the annual cost of keeping the 12 extra machines was not $72,000 but $132,000.

Furthermore, a study of the hours of use indicated that the equipment was operated 3,800 hours per year rather than 24,000. Management's evaluation of $3 per machine hour as the operating cost turned out to be closer to $35 per hour ($132,000 divided by 3,800 hours).

This example should not be interpreted to mean that excess equipment is never justified. There are many instances in which frequent changeovers from one set of tools to another justify extra machines even if utilization is lowered. By leaving tools in the machine until the next run, high costs required in the setup and teardown operations can be eliminated. While there is a point of diminishing returns in retaining excess equipment, no pat formula can be applied to determine that point. Each situation must be judged on its own merits.

Impact of Expansion on Utilization

More and more companies have dismantled old plants and moved into new facilities often located in a different part of the country. Such moves are usually accompanied by replacement of existing machines with newer and faster equipment. Machine utilization is frequently lowered when moves are made. The following are some of the reasons for the decrease in utilization:

- The labor force in the new location may be entirely unfamiliar with machine operation, particularly when one operator is expected to tend several machines and to monitor the quality of the product being fabricated.
- Setup and maintenance men are usually not available in sufficient numbers. Those who are available may have to be trained. The inability of the company to fill the need for such men is reflected in the efficiency with which the machines can be operated.
- The introduction of tools and equipment of greater precision makes the problems of the setup man and toolmaker even more critical and makes it necessary to have a larger quality assurance staff. Pinpointing poor machine utilization raises questions which can lead to quicker solutions of chronic problems than might otherwise be obtained. Some examples are as follows:

  - Utilization reports revealed that an operator charged with tending six machines could not maintain the desired rate of utilization because the machines were spread over a 50-foot area. Naturally, utilization dropped, with no corresponding reduction in the direct labor cost.
  - Watching utilization reports indicated to one plant manager that the cataloging and storage of tools were so inefficient that delays frequently occurred while tools were being sought. As a remedial measure, the floor area of the tool crib was tripled and an additional man assigned to make certain that tools could be found when needed. The returned tools were inspected to ensure that they would be in good condition when reissued.
  - In another situation, monitoring the utilization of equipment on a systematic and analytical basis revealed that machines in one department could not function at full capacity because of shortages in material flowing to it from another department. When this situation occurred frequently, management had to decide whether to add another machine in the deficient department, increase the hours of operation of the existing equipment, or subcontract some of the work.

Many companies, particularly those using expensive automated equipment, have found that the machine utilization report is one of the most important management control tools of all the reports available to them. Such a report will be discussed in the section which follows.

Preparation of the Utilization Report

The purpose of a utilization report, stated simply, is to compare the actual hours that a machine or group of similar machines operated with the number of hours they should have been run. The determination of the number of hours the machines should have operated is dependent on what should reasonably be expected. For instance, when equipment is purchased, certain minimum standards of output are established to justify the purchase. A very expensive machine, for example, may be required to operate two or three shifts in order to justify its purchase. Using such data as a guideline with a further adjustment to allow for a reasonable amount of downtime for changeovers, adjustments, and repairs, the hours of utilization can be determined. Exhibit 3 shows how the utilization base can be determined. The daily or weekly comparison of this figure with actual hours would provide management with a useful control tool.

Note in the exhibit that the types of machines are listed with the number of shifts

EXHIBIT 3
CALCULATION OF MACHINE HOURS

	Machines Available for Production	Number of Shifts	MHR Available per Day	% Utilization of Equipment	MHR per Day Available for Production
Compression Molding					
Rotaries	16	3	384	75%	288
Stokes	9	3	216	81	176
Transfer Press	8	3	192	63	121
Strauss	10	3	240	75	180
Total	43	3	1,032	74%	765
Injection Molding					
4 ounce	6	3	144	80%	115
8 and 12 ounces	3	3	72	70	50
96 ounce	1	3	24	60	14
Total	10	3	240	74%	179
Assembly					
Automatic Stakers	9	2	144 ⎫		
Semiautomatic Stakers	4	2	64 ⎬	70%	168
Hand Stakers	4	1	32 ⎭		
Closure Liners	6	1	48	75%	36
Total	23	—	288	71%	204
Metal Fabrication					
Z&H—9 Ton Presses	18	1	144 ⎫		
V&O—#0, #1, 25 Ton & 50 Ton	8	1	64 ⎪		
Minster—22-Ton	5	1	40 ⎬	28%	81
Benchmaster—4 Ton & B&J	3	1	24 ⎪		
Brandeis—30 Ton	1	1	8 ⎪		
Henry & Wright—60-Ton	1	1	8 ⎭		
Pin Machines	9	2	144	86%	124
Total	45	—	432	47%	205

MHR = Machine Hours

indicated. These are the shifts which were assumed when the equipment was purchased. Should management now find that it cannot justify operating this number of shifts, it will be at a competitive disadvantage.

The number of machines multiplied by the number of daily hours of operation yields the machine hours available per day. Obviously, no company can operate all its machines for all the hours which such a calculation will show. An adjustment is needed to reduce the available hours to a more realistic figure which takes into account the changeover time, time needed for repairs to equipment, and other normal delays which cannot be avoided. Ideally, the determination of the amount of adjustment should be based on records of machine downtime classified by cause. If such records are not available, an estimate should be made by an industrial engineer or foreman familiar with the equipment. This adjustment can best be expressed as a percentage. The available hours for production are determined by multiplying the available hours by the percentage of utilization.

The "Metal Fabrication" section of Exhibit 3 shows only a 28% utilization factor, which raises a question of credibility. This illustrates a situation where excess low-cost "inherited" equipment is retained to reduce setup and changeover requirements. Since the management is satisfied that the low utilization is offset by other savings, the resulting machine hours based on 28% utilization can be used as a norm for this group.

With the basic machine hours determined for the various types of equipment listed in Exhibit 3, the only step left is to accumulate the actual hours of operation of the various machines and to compare these with the norm. This can be done on a daily basis for problem areas until the situation is remedied and on a weekly basis for other areas.

Interplay of Utilization and Efficiency

Once machine utilization has been reasonably controlled and major periods of downtime have been eliminated, management should focus more of its attention on machine productivity during the hours that the machines are running. It is entirely possible that a machine being reported as operating at 100% capacity is actually producing at a substantially lower rate because:

- Periods reported as running hours may not be producing product because the material may be feeding improperly.
- Machines with variable-speed controls may be running at lower speeds.
- Short periods of downtime may be reported as running time, resulting in overstatement of the hours reported as running time. This may be desirable in order to eliminate paperwork.

Exhibit 4 illustrates alternative methods of reporting which can show utilization and machine efficiency at variance with each other. In the first instance, Reporting Procedure "A," utilization is shown as 100% because the machine has been reported as running for 70 hours against an available number of 70 hours. Comparison of the actual units produced with the number that should have been produced if the machine had run for 70 hours reveals that the machine, while running, operated at an efficiency of 70%. The overall percentage, obtained by multiplying the utilization percentage by the efficiency percentage, is 70% (100% × 70%).

EXHIBIT 4
COMPARISON OF ALTERNATIVE METHODS OF REPORTING
MACHINE UTILIZATION AND EFFICIENCY

Assumptions: Total available hours   70
Standard production per hour 300

Reporting Procedure "A"		Reporting Procedure "B"	
Running hours	70	Running hours	49
Machine utilization (70 divided by 70) = 100%		Machine utilization (49 divided by 70) = 70%	
Standard production:		Standard production:	
70 hours × 300 per hour	= 21,000	49 hours × 300 per hour	= 14,700
Actual units produced	= 14,700	Actual units produced	= 14,700
Machine efficiency $\dfrac{14{,}700}{21{,}000} =$	70%	Machine efficiency $\dfrac{14{,}700}{14{,}700} =$	100%
Overall efficiency:		*Overall efficiency:*	
Machine utilization 100% ×		Machine utilization 70% ×	
Machine efficiency 70% = 70%		Machine efficiency 100% = 70%	

Under Reporting Procedure "B," in which running hours are accounted for on a more meticulous basis, utilization is shown as 70%. The standard units of production, therefore, are based on 49 running hours rather than 70. Thus, the actual units produced (14,700) compare exactly with the standard based on 49 hours times 300 units per hour. The high machine efficiency percentage offsets the low utilization percentage.

Exhibit 4 illustrates that disparities in reporting—a situation that can never be entirely eliminated—require further evaluations of performance which will account for differences in reporting. The equating factor in this instance is the calculation of overall efficiency.

Profits are very closely related to the effectiveness with which a company utilizes its facilities. Although this chapter prescribes methods that can be used in measuring the effect on profits of changes in capacity, pure arithmetic is not the only criterion for making management decisions.

This situation will be discussed further in the following chapter.

12
Common Errors in Projecting the Productivity of Capacity Increases

Cost studies made to justify the purchase or rebuilding of capital equipment frequently overlook important cost factors. A typical cost that may not be considered is debugging of equipment. This can result in long periods of excessive machine downtime. New equipment may also require modification to fit the peculiarities of the product being run. Another overlooked cost is the requirement for tighter specifications in making the parts to be fed into automatic machines.

The same principles that apply to expansion from within apply with equal force to expansion through acquistion.

A calculated payback period which does not take factors such as the foregoing into account can overstate the savings and have a deleterious effect on profits and cash flow. While it may still make sense to expand capacity, management should know the true facts.

EXPANSION FROM WITHIN

The analytical procedures required in evaluating the economics of each purchase of new fixed assets or rebuilding existing machines can vary greatly because of the nature and mix of the types of assets being considered. Although a company may spend large sums on such purchases each year, it will frequently find that the analytical considerations used in the previous year cannot be applied to the current year. One year's plans may involve the purchase of an automatic assembly machine to reduce the labor cost of making a product. This was the case with the Erco Company (name disguised). The second year's fixed asset expenditures may involve the rebuilding of worn equipment, while the third year's program may be the acquisition of another company.

The factors that must be taken into account vary with the mix of the types of assets being considered for purchase. Many of the factors that must be given heavy weight in the analysis can go by unnoticed, making the analysis incomplete. It is therefore entirely possible, and frequently happens, that what appears to be a highly profitable purchase on paper can in actuality turn out to be substantially less profitable than indicated by the analysis.

The Erco Company provides a relatively simple example in analyzing the purchase of an automatic assembly machine. The purchase was recommended by Erco's Press Department foreman. The study approach pursued by the foreman, and presented to the general manager, was based on the assumption that purchase of a new automated assembly machine costing $150,000 would increase production and eliminate seven of the eight employees now performing the assembly operation manually. The supporting assumptions were as follows:

1. The press would operate 250 days per year.
2. After allowances for setup, the press would be utilized 75% of the available hours per day, or six hours.

3. The useful life of the press was assumed to be 10 years. This was considered to be conservative because the Internal Revenue Service (IRS) guidelines listed this type of equipment in its guidelines for depreciation as having a useful life of 12½ years.

Based on the foregoing assumptions, the foreman calculated a machine cost per hour as follows:

$$\text{Machine cost per hour} = \frac{\$150,000}{(10 \text{ years})(250 \text{ days})(6 \text{ hours})} = \$10 \text{ per hour}$$

The $10 per hour rate appeared to be a small cost in relation to labor because operators to be displaced by this machine were being paid $8.50 per hour. The foreman reasoned that the $8.50 would increase each time a new labor contract was negotiated but that the machine cost per hour would remain fixed.

Common Flaws in Many Analyses

The general manager felt that two factors were omitted from consideration in arriving at the $10 per hour machine cost:

1. Maintenance costs. As machines, particularly the more complex automated types, grow older, maintenance costs accelerate.
2. With technological advances being introduced at increasing rates, many machines become obsolete long before the end of their useful lives.

Although the general manager felt strongly about these flaws, he expressed interest in this approach to calculating a machine cost per hour. His chief objection was the assumption of a 10-year useful life. The argument advanced was that no one could predict how soon the new machine would become obsolete because of further technological changes in the method of manufacturing. He felt, further, that since products of the type to be assembled on the machine had an average life cycle of 2.6 years, there was no assurance that successor products could be assembled on this type of equipment. He therefore requested that the foreman recalculate the machine cost per hour based on a 2-year life—which was another way of showing a 2-year payback on the investment made in this machine. The revised calculation is:

$$\text{Machine cost per hour} = \frac{\$150,000}{(2 \text{ years})(250 \text{ days})(6 \text{ hours})} = \$50 \text{ per hour}$$

To Purchase or Not to Purchase

Simply comparing the hourly direct labor cost with the machine cost per hour as a means of justifying the purchase of the machine serves no useful purpose. The more significant criterion would be the cost saving per unit of production. But there is also a second consideration—will the production volume be sufficiently high to utilize the machine fully?

Comparison of the cost per unit by the two methods
Present method

8 employees at $8.50 per hour	= $68.00
Production per hour	= 240 units
Cost per unit ($68 divided by 240 units)	= $0.2833

Proposed method

1 machine operator at $8.50 per hour	= $ 8.50
Machine cost per hour at $50.00 per hour	= 50.00
	$58.50
Production per hour	= 360 units
Cost per unit ($58.50 divided by 360)	= $0.1625

Comparison of the total annual cost by the two methods
Present method
Total annual production of 625,000 units at $0.2833/unit = $177,060
Proposed method
Total annual production of 625,000 units at $0.1625/unit = 101,560
          Annual saving = $ 75,500

The total savings for the two-year payback period amount to $151,000, or $1,000 more than the purchase price of the machine. The required number of machine running hours per year needed to produce 625,000 units was calculated to be 1,736 (annual production of 625,000 units divided by 360 units per hour). The 1,736 hours were considered to be sufficiently close to the 1,500 hours (250 days × 6 hours per day) used as the basis for arriving at the machine cost of $50 per hour.

The Indirect Costs

The cost per hour of the eight direct labor employees under the present method and the cost of the one employee under the proposed method did not include the fringe benefits which are part of the indirect labor costs. The fringe benefits amounted to approximately 20% of the direct labor payroll. There is a savings in the fringe benefits as well as in the direct labor costs. The savings calculations are:

TOTAL UNITS DIVIDED BY UNITS PER HOUR	= LABOR HOURS ×	HOURLY DIRECT LABOR RATE	= TOTAL DIRECT LABOR COST	FRINGE BENEFITS AT 20%
Present method:				
$\dfrac{625,000 \text{ units}}{240/\text{hour}}$ =	2,604 ×	$68.00	= $177,072	= $35,414
Proposed method:				
$\dfrac{625,000 \text{ units}}{360/\text{hour}}$ =	1,736 ×	$ 8.50	= $ 14,756	= $ 2,951
	Total saving in fringe benefits			$32,463

Since seven of the eight direct labor employees were eliminated by the introduction of the automatic assembly machine, this resulted in a saving of $32,463 per year in fringe benefits.

Inasmuch as the machine cost of $50 per hour included provision for depreciation based on a two-year payback, the general manager concluded that the annual savings of $75,500 plus $32,463, in addition to a conservatively calculated machine costing rate, would more than cover any unexpected contingencies.

Why a Bright Outlook Turned Bleak

In spite of the optimistic results projected by the cost study relative to the purchase of the automatic assembly machine, unanticipated problems were revealed soon after the machine was set up. Although Erco's general manager did recognize the possibility of early obsolescence of the product as well as accelerating maintenance costs as the machine grew older, there were some other factors that were overlooked.

- Debugging problems. Any complex piece of machinery, such as an automatic assembly mechanism, requires a period of debugging that can substantially reduce production anywhere from one to three (or more) months.
- Modification is needed to fit the peculiarities of the product being assembled. In some instances, there may be a need to change the design.
- Closer tolerances are required in fabricating the parts assembled on automatic equipment.

Debugging

The general manager and his foreman did not allow for the possibility that a complex piece of equipment must go through a possibly long breaking-in period. Such a period may require numerous adjustments in the feeding and indexing mechanisms to assure that the parts to be assembled will come together at the proper time. Some of the adjustments may require disassembly and reassembly of various sections of the machine before proper functioning can be achieved. The downtime can be extensive.

Modification and/or Redesign

Many companies embarking on automation programs have found that they must redesign sections of the equipment to accommodate the peculiarities of their products. In one company that purchased automated foundry equipment, for example, it took three years and a lawsuit before the new equipment ran at anywhere near the production rate that was warranted by the supplier. Admittedly, this was an extreme case.

Need for Tighter Specifications of the Parts to be Assembled

The parts being made in Erco's Fabrication Department were satisfactory for manual assembly. However, those parts that had rough edges or were slightly out of dimension stuck in the feed mechanism, requiring the operator to stop the machine and remove the faulty parts. When several parts jammed together—a frequent occurrence—it was necessary for a maintenance man to disassemble part of the machine in order to remove the faulty parts. Because of the frequency of this type of occurrence, it was necessary to inspect and sort hundreds of parts each day.

It became obvious that the manual assembly operation could not be shut down. Debugging revealed that the gravity slides had to be set at a higher angle because the parts were light and frequently stopped midway. This required returning a section of the machine to the manufacturer for modification. It was also necessary to order new tooling for the fabrication department to meet the tighter specifications required in automatic assembly.

During the first two months spent in the debugging operation, the new machine averaged a production rate of between 100 to 150 units per hour, compared with the 360 units used as the basis for calculating the savings. Modification of the section to steepen the slope of the gravity slides required that still another section be returned to the manufacturer to assure proper interaction between the two sections. It took four weeks before these sections were completed and installed in the machine. The new tooling prints had to be redrawn. It took eight weeks before the new tools were received.

Could These Problems Have Been Avoided?

Problems of this type cannot be completely avoided. However, they could have been greatly minimized if the general manager or the foreman had had a better background in automatic assembly. Anytime a manually performed operation is transferred to automatic equipment, the tolerances of the parts must be tightened to avoid burrs and to assure that the parts are within the specifications required for proper movement through the machine. The general manager should have anticipated this situation.

The manufacturer had received a few parts and a sample of the completely assembled parts in order to design and build the equipment. A more knowledgeable general manager would have sent one of his representatives to watch the completed machine in operation for several hours before accepting delivery.

No record of the cost of these delays was available. However, the profits for the year declined by 5%. In the following year, they improved by 7%. This included recovery of the previous 5% reduction plus a gain of 2%. As might be expected, the return on investment was reduced during the year in which all the changes had to be made. It wasn't until the third year of operation that the machine attained its projected profitability.

The foregoing account emphasizes the importance of in-depth analyses when making studies to justify the acquisition or construction of fixed assets. Further, the nature and mix of the fixed assets can vary widely from year to year. This situation introduces new factors each year that must be taken into account. In the Erco Company example, several important factors were overlooked, thus creating a long delay and reducing the anticipated profitability.

Rebuilding Versus Purchasing New Equipment

The next case is related to one of the plants in the RG Company (name disguised). The manufacturing superintendent submitted an appropriation request for authorization to rebuild nine presses which were worn after years of service. The rebuilding would be done by the existing in-house maintenance staff at a cost of $165,000. This included the maintenance payroll and estimated cost of replacement parts. The justification was based on a comparison with the cost of purchasing new presses for a total cost of $225,000—a saving of $60,000.

The manufacturing vice-president reviewed the figures and the accompanying brochures of the manufacturer that quoted the price of $225,000. He noted that the brochures were not current. He then contacted the company to determine if there had been any state-of-the-art improvements since the previous brochures had been issued. The response was that an automatic feature had been added which would permit one operator to tend three to four presses at one time.

In the event of a jam, the buckling action of the metal being fed into the press would exert pressure against a solenoid which would stop the machine before damage could be done to the die. The additional cost with this added feature was approximately $20,000—raising the total cost from $225,000 to $245,000—$80,000 more than the cost of rebuilding the old presses. Since the annual pay for each operator, including fringe benefits, was $19,000, there would be a reduction of six operators (three on each of the two shifts) totaling $114,000. The $245,000 cost for the new presses less the saving of $114,000 in payroll meant a net cost of purchasing on the outside of $131,000. This was $34,000 below the $165,000 expenditure for rebuilding the old presses.

The manufacturing vice-president made the decision to purchase the presses. When he advised his plant superintendent of this decision, he also commented that if the maintenance staff was large enough to rebuild nine presses, there must be some over-staffing. He requested that the maintenance group be reduced to meet only the normal preventive and emergency repair needs. The superintendent reluctantly dropped two people—a further saving.

THE PLACE OF IN-HOUSE EQUIPMENT CONSTRUCTION AND REBUILDING

The preceding example of the RG Company should not be interpreted as an injunction against the involvement of maintenance departments in any machine rebuilding and construction. Maintenance departments in many companies make jigs and fixtures for use in fabrication and assembly of products. The crafts involved in this type of work have skills that can be productively employed in making improvements in some specialized types of equipment. The Electronics Division of Excel-Tech Products, Inc. (name disguised) provides such a case example.

The manufacturing superintendent of the Electronics Division wanted to purchase a new machine to replace what he considered to be a "Rube Goldberg" invention. This machine was used to put a solder coating on contact pins extending from the base of a molded plastic socket body. The solder coating process was performed by inserting the pins of the socket into openings on a lever. When the operator depressed a pedal, the lever was lowered into the solder pot to the depth needed to coat the pins. When the pedal was released, the lever, through spring action, catapulted the socket against a canvas backdrop to shake off the excess solder. Invariably, the plastic body was splattered with droplets of solder—requiring rework that took almost as much time as the solder dip operation. One of the maintenance workers who periodically worked on this equipment became aware of the plan to purchase a machine that would perform the solder coating without splattering the plastic body. The estimated cost of this machine was $27,000. In discussing this with his supervisor, the worker suggested modifying an obsolete drill press to perform this operation rather than paying $27,000 for a specially designed machine. Since the conversion of the press required only a day or two, the Maintenance Department obtained authorization to proceed.

The drill press was modified so that the socket could be slid into position in a fixture held in place by the chuck. The operator then lowered the fixture holding the socket into the solder pot to the proper depth. When the fixture was raised, the drill press head automatically rotated and shook off the excess solder against a heated circular metal shield. The droplets of solder that hit the shield remained in liquid form and flowed back into the solder pot. This process eliminated the need for rework because the centrifugal force of the spinning action forced the droplets of solder to fly off horizontally away from the socket.

Some companies using specialized manufacturing equipment have established their own equipment shops. The mission of these shops is to continually improve on the design of the equipment to conform with the changes in the products and thus improve the company's competitive position. The principles of managing fixed assets apply with equal force to both company-operated equipment shops and equipment purchased on the outside.

EXPANSION THROUGH ACQUISITIONS

The desire of management for bigness can be the by-product of a desire for a place in the sun. The bigger the company, the more important its executives become in the business community. Bigness, in this case, is a matter of pride coupled with aggressiveness and ambition. The need for bigness can also be ordained by the forces of competition, which continually squeeze out the marginal producer who does not have the resources to keep up with the growth of technology. This competitive situation forces companies to do more forward planning than they might otherwise do.

It is fortunate that the importance of forward planning is attracting so much management attention. However, because of the emphasis on the future, there is a tendency to discount the importance of past history. This is unfortunate because history frequently contains a wealth of information on past errors in judgment which can be overlooked in future planning.

The Case of the Durard Company

Take the case of the Durard Company, whose products consist of plastics molding, metal forming, and related hand assembly operations. The product line includes such items as push buttons for electronic and communications equipment, plastic knobs for appliances, electric shaver parts, camera parts, and a variety of formed metal parts used in the electronics industry.

The management of this company wanted to increase its share of the market. It planned to achieve this goal through the purchase of established companies as well as expansion from within. As each acquisition was digested, the plan was to move the operations to the town of Durard, for which the parent company was named. The management of the company was disappointed in the progress and changed general managers three times during a six-year period. The chronology of events leading to management dissatisfaction was as follows:

Purchase of Acme Plastics and expansion within Durard

Acme Plastics became a part of Durard in August of the first year shown in Exhibit 1. This acquisition resulted in a substantial increase in sales volume as well as profits. Since plans called for all Acme activities to be moved to Durard, a building expansion program was undertaken. This was completed in the spring of the second year, and the move was made. Concurrently with the completion of this move, 12 injection molding presses were purchased and set up in the expanded plant. The combination of the Acme move and the establishment of an injection molding department proved to be too big a bite. Since only key supervisory personnel of the Acme Company were transferred, critically needed personnel such as setup men and die/mold repairmen were in short supply. Utilization of equipment, which had normally been running at 95%, now dropped to an average of 45 to 50%. The new injection molding presses ran less than 25% of the time for several months

EXHIBIT 1

DURARD COMPANY ACTUAL AND PROJECTED SALES FOR TEN YEAR PERIOD

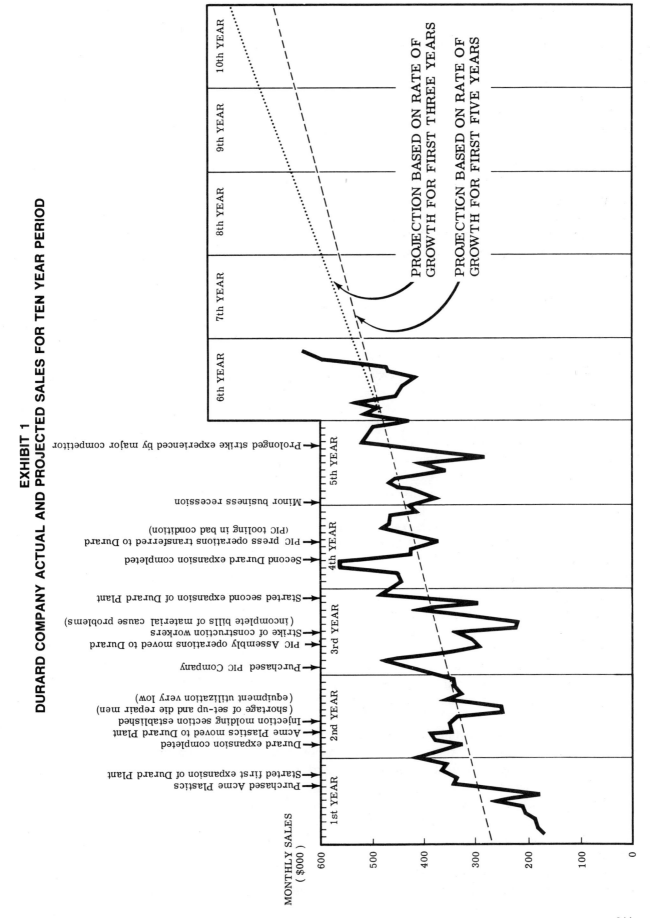

following installation, while operators and setup men were being trained and equipment problems were handled.

These problems were reflected in a reduced sales volume as well as reduced profits. As a result, the second year ended with a loss. Sales slipped throughout the second year because of the company's inability to make shipments to customers. Some improvement was experienced during the third year. Utilization of the equipment transferred from Acme increased to 75%—somewhat short of the desired 80 to 85%. The newly purchased injection molding equipment still lagged at 65%. The company anticipated that it would take six to nine months more before utilization of the equipment could attain optimum levels. The profit outlook still was not good, but improvement seemed in sight. Because the Durard Company was in sound financial condition, it was able to weather the storm. Under similar conditions, other companies might have failed.

Purchase of the PIC Company

The general manager who had been with Durard for two years had been replaced by a new man. The new man was advised of the company's interest in growth and of the recent problems that had been encountered.

Shortly after taking over, the new general manager learned that the PIC Company, which was in financial straits and losing money, could be purchased at a bargain price. This purchase would permit Durard to get into another related product line immediately and gain PIC's customers. With the Acme move out of the way, the decision was made to purchase PIC and to transfer the operations to Durard as soon as possible. Within two months, the unprofitable hand assembly items were moved. It was felt that the high labor rates paid at PIC's present location made profits out of the question. The substantially lower rates in the Durard area would help considerably. Although the rates were lower, management miscalculated in two other ways:

1. Bills of material were incomplete because PIC personnel had kept this information in their heads to reduce paperwork. Purchasing and production scheduling personnel could not work efficiently because of the absence of such up-to-date information.
2. The Durard plant could not accommodate the PIC press operations. The difficulty was not lack of space but the wrong type of floor construction. PIC's heavy presses required heavily reinforced floors.

PIC press operators and tool shopmen were leaving as soon as they could find other employment, knowing that their tenure was limited. Downtime on presses, because of the shortage of skilled personnel, increased greatly.

Plans for the second Durard expansion were hurriedly made, but actual work could not start because of an unexpected strike which closed down all construction in the area. Finally, with the settlement of the strike, construction began late in the year. Durard made a small profit that year, but its working capital was becoming strained.

The second expansion was completed late in the spring of the fourth year. Production schedules were firmed up, and certain PIC items were now running at high volume.

But then problems began to mount again. The tools used at PIC were of a poor quality—no longer meeting the tighter requirements of the industry, which had increased the use of automated equipment. As a result, many fabricated parts that did not meet the tighter tolerances had to be scrapped or reworked. It was obvious that a substantial retooling program was required. In the meantime, productivity dropped and production schedules had to be juggled frequently to satisfy specific customer demands. The tooling program would require 8 to 10 months for completion. In the meantime, production output continued to drop, with a resultant slippage in sales and profits. To add to the problems, a business recession developed near the end of the fourth year during what was normally a high-volume production period. Although the recession was relatively mild, productivity continued to slip, while the company frantically tried to find competent toolmakers to speed up the retooling program. The original forecast of 8 to 10 months for completion was now changed to 15 to 18 months. At this point, the general manager was released and still another new man brought in.

The new general manager (let's call him Norm Bayard) was somewhat surprised to learn that his predecessors had had such short tenures. He realized that if he simply picked up the reins without doing some deeper investigation, he might fall victim to the same problems that resulted in the release of the earlier general managers.

In his get-acquainted interviews with the members of his staff, Bayard decided that he would attempt to determine exactly what the problems were and how they might have been prevented—or at least greatly minimized. He sensed that some of the staff would undoubtedly apply 20/20 hindsight to impress him. To avoid being misled, Norm double-checked all statements that were made. When he was told that bad tools had been at fault, he asked such questions as the following:

- Were the tools poorly designed, or were they merely worn out and in need of maintenance?
- Could better maintenance have prevented the problem?
- Is it possible that only some of the key high-volume tools were the source of the problems? In that case, would the availability of a duplicate set of tools have allowed the needed maintenance?

By asking questions such as these, statements could be cross-checked with more factual data. Without being obvious, Norm gradually accumulated a volume of information which was correlated with past sales. To this he added the data accumulated during his own tenure. Exhibit 1, referred to earlier, was actually developed by Norm. Since growth seemed to be paramount in the minds of top management, two projections were made for the balance of the 10-year period. These were based on.

- The rate of growth for the first three years.
- The rate of growth for the first five years.

The first three years would project the trend if the high rate of sales increase experienced in this period could be duplicated. The five-year period, however, involved a more conservative estimate because it reflected the problems incident to the PIC move and the effect of a business recession. The favorable effect of a major competitor's strike, which occurred in the sixth year, was not included because this was considered to be a nonrecurring windfall.

A Period of Consolidation

The corrective programs instituted by Norm and his predecessor gradually began to take hold. Although the production volume continued to slip, defective production was reduced considerably. It was now only a matter of time before the problems of tooling and setup would be corrected. The Durard Company had profited immensely from the long strike of its competitor because it was able to accept business on a more selective basis and set up certain equipment to run continuously. One-shift operations were expanded to two shifts—some to three shifts—and the toolroom work week was extended to 45 hours. Sales and profits soared, somewhat relieving a serious shortage of working capital.

GUIDELINES FOR PROFITABLE EXPANSION

The new general manager felt that the pictorial representation of the problems experienced by the Durard Company, which are depicted in the exhibit, served a twofold purpose:

1. It dramatized the history of past events and demonstrated their effect on operations.
2. The availability of this type of information would be helpful at management meetings to reinforce the need for solid planning.

It was obvious that the previous two general managers had moved too quickly to fulfill the company's desire for growth—with the result that the company's working capital became seriously impaired. As a result of this and the other observations made by Norm, the following guidelines for expansion were established:

1. Coordinate engineering and production activities. Make certain that bills of material and process specifications are documented.
2. If the design of a product is changed, modify the tooling immediately. Waiting until the order is processed can mean expensive delays and problems in scheduling.
3. Don't expand beyond the limits of available skills. Hold expansion within the limits of the skills that can be made available in the foreseeable future; otherwise productivity will suffer.
4. Transfer the required skills—hourly as well as salaried. If some employees are reluctant to relocate, ask them to stay on for an additional six-month period to train employees at the new location of the operations being moved. The extra travel and living expenses will be far less than the high cost of poorly utilized equipment.
5. Evaluate the company's financial resources. Determine the potential effect on working capital if things don't go according to plan.
6. Check what your competitors are doing. If they have already embarked on a major expansion program, you may want to take a different course in order to avoid a large investment in excess facilities of that particular product.
7. Don't expand just for the sake of growth. Nothing is to be gained by increasing the sales volume at the sacrifice of profits.

Durand's management acknowledged that its policies emphasizing growth may have been overambitious. To avoid a recurrence of past problems, the above guidelines were issued in the form of a policy letter to all key members of management. All subsequent plans for expansion were reviewed by a committee headed by the executive vice-president and made up of representatives of manufacturing, engineering, production control, purchasing, sales, and finance. This group met approximately once a month to evaluate plans for future expansion and to review progress on current moves. The results of these meetings were summarized and distributed to the appropriate individuals.

Establishing and formalizing the above guidelines had a salutory effect. The rate of growth for the balance of the 10-year period was not as great as the company had hoped for originally. However, it did exceed the growth rate of the first five-year period. Profits, however, more than doubled. The experience of the Durard Company provides an object lesson for other companies intent on rapid growth. The question that should be asked is: "Am I interested in rapid expansion of sales volume, or am I interested in more profits?" It may be more judicious, for reasons outlined in this chapter, to slow the rate of sales growth in order to maximize productivity and its by-product—greater profits.

13
Productivity Management by Level of Responsibility

The first part of this chapter discusses some of the measures of productivity that are suitable for segments of the company's operations.

But division and corporate-level executives with profit responsibility do not have the time to deal with all the factors that add up to total productivity in their area.

The second part of the chapter therefore explains how gains and losses in productivity can be determined in two simple steps by analyzing the income statement. The first step calculates the effect of changes in the cost/selling price relationship, while the second determines the portion of the profit or loss that is attributable to a productivity gain or loss.

Usage of the term "productivity" has increased greatly in recent years because of intensified competitive pressures. Many companies, as well as government statistical reports, use labor hours as the denominator for measuring productivity. Companies using high-technology automatic equipment are turning to machine hours as the denominator.

There will always be some need for measuring productivity in terms of labor hours and machine hours. However, it is becoming more and more important for the executive with profit responsibility to know the breakdown of profits in two segments that will tell:

1. To what extent the company has been able to maintain or improve the cost/ selling price relationships that were planned.
2. The amount of profit (or loss) due to increases or decreases in productivity.

The profit for these two segments cannot be denominated in terms of labor or machine hours; they must be expressed in dollars. This chapter not only discusses productivity in denominators that are useful in the smaller segments of the operations; it also identifies the portion of the profit due to changes in the cost/selling price relationship and the portion due to changes in productivity.

WHAT IS PRODUCTIVITY?

Productivity is the difference between the quantity or value of input and the quantity or value of output. When output increases faster than input, there is a productivity gain. When the reverse occurs, there is a productivity loss. There are some important factors, however, that must be taken into account. The introduction of automation, for example, causes a spectacular increase in output since labor hours are reduced and the rate of production is increased. There is a less dramatic increase in value output when the cost of the equipment, its maintenance, and other associated costs are taken into account.

Productivity can be measured for an entire nation or for segments of the economy. As with any type of statistical measure, there are intangibles that defy expression in terms of a statistic. The productivity improvement of a nation can be expressed as, say, 3% in a particular year. But this figure on a national average will include the cost of welfare and pollution control devices—which represent negative factors.

Measurement of productivity increases (or decreases) becomes simpler and more definitive as smaller segments of the economy are considered because the effect of many intangibles is usually not included. Manufacturing is a good example. But even here, there are problems. We have already mentioned the effect of automation on increasing the volume of output. There are other methods that can increase productivity by cutting costs (the economists' definition). Use of sonics or lasers for cutting material, for example, can reduce the waste and losses characteristic of more conventional cutting methods. More efficient use of material, use of lower-cost material, and better buying practices are some of the other techniques that can result in lower unit costs. On the other hand, increased productivity of labor through automation can sometimes result in higher unit costs of material because material specifications will have to be tightened when automatic equipment performs assembly operations.

METHODS OF MEASUREMENT

There are numerous methods that can be used in measuring productivity. Some are quite simple and appropriate for the simpler one-company or one-industry situation. Others cover broader areas and require certain adjustments to the basic figures before productivity can be measured. The methods that will be discussed are:

- Units of output per labor hour
- Weighted labor hours per unit
- Productivity trend control for direct labor
- Sales per labor hour
- Productivity based on analysis of the profit

Units of Output Per Labor Hour

Many productivity measures are based on sales value per labor dollar expended. The use of dollars can distort the results because of changes in prices and in labor rates. Under certain conditions, units produced per labor hour would eliminate such dollar distortions. An illustration of this method is shown below:

	PERIOD 1	PERIOD 2	PERIOD 3	PERIOD 4
Units produced	2,400	2,450	2,500	2,750
Labor hours	5,200	5,200	5,150	5,500
Units per labor hour	0.462	0.471	0.485	0.500
Productivity change		+1.9%	+3.0%	+3.1%

This example is suitable when the units are fairly homogeneous—pairs of shoes produced, for example. The next illustration will deal with the nonhomogeneous types of products.

Weighted Labor Hours Per Unit

This method equates for differences in the products by using the standard labor hours required to produce each product type. It also assumes a balanced mix of products for which the weighted labor hours per average unit of product contains only minor fluctuations.

	PERIOD 1	PERIOD 2	PERIOD 3	PERIOD 4
Weighted labor hours per unit of product	1.980	1.945	1.907	1.851
Change in labor hours per unit of product		−0.035	−0.038	−0.056
Percent change in productivity		+1.8%	+1.9%	+2.9%

Each period's output is weighted by multiplying the production of each product by the standard labor hours required to produce it. If there are any changes in the methods used to produce a given product, the results of such changes will be reflected in the productivity until such time as the standards are changed.

Note in the above figures that the labor hours per unit of product were reduced in periods 2, 3, and 4. The percentage change in productivity was therefore favorable. This change was calculated by dividing the reduced labor hours of 0.035 in period 2 by the weighted labor hours per unit of product in period 1 of 1.980, to arrive at the increase of 1.8% in productivity. The weighted labor hours per unit of product are a better measure of productivity than the units per unweighted labor hours because they recognize product differences.

Productivity Trend Control (Earned Versus Actual Direct Labor Hours)

It should be recognized that all measures of productivity are affected by a mixture of factors. These include changes in personnel efficiency, in work methods, and in raw material specifications. There is also another factor that must be considered—volume of production, as well as the length of production runs.

When production is automated, it is possible for an operator to run two, three, four, or more machines simultaneously. A worker who normally runs four machines may have to run only two if the level of business activity drops. This worker's productivity would drop radically, yet he is actually putting in the same hours and working at the same relative efficiency. A similar situation exists when a company uses highly skilled employees who cannot be dismissed and recalled each time business dips and then improves.

The Productivity Trend Control, illustrated in Exhibit 1, shows how productivity can be monitored on a regular basis—weekly, monthly, or quarterly—to provide data that are far more meaningful than the broad overall measures such as units of output per labor hour and weighted labor hours per unit discussed earlier.

The figures shown in the Productivity Trend Control report are the actual results in a company using such a report. Note in column 5 (earned hours as a percentage of actual hours) that the total percentages for the weekly figures rise from 77.8% in week 1 to 81.6% in week 3 and 90.8% in week 4. Some of the departmental figures are erratic, as in the case of departments A and B in week 4, in which the efficiency jumps over 100%. This is due to an accumulation of production in week 3, which required a final step before the worker could be given credit for his completed production. In week 4, the backlog was given the finishing touches and counted as production in that week.

EXHIBIT 1
PRODUCTIVITY TREND CONTROL (EARNED VERSUS ACTUAL DIRECT LABOR HOURS)

	Earned Hours Scheduled (1)	Earned Hours Produced (2)	Produced Percent of Scheduled (3)	Actual Hours (4)	Earned % of Actual Hours (5)	Direct Charged to Indirect (6)	Total Labor Hours Available (7)	Earned % of Available Hours (8)
Week 1								
Total	2,762	2,608	94%	3,348	77.8%	5,073	8,421	31%
Dept. A	196	173	88	200	86.7	175	375	46
Dept. B	784	674	86	900	74.9	2,370	3,270	21
Dept. C	1,362	1,349	99	1,664	81.0	1,815	3,479	40
Dept. D	420	412	98	584	70.5	713	1,297	32
Week 2								
Total	2,841	2,601	92%	3,365	77.3%	4,649	8,013	34%
Dept. A	265	164	62	186	88.2	186	372	44
Dept. B	765	682	89	928	73.4	2,160	3,088	22
Dept. C	1,521	1,428	94	1,767	80.8	1,560	3,326	43
Dept. D	290	327	113	484	67.6	743	1,227	26
Week 3								
Total	3,120	3,020	97%	3,700	81.6%	5,011	8,711	35%
Dept. A	184	193	104	213	90.6	180	393	49
Dept. B	1,003	1,013	101	1,205	84.0	2,330	3,535	29
Dept. C	1,246	1,222	98	1,493	81.8	1,690	3,183	38
Dept. D	687	592	86	789	75.1	811	1,600	37
Week 4								
Total	3,630	3,529	97%	3,886	90.8%	4,407	8,293	42%
Dept. A	242	200	83	193	103.7	158	351	57
Dept. B	1,165	1,070	92	1,060	101.0	2,129	3,189	34
Dept. C	1,642	1,739	106	1,880	92.5	1,465	3,345	52
Dept. D	581	520	89	753	69.2	655	1,408	37

$$\text{Column 3} = \frac{\text{Column 2}}{\text{Column 1}} \quad \text{Column 5} = \frac{\text{Column 2}}{\text{Column 4}} \quad \text{Column 7} = \text{Column 4} + \text{Column 6} \quad \text{Column 8} = \frac{\text{Column 2}}{\text{Column 7}}$$

The Productivity Trend Report contains the following:

Earned hours scheduled (column 1): This indicates the number of earned hours of production that were scheduled. Note the increasing trend of earned hours scheduled—from 2,762 in week 1 to 3,630 in week 4. Column 3 shows earned hours produced as a percentage of earned hours scheduled.

Earned hours produced (column 2): The production in each of the four departments has been extended by the standard or earned hours. The earned hours are based on time studies made by the industrial engineers.

Produced percent of scheduled (column 3): Shows the percentage of production to the amount scheduled.

Actual hours (column 4): These are the actual hours of direct labor required to achieve the earned hours produced in Column 2. They do not include downtime of any kind.

Earned percent of actual hours (column 5): The efficiency or productivity percentage is obtained by dividing the actual hours in column 4 into the earned hours produced in column 2.

Direct charged to indirect (column 6): This column shows the nonproductive direct labor. These are the hours during which no products could be produced because of delays due to such factors as lack of material, machine breakdowns, tools in bad condition, cleaning up, and setting up short runs. Each of these items is reported separately in the underlying records. This permits management to monitor each of these causes of lost time in order to prevent them from getting out of line.

Total actual direct labor hours available (column 7): This column shows the total hours of employees classified as direct labor, whether charged as productive or nonproductive. The figures in this column are made up of column 4 plus column 6.

Earned percent of available hours (column 8): Companies that measure productivity without considering the nonproductive portion of direct labor can be deceived into thinking that the productivity of the direct labor is greater than it actually is. In the company used for illustrative purposes in this case example, the percent earned to total actual direct labor was also calculated as shown in column 8. Note that the percentages in this column are generally less than half those shown in column 5. This was a shocking revelation to management when the initial report was demonstrated on this basis. Instead of burying the direct labor charged to indirect labor in the overhead category, as in the past, these items are now analyzed individually—as noted above in the explanation of column 6.

The Productivity Trend Control* report provides a fairly sophisticated measure of the productivity of direct labor—for both the "productive" portion and the total labor, which includes the nonproductive as well as the productive portion.

As products and manufacturing operations increase in complexity, the horizon for measuring productivity must be broadened. Two illustrations of this process will be discussed. The first covers the measurement of sales per labor hour and how to cope with the impact of changes in sales prices on the two successive time periods illustrated. The second demonstrates the determination of productivity from information contained in the income statements, in which adjustments must be made not only for changes in selling prices but for changes in costs as well.

Sales Per Labor Hour

In Exhibit 2, period 1 has been used as the base period from which productivity in period 2 will be measured.

The base period: To simplify the illustration, only four products have been used. The labor hours required in period 1 to produce each of the four products are listed immediately below the listing of sales. These labor hours are then divided into the respective products to arrive at the dollar sales per labor hour in the base period.

---

* Permission granted by AICPA to reuse Exhibit 1, previously printed in the December, 1985 issue of the Journal of Accountancy.

EXHIBIT 2
SALES PER LABOR HOUR

Product #		Sales in Period 1	Sales in Period 2		
		Base Period	Current Period Prices	Percent Price Changes	Adjusted to Base Period Prices
17289		$ 713,760	$ 765,640	102%	$ 750,627
01651		320,670	319,615	103	310,306
02608		9,888	18,440	—	18,440
15734		1,770,480	967,040	101.5	952,749
	Total	$2,814,798	$2,070,735		$2,032,122

Product #		Labor Hours in Period 1			Labor Hours in Period 2
17289		10,935			10,890
01651		2,833			2,684
02608		165			365
15734		19,520			11,620
	Total	33,453			25,559

Product #		Sales Per Labor Hour in Period 1			Sales Per Labor Hour in Period 2
17289		$ 65.27			$ 68.93
01651		113.19			115.61
02608		59.93			50.52
15734		90.70			81.99
Weighted Average		$ 84.14			$ 79.51

Period 2: Since the sales for period 2 are stated in period 2 prices, they must be adjusted by factoring each product's sales by the percentage by which prices have been increased (or decreased). These percentages are shown in the column headed "Percent Price Changes." They include a 2% price increase for product #17289, a 3% increase for #01651, no change for product #02608, and a 1.5% increase for #15734. The period 2 sales are then divided by 1.02, 1.03, 0, and 1.015, respectively. The result of these computations is that period 2 sales are based on period 1 selling prices.

These sales at the base period prices are then divided by the period 2 labor hours incurred for each product. The resulting sales per labor hour are shown in the lower third of the column.

Use of labor hours as the base for measuring the productivity of sales can be a valid practice in companies that are highly labor intensive. If, however, there is a high degree of automation in which the ratio of labor hours to machine hours varies widely from product to product, the use of labor hours can have a distorting effect.

Productivity Based on Breakdown of Profit

The discussions and illustrative examples pertaining to measurement of productivity have, thus far, dealt with segments of manufacturing or other activities. These measurements illustrate how segments of a company management can monitor productivity in various stages of the manufacturing process. Although these segmental measurements are valuable to foremen, plant managers, and general managers, they are too fragmented for use by top management. The measurement of productivity at this level must be directly identifiable with its impact on profitability.

The income statement is the logical vehicle for identifying the portion of the profit (or loss) associated with productivity. A method for isolating the portion of the profit that reflects productivity consists of two steps:

1. Calculate the profit increase or decrease between the base period and the current period.
2. Adjust the current period's figures by sales price changes and the impact of inflation on costs.

The breakdown of profit in order to identify productivity is best made at the gross profit level, since this reflects the productivity of the manufacturing operations—unburdened by allocations of SG&A expenses. Determination of the profit increase or decrease and the contribution of productivity requires a comparison of two periods—one of which will be called the "base period," the other the "current period." The portion of the profit due to productivity can be identified by comparing year-to-year or quarter-to-quarter figures. The year-to-year figures are likely to be more accurate because the annual physical inventory corrects for any discrepancies between book and physical inventories that may have occurred during the year.

Month-to-month calculations of productivity tend to be more erratic than those of the longer intervals because the manufacturing costs incurred in any single monthly period may be greater or less than the cost of sales due to inventory increases or decreases.

Month-to-month measurement of productivity is not useless, however. A manufacturing income statement can be prepared by comparing the manufacturing costs incurred during the month with the sales value of finished products moved into inventory in the same month.

Admittedly, the amount of profit will differ between the two types of income statements. But on a cumulative basis, they should even out. The author prefers the manufacturing income statement for two reasons:

• The manufacturing income statement is more acceptable to the plant management because it more closely reflects the current month's operations.
• Calculation of productivity requires that the impact of inflation on costs be determined. It is more difficult to make this determination for the cost of sales than for the cost of production because the cost of sales figure in most companies is not readily identifiable by material and payroll costs.

Determining the Portion of Profit Attributable to Productivity

The abbreviated income statement summary below shows the sales, cost of sales, and gross profit for two successive periods. The first column, "Base Period," is treated as a standard for measuring the results in the second column, "Current Period."

INCOME STATEMENT SUMMARY*
($000)

	BASE PERIOD	CURRENT PERIOD
Net sales	$102,540	$162,514
Cost of sales	82,596	126,419
Gross profit $	$ 19,944	$ 36,096
Gross profit %	19.45%	22.21%

* If a manufacturing income statement were used rather than the conventional type, net sales would become sales value of production and cost of sales would become cost of production or manufacturing costs incurred.

Step 1: Calculating the profit increase or decrease. The current period's sales ($162,515) are multiplied by the base period's gross profit percentage (19.45%). The cost of sales then becomes 80.55% of sales—the same percentage as the cost of sales in the base period (see columns 1 and 2 below).

INCOME STATEMENT SUMMARY

	(1) BASE PERIOD		(2) CURRENT PERIOD AS ADJUSTED		(3) CURRENT PERIOD AS REPORTED	
	$	%	$	%	$	%
Net sales	$102,540	100.00	162,515	100.00	162,515	100.00
Cost of sales	82,596	80.55	130,906	80.55	126,419	77.79
Gross profit	$ 19,944	19.45	31,609	19.45	36,096	22.21

Since the actual cost of sales in the current period (column 3) is lower than the adjusted amount in column 2, the gross profit in column 3 is higher than that in column 2:

Gross profit in current period as reported	= $36,096
Gross profit in current period after adjustment to base period =	31,609
Gross profit increase (improved cost/selling price ratio)	$ 4,487

Step 2: Calculating the productivity. The impact of productivity on profits is measured by adjusting the sales by the price increases (or decreases) for the current period; the cost of sales is adjusted by the inflation rate.

	CURRENT PERIOD (1)	ADJUSTING FACTORS (2)	DEFLATED FIGURES (3)	ADJUSTED TO BASE PERIOD PROFIT % (4)
Net sales	$162,515	109.2%	148,823	148,823
Cost of sales	126,419	104.7	120,744	119,877
Gross profit $	$ 36,096		28,079	28,946
Gross profit %	22.21%		18.87%	19.45%

The adjustment to sales prices and to the cost of sales is illustrated in columns 1 to 3.

Column 1 shows the current period's figures as they appeared on the income statement. The adjusting factors in column 2 show that prices were increased by 9.2% during the current period, while cost increases due to inflation rose by 4.7%. The resulting adjusting factors, which are shown in column 2, were divided into the figures in column 1. Column 3 shows the deflated figures, which result in a gross profit percentage of 18.87%.

To determine the amount of profit increase or decrease due to productivity changes, the deflated figures in column 3 must be adjusted to reflect the profit margin of 19.45% in the base period. When this adjustment is made, it shows that the cost of sales would have been $119,877 (see column 4). Column 3, however, shows that when the actual costs are deflated, they show a cost of sales amounting to $120,744, or $867 more than in column 4. In summary, then, the productivity calculation is:

Deflated cost of sales	$120,744
Deflated cost of sales adjusted to base period profit %	119,877
Decrease in profit due to reduced productivity	$ (867)

GUIDELINES FOR MEASUREMENT OF PRODUCTIVITY

The productivity measurements discussed in this chapter are based on total units produced, on departmental efficiency, and on measures based on the use of dollar values. The guidelines that apply to these are as follows:

1. In measuring units of output in terms of finished units per labor hour or per employee, restrict this method to homogeneous units.
2. If productivity measurement of nonhomogeneous units is desired, use total labor based on a weighting of the labor by the type and quantity of the various kinds of units produced.
3. In calculating productivity by departmental responsibility, do not limit the calculation to a comparison of the actual labor while on standard with the earned hours. This type of measurement, which is used by many companies, understates the measurement of productivity in two ways:
   a. It does not compare the earned hours with the earned hours scheduled, a measure of utilization.
   b. It does not include the direct labor charged to indirect labor. This labor should also be included in the base for calculating productivity because it is direct labor and should have been utilized for productive work (see Exhibit 1).
4. When using dollar figures in measuring productivity, whether sales or costs, they must be adjusted for price changes and inflation, respectively, to assure comparability from period to period.

SECTION 4
KEY MANAGEMENT REPORTS AND HOW TO PRODUCE THEM

"Is your manufacturing services staff earning its keep?" is the question posed by Chapter 14. It discusses the functional responsibilities of the manufacturing services staff in performing operations audits at the various manufacturing locations and preparing a report of its findings and recommendations to management—both local and corporate. This is a key management report because it specifically identifies weaknesses and recommendations for correction. These are not readily discernible in the conventional types of reports because they merely reflect the symptoms.

Chapter 15 discusses another type of "customized" report which creates individual profit centers for manufacturing and marketing. This segregation of profit responsibility may not completely eliminate the historical adversarial relationship between these two functions, but it can appreciably narrow the principal reasons for disagreement.

The old cliche that "there are liars, damn liars, and statisticians" could very well be applied to the graphic presentation of data. In most cases, the deficiencies in graphic presentations are not intentional. Chapter 16 illustrates the common errors made in preparing graphs and how they can be corrected.

Chapter 17 highlights the major areas of weakness in the cost accounting system. More importantly, it points out that the principal underlying weakness is the failure of many cost accountants to become sufficiently familiar with the manufacturing operation. The 10 guidelines listed in this chapter describe the steps to be followed in obtaining the necessary familiarity.

14
Is Your Manufacturing Services Staff Earning its Keep?

Corporate executives of large companies must rely on their manufacturing services staff to keep them abreast of "soft spots" in the field. This chapter discusses the duties of such staff personnel, with specific case examples illustrating the kind of information that is expected. It also presents 10 guidelines that should be helpful in assuring that the manufacturing services staff earns its keep.

In large manufacturing corporations, as well as many small ones, executives responsible for profitable operations are faced with a wide range of mind-boggling problems due to the complexity of business, rapidity of change, and competitive pressures. No matter how brilliant such individuals may be, they do not have the time to keep informed in depth on the complexities of their manufacturing operations, which may be spread throughout the country. They must therefore rely heavily on the manufacturing services staff, who must "live" in the factories in order to monitor adherence to sound procedures and good interdisciplinary relationships, study operational performance by the various disciplines, and evaluate the cost and operating controls.

MISSION OF THE CORPORATE MANUFACTURING SERVICES STAFF

The principal mission of this group is to act as "operations auditors" (as opposed to financial auditors). In this role, they spend the majority of their time at the manufacturing locations. Their investigations include:

- Evaluating the systems and procedures.
- Determining whether these are being complied with and if they are adequate.
- Monitoring interdisciplinary relationships to assure that one discipline does not violate procedures that affect the efficient functioning of another one.
- Studying the operational performance of the various disciplines to determine if the functions are being performed efficiently.
- Appraising and evaluating the cost and operating controls.

The following case example illustrates some of the problems that can be disclosed.

The ESKO Division (name disguised) is a manufacturer of kitchen and bathroom hardware as well as related fixtures. As with the products of many companies, design changes are introduced periodically to spur sales and to meet competitive challenges. In this division, forecasts used as a basis for planning material requirements proved to be incorrect because the materials manager and the design engineer failed to work together closely enough. As a result, material purchases were based on the assumption that the existing design of one of the products would remain in the line longer than was actually the case. When the materials manager learned that a new line was to be launched sooner than he anticipated, it was too late to stem the flow of incoming material for a product line that was now obsolete.

It is obvious that there was a serious lack of interdisciplinary coordination between the design engineering function and the group responsible for purchasing and inventory management. Procedures did exist for alerting all concerned departments sufficiently in advance when the design of an existing product was to be changed, when a new product was to be launched, and when an existing product was to be replaced by a new one. However, the paperwork was continually issued late. In short, the design engineering group did not follow procedures on a timely basis, with the result that interdisciplinary relationships were not properly synchronized.

Another inventory-related finding at the same location disclosed that modifications in existing products were scheduled for implementation without first determining the quantity and dollar value of component parts and finished products that would be rendered obsolete by the change. A test showed that in the course of a year, it was estimated that modifications in products occurred about twice a month on the average. The potential value of the resulting inventory obsolescence was as high as $110,000 per year.

The report for this division, which was reviewed with the general manager prior to submission to the corporate vice-president of manufacturing, made the following recommendations:

1. All concerned disciplines should be notified well in advance of the planned introduction of new products in order to facilitate better coordination.
2. All product change notices should contain a section showing the quantity and value of all components and finished products in inventory that would be rendered obsolete by the change.

RESPONSIBILITY OF THE CORPORATE EXECUTIVE

The vice-president of manufacturing, executive vice-president, chief operating officer, or other executive to whom such reports are addressed should assume that if a deficiency exists at one location, there is a good possibility that it exists at other locations. Accordingly, the pragmatic executive will issue a special letter or bulletin to all general managers requesting that they report to him on the procedures being followed to minimize inventory obsolescence when new products are introduced or existing products are modified.

STAFFING AND QUALIFICATIONS OF THE CORPORATE MANUFACTURING SERVICES GROUP

The staffing of this group is determined by the number of manufacturing locations rather than by the total dollar value of sales. The group should be organized in teams of two—each team performing an operations audit of each of 12 locations once a year. This allows an average of four weeks per review. The less complex operations might require less than four weeks—allowing the excess time for the more complex plants. The larger company with, say, 72 manufacturing locations would require six teams plus the group head, who would direct and schedule the assignments.

The teams would consist of a factorywise cost accountant and an experienced industrial engineer. Both should be comfortable in the factory environment and should be good listeners as well as good communicators. There are further qualifications that can only be determined after a period of time on the job. Even some highly qualified persons cling to the corporate office atmosphere and attempt to fulfill their responsibilities by long-distance telephone, correspondence, and periodic overnight trips to visit the plant locations. This can be illustrated with an actual example related by the manufacturing superintendent of the X-ray tube plant of a large company.

"This staff guy from Corporate was designing a performance report for the cathode ray tube plant which supplies the plant that makes the computer terminals. He wanted to avoid an out-of-town trip, so he called me to ask if I would have someone take him through our plant, which is near the corporate offices. When he told me that he was going to apply what he learns from seeing my X-ray tube operation to develop a report for the cathode ray tube plant, I almost split my gut. These two products are as different as night and day. I had someone give him the 25-cent tour, but when the story got around, the corporate staff became the laughingstock of the company."

The plant manager of another company complained about the number of telephone calls he had been receiving from the corporate staff personnel, with special reference to one member of the manufacturing services staff. This individual, according to the plant manager, was so unfamiliar with the operation that he didn't even know what questions to ask. "One of my department heads gave him an answer to what he thought the caller wanted to know, but we have doubts that he knew what to do with the information after he received it."

These two examples hark back to the reference made at the beginning of this chapter that the members of the manufacturing services staff (like the traveling salesman) must "live" in the field. Companies with a manufacturing services staff should seriously consider giving newly hired staff members rotation assignments in manufacturing departments such as production scheduling, inspection, and production control.

STEPS IN AN OPERATIONS AUDIT

A systematic program must be followed by the manufacturing services teams. Such a program must include the following steps:

- Plant tour to become familiar with the manufacturing processes and the products being manufactured.
- Interviews with key factory personnel.
- Preparation of draft reports as the work progresses.
- Review of findings and recommendations with the general manager of the plant.
- Final report containing the findings and recommendations.

The Plant Tour

Corporate personnel visiting a factory location often breeze through a plant tour, not realizing the wealth of information that can be obtained by being observant. Take the Electrical Products Division (name disguised), for example. This division produced ground rod, a type of lightning arrestor that carries off excess current into the ground. This product was manufactured by running coils of steel through a copper plating tank. The plating thicknesses varied depending on the application of the copper plated rod. The overhead costs of plating such as energy, depreciation, maintenance, occupancy costs, and chemicals were applied to the product on a per pound basis of plated rod. Since the rod with the thinner plating ran through faster and accumulated more poundage in a given time period than the heavier plating, the overhead cost charged to the lightly plated rods was excessive. Conversely, the heavier-plated rods, which ran through at a slower rate, accumulated less poundage in the same time period. The heavier-plated product, therefore, was assigned less overhead than the lighter-plated types. Management was thus being deceived as to the true cost/selling price relationships of the various thicknesses of ground rod plating. It was obvious, merely by observing the operation, that the costing procedures were deficient. A recommendation was made to change the method of applying the overhead costs on the basis of machine hours rather than on the weight of the products.

The foregoing example is illustrative of weaknesses in product costing that can be uncovered during a plant tour. A plant tour can reveal weaknesses in operational performance in the same way. A company whose products included steam irons utilized a moving conveyor on which the fully assembled irons were hung. At the testing work station, the irons that passed inspection were removed from the conveyor and placed on carts that were wheeled to the packing area. The defective irons were left on the conveyor to be transported to the repair station. It was obvious to the perceptive observer that it would make more sense to extend the conveyor to the packing area and place the defective irons in the carts for transfer to the repair station.

An individual with some feel for the factory environment could readily make similar observations relating to work pace, unbalanced assembly lines, inefficient work flow, poor layout at the workplaces, and the like.

Interviews With Key Factory Personnel

The observations gleaned and questions raised as a result of a review of notes made during the plant tour provide an excellent base for the interviews with key factory personnel. These cover such disciplines as cost accounting, industrial engineering, quality control, purchasing, production control, and maintenance.

In an interview, the quality control manager of the industrial air conditioning division of a large manufacturer was asked why so much rework was being done on air conditioners that had already been packed for shipment. He explained that there had been failures in the field in the three new industrial air conditioners that were recently developed by the New Products Group, a corporate-level function. When the new products were turned over to the factory for production, the Quality Control Department at the factory did not receive testing specifications because the New Products Group claimed it was too busy. As a result, the plant Quality Control Department established its own parameters for inspection—without the benefit of the background knowledge amassed by the development engineers.

The testing specifications established by the plant proved to be deficient. As a result, a large number of units failed in the field. The company had to recall many of them and rework those that were completed but had not yet been shipped. This was obviously a case of lack of interdisciplinary coordination between the New Product Group at the corporate level and the Quality Control Department at the manufacturing location. The quality control manager was only too happy to point out this problem to the Manufacturing Services staff personnel who would include this in their report.

Further discussion with the quality control manager revealed that he had complained to his general manager, who was reluctant to criticize corporate-level personnel.

Upon receipt of the report covering the operations audit of this division, the vice-president of manufacturing, who had been pressured to improve profits, lost no time in making a personal investigation of the problem. He quickly replaced the general manager.

Preparation of the Draft Report

Staff personnel making reviews at plant locations frequently overlook the importance of taking notes as the review progresses. There are two important advantages in making such notes:

1. Memories are short. To wait until the completion of the assignment takes too long.
2. Writing a draft report as the job progresses has the advantage of pointing out gaps in the review. Too often, such gaps are not discovered until the individual is queried about the findings upon his return to the corporate office, a circumstance that raises questions about the credibility of the report.

The manufacturing services staff personnel should, after the first interview, leave the door open for a second review. This likewise, has two advantages:

1. When gaps in the information are found in the draft report, there is an opportunity for further discussion to fill them in.
2. When reviews with other department heads indicate differences of opinion between two disciplines, the second session provides the opportunity to obtain a broader picture of both points of view.

Even if no gaps or differences of opinion occur, it is advantageous to summarize with each department head interviewed the notes that will appear in the final report. In the event of a misunderstanding on the part of the interviewer, the interviewee will have the opportunity to clarify the facts.

Often the individual being interviewed will be more relaxed in the second session and will expound on the problems he may be encountering—as in the case of the quality control manager who was having difficulty obtaining testing specifications from the New Product Group.

Review of Findings and Recommendations with the General Manager

Staff people should, as a courtesy to the general manager (or equivalent), review their completed findings and recommendations with him. This provides the general manager with an opportunity to correct erroneous assumptions and to confirm those observations that are correct.

Final Report

The requirement of a formal report on the findings and recommendations resulting from an operations review lends a touch of professionalism to the work of the manufacturing services staff group. It also keeps corporate executives abreast of the problems in the manufacturing locations.*

The report should include the following:

- A statement of the objectives of the review.
- A short summary pointing out the strong points and the areas of weakness observed.
- Highlights of the findings and recommendations.
- Background material concerning the plant. This includes statistics on the size of the plant in terms of sales volume, types of products manufactured, share of the market, closest competitors, problems in the industry, and any other pertinent data.
- Detailed findings and recommendations accompanied by any exhibits or other documentation that may be helpful for further clarification.

The letter of transmittal, which should be written by a corporate executive (in this case, the vice-president of manufacturing), is addressed to the general manager of the manufacturing location covered by the plant review. The transmittal letter should request the following information from the addressee:

- There should be an indication of agreement or disagreement with each of the findings and recommendations.
- In all instances in which there is agreement with the findings and recommendations, the implementation program should be stated in writing.
- In the event that there is disagreement with a particular recommendation, the reason should be given in writing.

One company has developed a standardized form for use in making responses. The corporate office lists the findings and recommendations down the left column. The second and third columns are headed "Agree" and "Disagree," respectively. One of them must be checked. The fourth column provides space for the implementation date if there is agreement with the recommendation. The final column, "Comments," is provided to enter the reason for disagreement.

Another company, in its quarterly financial review meetings with all general managers, schedules a separate submeeting with the general managers whose plants had been reviewed since the previous quarterly meeting. The individuals in attendance at these submeetings are the group vice-president, the vice-president of manufacturing, and the operations audit team that prepared the report. The general manager is requested to bring to the meeting any member of his staff who has expressed disagreement with any portion of the report, if he chooses. If, in the course of discussing the report, a question is brought up concerning a corporate department (the product development group that failed to furnish electrical testing specifications to the plant, for example), a representative of that department is called into the meeting. These discussions have been found to have a highly salutary effect.

---

* For a specimen copy of a final report, see Thomas S. Dudick, "A Consultant's Review of Cost and Operating Controls," in *Controller's Handbook,* ed. by Sam R. Goodman and James S. Reece. Dow Jones-Irwin, Homewood, Ill. 1978.

GUIDELINES FOR MORE EFFECTIVE MANUFACTURING SERVICES STAFF WORK

The introduction to this chapter emphasized that the corporate manufacturing services staff is made up of a group of specialists whose mission is to deal with problems in the field and thus relieve the corporate officials of most of their direct involvement in problems that could be resolved by the corporate staff. The 9 guidelines to help assure that their mission will be successfully accomplished are as follows:

1. Prior to embarking on an assignment at one of the plant locations, this staff should learn as much about the product line as possible. They should review the income statement and study the catalog of products in order to become more familiar with the operations.
2. Arrangements should be made in advance for a plant tour to be conducted by someone who is intimately familiar with the operations.
3. Time should be taken at the various work stations to learn how the product is made and the paperwork that controls its movement from one process to another.
4. In the course of the plant tour, a list of questions that might be asked in the interviews with the various departmental managers should be made. For example, the quality control manager could be asked to point out the most important causes of production losses and the work stations at which these occur. This could lead to questions about what corrective steps are being planned.
5. During the interviews, the interviewee should be encouraged to discuss the nature of the problems being experienced. A frustrated purchasing agent might point out and provide examples of very short lead times given to him in which to place orders at the lowest prices. The materials manager might provide examples of many back orders resulting from a failure of the production departments to abide by the scheduled dates of completion. This situation can be probed further by discussions with the foremen of the production departments.
6. Copious notes should be taken of the important points covered in each interview.
7. Whenever possible, documentation in which the problem is illustrated should be obtained. This might be an inspection report, efficiency report, or some other document that could be reproduced in the final report.
8. Upon completion of each interview, the staff man should summarize for the interviewee his understanding of the points that were discussed. If there was a misunderstanding, it can be cleared up. In some cases, interviewees have added important points that the recapitulation brought to mind.
9. The final report prepared for local management, as well as corporate management, should include a list of the weaknesses found and recommendations for correcting them.

It should be obvious from this discussion that good staff work cannot be done by long distance from behind a desk at headquarters. It requires that the staff member be a detective, psychologist, diplomat, and good listener. These qualities are necessary to assure that the corporate staff services will earn their keep.

15
Management's Need for Separate Income Statements for Manufacturing and Marketing

The present format of the external income statement intermingles manufacturing and marketing costs, making it difficult to hold the heads of these two functions accountable for their respective contributions to profits.

This chapter describes the format of an internal income statement that separates these two functions. This, in effect, establishes Manufacturing and Marketing as two separate businesses with their own income statements. Manufacturing sells to Marketing at an agreed-upon price. Manufacturing is responsible for the raw material inventory, work-in-process, and net fixed assets, while Marketing is responsible for the finished goods and accounts receivable. Both are charged an interest rate based on the amount of assets in their charge. The total interest charge made to each becomes the allocation to cover the corporate office costs.

When profits decline and management attempts to find the cause, an adversarial relationship frequently develops between Manufacturing and Marketing, each pointing the finger at the other. Management becomes more confused than enlightened; it must spend valuable time sorting out and evaluating the arguments advanced by both sides to determine the reason for the profit deterioration. While this adversarial relationship can never be completely eliminated, it can be somewhat diminished by establishing separate income statements wherein both functions become individual profit centers.

DEVELOPING A FUNCTIONAL INCOME STATEMENT FORMAT

Under a functional responsibility, there is a complete separation of the manufacturing and sales functions. This permits a top manufacturing executive to head up all manufacturing. It likewise permits a strong sales personality, who might be devoid of manufacturing know-how, to spark the selling effort without being concerned with the problems of manufacturing. The relationship between the two functions would be that of seller and buyer with the buyer having the option of purchasing from a competitor if need be.

Manufacturing as the Seller

Manufacturing would sell finished products to Marketing at an agreed-upon price. This price, in addition to covering the cost of material, direct labor, and overhead, would include a surcharge to cover the interest on the factory investment. The items considered as factory investment would consist of net fixed assets, raw material, and work-in-process inventories.

Marketing as the Buyer

The marketing income statement, in addition to showing the actual sales for the period, would base the cost of those sales on the agreed-upon transfer price from Manufacturing, adjusted by the cost of any finished goods losses and writeoffs due to obsolescence. Below the cost-of-sales line, the statement would list the usual selling expenses, advertising, commissions, freight, warehousing costs, bad debts, and the like. Charges from engineering for product development would also be included on a separate line. Marketing, like Manufacturing, would be charged an interest rate on its investment in finished goods inventory and accounts receivable.

Establishing the Transfer Price

Establishing an agreed-upon price can present problems. It is only natural that the Marketing Department will exert pressure to obtain lower prices than Manufacturing is willing to accept. To keep such problems at a minimum, one company mandated that the transfer prices would be based on competitive prices less the selling and advertising expenses. This recognizes that selling and advertising are not required to sell within the company. Other companies allow the buying division to purchase from outside sources if they can obtain lower prices. Disagreements will not be eliminated entirely, but measures such as these can help.

Charging Interest on Investment by Function

The rate of interest charged to Manufacturing and Marketing would be based on the anticipated Manufacturing and Marketing investment for the year divided by the budgeted corporate expenses. These would include the residual administrative expenses of the central headquarters staff after all direct charges have been made to Manufacturing and Marketing for specific services rendered to these two functions. The aggregate of the interest charges made to Manufacturing and Marketing would then be compared with the actual corporate expenses incurred. One company considers the aggregate of the interest charges as the budget for corporate expenses.

FORMAT OF THE FUNCTIONAL INCOME STATEMENT

The two income statements are placed side by side, as shown in the first two columns of Exhibit 1. "Intracompany Elimination," the third column, eliminates the duplication in the first two columns. The items that are eliminated are the manufacturing net sales, cost of sales, and resulting profit. The net sales are composed of the transfer of finished products to Marketing. The cost of sales is the material, direct labor, and overhead cost of manufacturing, while the profit that is eliminated is the difference between the two.

Over- or Underabsorption of Overhead

Had there been sufficient production volume to fully absorb the overhead, Manufacturing would have shown a $50,000 profit rather than a $10,000 loss. The combined results would have shown a $55,000 profit rather than a $5,000 loss.

Over- or underabsorption of overhead is usually correlatable with the level of order

EXHIBIT 1
FUNCTIONAL INCOME STATEMENT

	Manu-facturing	Marketing	Intra-company Elimination	Combined Results
Gross Sales	$	• 2,000,000		2,000,000
Less Returns		60,000		60,000
Net Sales	1,500,000	1,940,000	1,500,000	1,940,000
Cost of Sales				
Material	940,000	960,000	940,000	960,000
Direct Labor	100,000	120,000	100,000	120,000
Overhead	360,000	370,000	360,000	370,000
Total Cost of Sales	1,400,000	1,450,000	1,400,000	1,450,000
Overhead Incurred	360,000			360,000
Overhead Absorbed	300,000			300,000
Overhead (Over) or Underabsorbed	60,000			60,000
Distribution Costs				
Selling Expenses		90,000		90,000
Advertising Expenses		10,000		10,000
Commissions		50,000		50,000
Freight		20,000		20,000
Warehousing		10,000		10,000
Bad Debts		5,000		5,000
Total Distribution Costs		185,000		185,000
Product Development		120,000		120,000
Operating Profit	40,000	185,000	100,000	125,000
Interest on Investment	50,000	80,000		130,000
Company Profit or (Loss)	$ (10,000)	105,000	100,000	(5,000)

intake and is normally considered to be controllable by Marketing. However, the $60,000 underabsorption is shown in Manufacturing because it relates directly to manufacturing overhead—and is carried over to the "Combined Results" column. It is analyzed to determine where the cause of underabsorption might lie. Order intake would be reviewed first to ascertain if there was a decline in incoming orders. If the order receipts were found to be at the budgeted level, then factory efficiency would become suspect. Pointing the finger in the right direction is not easy, however.

If Marketing could prove that its volume of order intake met the budgeted dollar volume, Manufacturing could counter by pointing out that the orders contained many short runs which consumed more than the normal amount of set-up time—thus reducing machine utilization. Such differences of opinion, though sometimes difficult to resolve to the complete satisfaction of one side or the other, usually have a salutary effect.

THE BUDGETING PROCESS

In making up the budget for the coming year, Manufacturing, Marketing, and the corporate office prepare annual figures only. Working with annual amounts at first eliminates the time-consuming monthly detail. Once the annual figures have been approved, the month-by-month breakdown can be made.

Sales Projections: The Starting Point

Each product manager in Marketing prepares as realistic an estimate of anticipated sales as possible. The need for realism is emphasized by the marketing manager because he realizes that an overoptimistic forecast bears the penalty of a corresponding amount of underabsorbed overhead if the sales fall below the amount that was forecasted. Overoptimism could also mean an excessive inventory of finished products. This would result in a higher interest charge because the investment in inventory would be higher. It could also mean obsolescence of some of the inventory, as well as higher warehousing costs. On the other hand, too low an estimate would cause the overhead rates used for calculating the transfer prices to be high.

THE MANUFACTURING BUDGET

When the approved sales forecast is received by Manufacturing, it is adjusted by the inventory on hand to produce a production schedule. From this schedule, the Material Control Department can determine the material requirements and Manufacturing Engineering can project the direct labor levels.

Breaking Down the Material and Direct Labor by Month

Since material must be ordered in time to meet customer shipping dates, this provides the basis for breaking down the material requirements by months. The direct labor requirements would likewise be linked to the production schedule. Production hours would be denominated in terms of direct labor hours if the operation is labor paced or in machine hours if machine paced.

Budgeting the Overhead by Month

Flexible budgets provide a more meaningful measure of overhead requirements than conventional budgets. Exhibit 2 shows the flexible budget formula for the manufacturing operation, in which each overhead expense is broken down into its fixed and variable segments. Each variable cost is then divided by the production hours to arrive at a variable cost per production hour. The production hours used to make this calculation were based on the production schedule requirements for the year divided by 12 months.

Exhibit 3 illustrates a precalculated table of flexible budget allowances for nine levels of activity at increments of 1,000 hours. This type of table can help the manufacturing manager obtain an overview of the overhead expenses that can be expected at various levels within the normal range of production.

The budget formula shown in Exhibit 2 was used to make these calculations. Using the 35,970-hour level, the calculations would be as follows:

$$35{,}970 \text{ hours} \times \$5.187 \text{ per hour} = \$186{,}576$$

$$\begin{aligned} &\$186{,}576 \text{ (variable allowance)} \\ &\underline{225{,}747} \text{ (fixed cost)} \\ &\overline{\underline{\$412{,}323}} \text{ (total overhead allowance)} \end{aligned}$$

There is a small error in the variable allowance because of rounding of the variable cost per hour.

EXHIBIT 2
MANUFACTURING FLEXIBLE BUDGET FORMULA

	Total Monthly Fixed and Variable	Total Fixed Cost	Total Variable Cost	Variable Cost Per Prod'n Hour (1)
PRODUCTION DEPARTMENTS:				
Fabrication	$ 14,395	11,905	2,490	.069
Assembly	38,024	25,418	12,606	.350
SERVICE DEPARTMENTS:				
Manufacturing Administration	20,640	20,640	—	—
Industrial Relations	14,666	10,994	3,672	.102
Cost Accounting	16,024	11,214	4,810	.134
Material Control	35,308	16,882	18,426	.512
Manufacturing Engineering	18,469	12,064	6,405	.178
Quality Assurance	29,876	20,174	9,702	.270
Purchasing	10,864	6,264	4,600	.128
Maintenance	48,344	29,479	18,865	.524
Receiving and Incoming Inspection	24,987	10,643	14,344	.399
TOTAL PRODUCTION & SERVICE DEPT. PAYROLL	$271,597	175,677	95,920	2.666
NONPAYROLL EXPENSES:				
Disability Payments	920	600	320	.009
Payroll Taxes	8,510	5,550	2,960	.082
Compensation Insurance	506	330	176	.005
Employee Benefits	3,588	2,340	1,248	.035
Factory Supplies	200	200	—	—
Office Supplies and Forms	7,500	7,500	—	—
Other Purchased Supplies	500	500	—	—
Postage	50	50	—	—
Depreciation	1,500	1,500	—	—
Freight-in	68,000	—	68,000	1.890
Dues and Subscriptions	150	150	—	—
Purchased Services	150	150	—	—
Fire Insurance	1,000	1,000	—	—
Travel	18,200	10,200	8,000	.222
Telephone	30,000	20,000	10,000	.278
TOTAL NONPAYROLL EXPENSES:	$140,774	50,070	90,704	2.521
TOTAL MANUFACTURING OVERHEAD	$412,371	225,747	186,624	5.187

(1) TOTAL VARIABLE COST DIVIDED BY 35,970 BUDGETED PRODUCTION HOURS.

The same type of calculation would be made for each month's actual level of activity, showing the budgeted overhead expenses compared with the actual expenses incurred—not only for the current month but for the year-to-date as well.

Material and direct labor would be controlled by standard costs which are extended by the production and then compared with the actual costs.

THE MARKETING BUDGET

Fixed and variable costs in Marketing would be identified by cost behavior, as was done for Manufacturing. The base used for denominating the variable costs would not be production hours. The alternative methods are sales, cost of sales, and conversion costs (direct labor and overhead content of the cost of sales). These three methods

EXHIBIT 3
MANUFACTURING OVERHEAD

Monthly Budget Allowance for Various Activity Levels

PRODUCTION HOURS PER MONTH	31,970	32,970	33,970	34,970	35,970	36,970	37,970	38,970	39,970
PRODUCTION DEPARTMENTS:									
Fabrication	$ 14,119	14,188	14,257	14,326	14,395	14,464	14,533	14,602	14,671
Assembly	36,624	36,974	37,324	37,674	38,024	38,374	38,724	39,074	39,424
SERVICE DEPARTMENTS:									
Manufacturing Administration	20,640	20,640	20,640	20,640	20,640	20,640	20,640	20,640	20,640
Industrial Relations	14,258	14,360	14,462	14,564	14,666	14,768	14,870	14,972	15,074
Cost Accounting	15,488	15,622	15,756	15,890	16,024	16,158	16,292	16,426	16,560
Material Control	33,260	33,772	34,284	34,796	35,308	35,820	36,332	36,844	37,356
Manufacturing Engineering	17,757	17,935	18,113	18,291	18,469	18,647	18,825	19,003	19,181
Quality Assurance	28,796	29,066	29,336	29,606	29,876	30,146	30,416	30,686	30,956
Purchasing	10,352	10,480	10,608	10,736	10,864	10,992	11,120	11,248	11,376
Maintenance	46,248	46,772	47,296	47,820	48,344	48,868	49,392	49,916	50,440
Receiving and Incoming Inspection	23,391	23,790	24,189	24,588	24,987	25,386	25,785	26,184	26,583
TOTAL PRODUCTION & SERVICE PAYROLL	$260,933	263,599	266,265	268,931	271,597	274,263	276,929	279,595	282,261
NONPAYROLL EXPENSES:									
Disability Payments	884	893	902	911	920	929	938	947	956
Payroll Taxes	8,182	8,264	8,346	8,428	8,510	8,592	8,674	8,756	8,838
Compensation Insurance	486	491	496	501	506	511	516	521	526
Employee Benefits	3,448	3,483	3,518	3,553	3,588	3,623	3,658	3,693	3,728
Factory Supplies	200	200	200	200	200	200	200	200	200
Office Supplies and Forms	1,500	1,500	1,500	1,500	1,500	1,500	1,500	1,500	1,500
Other Purchased Supplies	500	500	500	500	500	500	500	500	500
Postage	50	50	50	50	50	50	50	50	50
Depreciation	7,500	7,500	7,500	7,500	7,500	7,500	7,500	7,500	7,500
Freight-in	60,440	62,330	64,220	66,110	68,000	69,890	71,780	73,670	75,560
Dues and Subscriptions	150	150	150	150	150	150	150	150	150
Purchased Services	150	150	150	150	150	150	150	150	150
Fire Insurance	1,000	1,000	1,000	1,000	1,000	1,000	1,000	1,000	1,000
Travel	17,312	17,534	17,756	17,978	18,200	18,422	18,644	18,866	19,088
Telephone	28,888	29,166	29,444	29,722	30,000	30,278	30,556	30,834	31,112
TOTAL NONPAYROLL EXPENSES	$130,690	133,211	135,732	138,253	140,774	143,295	145,816	148,337	150,858
TOTAL MANUFACTURING OVERHEAD	$391,623	396,810	401,997	407,184	412,371	417,558	422,745	427,932	433,119

were discussed in Chapter 5. It might be well, nonetheless, to summarize the key features of the three methods.

Sales

If the products in the line are fairly homogeneous, with material, direct labor, overhead, and markup bearing about the same percentage of sales for all products, the variable costs can be measured as a percentage of sales dollars.

Cost of Sales

Use of the cost of sales will correct for any wide variations in the markups.

Conversion Costs

The advantage of conversion costs over sales and cost of sales is that distortions due to large variations in the material content of the products and in the gross profit markup are avoided.

Corporate Expenses

The residual corporate headquarters expenses, after chargeouts for services rendered to Manufacturing and Marketing, are usually highly fixed. For this reason, flexible budgets would show a smaller amount of variability in costs.

ADVANTAGES OF THE FUNCTIONAL INCOME STATEMENT

The functional income statement is a more sophisticated tool than the conventional statement used for outside reporting. Following are some of the advantages:

1. The size of the finished goods inventory becomes the responsibility of the marketing function. This is logical, since Marketing is responsible for the forecasts that generate the production of finished products.
2. Using the total assets as the numerator and corporate expenses as the denominator for calculating the interest rate provides a more stable basis for allocating corporate expenses.
3. Since both Manufacturing and Marketing are charged an interest rate based on the size of their respective investments, there is a more compelling reason for each to hold down the amount of the assets.

GUIDELINES FOR USING THE FUNCTIONAL INCOME STATEMENT

Although the functional statement measures the profit contributions made individually by Manufacturing and Marketing, it does not entirely eliminate disagreements between the two. Management must still look behind the figures for answers to questions such as these:

1. Are the production runs too short to be economically produced? If so, transfer prices to Marketing should include set-up charges for such uneconomical orders.
2. Are orders being accepted with incomplete specifications and only sketchy drawings? This occurs with surprising frequency. If Marketing accepts orders with incomplete specifications, these should be routed through the Product Development Group prior to acceptance by Manufacturing. Since Product Development costs are part of the Marketing income statement, the industrial engineers in Manufacturing will be relieved of this task.
3. Does the manufacturing manager have the opportunity to review customer orders for new products? Selling prices are sometimes prepared on the supposition that the product being quoted is like another product with some minor differences. Frequently, the "minor" differences result in major differences in manufacturing cost.
4. Does Marketing reduce prices to obtain a larger share of the market? If so, the reduced profit should be reflected in the Marketing income statement unless Manufacturing agrees, in the interest of increasing its volume, to reduce its transfer price.

The procedures outlined here can be applied to almost any corporate entity making and marketing a commercial product (or performing a service). The key to success in any type of control is management follow-up. Inasmuch as the income statement is the focal point of control, the degree to which profit responsibility can be assigned by function determines the degree of follow-up that is available to management.

16
Computerized Graphics: Will They Correct the Deficiencies in Manually Prepared Graphs?

Graphs are used in annual reports, business publications, newspapers, government publications, and other media. A surprising number of such graphs distort the data being presented because of the use of incorrect scales, omission of part of the vertical scale, and the use of an incorrect graphic format. This chapter illustrates examples of the major types of distortions which are being perpetuated in much of the present software on business graphics.

Tremendous progress has been made in computer technology. Modern computers are much smaller, far less expensive, and more flexible in their applications than those of even a few years ago. Their lower price and greater flexibility has increased the demand for them—with the result that numerous manufacturers have sprung up, both domestic and foreign, all vying for a larger market share.

With the increase in competition, marketing strategy has been directed toward exploitation of various features and their application to business. One of these features is business graphics. Computer manufacturers in full-page ads point out the existence of packages that can take numerical/statistical data and display them in line graphs, bar charts, and pie charts. They stress that trends can be highlighted instantaneously and that the pictorial output furnishes management with a method that is unsurpassed for recognizing important patterns within a mass of numbers in an expeditious and efficient manner.

Unfortunately, most of the present packages have merely computerized existing manual procedures without building in safeguards to prevent many of the distortions that are characteristic of existing manual methods followed in producing line graphs, bar charts, and pie charts. This chapter discusses some of the major types of distortions that are prevalent in manually produced graphics, using actual cases in which such erroneous graphics were found.

LINE GRAPHS

Natural Scales versus Semilogarithmic Scales

When two or more variables (lines) of different magnitude are being compared, the semilogarithmic (percentage) scale, rather than the natural (arithmetic) scale, should be used. The natural scale emphasizes absolute rather than percentage differences. An increase in sales, for example, ranging from $500,000 to $750,000 (a 50% increase) would show a spread on the vertical scale of Exhibit 1 of 1½ inches. But an increase of 50% in selling expenses from $5,000 to $7,500 would show a spread of only $\frac{1}{16}$th of an inch. On the semilogarithmic scale of Exhibit 2, the spread of both would

---

Note: The following pairs of terms are used interchangeably: "charts and graphs," "natural scale and arithmetic scale," "semilogarithmic and percentage scale."

be the same. Note, for example, that the distance from \$10,000 to \$20,000 along the vertical scale is exactly the same as the spread from \$100,000 to \$200,000.

The figures shown in Exhibits 1 and 2 reflect a three-year comparison of selling expenses with sales for one of the divisions of a consumer products manufacturer. The sales manager was being criticized because the increase in his selling expenses was greater over the three-year period than the increase in profits. The sales manager therefore had a graph similar to Exhibit 1 prepared in order to prove that sales had moved substantially higher over the three-year period but that selling expenses to attain these sales had moved very little. When the sales manager's graph was redrawn on semilogarithmic paper, as shown in Exhibit 2, selling expenses were shown to have increased at a substantially greater percentage rate than sales.

Had computerized graphics (based on presently available packages) been utilized in comparing the sales with the selling expenses, the natural scale would have been used. If a bar chart rather than line drawings had been used, the comparison would still have been distorted because the natural scale is always used in constructing bar charts.

Alternative to Semilogarithmic Scales

Exhibits 1 and 2 illustrated the importance of using semilogarithmic scales when two or more lines of different magnitude are being compared. The advantage of semilogarithmic scales is that the plotted data will show fluctuations in the variables based on the percentage of change rather than on the absolute amounts involved in the change.

There is another alternative that does not require the use of semilogarithmic scales. This is illustrated in Exhibit 3, in which the selling expenses are plotted as a percentage of sales. This is done by finding the percentage of selling expenses in each period to the sales in the same period and plotting them. Sales, in effect, becomes the base from which the selling expenses are measured. In Exhibits 1 and 2, the plotting of selling expenses measures the deviations from one period to the next. In Exhibit 3, the measurement is not only based on the variations of these expenses from one period to another but takes into account deviations from sales.

This alternative, using a single line on natural scale paper, tells the story in a simple and effective fashion. The writer is not aware of any graphics software that presently includes this method. It would be well if producers of software packages gave serious consideration to this method as well as semilogarithmic scales.

How the Same Set of Figures Could Lend Credence to Opposing Arguments

Exhibits 4 and 5 show the comparison of the annual payroll per employee (including benefits) with the average selling price of vehicles for the years 1971 through 1980. Although these figures were taken from the subject company's annual reports, the company's reports do not include the use of graphs, nor has it published such graphs, to the author's knowledge. The principle illustrated in Exhibits 4 and 5 is similar to that used in Exhibits 1 and 2, except that it illustrates how data can be manipulated to influence public opinion by merely changing the scales in presenting the graphics.

In Exhibit 4, these figures were plotted to a semilogarithmic scale in which percentage changes, rather than the magnitude of the dollars, are emphasized. Note in this exhibit that the annual payroll per employee and the selling price per vehicle move

COMPARISON OF SALES WITH SELLING EXPENSES

NATURAL SCALE

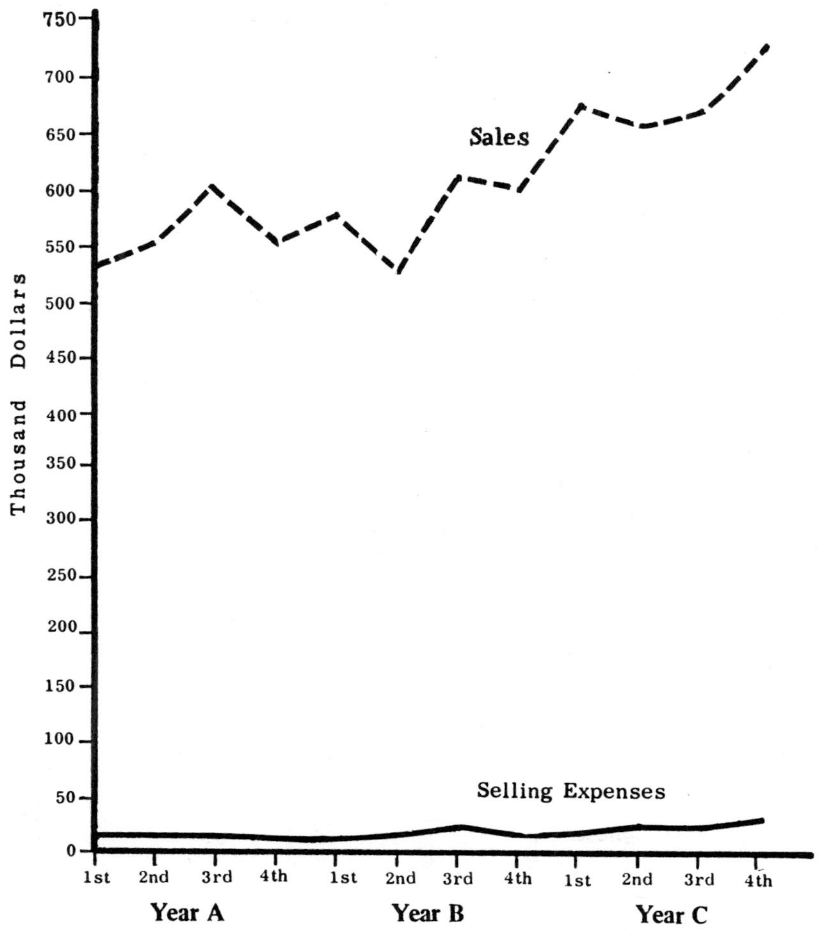

SEMI-LOGARITHMIC SCALE

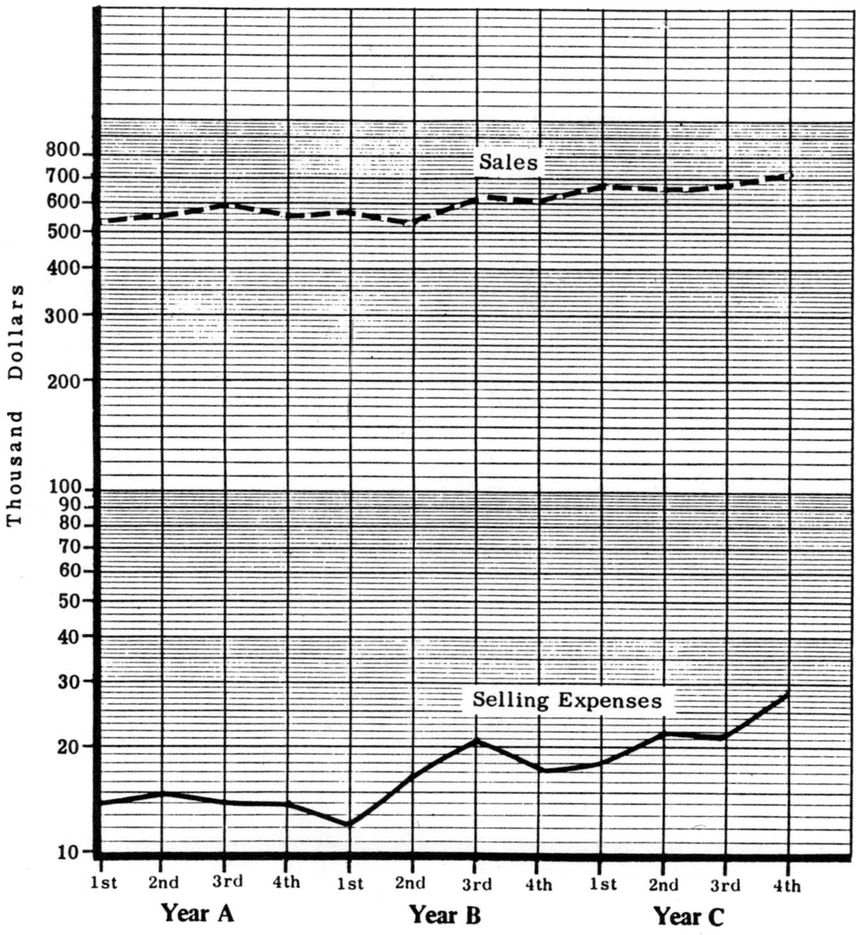

EXHIBIT 1

EXHIBIT 2

EXHIBIT 3
SELLING EXPENSES AS A PERCENTAGE OF SALES

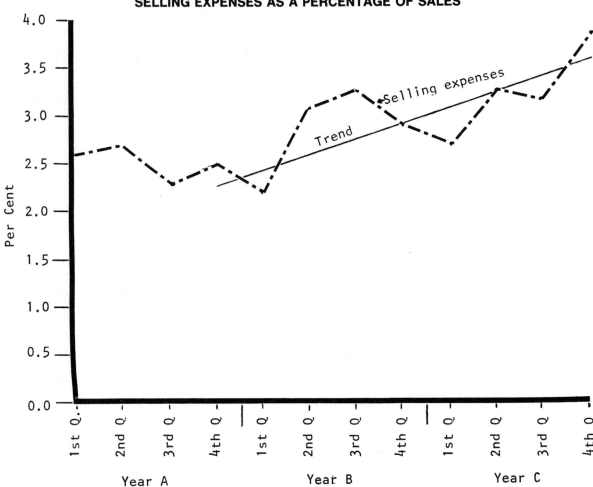

almost identically. The argument that could be propounded by the use of this graph is that selling prices of cars are being forced upward by persistent union pressures to drive labor rates up.

Exhibit 5 shows the same figures plotted to an arithmetic scale, which gives greater emphasis to changes in the larger of the two figures. Since the payroll of the average employee is about three times the price of the average vehicle, increases in payroll figures will move up faster when plotted to the natural scale. This graph can be used to support the argument that factory selling prices of cars are being held down, while salaries and wages are rising uncontrollably.

From a statistical point of view, Exhibit 4 shows the proper method for plotting these two variables. Since existing software does not provide for plotting on logarithmic scales, computer graphics would produce results similar to those in Exhibit 5, whether a line graph or bar chart format is used.

How the Message Can Be Distorted by Omitting Part of the Scale

Line charts in which the variables are additive to a total, which is also plotted, can show distorted results when part of the scale is omitted. Such a line graph is quite

EXHIBIT 4
COMPARISON OF ANNUAL PAYROLL PER EMPLOYEE
WITH FACTORY SELLING PRICE PER VEHICLE

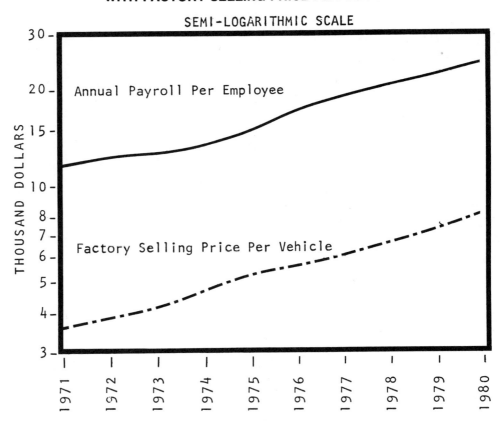

SEMI-LOGARITHMIC SCALE

EXHIBIT 5

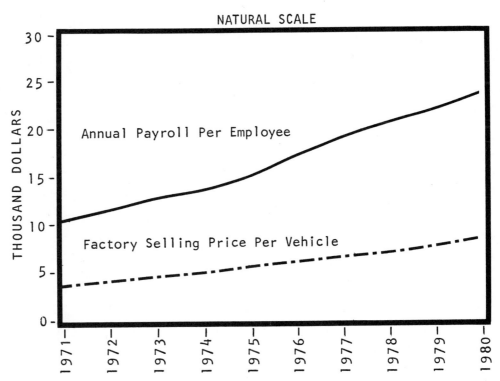

NATURAL SCALE

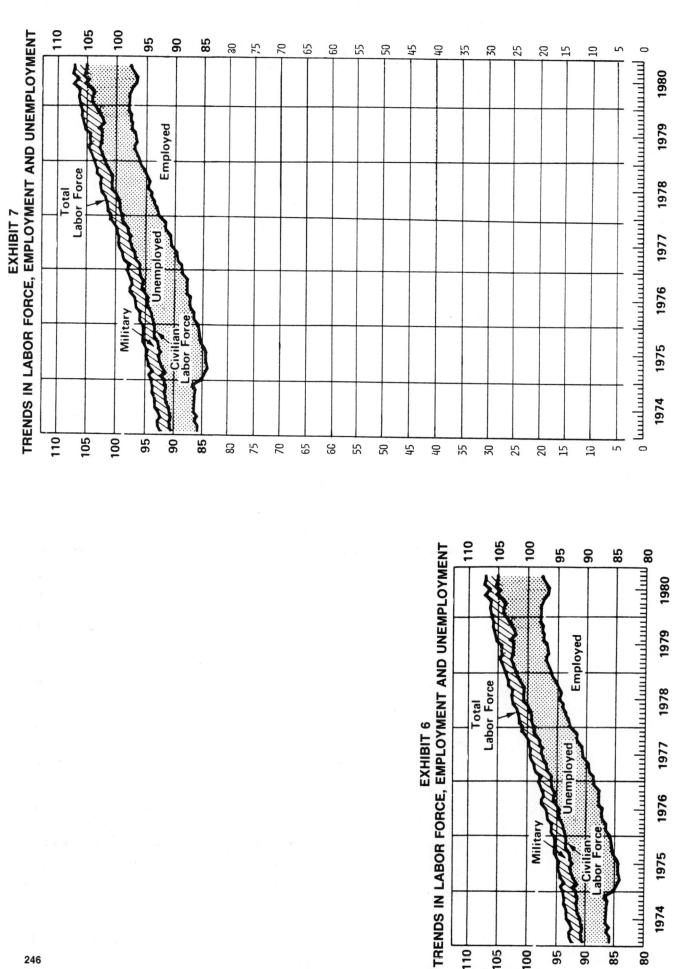

EXHIBIT 7

TRENDS IN LABOR FORCE, EMPLOYMENT AND UNEMPLOYMENT

EXHIBIT 6

TRENDS IN LABOR FORCE, EMPLOYMENT AND UNEMPLOYMENT

Millions of Persons 16 Years of Age and Over, Seasonally Adjusted

246

similar to a bar chart in that omission of part of the scale also distorts the message.

This is illustrated in Exhibit 6, which depicts the trends in the total labor force, unemployment, and employment. Note that in this exhibit the scale from 0 to 80 has been omitted. The omission of almost 80% of the scale in the employed category results in distortion of this category. Note that the unemployed category takes up approximately ½ inch of the vertical scale in both periods of rising unemployment—most of 1975 and mid-1980. The employed category, on the other hand, takes up ¼ inch of the scale in 1975 and about 1 inch in mid-1980. This gives the visual impression that the employed category has increased four times in 1980 over 1975, obviously an erroneous assumption.

Exhibit 7, which is drawn with a complete scale, shows the same picture for total labor, military, and unemployed groups. However, the growth of the employed category, based on the use of the full scale, is not four times as great in 1980 but only 15% greater.

This points up an important guideline in graphing: include the full scale when plotting line graphs when the data are additive. The same applies to bar graphs, which will be discussed next.

BAR CHARTS

The Same Principle Illustrated in Exhibits 1 and 2 Applies to Bar Charts

In bar charts, as in line charts, variables with wide differences in magnitude should be plotted on semilogarithmic scales; or the variables should be converted to percentages of the base variable and plotted on natural scale paper (see Exhibits 2 and 3).

Exhibit 8 is a reproduction of an advertisement in two well-known newspapers. The only change was to disguise the years to allow the company to remain anonymous. Although no scales are shown, the actual dollar value for the bars is indicated on each bar. The use of variables with a wide difference in magnitude is obvious when one notes that the $6.7 million representing profits in the year 19x1 is about twice as high as the bar for assets in the same year, which amounts to $165 million. This makes it appear as if the profits greatly exceed the assets—a very unlikely circumstance.

The first alternative—plotting the bar chart data to a semilogarithmic scale—will not be practical when one of the variables is profits. The reason is that semilogarithmic scales do not provide for negative quantities. The logical substitute, when profits turn to losses, would be a tabular presentation such as the one shown in Exhibit 9. In this exhibit, the profits for each of the years shown in Exhibit 8 are divided by the assets to arrive at the percentage return on assets. Note that instead of a rising trend in profits, as reflected by Exhibit 8, the return drops from 4.06% in the first year to 1.95% in the second year. It then falls to 1.61% in the third year, to 1.33% in the fourth year, and then rises to 1.55% in the fifth year. Although these percentages could have been plotted in the form of a graph on natural scale paper in the same manner as Exhibit 3, the tabular form was illustrated because it shows both the assets and the profits in dollar value as well as the percentage return.

WHEN RATIOS (PERCENTAGES) ARE PLOTTED, NATURAL SCALES WITHOUT A ZERO BASE LINE CAN BE USED

The requirement of common scales when making comparisons of two or more variables on a single chart applies with equal force to "stand-alone" charts presented separately.

EXHIBIT 8
COMPARISON OF PROFITS WITH ASSETS

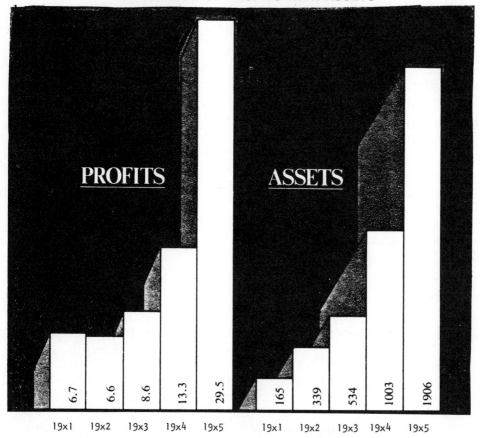

	PROFITS					ASSETS			
6.7	6.6	8.6	13.3	29.5	165	339	534	1003	1906
19x1	19x2	19x3	19x4	19x5	19x1	19x2	19x3	19x4	19x5

(FIGURES IN MILLION DOLLARS)

EXHIBIT 9
PROFITS AS A PERCENT OF ASSETS

	Profits	Assets	Percent Return on Assets
19x1	6.7	165	4.06
19x2	6.6	339	1.95
19x3	8.6	534	1.61
19x4	13.3	1,003	1.33
19x5	29.5	1,906	1.55
FIVE-YEAR AVERAGE			1.64

Figures for profits and assets are in million dollars

If the scales are not the same, the old cliche of comparing "apples and oranges" applies.

The four charts shown in the upper half of Exhibit 10 are reproductions taken from a well-known newspaper. The horizontal scales show the first five years in the form of line charts, while the sixth year is shown in bar chart form by months. In scanning these four charts, it appears that the interest rate on utility bonds is the highest, with treasury bills next and federal funds third. In studying the vertical

EXHIBIT 10
COMPARATIVE INTEREST RATES OF VARIOUS OFFERINGS
AS CHARTS APPEARED IN NEWSPAPER

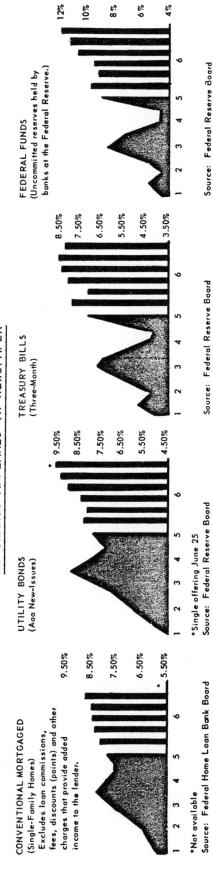

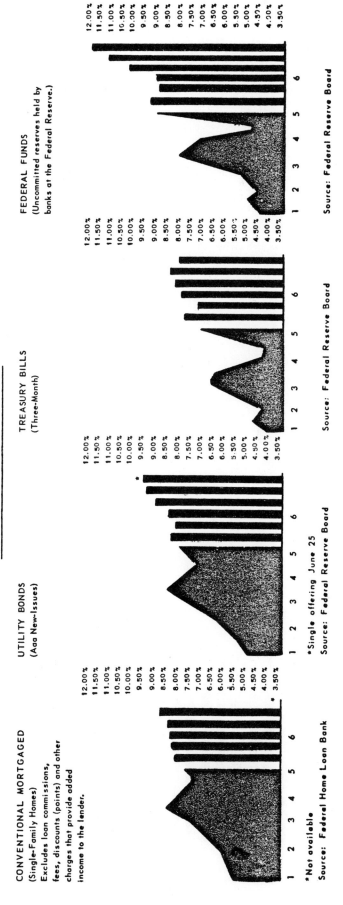

CONVENTIONAL MORTGAGED
(Single-Family Homes)
Excludes loan commissions,
fees, discounts (points) and other
charges that provide added
income to the lender.

*Not available
Source: Federal Home Loan Bank Board

UTILITY BONDS
(Aaa New-Issues)

*Single offering June 25
Source: Federal Reserve Board

TREASURY BILLS
(Three-Month)

Source: Federal Reserve Board

FEDERAL FUNDS
(Uncommitted reserves held by
banks at the Federal Reserve.)

Source: Federal Reserve Board

REDRAWN TO COMMON SCALES

CONVENTIONAL MORTGAGED
(Single-Family Homes)
Excludes loan commissions,
fees, discounts (points) and other
charges that provide added
income to the lender.

*Not available
Source: Federal Home Loan Bank

UTILITY BONDS
(Aaa New-Issues)

*Single offering June 25
Source: Federal Reserve Board

TREASURY BILLS
(Three-Month)

Source: Federal Reserve Board

FEDERAL FUNDS
(Uncommitted reserves held by
banks at the Federal Reserve.)

Source: Federal Reserve Board

scales, one finds an inconsistency which distorts the observations made at first glance. Following is a comparison of the scales:

OFFERINGS	RANGE OF SCALES USED
Conventional mortgages	5.50 to 9.50%
Utility bonds	4.50 to 9.50%
Treasury bills	3.50 to 8.50%
Federal funds	4.00 to 12.00%

When the charts are redrawn to a common scale ranging from 3.50 to 12.00%, as shown in the lower half of Exhibit 10, first-glance observations show a different picture. Note that since we are dealing with scales that measure a return rather than dollars that are additive, failure to start at zero is not a serious distorting factor. A comparison of the ranking of the published and the redrawn graphs in Exhibit 10 is shown at the top of page 251.

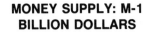

MONEY SUPPLY: M-1
BILLION DOLLARS

EXHIBIT 11   **EXHIBIT 12**

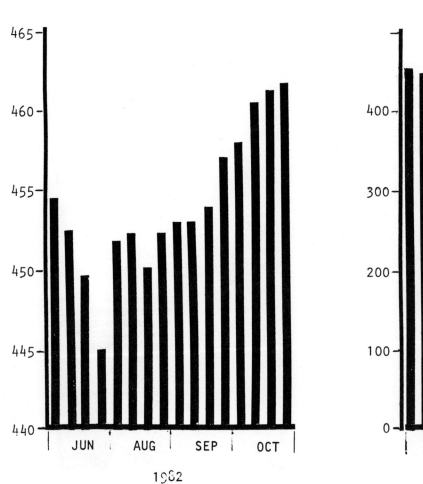

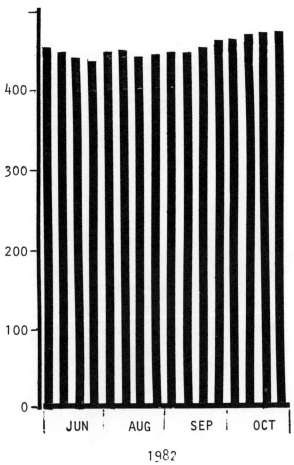

VISUAL RANKING AS PUBLISHED	OFFERINGS	VISUAL RANKING AS REDRAWN
#4	Conventional mortgages	#3
#1	Utility bonds	#2
#2	Treasury bills	#4
#3	Federal funds	#1

Since the purpose of graphics is to condense a mass of information into a simple visual presentation, the scales used in the graphics cannot be haphazardly applied, as has been done in Exhibit 10.

OMISSION OF PART OF THE SCALE IN BAR CHARTS CAN DISTORT THE MESSAGE JUST AS MUCH AS IN LINE CHARTS

Omission of part of the scale in a bar chart magnifies the variations in the remaining portion of the bar chart presentation. The greater the portion of the scale that is omitted, the greater the magnification of the portion that is shown. If, for example, half of the scale were omitted, the remaining half of the bar chart would double the magnitude of the variations in the portion of the chart that is shown.

This is demonstrated by an actual example in Exhibit 11, in which the money supply (M-1) is shown in bar chart form by weeks for four months of 1982. The scale in this chart starts at $440 billion, thus allowing approximately the same vertical space for the remaining $25 billion ($465 billion − $440 billion) as was used in Exhibit 12 to show the total money supply for the entire $465 billion.

Since the scale in Exhibit 11 provides scale gradations of $5 billion compared with $100 billion in Exhibit 12, the variations in Exhibit 11 are magnified 20 times ($100 billion ÷ $5 billion). As a result, the variations between peaks and troughs in Exhibit 11 are 20 times greater than those in Exhibit 12.

Like several other charts discussed earlier, Exhibit 11 is a reproduction of a chart taken from a well-known newspaper. The state of the art in computer graphics must be improved in order to guard against such distortions.

PIE CHARTS

Pie charts are relatively simple presentations in which the "pie" is cut up into segments expressed in percentages that add up to 100%. This eliminates the problem of inconsistency of scales and omission of part of the scale. Pie charts being compared must be the same size, and comparisons should be limited to two charts.

Exhibit 13 illustrates how the use of more than two pie charts reduces their usefulness because the analysis of the data becomes more complex. This exhibit is a reproduction of a page in the annual report of a mining company. The intent of these pie charts is to show, for each of five years, the percentage of sales revenues derived from five different metals. Note the difficulty in determining the trend of sales revenues for each of the metals over this period.

Exhibit 14 shows the same data presented in bar chart form in which each bar is the same height, with the scale running from 0 to 100%. Note how much easier it is to make comparisons over the five-year period for the trend of sales for the metals.

EXHIBIT 13
TOTAL SALES REVENUES BY TYPE OF METAL

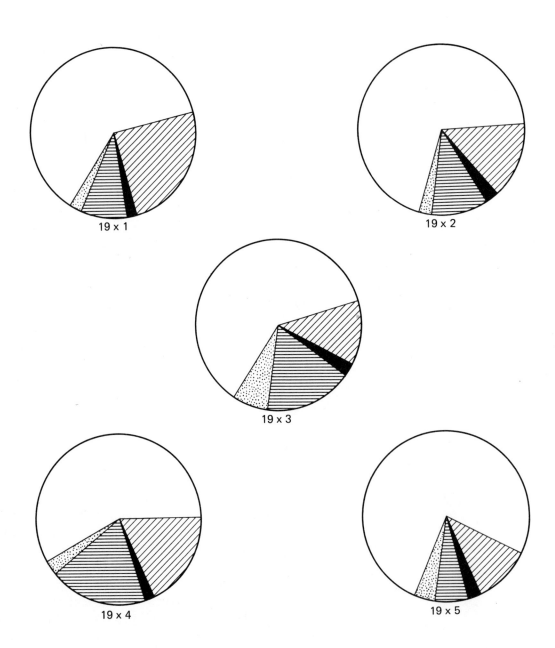

MOLYBDENUM   NICKEL   TUNGSTEN   PALLADIUM   COPPER

19 x 1

19 x 2

19 x 3

19 x 4

19 x 5

EXHIBIT 14
TOTAL SALES REVENUES BY TYPE OF METAL

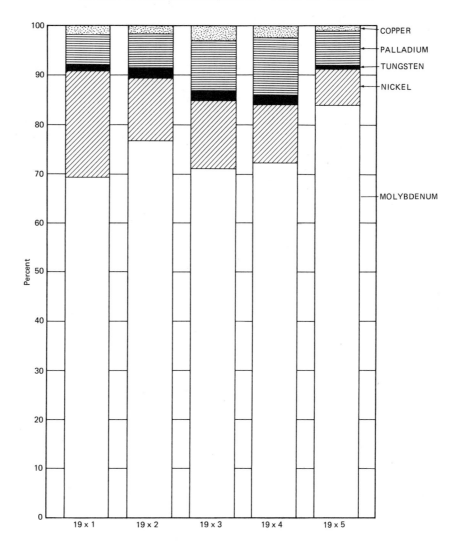

CONCLUSIONS

The business computer graphics market is projected to increase 40% annually during the 1980s (Management Information Systems, March 1983 issue of *Management Accounting;* editor: Grover L. Porter). Present computer graphics packages provide for line graphs, bar charts, and pie charts—all of which represent the major types of business graphics in use.

The cathode ray tube (CRT) display advertisements have shown line graphs plotted to arithmetic (natural) scales even when the variables being compared have wide differences in magnitude—thus distorting the true relationship, as demonstrated in Exhibits 1 and 2. Likewise, bar charts have been shown with a portion of the scale omitted, with similar distortions in the data being presented. This was demonstrated in Exhibits 11 and 12. Exhibit 15 summarizes the general guidelines for presenting graphics for line charts, bar charts, and pie charts to minimize distortions.

It is unfortunate that the same deficiencies that are present in manually prepared graphics shown in our best-known newspapers, annual reports, and other media are

EXHIBIT 15

GENERAL GUIDELINES FOR PRESENTING GRAPHICS

Type of Graphics	Natural Scale	Semilog Scale	Converting Data to Percentages	Omission of Part of the Scale
LINE GRAPHS	WHEN VARIABLES HAVE WIDE DIFFERENCES IN MAGNITUDE, NATURAL SCALES WILL SHOW A DISTORTED PICTURE (See Exhibits 1 and 5)	SUCH DISTORTIONS CAN BE AVOIDED BY PLOTTING ON SEMILOG SCALES. (See Exhibits 2 and 4)	VARIABLES CAN ALSO BE PLOTTED AS PERCENTAGES OF A BASE VARIABLE. (See Exhibit 3)	WHEN DATA ARE ADDITIVE, AS IN EXHIBIT 6, A FULL SCALE AS IN EXHIBIT 7 MUST BE SHOWN TO AVOID DISTORTION OF DATA
BAR CHARTS	WHEN TWO OR MORE VARIABLES COMPARED IN BAR CHART FORM HAVE WIDE DIFFERENCES IN MAGNITUDE, THE DATA CAN SHOW LARGE DISTORTIONS. (See Exhibit 8.)	SUCH DISTORTIONS CAN BE AVOIDED BY CONVERTING THE DATA TO LINES AND PLOTTING ON SEMILOG SCALES (See Exhibits 2 and 4)	VARIABLES CAN BE PLOTTED AS PERCENTAGES OF A BASE VARIABLE, AS IN EXHIBIT 3. OR, IF THE VARIABLES ARE ADDITIVE TO A TOTAL, THEY CAN BE PLOTTED AS PERCENTAGES OF THE TOTAL IN BAR CHART FORM (See Exhibit 14)	OMISSION OF PART OF THE SCALE CAN RESULT IN DISTORTIONS IN THE DATA BEING PRESENTED (See Exhibit 11)
PIE CHARTS	NOT APPLICABLE TO PIE CHARTS	NOT APPLICABLE TO PIE CHARTS	PIE CHARTS ARE PRESENTED IN PERCENTAGE FORM. (See Exhibit 13.) IF MORE THAN TWO PIE CHARTS ARE TO BE COMPARED, THEY SHOULD BE CONVERTED TO BAR CHARTS SHOWING THE VARIABLES BROKEN DOWN IN PERCENTAGE FORM, AS IN EXHIBIT 14	THE FULL SCALE, FROM ZERO TO 100%, MUST BE SHOWN (See Exhibit 14)

Note: The term "variable" refers to the data being plotted.

being perpetuated in computerized graphics packages. Automation does not promote progress when it merely speeds up production without first correcting the underlying weaknesses in existing procedures.

The steps required to correct these weaknesses are summarized in the guidelines shown in Exhibit 15.

17
Summing Up

A substantial part of the accounting function requires the processing of a large volume of transactions each month. These must be checked, categorized, processed through the books, and summarized for reporting purposes in time for each month's closing of the books. A high percentage of accounting tasks are therefore, by necessity, processed on a "production line" basis.

REASON FOR PRODUCT COSTING DEFICIENCIES

Because of the highly routine nature of accounting, there is a tendency in many companies to oversimplify even the tasks that require special treatment. This oversimplification applies to the development of overhead costing rates, allocation of SG&A, and use of the wrong cost system when companies making standard products add highly engineered products to their line.

Overhead Costing Rates

When automatic equipment is installed to reduce labor costs, many companies continue to allocate overhead to products using a single plantwide overhead costing rate based on direct labor. Failure to recognize the need for special treatment of machine-paced versus labor-paced operations results in labor-paced operations absorbing a disproportionate amount of the total pool of overhead costs.

An automated operation in which one operator can operate, say, four machines absorbs a much smaller portion of the overhead pool because of the smaller direct labor base—in spite of the fact that the overhead pool is larger because of the addition of the automatic equipment. Labor-paced operations, on the other hand, absorb a larger share than previously because their labor is now a larger percentage of the total labor. This penalizes the products that require a greater amount of labor (see Chapters 1 and 2).

Allocation of SG&A

"Broad-brush" allocations of SG&A can also result in product cost distortions because of the use of arbitrary bases for such allocations. Many companies that sell to different markets, such as original equipment manufacturers, distributors, and the replacement market fail to recognize the differences in costs attendant on selling in different markets (see Chapter 5).

Using the Wrong Cost System

The increased defense effort, space exploration, and the production of nuclear components has resulted in a greater demand for these highly engineered products.

Companies making standard commercial products generally use a standard cost system. When they accept orders for highly engineered products even with their tight specifications, they frequently extend the standard costing procedures to include these products, rather than using a job cost system. Job costing is required because certain indirect labor costs—quality assurance and engineering, for example—require substantially more cost than the overhead costing rate would show. A job cost system would treat such costs as direct labor—allowing the actual amount of time spent on each product to be charged to the individual jobs (see Chapter 4).

INVENTORY MANAGEMENT AND MISMANAGEMENT

Too much reliance is placed on production reject reports to remove spoiled production from the inventory. This often results in a buildup of phantom inventory on the books. The physical to book differences then remain on the books until a physical inventory is taken—usually at year-end. These differences can be minimized by booking into inventory only the good components and assemblies accepted into stock (see Chapter 6).

Computerized MRP procedures are often highly transaction oriented, with no built-in analytical capability to highlight erroneous figures appearing on the inventory status reports. The most common errors are described in Chapter 7. The following chapter provides actual illustrative reports showing the steps used in developing the computer program, as well as the various output reports required to interface inventory management with the cost accounting system.

PRODUCTIVITY AND PROFITS

Many companies that make profit projections based on increases in capacity rely on theoretical expectations based on arithmetic. They often overlook many of the real-world problems that must also be considered. This section deals with the common errors in projecting profitability not only from within but through acquisitions as well (see Chapters 11 and 12).

HOW TO PRODUCE KEY MANAGEMENT REPORTS

Management reports are often visualized as preprinted forms containing standardized information—usually in statistical form. Management is already swamped with statistics. What it needs is customized reports that provide them with information on the weaknesses at the various locations, together with recommendations for correcting these weaknesses. This is the mission of the manufacturing services staff. The guidelines for effective performance by this group are presented in Chapter 14.

When profits drop, management must frequently play the role of mediator between Manufacturing and Marketing to determine the reason. Chapter 15 describes an internal income statement that establishes Manufacturing and Marketing as separate profit centers to assist management in pinning down the responsibility. While there will always be disagreements, this type of segregation by responsibility should eliminate most of it (see Chapter 15).

The graphic presentation of key management figures can be very helpful because graphs are effective in condensing masses of data and portraying trends (see Chapter 16). This chapter also illustrates how graphs can be deceptive, whether manually prepared or prepared on the computer from currently available software on business graphics. See the general guidelines for presenting graphics in this chapter.

TEN GUIDELINES FOR IDENTIFYING AND CORRECTING WEAKNESSES IN THE SYSTEM

Manufacturing executives with profit responsibility frequently complain that they don't know what their costs are. One general manager made the following comment:

> When I first took over as general manager, I asked the cost accountant for some cost information. What I received was several computer output reports containing unanalyzed raw data. There was no question about the accuracy of the numbers, but what surprised me was how unfamiliar this individual was with the manufacturing process for making the products. He had difficulty in associating the figures contained in the reports with the factory operations behind the figures.

This is not an unusual situation. It points up the need for cost accountants to develop a greater familiarity with the operational aspects of the business. This familiarity can be achieved by taking the following steps:

1. Arrange to have a knowledgeable individual (an industrial engineer, for example) explain the various steps in the manufacturing operation. This can be done by a comprehensive plant tour—not a quick walk-through.
2. Take along brochures of the company's key products so that the steps in the manufacturing process can be directly associated with the products.
3. Inquire about the machine-to-operator ratios in the machine-paced operations. Within the labor-paced operations, take note of any differences in the nature of the processes that might indicate the need for separate costing rates. Discussion with the industrial engineer is recommended.
4. Make a list of the machine-paced and labor-paced departments for which you would establish costing rates. Review this list with the industrial engineer. If any question or difference of opinion arises, revisit the operations in question and discuss them further.
5. In the course of the plant tour, review paperwork such as production reports, routings, and scrap reports. Obtain copies of a typical set of these reports for further study.
6. Upon completion of the tour, review the paperwork with the respective departments that issue it. Find out how the information is used.
7. Upon reaching an agreement on what costing rates are required, obtain machine and labor utilization percentages from the industrial engineer. In some instances, it may be necessary to consult the foreman of the department.
8. Upon completion of the plant tour and the determination of how many costing rates are required, prepare a budget for the direct labor and machine-hour requirements in each production center. Determine the amount of the various overhead items required to meet the anticipated level of production for the coming year.
9. Discuss the required allocation bases with the individual most familiar with each expense.
10. Upon completion of the direct labor and overhead costing rates, work with the marketing department in developing the allocation bases for allocation of SG&A to the various product lines.

These 10 guidelines focus mainly on correcting product costs that are deficient because of improper allocation of manufacturing and nonmanufacturing overhead. These suggested guidelines, if followed, will provide the accountant with a much better understanding of the manufacturing process. This will be invaluable not only in achieving more meaningful product costing but in preparing other analyses as well.

Index

Index

Accounting for inventory, 87
  overstatement of input,
  overstatement of output, 87–88
Acquisitions
  expansion through, 210–214
Activity level,
  determination of
    labor-paced operations, 26–28, 44
    machine-paced operations, 26–28, 44
Allocating overhead, 33–37, 46–48
  controversial aspects, 37
American Society of Mechanical Engineers, 55
Atomic Energy Commission (AEC), 55

Breakeven, 52–53, 157, 197
Budgeting
  annual figures, 236
  manufacturing, 238–239
  marketing, 238

Capacity
  fallacy of excess equipment, 199
Corporate expenses, 240
Cost accounting
  computerization
    cost of sales, 131–133
    cost routing sheet (roll-up), 124–125
    fabricated parts transfer, 131–132
    inventory management interface, 117
    product costing, 126–129
    material receipts compared to plan, 136
    product structure, 121
    purchased parts price history, 131–133
    purchased price variance report, 134–135
    raw material issues, 130
    vendor delivery performance, 138
    where used file, 119
Cost accumulation for product costs
  transfer of material, labor and overhead to next department
    as material, 150–151, 157
    by individual element, 150, 154
Cost history record, 67–69
Cost reduction, 155–157
Cost system, using the wrong system, 256
Customer returns, improper handling of, 88

Debugging problems, 207
Distributor sales, 74–75
Downtime, minimization of, 208–209

Efficiency and utilization, interplay of, 195, 202–203
Engineered products, 55
Electro Company, 74–75, 77

Estimating, 66
Expansion
  from within, 204
  overtime, in lieu of, 199

Factory ledger accounts, 147
FIFO versus LIFO
Fixed assets
  allocation by market, 78
  construction versus rebuilding, 208–209
  rebuilding versus purchasing, 208–209
Flexible budget formula, 50–51
Fluorescent light fixtures
  costing two different fixtures, 9–10
  manufacturing operations, 8–9

General Electric Company, 163
Graphics
  bar charts, 247–251
  computerization of graphs, 241
  line graphs on natural scale paper, 241, 244–245
  omitting part of the scale, 244–246
  pie charts, 251–252
  projected increase of computer market, 252
  semi-logarithmic scale paper, 241–245

IBM annual report, 72
Incandescent lamp manufacture
  automatic mount assembly, 4–6
  manual mount assembly, 6–8
Income statement
  advantages of functional format, 240
  breakdown by market, 76
  need for functional format, 76
Increments, pricing of LIFO inventory, 175–177, 180
Indirect costs, 206
Indirect labor
  production departments, 28–29, 45
  service departments, 31–33, 45
Inflation versus deflation, 161
Internal Revenue Service (IRS), 164–171, 191, 205
Interviews, importance of, 230
Inventory
  allocation by markets, 78
  annual physical, 85
  book to physical adjustments, 85, 94
  cycle counting, 110
  management and mismanagement, 257
  monitoring cost flow, 90
  overcosting production, 92
  unaccounted-for production rejects, 92
Inventory management—computerization
  common errors, 102
  pick lists, 102

shop floor controls, 102
stock status reports, 103
strengths of, 102
weaknesses of, 106
Inventory valuation, matching costs and revenues, 162
Investment
  control of, 195
  effective utilization of, 195
  payback, 205

Job costs
  customized products, 91
  estimating, 49–50
Jones, Reginald H., 163
Journal entries, 139–142, 144

Labor intensive operations, 78
LIFO costing methods
  advantages and disadvantages, 163–165, 174–175
  distributors, 187–189
  dollar value method, 177
  double extension, 177–179
  indexing, 181
  link-chain method, 181–183, 186–187
  multiple pools, 193–194
  natural business unit, 191–193
  specific goods methods, 172–174, 184
  wholesalers and retailers, 194
LIFO costing with standard costs, 189–191

Machine hours
  adjustment of, 202
  available, 202
  calculation of, 201
Machine-paced operations, 78
Maintenance costs, 205
Make or buy studies, 155
Management Accounting, 253
Management reports, how to produce key reports, 257
Manufacturing cost overview, importance of, 23–26
Manufacturing and marketing, need for separate income statements, 234, 257
Manufacturing operations, automated versus manual, 7–8
Marketing and manufacturing, need for separate income statements, 234, 257
Manufacturing services staff
  guidelines for greater effectiveness, 233
  is it earning its keep? 225
  mission of, 227
Marginal costing and pricing, 155
Marginal income, 197
Material requirements planning (MRP)
  bill of material explosion, 100–103, 119
  inventory reduction, 103, 105
  shop floor control, 103, 105
  stock status reports, 103

Non-destructive testing (NDT), 59, 63
Nonmanufacturing costs
  packing and shipping expenses, 18–20
  selling, general and administrative expenses, 20–21
Nuclear components, 55–56, 62–64

Operations audit, steps in, 229
Original equipment manufacturers (OEM), 229
Overhead
  costing rates, 256
  over or underabsorption of, 235
Overhead rates,
  calculation of
    differential rates, 38, 40
    increasing six overhead rates to twelve, 10–13
    labor-paced rates, 4, 8–9, 26–28, 39, 48
    machine-paced rates, 4, 26–28
    single-plantwide rates, 6

Payback on investment, 195
Pfizer annual report, 72
Plant tour, importance of, 229
Printing-Binding, Inc., 42–43
Process costing, 85, 92
  standard products, 91
Production flow into inventory, monitoring cost input, 94–96
Product costing, deficiencies in, 256
Product line profitability, 71
Productivity
  measurement of, 222–224
    errors in projecting capacity, 204
    guidelines for measurement of, 224
  identification of,
    portion due to changes in profit, 216
    portion due to change in cost/selling price relationship, 216
  maximization of, 195
    methods of measurement, 217
    output per labor hour, 217
    sales per labor hour, 220, 221
    trend analysis, 218–220
    weighted labor hours per unit, 217
Productivity and profits, 195, 257
Profits, effect of changes in capacity, 198

Replacement market, 74–75
Return on investment, by market, 77–78

Sales projection of, 237
Securities Exchange Commission (SEC), 86
SG&A allocation, 256
  allocation problems, 73
  allocation method too arbitrary, 71–74
  percent breakdown by market, 73, 78
Standard cost system, 55

Transfer price, 235

Utilization
  impact of expansion, 200
  Interplay of utilization and efficiency, 195, 202–203
Utilization of equipment, monitoring, 195
Utilization of facilities, optimum level of, 197
Utilization report, preparation of, 201

Variance analysis, 146–147

Warner-Lambert annual report, 72
Work-in-process, breakdown of, 93

Xerox annual report, 72